CRISIS INTERVENTION AND PREVENTION

Lisa R. Jackson-Cherry
Marymount University

Bradley T. Erford
Loyola University Maryland

Boston   Columbus   Indianapolis   New York   San Francisco   Upper Saddle River
Amsterdam   Cape Town   Dubai   London   Madrid   Milan   Munich   Paris   Montreal   Toronto
Delhi   Mexico City   Sao Paulo   Sydney   Hong Kong   Seoul   Singapore   Taipei   Tokyo

Editor in Chief: Jeffrey W. Johnston
Acquisitions Editor: Meredith D. Fossel
Editorial Assistant: Nancy Holstein
Vice President, Director of Marketing and Sales Strategies: Emily Williams Knight
Vice President, Director of Marketing: Quinn Perkson
Marketing Manager: Amanda Stedke
Senior Managing Editor: Pam Bennett
Production Editor: Mary Irvin
Project Manager: Susan Hannahs

Art Director: Jayne Conte
Cover Designer: Diane C. Lorenzo
Cover Art: Ferrell McCollough/SuperStock
Full-Service Project Management: Suganya Karuppasamy/GGS Higher Education Resources, A division of PreMedia Global, Inc.
Composition: GGS Higher Education Resources, A division of PreMedia Global, Inc.
Printer/Bindery/Cover Printer: Courier Corporation, Inc.
Text Font: Palatino

Credits and acknowledgments borrowed from other sources and reproduced, with permission, in this textbook appear on appropriate page within text.

Every effort has been made to provide accurate and current Internet information in this book. However, the Internet and information posted on it are constantly changing, so it is inevitable that some of the Internet addresses listed in this textbook will change.

Library of Congress Cataloging-in-Publication Data
Erford, Bradley T.
   Crisis intervention and prevention / Bradley T. Erford, Lisa R. Jackson-Cherry. — 1st ed.
      p. cm.
   Includes bibliographical references and index.
   ISBN-13: 978-0-13-243177-4
   ISBN-10: 0-13-243177-7
   1. Crisis intervention (Mental health services)   I. Jackson-Cherry, Lisa R.   II. Title.
   RC480.6.E74 2010
   616.89'14—dc22

                                                                2009022502

10 9 8 7 6 5 4 3 2 1

ISBN-10:   0-13-243177-7
ISBN-13: 978-0-13-243177-4

To all crisis counselors who give selflessly to alleviate the pain of others. This work is dedicated to my family, which has sacrificed and continues to be my source of support, particularly my husband, Jim; my daughters, Gabrielle and Alexandra; my parents, Barbara Jackson and Francisco Japzon, M.D.; my grandmother Mary Manford; and in memory of my grandfather Grover Beggarly; while ever-mindful that all my fortunes and blessings are gifts from God.

LRJC

This effort is dedicated to The One: the Giver of energy, passion, and understanding; Who makes life worth living and endeavors worth pursuing and accomplishing; the Teacher of love and forgiveness.

BTE

PREFACE

The purpose for constructing this text was to convey the practical implications of and applications for dealing with crisis situations. Prior to September 11, 2001, crisis counselors' and university faculty members' conceptualization of crisis was generally limited to individual clients, primarily addressing suicidal client needs. But recent events (e.g., terrorism, school shootings, natural disasters), coupled with renewed societal concerns over continuing violence (e.g., homicide, intimate partner violence, rape, sexual abuse), have expanded our conceptualization of crisis and the needs of the new generation of counselors. This book is written to address this expanded concept of crisis in today's world and includes the practical applications that will help crisis counselors immediately be able to serve diverse clients in a changing world.

Preservice students and mental health professionals in the field need all the crisis management help they can get in order to hit the ground running. This short text provides vital information on assessing and reacting to various crises involving suicide, homicide, intimate partner violence, sexual assault/abuse, bereavement/grief, substance abuse, natural disasters, war, and terrorism. The text provides practical applications for various crisis situations experienced by crisis workers. The book allows students to become familiar with various crisis issues and situations and to practice necessary skills before encountering the problem for the first time in the field. The text features numerous crisis situations not found in other crisis texts and is of benefit to various counseling specialties (e.g., school, mental health, pastoral). Students see the process as a whole and are exposed to crucial information, clinical considerations, and practical experiences on every crisis topic.

The book is divided into two parts. Part I: Elements of Crisis Intervention, which includes Chapters 1–5, reviews the fundamental information related to crises and crisis intervention. In Chapter 1: Overview of Crisis Intervention, by Stephanie Puleo and Jason McGlothlin, the authors acknowledge that crises occur in a variety of settings for a variety of reasons. Responses to crises are equally variable. In Chapter 1, basic frameworks for assessing and conceptualizing crises are presented, along with a discussion of how crisis intervention may differ from traditional counseling. Chapter 2: Reacting in Crisis Situations was written by Charlotte Daughhetee and Mary Bartlett. When responding to a crisis, counselors need to be able to act promptly; meaning that crisis preparedness is essential to best practice during emergency situations. A brief overview of crisis planning guidelines and crisis counselor safety procedures is presented in Chapter 2, along with a review of transcrisis issues, ethical considerations in crisis treatment, and counselor self-care concerns.

Chapter 3: Essential Crisis Intervention Skills, by Joseph Cooper, provides an overview of the fundamental skills needed to engage in effective crisis intervention work. The skills covered in Chapter 3 focus on Ivey and Ivey's (2007) microskills hierarchy. At the heart of this hierarchy is the basic listening sequence, an interrelated set of skills that will not only foster the development of rapport with clients but also aid in the identification of interventions to help achieve a successful resolution to the client's crisis state. Examples of the skills in use, as well as practice exercises to foster individual skill development, are provided.

Whenever we lose, we grieve. Chapter 4: Grief and Loss, by Lourie W. Reichenberg, covers approaches to crisis counseling with mourners, theories of grieving, and the variables that affect how a bereaved person mourns. Also addressed is how timing, cause of death, and the role the relationship played in a person's life all mediate the mourning process, followed by an attempt to distinguish between "normal grief" and complicated mourning.

Finally, Part I concludes with Chapter 5: Intervention with Clients: Suicide and Homicide, by Mary Bartlett and Charlotte Daughhetee. Chapter 5 recognizes that suicide and homicide continue to play increasingly important roles in American society and on the world stage. Suicide and homicide affect us personally as we, family members, friends, and those in extended social networks struggle with the ever-increasing challenges of modern life. As personal liberty has increased, the chance for violent responses to stressful situations has increased. The effectiveness of the care given by professional emergency first responders, as well as the effectiveness of ordinary people in responding to their own crises and the crises of those about whom they care, is improved by background knowledge involving current trends in and treatments for suicide and homicide impulses.

Part II: Special Issues in Crisis Intervention comprises Chapters 6–9. In Chapter 6: Intimate Partner Violence, by Amy L. McLeod, John Muldoon, and Danica G. Hays, intimate partner violence (IPV) is defined as the infliction of physical, sexual, and/or emotional harm to a person by a current or former partner or spouse with the intent of establishing power and control over the abused partner. IPV is a major public health concern, and it is imperative that crisis counselors be able to recognize and respond to IPV survivors competently. Chapter 6 provides an overview of the facts and figures associated with IPV, discusses the cycle of violence commonly experienced in abusive relationships, and explores various perspectives on survivors who stay in relationships with abusive partners. Common crisis issues experienced by IPV survivors, including dealing with physical injury, establishing immediate safety, and reporting IPV to the police are also highlighted. In addition, this chapter explores special considerations regarding IPV in lesbian, gay, bisexual, and transgender (LGBT) relationships, relationships characterized by female-to-male violence, abusive relationships in racial and ethnic minority populations, and abusive dating relationships among adolescents and young adults. Guidelines for crisis counselors who are conducting IPV assessment, responding to IPV disclosure, planning for client safety, and addressing the emotional impact of IPV are provided. Finally, the goals, theories, and challenges associated with IPV offender intervention are discussed.

Chapter 7: Sexual Assault and Sexual Abuse, by Carrie Wachter and Robin Lee, reveals that sexual assault and child sexual abuse are two of the most underreported crimes, with survivors facing a number of potential physical, psychological, cognitive, behavioral, and emotional consequences. Crisis counselors who work with survivors of sexual assault and child sexual abuse need to be aware of the multitude of challenges these individuals face, best practices for treatment, and support services available in the local community. In Chapter 7, sexual assault and child sexual abuse are defined, signs and symptoms described, treatment interventions discussed, and guidelines for working with law enforcement and child protective services personnel provided. In addition, this chapter addresses sexual offenders, their patterns of behavior, and common treatment options.

Chapter 8: Addressing Substance Abuse and Dependence Within the Crisis Context, by Edward Cannon, reviews Substance Use Disorders and the disease of addiction, including causes, manifestations, and treatment. There are numerous models and theories about the causes of alcoholism and drug addiction, and this chapter introduces the medical and moral/legal models as well as important genetic, sociocultural, and psychological theories.

Finally, in Chapter 9: Emergency Preparedness and Response, by Jason McGlothlin, Lisa Jackson-Cherry, and Michele Garofalo, the information and interventions from the preceding eight chapters are integrated into an overview of the various disasters and crises that crisis counselors may need to address. In the first section of Chapter 9, crisis intervention models and clinical implications for disasters and hostage situations are explored. In the second part of Chapter 9, crisis management in the school is explored, including the components of a crisis plan and the role of school counselors and other school officials. Finally, the chapter concludes with an outline of the components that should be implemented when preparing for and providing death notifications.

ACKNOWLEDGMENTS

We thank Emily Miller, graduate assistant extraordinaire, for her tireless assistance in the preparation of the original manuscript. All of the contributing authors are to be commended for lending their expertise in the various topical areas. As always, Meredith Fossel, our editor at Pearson has been wonderfully responsive and supportive. Finally, special thanks go to the outside reviewers whose comments helped to provide substantive improvement to the original manuscript: Al Carlozzi, Oklahoma State University; George K. Hong, California State University, Los Angeles; Nicholas Mazza, Florida State University; Eric Ornstein, University of Illinois at Chicago; Toni R. Tollerud, Northern Illinois University; and Barbara F. Turnage, Arkansas State University.

BRIEF CONTENTS

CONTENTS

Part II   Special Issues in Crisis Intervention

Chapter 6   Intimate Partner Violence   135

Amy L. McLeod, John Muldoon, and *Danica G. Hays*

Chapter 8   Addressing Substance Abuse and Dependence Within the Crisis Context   193

Edward Cannon

ABOUT THE EDITORS

Lisa R. Jackson-Cherry, Ph.D., LCPC, NCC, ACS, NCSC, is an associate professor of psychology and Chair of the Department of Counseling in the School of Education and Human Services at Marymount University in Arlington, Virginia. She coordinates the community counseling and pastoral counseling programs. She is the recipient of the American Counseling Association's Carl Perkins Government Relations Award for her initiatives in psychological testing. Dr. Jackson-Cherry is a Licensed Clinical Professional Counselor, National Certified Counselor, Approved Clinical Supervisor, and National Certified School Counselor. She is approved as a Pastoral Counselor Educator by the American Association of Pastoral Counselors and is certified as a Disaster Mental Health Counselor by the American Red Cross. She is the President-elect (2009–2010) of and delegate to the American Association of State Counseling Boards and is the current President (2008–2009) of the Association for Spiritual, Ethical, and Religious Values in Counseling. She is a member of the Board of Professional Counselors and Therapists in Maryland and currently serves as the Board Chair and Ethics Chair. She is the past Membership Co-Chair and Southern Regional Representative for the Counseling Association for Humanistic Education and Development and has served as past Secretary and Legislative Representative for the Licensed Clinical Professional Counselors of Maryland. Her research focuses mainly on the areas of ethical and legal issues in counseling and supervision, military deployment and reintegration issues, and risk assessment. She teaches courses primarily in the areas of crisis intervention, pastoral counseling integration, and clinical internship experiences for community counseling and pastoral counseling programs. She is currently in private practice in Maryland, where she works with children and couples. She is involved with COPS Kids during National Police Week, providing group counseling to children who lost a parent in the line of duty. Her previous clinical experiences consisted of clinical director for mobile crisis teams, behavioral specialist (grades K–5) and conflict resolution coordinator/counselor (grades 9–12), group co-facilitator for a women's correctional facility, and crisis intervention training for law enforcement basic trainees and hostage negotiators.

Bradley T. Erford, Ph.D., NCC, LCPC, LPC, LP, is a professor in the School Counseling Program of the Educational Specialties Department at Loyola University Maryland. He is the recipient of the American Counseling Association (ACA) Research Award, ACA Hitchcock Distinguished Professional Service Award, ACA Professional Development Award, and ACA Carl D. Perkins Government Relations Award. He has also been inducted as an ACA Fellow. In addition, he has received the Association for Assessment in Counseling and Education (AACE)/Measurement and Evaluation in Counseling and Development Research Award, the AACE Exemplary Practices Award, the Association for Counselor Education and Supervision's Robert O. Stripling Award for Excellence in Standards, Maryland Association for Counseling and Development (MACD) Maryland Counselor of the Year, the MACD Counselor Advocacy Award, the MACD Professional Development Award, and the MACD Counselor Visibility Award. He is the editor of six texts: *Transforming the School Counseling Profession* (Merrill/Prentice-Hall, 2003, 2007); *ACA Encyclopedia of Counseling; Orientation to the Counseling Profession* (Merrill/Pearson, 2010); *Group Work in the Schools* (Merrill/Pearsonl, 2010); *Multicultural Counseling Competence; Professional School Counseling: A Handbook of Principles, Programs and Practices* (Pro-Ed, 2004, 2008); *Assessment for Counselors* (Houghton Mifflin/Lahaska Press, 2007); *Research and Evaluation in Counseling* (Houghton Mifflin/Lahaska Press, 2008); and *The Counselor's Guide to Clinical, Personality and Behavioral Assessment*

(Houghton Mifflin/Lahaska Press, 2005). His research specialization falls primarily in development and technical analysis of psychoeducational tests and has resulted in the publication of numerous refereed journal articles, book chapters, and published tests. He is an ACA Governing Council Representative; Past President of the AACE; Past Chair and Parliamentarian of the ACA—Southern Region; Past President of the MACD; Chair of ACA's Task Force on High Stakes Testing; Past Chair of ACA's Standards for Test Users Task Force, Interprofessional Committee, and Public Awareness and Support Committee (Co-Chair of the National Awards Subcommittee); Chair of the Convention and Past Chair of the Screening Assessment Instruments Committees for the AACE; Past President of the Maryland Association for Counselor Education and Supervision; and Past President of the Maryland Association for Mental Health Counselors. Dr. Erford has been a faculty member at Loyola since 1993 and is a Licensed Clinical Professional Counselor, Licensed Professional Counselor, Nationally Certified Counselor, Licensed Psychologist and Licensed School Psychologist. Prior to arriving at Loyola, Dr. Erford was a school psychologist/counselor in the Chesterfield County (Virginia) Public Schools. He maintains a private practice specializing in assessment and treatment of children and adolescents. A graduate in counselor education (Ph.D.) of The University of Virginia and in school psychology (M.A.) of Bucknell University, he teaches courses in testing and measurement, psychoeducational assessment, lifespan development, research and evaluation in counseling, school counseling, counseling techniques, and stress management (not that he needs it, of course).

ABOUT THE CONTRIBUTING AUTHORS

Mary Bartlett, Ph.D., LPC-CS, NCC, CFLE, is an assistant professor and coordinator of the community counseling track in the Department of Counseling, Leadership, and Foundations at the University of Montevallo in Montevallo, Alabama. She is a licensed counselor in several states, a counseling supervisor, and an educator in family life matters. Her area of research is suicide, and she speaks nationally on suicide prevention, clinical assessment of suicidality, and various related topics. She is an authorized trainer for the American Association of Suicidology and the Suicide Prevention Resource Center and also serves on the Alabama Suicide Prevention Task Force Speakers' Bureau. Dr. Bartlett's clinical experience includes working with a wide variety of populations in crisis intervention throughout her career, both in the United States and in Europe.

Edward Cannon, Ph.D., LPC, LMFT, is an assistant professor in the Department of Counseling at Marymount University in Arlington, Virginia. Prior to completing his Ph.D. at the College of William and Mary, he worked as director of the New Horizons Family Counseling Center as well as a substance abuse counselor and crisis counselor for a local community mental health center.

Joseph Cooper, Ph.D., LPC, NCC, is an assistant professor in the Department of Counseling at Marymount University in Arlington, Virginia. He received his Ph.D. in counselor education at the University of North Carolina at Charlotte. Prior to completing his Ph.D., Dr. Cooper worked for 10 years providing individual, family, and group substance abuse and mental health counseling in both agency and school settings. His current research interests include motivational interviewing, attachment theory, intensive short-term dynamic psychotherapy, and neurophysiology.

Charlotte Daughhetee, Ph.D, NCC, LPC, LMFT, is an associate professor of counseling and foundations at the University of Montevallo in Montevallo, Alabama, where she has been on the faculty since 1999. She graduated from the University of South Carolina with a doctoral degree in counselor education and has clinical experience in school, college, and agency settings. She maintains a part-time private practice where she provides individual, couples, and family counseling. Her interests include lifelong continuing competency for counselors, evaluation of counselor trainees, supervision, and disaster mental health intervention.

Michele Garofalo, Ed.D., LPC, NCC, is the Assistant Chair in the Department of Counseling and School Counseling Program Director at Marymount University in Arlington, Virginia. She has worked as a school counselor at the elementary and middle school levels in both independent and public schools. She consults with area schools on a variety of school-related topics and mental health issues. Dr. Garofalo is a Licensed Professional Counselor and maintains a private practice where she works with adolescents and families. She teaches school counseling courses and provides supervision for school counseling practicum and internship students. Her research interests include adolescent stress, counselor training and supervision, ethical and legal issues, and character education.

Danica G. Hays, Ph.D., LPC, NCC, is an associate professor in the Department of Educational Leadership and Counseling at Old Dominion University. She has conducted individual and group counseling in community mental health, university, and hospital settings. Her research interests include qualitative methodology, assessment and diagnosis, domestic violence intervention, and multicultural and social justice issues in counselor preparation and community mental health.

Robin Lee, Ph.D., LPC, NCC, is an associate professor in the professional counseling program at Middle Tennessee State University. She received her doctoral degree in counselor education and supervision from Mississippi State University. Her interests include counselor training issues, ethical and legal issues, counseling supervision, women's issues, and generational characteristics.

Jason McGlothlin, Ph.D., PCC-S, is an associate professor in the counseling and human development services program at Kent State University (KSU). He also serves as the coordinator of the community counseling and school counseling programs at KSU. He earned his doctorate in counselor education from Ohio University and is currently a Professional Clinical Counselor with Supervisory endorsement (PCC-S) in Ohio. Prior to joining the KSU faculty, he practiced in community mental health, private practice, and suicide prevention/hostage negotiation facilities. Dr. McGlothlin has had a variety of local, state, and national leadership positions in the counseling profession. His current areas of teaching, publication, and research include the assessment, prevention, and treatment of suicide and counselor education accreditation. He is the author of a text titled *Developing Clinical Skills in Suicide Assessment, Prevention and Treatment*, which was published in 2008 by the American Counseling Association.

Amy L. McLeod, Ph.D., is an assistant professor at Argosy University in Atlanta, GA. Her research interests include women's issues, crisis counseling, assessment and diagnosis, and multicultural issues in counselor education and supervision. Ms. McLeod's clinical experience includes work in a private practice and at Ridgeview Institute, a mental health and substance abuse hospital.

John Muldoon, Ph.D., LPC, CAAP, received his Ph.D. in counselor education. He is an assistant professor at Kean University in Union, New Jersey. Formerly, he worked for the behavioral services unit for a regional hospital system, facilitating intensive outpatient and outpatient recovery groups, as well as maintaining an individual caseload, the majority of who were dually diagnosed. His most significant experience was as the director of Alternatives to Violence, a program for domestic violence offenders, for seven years. In this position, he presented at local, state, and national conferences on topics including offender intervention, fatherhood programs, and substance abuse counselor training. He has also conducted research projects on the effectiveness of offender intervention and the correlation between substance use and dependence. His professional experience also includes approximately five years working with individuals with substance abuse problems and their significant others as well as working as a school counselor providing groups for students on issues ranging from substance use to conflict resolution and bullying. Dr. Muldoon is a Certified Associate Addictions Professional and is a Licensed Professional Counselor in several states.

Stephanie Puleo, Ph.D., is a professor in the Department of Counseling, Leadership, and Foundations at the University of Montevallo in Montevallo, Alabama. She is a Licensed Marriage and Family Therapist, Licensed Professional Counselor, and National Certified Counselor and is certified by the American Red Cross in Disaster Mental Health. Dr. Puleo earned her Ph.D. in counselor education at the University of Alabama. She also has earned master's degrees in community counseling and in school psychology. In addition to coordinating the marriage and family counseling program track at the University of Montevallo, she provides counseling and psychometric services to individuals, couples, and families in the Birmingham and central Alabama area.

Lourie W. Reichenberg, M.A., LPC, NCC, received her undergraduate degree in psychology from Michigan State University and her M.A. degree in counseling psychology from Marymount University, where she is currently an adjunct faculty member in the School of Education and Human Services. She teaches counseling theories, abnormal psychology, and crisis management. Her specific interest areas include loss and life transitions, crisis management, and suicide prevention and postvention. She is co-author of two books and editor of more than 20 books, has published numerous articles, and has conducted more than 50 presentations on various topics. She is a Licensed Professional Counselor in several states and has a private practice in Falls Church, Virginia.

Carrie Wachter, Ph.D., NCC, ACS, is an assistant professor in the counseling and development program at Purdue University. She received her doctoral degree in counseling and counselor education from the University of North Carolina at Greensboro. Her clinical experience includes work in schools and at an inpatient behavioral health center for children, adolescents, and adults. Her research interests include crisis prevention and intervention in the schools and school counselor collaboration with other educational and mental health personnel.

1

Overview of Crisis Intervention

Stephanie Puleo and Jason McGlothlin

PREVIEW

Crises occur in a variety of settings for a variety of reasons. Responses to crises are equally variable. In this chapter, basic frameworks for assessing and conceptualizing crises are presented, along with a discussion of how crisis intervention may differ from traditional counseling.

A BRIEF INTRODUCTION TO CRISIS INTERVENTION

If asked to think about a crisis, what comes to mind? Hurricane Katrina? September 11, 2001? Suicide? Homicide? Domestic violence? How do some people survive such apparent trauma adaptively and with resilience, while others endure mental health issues for months or years afterward?

To begin, situations such as Hurricane Katrina, the terrorist attack of September 11, suicide, and domestic violence, although sharing traumatic characteristics, in and of themselves do not constitute crises. These are, instead, events that trigger crises. Typically, a crisis is described using a trilogy definition; that is, there are three essential elements that must be present for a situation to be considered a crisis: (1) a precipitating event, (2) a perception of the event that leads to subjective distress, and (3) diminished functioning when the distress is not alleviated by customary coping resources.

When terrorists bombed the World Trade Center in New York City in 1993, crises ensued for some individuals and families. Six families lost loved ones, approximately 1,000 individuals were injured, and the jobs, careers, and work of countless people were interrupted. Using the trilogy definition, it is obvious that all of those who experienced diminished functioning following the event were in crisis. People throughout the rest of the world, however horrified, continued to function as normal and therefore were not in crisis.

The trilogy definition is reflected in the work of several notable contributors to the crisis intervention literature and applies both to individuals and to families (Boss, 1987, 1988, 2002; McKenry & Price, 2005). Recently, James (2008) reviewed a number of definitions that

CASE STUDY 1.1

The Nguyens

Vin and Li Nguyen are recent immigrants to the United States. They reside in a small town along the Gulf Coast of Mississippi, where a number of other Vietnamese immigrants have settled. Like many members of the community, the Nguyens are learning to speak, read, and write English and are hoping to become naturalized citizens of the United States some day. After arriving in the United States, the Nguyens invested all of their money in an old shrimp boat in order to support themselves by selling their daily catch to local seafood processing facilities.

In 2005, the shrimp boat was heavily damaged, and the seafood processing facilities were destroyed by Hurricane Katrina. Subsequently, the Nguyens had no income for quite awhile. With limited income and no health insurance, they relied on the county department of public health for prenatal care when Li became pregnant. Li's pregnancy progressed normally; however, her daughter was born with Spina Bifida.

As you read this chapter, try to conceptualize the Nguyens' situation according to the crisis models presented.

Discussion Questions

- What incidents have occurred in the Nguyens' lives that could be considered provoking stressor events?
- Beyond the provoking stressor events, are there additional stressors that the Nguyens must address?
- What resources are the Nguyens utilizing? What further information do you need to determine if the Nguyens are in crisis?
- What factors will predict the outcome for this family?

exist in the literature and summarized crisis as "a perception or experiencing of an event or situation as an intolerable difficulty that exceeds the person's current resources and coping mechanisms" (p. 3).

According to Slaikeu (1990), a crisis is "a temporary state of upset and disorganization, characterized chiefly by an individual's inability to cope with a particular situation using customary methods of problem-solving, and by the potential for a radically positive or negative outcome" (p. 15). While it is always hoped that a positive outcome (McCubbin & Patterson, 1982) would occur, there are occasions when a radically negative outcome such as suicide happens, thereby precipitating further upset.

FOUNDATIONS OF CRISIS INTERVENTION THEORY

The study of crisis intervention began in earnest during the 1940s in response to several stressor events. During World War II, numerous families experienced distress and changes in functioning after individual family members left home to participate in the war effort. Families that seemed to experience the greatest degree of distress were those that had the most difficulty adapting to the absence of family members. Similarly, many families were forced to deal with losses brought about by a more acute stressor event, a nightclub fire that claimed nearly 500 lives in Boston, Massachusetts. These events led to Hill's proposal of a model through which family stress and crisis could be conceptualized and to Caplan and Lindemann's proposed recommendations for responding to crises at the community level. In the decades following the 1940s, these original models have been expanded, with more attention to contextual variables and to outcomes.

Basic Crisis Intervention Theory

Caplan and Lindemann often are credited as pioneers in the field of crisis intervention. Their work began after a tragic event in Boston in 1942, the Cocoanut Grove nightclub fire, in which 493 people died. Lindemann treated many of the survivors of the nightclub fire and noted that they shared similar emotional responses, along with the need for psychological assistance and support (Lindemann, 1944). His work created awareness that many individuals who suffer loss experience pathological symptoms but have no specific psychiatric diagnosis. It was his contention that responses to sudden grief are normal and transient and need not be considered pathological. Lindemann theorized that "normal" responses to grief include preoccupation and identification with the deceased, feelings of guilt and expressions of hostility, disorganization in daily functioning, and somatic complaints (Janosik, 1984). In essence, his paradigm for crisis intervention included an individual who was in a state of disorganization, brief therapy to assist the individual in working through grief, and ultimately restoration of equilibrium.

As Lindemann worked with others from Massachusetts General Hospital to assist survivors who had lost loved ones in the Cocoanut Grove fire, he began to realize that helpers other than psychiatrists could assist people in coping with their sudden grief. Lindemann's report describing common grief reactions to disaster, as well as the benefits of including clergy and other community helpers in intervention efforts, became a cornerstone in the conceptualization of community mental health.

Following the Cocoanut Grove fire, Lindemann worked with Caplan to establish a communitywide mental health program in Cambridge, Massachusetts, known as the Wellesley Project (Caplan, 1964). The aim of this project was to study and provide support to individuals experiencing traumatic events. The outcome of this project supported Caplan's notion of preventive psychiatry—that is, early intervention in an effort to promote positive growth and well-being.

Caplan (1961, 1964) expanded Lindemann's concepts by expanding their application to a wider field of traumatic events. According to Caplan (1961), "People are in a state of crisis when they face an obstacle to important life goals—an obstacle that is, for a time, insurmountable by the use of customary methods of problem-solving. A period of disorganization ensues, a period of upset, during which many abortive attempts at solution are made" (p. 18). What is important to note in Caplan's description is that the concept of crisis refers to an outcome of a precipitating event, not to the precipitating event itself. Similar to Lindemann, Caplan described the outcome, or the crisis, as the state of disequilibrium that the individual experiences.

The ABC–X Model of Crisis

Hill (1949, 1958) was among the first to conceptualize a crisis theory that applied to families. From his studies of families experiencing separation and reunion as a result of World War II, Hill postulated the ABC–X Model of Crisis (see Figure 1.1). According to

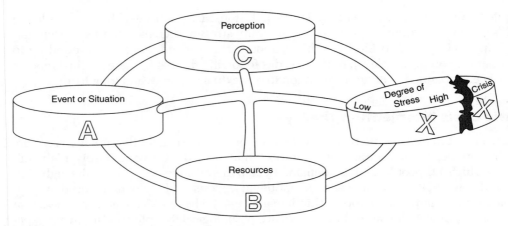

FIGURE 1.1   The ABC–X Model of Family Crisis.

this model, there is an interaction among (A) a provoking stressor event, (B) the family's resources, and (C) the meaning that the family attaches to the stressor event. The crisis (X), a state of acute disequilibrium and immobilization of the family system (Boss, 1988), is an outcome of this interaction. Although Hill's original research pertained to families, the concepts he proposed may be applied to individuals.

The Double ABC–X Model of Crisis

Hill's original ABC–X model continues to provide a framework for much research in the area of family stress and crisis; however, a few scholars (Boss, 1988, 2002; McCubbin & Patterson, 1982) have chosen to expand upon the model. Among the better-known variations of Hill's work is the Double ABC–X Model of Crisis proposed by McCubbin and Patterson (1982). Writing from a systems orientation, which assumes that systems naturally evolve and become more complex over time, McCubbin and Patterson considered recovery and growth following crisis. The concept of adaptation was introduced to describe lasting functional changes that occur in order to meet the demands of a crisis or stressful event. According to these scholars, Hill's original model was somewhat incomplete in that it outlined only those factors that contribute to a crisis or breakdown in functioning. Following a state of disequilibrium or incapacitation, additional stressors may accrue, and additional resources may be identified and acquired. Subsequently, new perceptions that take into account the original event and related hardships or stressors, along with the application of resources and coping strategies to meet the needs of those stressors, are formulated.

According to McCubbin and Patterson (1982), there is a "double A" factor that includes Hill's original concept of a provoking stressor plus the buildup of further stressors that must be addressed. These stressors may include unresolved issues related to the crisis-provoking event, changes that occur unrelated to the event, and any consequences of attempts to cope (McKenry & Price, 2005). The "double B" factor refers to resources available at the time of the provoking stressor, as noted by Hill, along with tangible and intangible resources that have been acquired or strengthened. Fortified coping resources would be included in this concept. The "double C" factor refers not only to perceptions and meanings assigned to the original provoking stressor but also to accumulated stressors, resources, coping, and the entire situation. Perceptions are influenced by religious beliefs, family and cultural values, and how the situation may have been reframed. In the model proposed by McCubbin and Patterson, the original crisis (Hill's X factor) constitutes a beginning point, while adaptation ("double X") occurs later in time. Adaptation is an outcome variable involving changes in functioning and perception. More than the simple reduction of stress, adaptation is the degree to which long-term change has occurred in response to the demands of stressor and crisis events.

Ecological and Contextual Considerations

In addition to considering the accumulation of stressors and resources, Boss (1987, 1988, 2002) and others (Collins & Collins, 2005) have suggested that stress and crisis are affected by contextual factors. Collins and Collins (2005) have advocated a "developmental-ecological" perspective to conceptualizing crises. According to these authors, some crises are triggered by stressor events that are developmental in nature; that is, these developmental crises are expected events in the life span of the individual or family. However, regardless of whether the stressor event is developmental or situational, life span variables must be considered to determine their meaning and impact on the stress or crisis situation. In addition to considering developmental factors, Collins and Collins have maintained that the context provided by environmental factors such as interpersonal relationships, community resources, and society at large must be recognized. This approach suggests that each crisis is unique, since the ecological determinants for each person will be unique. Therefore, crisis counselors need to be aware that even though many of the clinical considerations and approaches may be similar for a specific crisis and for many individuals experiencing that crisis (e.g., sexual assault), the person in crisis will experience the crisis differently than someone else due to the unique and personal ecological determinants. In essence, do not simply generalize and implement a generic approach to a particular crisis without first assessing the client's unique ecological factors.

Boss (1987, 1988, 2002) similarly proposed a contextual approach to the study of stress and crisis, stating that "factors in addition to the stressful event influence family vulnerability or breakdown" (2002, p. 28). According to Boss, stress is mediated by contextual dimensions, which may be either internal or external. The internal context includes three dimensions that may be controlled or changed: the structure of the family, psychological elements such as perception and assessment, and philosophical elements such as values and beliefs. The external context is composed of environmental or ecosystemic dimensions over which there is no control. External influences on stress and crisis include historical, economic, developmental, hereditary, and cultural contexts.

Elements of Stress and Crisis Theory

PROVOKING STRESSOR EVENTS   Stressor events are those occurrences that provoke change in the functioning of a system. Stressor events may be positive or negative, and while some are normal and predictable, others are unforeseen. In general, stressor events may be categorized as either normative stressor events (i.e., those stressors that occur at points of normal developmental transitions) or nonnormative stressor events (i.e., products of distinctive, unexpected situations). Many families anticipate normative stressor events such as children graduating from high school and beginning college, while few anticipate nonnormative stressor events such as the school shootings at Columbine High School and Virginia Tech.

Boss (1988) categorized stressor events and situations by source, type, and severity. Sources are either internal, originating within the family, or external, attributable to someone or something outside the family. Examples of internal stressors include partner violence and chemical dependency. These stressors begin within the family and are accompanied by changes in the way the family functions. Partners and family members often adopt various roles, behaviors, and communication styles in attempts to cope with and survive the actions of the abusive or addicted person. As familiar coping strategies become increasingly inadequate, families cease to function effectively and healthily. "Crises" in these families are rarely a one-time occurrence (James, 2008).

Another example of an internal stressor is infertility. Within the context of the family life cycle, most couples expect to be able to conceive and carry a pregnancy to term. Infertility is considered an internal stressor because the inability to achieve a successful pregnancy originates with one (sometimes both) of the partners as opposed to something outside of the family. It becomes a crisis situation because the partners face psychological and relationship changes that affect the way they function. Each menses is encountered as a crisis situation. In response to this crisis situation, many couples are able to redefine their relationships and reframe their meanings of pregnancy and parenting; unfortunately, however, many couples do not respond well and ultimately separate (Puleo & Wilcoxon, 1995).

External stressors originate outside the family but affect family functioning nonetheless. Examples of external stressors include natural disasters, terrorism, financial decline due to the stock market, and the rising cost of oil. Some external stressors are attributable to forces of nature (e.g., hurricanes, tornadoes, earthquakes), some to humans (e.g., violent crimes, job termination), and some to a combination of the two (e.g., global warming). Individuals and families typically have less control over external stressors than they do over internal stressors. For example, families have little control over the stock market. However, the ramifications of a declining stock market could have a substantial impact on a family's future.

As with internal stressors, however, the degree to which crises caused by external stressors are experienced is contingent on available resources and the meaning attached to the stressor event. In the United States, Hurricane Katrina, an external stressor, interrupted the normal functioning and triggered crises for thousands of families along the Gulf Coast of Louisiana, Mississippi, and Alabama. Families who seemed to be the most resilient and who seemed to have the least difficulty recovering from this crisis were those with available resources such as social support, housing, and financial assets.

Many stressors are normal, predictable, and developmental in nature. Stressor events of this type generally are an expected part of everyday life and of the family life cycle. Typical normative stressor events include "birth, puberty, adolescence, marriage, aging, menopause, retirement, and death" (Boss, 2002, p. 51). Although these events are expected, they have the potential to disturb the equilibrium of an individual or family and result in crisis.

The type of crisis-inducing stressor that initially comes to mind for many people is the catastrophic, situational, unexpected event. Such a situation tends to be unique, is not predicted, and is not likely to be repeated. Examples of catastrophic stressors include those that may be attributable to human behavior, such as the bombing of the Alfred P. Murrah Federal Building in Oklahoma City in 1995, or to natural disasters, such as the 2008 earthquake in China. Other nonnormative stressors may not be catastrophic at all, and may actually be positive, but nonetheless may still have the potential to disrupt equilibrium. Examples are finding a lost relative (Boss, 2002) and winning the lottery. Unexpected stressor events such as these also may be categorized as nonvolitional stressors. Volitional stressors, on the other hand, are recognized by the amount of choice and control the individual or family has over them. Examples include wanted changes in jobs or residences and planned pregnancies. Although volitional stressors are wanted and initiated, pursued, or orchestrated by the individual or family, they still have the potential to trigger a crisis if resources and meaning do not match needs and requirements. Changing jobs for the sake of career advancement, for instance, may require a move to a geographic location where housing is unavailable or unaffordable. Even if everything goes according to plan (i.e., no medical complications, a single birth, and a healthy baby), financial and social support for a planned pregnancy may be inadequate.

Beyond classifying stressors by their source and type, Boss (2002) described stressor situations according to their duration and severity. Some stressors are one-time events, happen suddenly, and resolve quickly; these are considered acute stressors. An automobile accident, for example, might disrupt a family's equilibrium as broken bones heal and alternate transportation is used, but ultimately, the family's balance is restored. Other stressors, such as lifelong illnesses, infertility, and poverty, persist over long periods of time and are considered chronic. Families caring for aging family members may experience chronic stress and may face disequilibrium and crisis each time the elderly family member's health takes a turn for the worse. The crisis is triggered by changes in health but is the result of additional demands for financial, social, and other resources as well as the perception and meaning the family attaches to the elderly person's decline. Finally, Boss (2002) suggested that it is important to consider whether a stressor situation is an isolated event or part of an accumulation of stressor events. It is often the case that any one stressor event may not be enough to trigger a crisis, but the cumulative effect of the pileup of stressors taxes resources, disrupts equilibrium and functioning, and results in crisis.

RESOURCES   Resources may be defined as traits, characteristics, or abilities that can be used to meet the demands of a stressor event (McCubbin & Patterson, 1982) and that can be available at the individual, family, or community level (McKenry & Price, 2005). They may be tangible (e.g., food, clothing, shelter) or intangible (e.g., social support, self-esteem). When resources are adequate to meet the demands created by a stressor situation, the situation is less likely to be perceived as problematic—and less likely to lead to crisis. Two types of resources are important: those that are available and used to mediate the initial stressor and those that are acquired, developed, or strengthened subsequent to a crisis situation (McCubbin & Patterson, 1982). Individual resources may include finances, education, health, and psychological qualities, whereas family resources include the internal, systemic attributes of cohesion and adaptability, along with resources such as financial management, communication skills, compatibility, and shared interests (Olsen, 1988). Community resources include external supports, such as social networks, on which the individual or family can draw.

MEANING OR PERCEPTION   Whether a stressor event results in crisis depends not only on available resources but also on the meaning attached to the event. The meaning attributed to a stressor event is subjective and comes from the way it is appraised through both cognitive and affective processes. Factors contributing to this qualitative variable include the ambiguity associated with the stressor situation, denial, and the belief and value orientation of the individual or family. Ambiguity occurs when facts cannot be obtained. It is often the case that specific information about the onset, development, duration, and conclusion of an unpredictable stressor event is unavailable. When information is unavailable, individuals may be uncertain in their perception of who is included in their families or social support systems. With limited understanding about who is in and who is out, it becomes difficult to ascertain how various roles, rules, and functions will be carried out. Whereas sometimes stressors themselves are ambiguous because data are not available, at other times facts are available but are ignored or distorted. The resulting denial may be a useful coping strategy in the short term but may be damaging if it prevents further action during a crisis situation (Boss, 1988, 2002; McKenry & Price, 2005).

COPING   In his original ABC–X model, Hill (1949, 1958) considered coping behaviors as part of the family's resources (represented by "B" in the ABC–X model) to be utilized in response to demands of a stressor event ("A"). While many researchers agree that coping behaviors are a subset of available resources, coping itself is a separate construct, often interacting with both resources ("B") and perception ("C"). According to Pearlin and Schooler (1978), any effort taken to deal with stress may be considered coping. Thus, coping is a process and requires cognitive as well as behavioral activities (McKenry & Price, 2005; Pearlin & Schooler, 1978). Cognitively, people experiencing stressor events must appraise what is happening and assess any potential for harm. They also must evaluate the consequences of possible response actions. According to Lazarus (1966, 1976), these appraisals occur before any coping mechanisms are employed. Following appraisal, there are three types of coping responses that may be used: direct actions, intrapsychic mechanisms, and efforts to manage emotions. Direct actions are those behaviors that typically are thought of as "fight or flight" responses. Examples include acquiring resources, asking for help, and learning new skills (McKenry & Price, 2005). These actions are used in relation to the environment in order to master stressors and are thought of as problem-focused coping strategies.

Emotion-focused coping strategies, conversely, involve mechanisms used to change feelings or perceptions when there is little that can be done to change a stressor. Intrapsychic responses are those responses that often are thought of as defense mechanisms (e.g., denial, detachment) and allow people to alter their interpretations of the stress-provoking situation (Boss, 2002; McKenry & Price, 2005). Additional emotion-focused strategies are used to manage emotions generated by the stressor. Examples include the use of resources such as social support or of alcohol and drugs. Obviously, specific coping responses are neither adaptive nor maladaptive; they are simply efforts to manage.

CASE STUDY 1.1 (continued)

The Nguyens

Stressor events are those occurrences—positive or negative, predictable or unforeseen—that provoke change in the functioning of a system. They may be categorized as normative or nonnormative. The Nguyen family has experienced a number of provoking stressors, some of which they chose, others of which they did not.

Stressors may be categorized by source, type, and severity and should be considered within context (Boss, 1988). There are many variables, such as culture, history, education, and heredity, over which the Nguyen family has no control. These compose the external context. Crisis counselors who work with the Nguyens need to take into account their Vietnamese culture as well as additional cultural issues related to being part of an immigrant community along the Gulf Coast of the United States. Imbedded in these considerations is the fact that the Nguyens chose to leave Vietnam for the United States some thirty years after the Vietnam War. What kinds of social prejudices and biases does this couple face simply by being Vietnamese? Are there additional biases that they endure by virtue of being immigrants in a post-9/11 U.S. society?

The Nguyens' situation is complicated by their economic status, another component of their external context. Prior to Hurricane Katrina, they were making a living in the shrimp industry. They had few bills and no debt; however, they had no medical insurance. On those rare occasions when they required medical attention, they were able to use community public health resources. In the aftermath of Hurricane Katrina and the tough economic times that followed, numerous public, nonprofit health agencies were forced to close their doors, making it difficult for the Nguyens to access prenatal care. When their daughter was born with a birth defect, they found it necessary to travel to a larger city to receive care for her needs. Thus, they incurred transportation and lodging expenses, further affecting their delicate economic status.

Having lost their livelihood as shrimpers to Hurricane Katrina, the Nguyens were forced to look for work elsewhere. They were fortunate in that they had a rather large social support network and that acquaintances helped them find employment once retail outlets began to reopen in the months after the hurricane. Unfortunately, the retail jobs they found paid little more than minimum wages and did not include medical insurance. The Nguyens' educational background and minimal fluency in English made it difficult for them to pursue higher-paying jobs.

Internal contextual factors are those that originate within the family and are accompanied by changes in the way the family functions. The Nguyens chose to leave their family and friends in Vietnam in order to move to the United States. In doing so, the structure and definition of their family became less clear, particularly given the limited opportunities they had to return for visits. They also were forced to wrestle with issues related to caring for their aging parents. Once living in the United States, the Nguyens' family structure changed further when they became parents themselves.

For the Nguyens, a relatively young couple, becoming parents could be considered a "normative" stressor. Normative stressors are normal, predictable, and developmental in nature. This stressor of becoming parents also could be considered volitional, as a degree of choice was involved. Conversely, nonnormative stressors are those that are unexpected. A catastrophic event such as Hurricane Katrina and all of its ramifications certainly should be classified as nonnormative. For the Nguyens, having a child with Spina Bifida also is a nonnormative and nonvolitional stressor, and its lasting implications will make its presence chronic.

To ameliorate their situation, the Nguyens have several resources, derived from both internal and external contexts, on which they may rely. Although they left friends and family behind in order to move to the United States, they are members of a fairly large immigrant community in Mississippi. From this community, they receive a tremendous amount of social support. In addition, the Nguyens have been able to utilize public community resources for health care and for other basic survival needs in the weeks and months after Hurricane Katrina. The Nguyens possess strengths such as initiative, resourcefulness, and a strong work ethic that help them to be resilient in the face of their stressors.

KEY TERMS RELATED TO CRISIS

To help plan effective crisis response strategies, it is important to keep a number of concepts in mind. A problem, however, is that many of the terms used in the stress and crisis literature are used inconsistently or without specificity (Boss, 2002). For example, in Western culture, the word *stress* is widely used to describe emotional phenomena ranging from feeling mild irritation and frustration to being frozen with fear. As the word relates to crises, however, it applies more to the ability to function than it does to affect. While the definitions of many terms seem intuitively obvious, some have unique connotations within the context of crisis intervention. In this section, key phrases and concepts used to describe crisis intervention theories and models are defined.

Stress

The terms *stress* and *crisis* often have been used interchangeably in the literature, thus creating a bit of confusion. Boss (1988, 2002), has attempted to distinguish between the two concepts, stating that stress is a continuous variable (i.e., stress may be measured by degree), whereas crisis is a dichotomous variable (i.e., there either is or isn't a crisis). Stress may be thought of as a process that exists over time, as, for example, the stress of having a loved one serving in the military in a hostile environment. Crisis, on the other hand, may be thought of as that temporary period of time during which typical coping ceases and there is intense disorganization and disequilibrium. A family accustomed to coping with the stress of having a loved one serving in the military overseas may experience crisis when that individual returns home. The family's boundaries, structure, and coping mechanisms may have changed during the loved one's absence, leaving the family inadequately equipped to function with that loved one's homecoming.

Stress is defined as pressure or tension on an individual or family system. It is a response to demands brought about by a stressor event and represents a change in the equilibrium or steady state of an individual or family system (Boss, 1988, 2002; McKenry & Price, 2005; Selye, 1978). The degree of stress experienced hinges on perceptions of, and meanings attributed to, the stressor event. While anything with the potential to change some aspect of the individual or family (e.g., boundaries, roles, beliefs) might produce stress, increased stress levels do not necessarily always lead to crises. Often, stress can be managed, and the family or individual can arrive at a new steady state.

Trauma

Traumatic events are one type of stressor event. Traumatic events are powerful and overwhelming, and they threaten perceptions of safety and security. Some may be single incidents of relatively short-term duration, whereas others may occur over longer periods of time, resulting in prolonged exposure to the threatening stressor (Collins & Collins, 2005). According to the *Diagnostic and Statistical Manual of Mental Disorders* (*DSM–IV–TR*; American Psychiatric Association, 2000), a traumatic event involves "actual or threatened death or serious injury, or a threat to the physical integrity of self or others" (p. 218). Traumatic events may be human-caused accidents or catastrophes, such as the 2003 ferry disaster in New York City. The ferry reportedly had not been running a straight course and struck a concrete pier while attempting to dock at the Staten Island end of its run. The crash killed 11 people and injured dozens of others. Other traumatic events include acts of deliberate cruelty. The terrorist attacks on the World Trade Center and Pentagon on September 11, 2001; the bombing of the Alfred P. Murrah Federal Building in Oklahoma City in 1995; and school shootings such as those at Westside Middle School in Jonesboro Arkansas, at Columbine High School in Littleton, Colorado, and at Virginia Tech all are examples of acts of deliberate human cruelty, as are the numerous homicides and sexual assaults that occur in the United States each year. Additional traumatic events include natural disasters—events such as Hurricane Floyd, which struck the Carolina coast in 1999 and resulted in 56 deaths; the F-5 tornado that left a trail of death and destruction in Oak Grove, Alabama in 1998; the flood that occurred in Cedar Rapids, Iowa in 2008; and the earthquake that resulted in tens of thousands of deaths in China in 2008.

Responses to Trauma

In general, people experiencing traumatic events respond with feelings of "intense fear, helplessness, or horror" (American Psychiatric Association, 2000, p. 219). Many of these individuals become significantly distressed and impaired, and a few develop illnesses such as Acute Stress Disorder (ASD) and Posttraumatic Stress Disorder (PTSD). The risk for psychological disturbance tends to increase with the magnitude or intensity of the traumatic stressor and with the degree to which the event was human caused and intended to harm (Norris et al., 2002).

Following the Cocoanut Grove fire in 1942, practitioners began to become aware of "common reactions to abnormal events" that do not necessarily constitute psychiatric illnesses. Reactions to traumatic events typically include physical, behavioral, cognitive, emotional, and spiritual responses, which tend to occur in stages, but ultimately are temporary. These transient reactions often are referred to as reactions to posttraumatic stress (PTS). Physical responses involve the autonomic nervous system as the person prepares to "fight or flee" and may be experienced through symptoms such as palpitations, shortness of breath, nausea, muscle tension, headaches, and fatigue. Behaviorally, individuals may experience sleep and dietary changes, social withdrawal, purposeful avoidance of or attention to reminders of the trauma, changes in relationships, and increased use of alcohol or other mood-altering substances. Cognitive responses include rumination, preoccupation, forgetfulness, and difficulty concentrating.

Emotional responses include distress, anxiety, impatience, irritability, anger, and symptoms of depression. Finally, spiritual responses are centered on existential questions and attempts to find meaning in the traumatic event. These reactions may transpire over a period as long as two years, but they are not considered pathological.

While most people return to a level of equilibrium and healthy functioning following a reaction to traumatic stress, some may experience consequences that impair their ability to function. Many of these individuals experience traumatic stress–related anxiety disorders. Two such disorders are described in the *DSM–IV–TR* (American Psychiatric Association, 2000): ASD and PTSD. These two disorders are similar in their symptomology and differ mainly in their temporal association with exposure to the traumatic event. According to the *DSM–IV–TR*, the diagnostic criteria for ASD and PTSD include hyperarousal (hypervigilance, difficulty concentrating, exaggerated startle responses, sleep disturbance), reexperiencing (flashbacks, nightmares, intrusive thoughts), and avoidance (attempts to avoid reminders of the traumatic event, inability to recall components of the event, detachment, dissociation, restricted affect)— symptoms that lead to distress and impairment in key areas of functioning such as work and interpersonal relationships. If these symptoms appear within one month of exposure to the trauma, ASD is diagnosed. If exposure to the traumatic event occurred more than a month prior to the development of these symptoms, PTSD is diagnosed. If symptoms persist for more than three months, PTSD is considered chronic.

Coping

All actions taken in an effort to manage stress, regardless of whether they are successful, are referred to as coping. Coping involves cognitive and behavioral components and is considered a process, not an outcome. Coping requires an assessment of the stressor event and its potential for harm as well as an assessment of the possible outcome of any response strategy chosen. Coping responses may be problem focused or emotion focused and may employ direct action behaviors that are used in relation to the physical or social environment or intrapsychic tactics that allow for the reduction of emotional arousal. Specific coping behaviors are chosen either to deal directly with the problem associated with stress (e.g., fight or flight) or to control emotions, in some cases by covering them up. Coping strategies are neither adaptive nor maladaptive, as adaptation is considered an outcome variable. Instead, coping behaviors should be considered in relation to the specific purpose for which they were chosen. Following the experience of a traumatic stress event, for example, some individuals may choose to increase their alcohol consumption. While this behavior does little to address the needs brought about by the stressor, it may be effective (albeit unhealthy) in keeping unwanted emotions at bay (Boss, 1988; Lazarus, 1966, 1976; McKenry & Price, 2005; Pearlin & Schooler, 1978).

Adaptation

Adaptation is an outcome of stress or crisis. It is the degree to which functioning has changed over an extended period of time and may be measured by the fit between the individual or family system and the environment. According to McCubbin & Patterson (1982), some families benefit from the challenges of adversity. Successfully dealing with adversity results in an outcome that is better than one that might have been reached without the adversity. These families have changed to the point where they have the resources to meet the demands of stressors while continuing to grow. Quite often, changes have occurred in functional behaviors such as rules, roles, boundaries, and interpersonal communication patterns, resulting in families being better equipped to meet the challenges of future stressors. Conversely, for some families an imbalance continues between stress demands and the capability to meet those demands. Many families may adopt unhealthy and unproductive responses to stress. Unhealthy coping behaviors, such as addictions or domestic violence, result in additional stress. Furthermore, it is often the case that coping behaviors that appear to be healthy contribute to stress. A parent, for example, might take a second job in order to increase the family's financial resources. Working extra hours, however, removes that parent from the home and may contribute to strained family relationships and a decrease in other nontangible resources.

Resiliency

How well an individual or family system bounces back from adversity is considered resiliency. Based on physiological strengths, psychological resourcefulness, and interpersonal skills (Cowan, Cowan, & Schultz, 1996), resiliency is that group of coping strengths that allows some people to benefit from having successfully dealt with stress. In addition to being considered an outcome of stress and crisis, resilience may be considered protective in that hardy individuals and families seem to be less vulnerable to stress. People who are resilient tend to be protected by their attribution, response, and cognitive styles as well as by their social and problem-solving skills (Boss, 2002). Very often, these protective factors have been acquired through the successful resolution of a crisis.

CRISIS INTERVENTION VERSUS TRADITIONAL COUNSELING

There are many differences between traditional counseling and crisis intervention. However, the overall differences rest in purpose, setting, time, and intervention plan. It is crucial for professionals to understand the purpose of crisis counseling, as it differs from that of traditional counseling, in order to intervene appropriately. Simply, the goal of traditional counseling is to increase functioning, whereas the goal of crisis counseling is to decrease suffering and increase stabilization in order to refer the client on for longer-term counseling. Imagine a car accident in which an individual may have experienced a severe medical trauma. It is essential for the EMT to stabilize the patient to prevent further injuries prior to transferring (referring) the patient to a surgeon at the hospital.

Traditional counseling is typically a scheduled event that lasts for a specific period of time (e.g., a 50-minute session), and it is expected to consist of more than one such session over a period of time. Traditional counseling sessions take place in mental health agencies, private practices, hospitals, correctional facilities, residential facilities, and other locations related to mental health services (Gladding, 1997).

Crisis intervention is quite different from traditional counseling. Crisis intervention happens at the spur of the moment and is not a scheduled event. Clients can present with symptoms of a crisis in traditional counseling, but typically crises are not planned. Crisis intervention can take place in all of the settings that traditional counseling takes place but has much broader borders. Crisis intervention can take place in one's home (e.g., after a child becomes missing), a makeshift shelter (e.g., after a hurricane), an emergency room (e.g., after a rape), or any one of numerous other contexts.

Treatment Planning

A treatment plan is a formal document that has the primary purpose of focusing the treatment of clients, setting realistic expectations of counseling, developing a tool for measuring progress in treatment, and establishing a measure of quality control (Maruish, 2002). A formal treatment plan typically consists of the referral source and reason for referral, the presenting problem and a prioritized list of all problems, a working diagnosis, goals and objectives, treatment strategies and interventions, client strengths, possible barriers to treatment, referral for evaluation, criteria for ending treatment, responsible staff, risk assessment, and treatment plan review date.

Clinicians conducting traditional counseling will use these treatment planning components to focus the progress of counseling. Counselors who work with clients experiencing crises will also use treatment plans but may modify a treatment plan to specifically address the crisis issues (Johngma & Peterson, 1999). When dealing with clients who are in a crisis situation or who are in a continual state of crisis, considerable time should be spent in developing a strength-based treatment plan highlighting protective factors and the positive aspects of the client's life (Greene, Lee, Trask, & Rheinscheld, 2005). In addition, treatment planning in crisis intervention may use a team approach involving multiple professionals to address the various needs of the person in crisis. For example, counselors, psychiatrists, case workers, clergy/pastoral counselors, first responders, and law enforcement and medical professionals may all be involved to address specific issues for one person or family unit in crisis. Table 1.1 illustrates additional differences in treatment planning between traditional counseling and crisis intervention.

ROLES OF AND COLLABORATION BETWEEN HELPING PROFESSIONALS DURING CRISIS

The roles of mental health providers are not clearly defined in the scholarly literature. However, one could assume that all of those who work in the mental health profession have been exposed to crisis intervention training or at least basic counseling skills that can help clients reduce crisis or stressful situations. Following are brief descriptions of how different mental health professionals—including professional school counselors, professional counselors, psychologists, social workers, psychiatrists, hotline workers, and paraprofessionals—can be helpful in crisis situations.

Professional School Counselors

Professional school counselors play a vital role in a comprehensive crisis leadership team (Kerr, 2009) and are key figures in a school building who provide leadership to the school through advocacy and collaboration. They work to maximize student achievement and also to "promote equity and access to opportunities and rigorous educational experiences for all students" as well as helping to facilitate "a safe learning environment and work[ing] to safeguard the human rights of all members of the school community" (American School Counselor Association, 2008, p. 2). School counselors

TABLE 1.1 Treatment Planning Differences Between Traditional Counseling and Crisis Intervention

Treatment Plan Component	Traditional Counseling	Crisis Intervention
Purpose	Increase functioning.	Decrease suffering; increase stabilization.
Referral Source and Reason	Indicate who sent the client to therapy and why the client is in counseling.	Same as traditional counseling, but indicate if such reason for referral is due to a crisis or is a temporary situation.
Presenting Problem and Prioritized List of All Problems	Define the main problem that the client is experiencing.	Typically, the presenting problem is the crisis, although it is important to determine what issues may have led up to the crisis. The clinician must also contextualize and triage client problems even though the client may not see them as significant. For example, if the client is depressed but becomes suicidal when the depression increases, the clinician would view suicide as more pressing than the depression.
Working Diagnosis	The clinician will develop a five-axis diagnosis.	Same as traditional counseling but more of a rapid crisis assessment that may require symptomology to be triaged. Specific attention will also be brought to those diagnoses that contribute to suicide, crisis, and spontaneity (e.g., Substance Abuse, Borderline Personality Disorder, Anxiety Disorders, Mood Disorders).
Goals and Objectives	The clinician and the client will develop short-term and long-term goals and objectives to make progress in therapy. These goals and objectives must be stated in realistic and measurable terms.	Same as traditional counseling, but more short-term goals and objectives will typically be indicated when a crisis occurs.
Treatment Strategies and Interventions	The clinician will indicate specific theory-driven strategies and interventions to progress toward positive outcomes in treatment. Such strategies and interventions should correspond to the established goals and objectives.	Same as traditional counseling, but include issues of crisis assessments, issues of safety and possible supervision, and the client's readiness to change his/her ability to handle crisis.
	Nondirective or collaborative approaches are ideal.	May employ a directive, nondirective, or collaborative approach.
Client Strengths	The clinician and the client will develop a list of the client's strengths.	Same as traditional counseling, but specifically include client protective factors and strengths that will facilitate coping with crisis circumstances.

(continued)

TABLE 1.1 Treatment Planning Differences Between Traditional Counseling and Crisis Intervention (*continued*)

Treatment Plan Component	Traditional Counseling	Crisis Intervention
Possible Barriers to Treatment	The clinician and the client will develop a list of general events, situations, people, etc., that may negatively interfere with treatment.	Same as traditional counseling, but specifically indicate events, situations, people, etc., that are not to be initiated when a crisis occurs. For example, typically cousin Sally is a good resource and listens to problems, but she does not provide the client with what is needed when upset.
Referral for Evaluation	The clinician will indicate what assessments are needed to assist the progression of treatment and what outside resources need to be consulted.	Same as traditional counseling, but also provide specific assessments for crisis, protective factors, and other resources that may relieve crisis situations. For example, if a client is in crisis because he or she lost his or her job, a career counselor may be warranted. Referrals are used more often, since the crisis symptoms may mask the actual presenting issue, which may warrant a person with specialized training.
Criteria for Ending Treatment	Typically, termination criteria will involve a significant decrease in the presenting problem symptoms.	Priority is to decrease the symptoms associated with the presenting problem and then refer the client to long-term counseling. Termination often occurs due to referring the client to another professional.
	Often, a formal termination process is the protocol and is explained during the initial visit. Termination is completed after issues have been resolved or after a referral is made that allows for closure.	Appropriate termination and closure are often missing in crisis counseling, since the problem may not be reconciled at this point.
Responsible Staff	Indicate what staff are involved in treatment and include their responsibilities.	Same as traditional counseling, but include specific individuals and agencies to contact in crisis situations.
	Often, an individual counselor.	Team approach utilizes numerous professionals to address the symptoms and issues related to the crisis.
Treatment Plan Review Date	Typically in an agency setting this occurs every three months.	If the client is in a serious crisis or is continually in crisis, review of the treatment plan should be more frequent; in some settings, this is done daily or multiple times throughout the same day.

frequently accomplish these goals by providing preventative and substantive programs that are imbedded in a comprehensive school counseling program.

Given their unique role, school counselors can be helpful in school crisis situations by using individual counseling, group counseling, and classroom guidance activities and by collaborating with key stakeholders. Individual counseling can be helpful to those who are directly affected by crises (e.g., by working with a student on expressing feelings after his or her house caught on fire). Providing group counseling to those who have been exposed to crises (e.g., by establishing a support group for students who have divorced parents) could ease the pain of the initial impact of the crisis and create a support network among the group members. School counselors could also provide classroom guidance activities such as these:

- Preventative programs via classroom guidance activities on crisis, suicide, handling stress, communication skills, expressing frustration, and the like, which are seen as ways to prevent crises from occurring.
- Classroom guidance activities in the aftermath of a crisis (e.g., providing students with resources after the town has been devastated by a flood).

Lastly, connecting with the community and collaborating with key stakeholders are a vital role for school counselors in the wake of a crisis. Such connective efforts could include the following:

- Collaborating with teachers, staff, principals, superintendents, and other school personnel on preventing and responding to crisis (e.g., by providing school staff with materials and training on recognizing suicidal behavior).
- Working with families and individuals in the Parent Teacher Organization on ways to prevent, respond to, intervene in, and manage crisis. This will help parents provide supportive care that is congruent with what their children are learning in school.

Professional Counselors, Psychologists, and Social Workers

For the purpose of this book, professional counselors, psychologists, and social workers are grouped in one category because each profession can provide short-term or long-term therapy and individual or group therapy. Each state may allow for a differing scope of practice, and it is beyond the purpose of this book to discuss each of the subtle differences. For example, some states may allow professional counselors to diagnose and treat mental and emotional disorders, while others may not allow this. Overall, this group of mental health professionals will need a minimum of a master's degree to become licensed and practice (Gladding, 1997) and must possess specific training in providing mental health services. These professionals can be helpful in crisis situations by

- Assisting clients in gaining insight into the ways crisis affects their life in a cognitive, behavioral, and emotional manner over a lengthy period of time.
- Providing specific treatment goals and objectives related to crisis.
- Monitoring and assessing the magnitude of severity of a crisis situation.
- Providing insight into co-occurring mental and emotional disorders and crisis (e.g., showing a client diagnosed with Bipolar Disorder how to cope with and monitor crisis).
- Providing specific crisis intervention strategies during a crisis and over a period of time.
- Providing clients in crisis with resources and preventative measures.
- Assisting in alleviating symptoms associated with the crisis.
- Preparing clients to handle future crises.

Some professional counselors, psychologists, and social workers may specialize in a particular area that would contribute to helping individuals in crisis. For example:

- Marriage and family therapists provide support for couples and families and may involve the family in the resolution of the crisis on a short- and long-term basis.
- Pastoral counselors provide religious or spiritual integration in times of a crisis. Often, a crisis involves a spiritual or religious disconnect or dimension that must be explored. It is also important to understand any religious or spiritual coping mechanisms that were effective in the past that could be applied to the present crisis. This is important for all counselors to explore and should not be limited to the pastoral counseling profession.
- Chemical dependency counselors specifically address the use of drugs and alcohol as a coping mechanism during crisis.
- Counselors or psychologists who specialize in treating children, adolescents, adults, or geriatric populations could specifically address the crisis needs of individuals at a specific age.

Psychiatrists

According to the American Psychiatric Association (2008), psychiatrists are physicians who have obtained specific training and experience in treating mental and emotional disorders. The key difference between the scope of practice of psychiatrists and that of other mental health practitioners is that psychiatrists can prescribe medication to clients. "Psychiatrists are especially suited to triaging direct and indirect victims in various settings, such as on consultation in hospitals' emergency rooms, intensive care and burn units, general medical floors or inpatient psychiatry units. Or psychiatrists may volunteer for agencies such as the American Red Cross, where they may be part of a mental health team providing grief support, notification of death to family members, or crisis intervention" (American Psychiatric Association, 2004, p. 21).

Hotline Workers

Hotline workers are often the first point of contact for many individuals experiencing a crisis and may handle any number of crises resulting from suicidal and homicidal ideation, domestic violence, substance abuse, and sexual assault. There are hotlines that specialize in specific crisis situations such as those mentioned previously. There are even crisis hotlines for specific age groups (e.g., a hotline dedicated to teen callers). Typically, hotline workers are not mental health professionals but volunteers who have undergone specific training in responding to crises. No matter what their focus, crisis hotlines play a vital role in assessing, intervening in, and preventing the occurrence of crises (Seeley, 1995). Crisis hotline workers are essential during a crisis situation to

- Assess the severity of the crisis situation and the lethality of the caller.
- Provide immediate crisis intervention to the caller in an attempt to deescalate the crisis. This is critical in a crisis situation because the caller does not have to make an appointment with a professional or wait to get help. Most hotlines are 24-hour services open 365 days a year.
- Provide resources to the caller that may help resolve the crisis (see Table 1.2 for a sample of national toll-free hotlines that serve those in crisis).

TABLE 1.2 Sample Toll-free Hotlines

General Crisis Intervention Hotlines for Youth (dealing with conflicts, family stressors, suicide, runaway youth, drugs and alcohol, homelessness, and so on)

- Boys Town Suicide and Crisis Line: 800-448-3000 (voice) / 800-448-1833 (TDD)
- Covenant House Hotline: 800-999-9999
- National Youth Crisis Hotline: 800-442-HOPE

Child Abuse Hotlines

- ChildHelp USA National Child Abuse Hotline: 800-4-A-CHILD (voice) / 800-2-A-CHILD (TDD)
- National Child Abuse Hotline: 800-25-ABUSE

Domestic Violence Hotlines

- National Domestic Violence/Child Abuse/Sexual Abuse Hotline: 800-799-SAFE (voice) / 800-787-3224 (TDD) / 800-942-6908 (Spanish speaking)
- Domestic Violence Hotline: 800-829-1122

Substance Abuse/Alcoholism Hotlines

- Al-ateen: 800-352-9996
- National Cocaine Hotline: 800-COCAINE
- National Drug Information Treatment and Referral Hotline: 800-662-HELP

Poison Control Hotline

- Poison Control: 800-362-9922

Rape Hotline

- National Rape Crisis Hotline: 800-656-4673

Suicide Prevention Hotlines

- National Suicide Hotline: 800-SUICIDE (voice) / 800-799-4TTY (TDD)
- National Suicide Prevention Lifeline: 800-273-TALK / 888-628-9454 (Spanish speaking)

Paraprofessionals

Some individuals within the mental health community have little professional mental health training but perform essential tasks (e.g., case management duties, residential care) for individuals in crisis. Paraprofessionals can

- Manage resources that help facilitate stabilization (e.g., make sure clients keep all medical, financial, emotional, environmental, and social service appointments).
- Ensure clients are aware of appropriate resources that could be seen as preventative actions to crisis (e.g., ensure a client has appropriate resources to pay a natural gas bill to have heat in the winter).
- Provide an outlet for a client to decrease isolation and talk to others (e.g., talk with individuals in crisis and provide assurance that someone cares for them and their situation).
- Participate in executing the modality and frequency aspects of the treatment plan—in other words, make the connections set out in the treatment plan. For

example, the professional counselor may develop a treatment plan for someone in a residential program that involves attending Alcoholics Anonymous groups daily, attending a group on a specified psychosocial issue three times per week, and addressing a medical issue. The paraprofessional case worker may be responsible for following through with the treatment plan by assisting the client in making the appointments and setting up transportation to the appointments or groups.

To be effective, a crisis worker, whether a professional or a paraprofessional, must be able to (a) rely on life experiences and emotional maturity to remain stable and consistent, (b) remain calm and poised in order to deescalate the situation, (c) use creativity and flexibility to adapt to rapidly changing situations, (d) maintain an energetic and resilient self to keep up with the rigor of working in a crisis situation, and (e) use effective clinical skills in a timely fashion in order to create a trusting and safe environment and suspend one's values just for the crisis time in order to stabilize the client and refer him or her on to another professional (James, 2008). Keep these characteristics in mind when doing Activity 1.1.

ACTIVITY 1.1
Who Does What and Why?

In the following crisis situations, what might be some activities, interventions, responsibilities, and considerations for each of the mental health professionals addressed above?

Crisis Situation 1

Alan and Mary have been married for three years. Alan has been cheating on Mary for the past six months, and Mary has been cheating on Alan for the past year. Each is unaware of the other's infidelity, but the stress in their house is severe. They yell constantly, and Mary throws objects during arguments. In the past month, Alan has begun to slap Mary during these arguments. Last night Alan hit her so hard that he knocked her unconscious. Mary is now in the hospital talking to a social worker. Mary states to the social worker, "I am afraid of my husband, but I don't have anywhere else to go; I feel so alone."

Crisis Situation 2

John F. Kennedy High School, located in a primarily low- to middle-class rural community, comprises approximately 1,000 students, most of whom know one another. Within the past four months, the school has been evacuated five times as a result of a call indicating that there is a bomb in the building and that "everyone should get out." As a result of these threats and evacuations, students are scared, parents do not want to send their children to school, and teachers and other school personnel are frightened to go to work. Students also have begun to accuse other students of calling in the bomb threats, and several students have been ostracized and bullied. The Parent Teacher Organization has called a meeting tonight to address this issue.

Crisis Situation 3

Walter Taylor is a 74-year-old African-American male who has worked all of his life as a plumber. Walter has been married to Martha for 52 years and has four children and six grandchildren. Due to intense flash floods within the past week from melting snow, the Taylor household is seven feet under water. When the water came, Walter, his 40-year-old daughter June, and his 13-year-old granddaughter Beverly had to be rescued from their house by boat. Walter's house is destroyed, Beverly is having nightmares and not wanting to leave her family, and June is recovering from a head trauma caused while being evacuated.

ASSESSMENT AND INTERVENTION

Attempts to intervene in crisis situations must begin with assessment. At a minimum, crisis counselors need to assess clients for disturbances in their equilibrium or mobility by evaluating their functioning in the areas of affect, behavior, and cognition. Through appropriate assessment, responders are able to gauge the severity of the crisis situation, the extent to which clients have been immobilized, available resources, lethality, and the effectiveness of the crisis workers' own efforts (James, 2008).

A Developmental-Ecological Model of Assessment

A number of models have been suggested for use in assessing crises, including the multidimensional model proposed by Slaikeu (1990) and the triage assessment model proposed by Myer, Williams, Ottens, and Schmidt (1992). The multidimensional model proposed by Slaikeu (1990) was based on Arnold Lazarus's multimodal approach to counseling. According to Slaikeu, it is important to approach crisis intervention from a systemic, contextual point of view. In addition, it is important to attend to behavior, affect, somatic responses, interpersonal interactions, cognitions, and spirituality. Similar to the multidimensional model, the triage assessment model (Myer et al., 1992) addresses affect, behavior, and cognition in response to crisis events. According to the triage assessment model, affective responses tend to be negative and centered around anxiety and fear, anger, or sadness. Behavioral reaction, in general, may be classified as approach, avoidance, or immobility. Cognitive perceptions, which often impact affective and behavioral responses, tend to emphasize the idea of transgression; that is, there is a sense of victimization or of rights being violated, threats to safety and security, and loss.

These models have strengths in that they stress assessment from a holistic perspective, but according to Collins and Collins (2005), neither has the collective qualities of being user-friendly, adaptable, comprehensive, and culturally sensitive. Thus, Collins and Collins have proposed a developmental-ecological paradigm for assessment as well as intervention. This model addresses the individual, the environment, and the interaction between the two.

The developmental-ecological model presented by Collins and Collins (2005) provides a framework for assessing clients, along with their environmental contexts. The framework includes five dimensions: affect, behavior, cognition, development, and the ecosystem or ABCDE. Common affective responses during crises include anxiety, anger, depression, sadness, fear, shame, and confusion. Behavioral responses range from inaction and immobility to lethal actions and are representative of how well clients are coping. Consideration of cognitions provides additional clues to coping, as clients engage in cognitive appraisal as one aspect of the coping process. Attention to cognitions also allows the crisis counselor to assess perceptions and the meaning that clients assign to the crisis situation.

In agreement with Boss (1987, 1988, 2002), Collins and Collins (2005) maintained that it is important to consider contextual variables in order to understand fully the crisis experience. As many crises are triggered by stressors that arise at transitional points during the life span, it is essential for crisis counselors to be familiar with theories of human and family development. Phenomena associated with various stages of development may contribute to the pileup of stressors but may present additional resources as well (McCubbin & Patterson, 1982).

CASE STUDY 1.1 (continued)

The Nguyens

If you were to work with the Nguyen family as a crisis counselor, you would need to assess Vin and Li and their environment from a contextual point of view. The ABCDE assessment model (Collins & Collins, 2005) is suggested for assessing the Nguyens' essential areas of function:

A (affect): Given the birth of a daughter with a disability in the context of the other hardships that the Nguyens have been dealing with, what feelings might this couple be experiencing?

B (behavior): What actions have Vin and Li taken to deal with their provoking stressors? Are any of these behaviors dangerous?

C (cognition): How do Vin and Li explain what has happened to them? Do their cultural and religious beliefs affect the meaning they have attributed to their situation? Since the Nguyens lost their livelihood to Hurricane Katrina, are they focused on loss, or has the birth of their daughter brought them new hope for the future?

D (development): Vin and Li are young adults and, in terms of the family life cycle, are at the developmental stage of becoming first-time parents. What additional stressors and resources come with this stage of development?

E (ecosystem): What is happening in the community in which Vin and Li live? Are the Nguyens supported in this community? Do they have friends and family? Are there other Vietnamese families in the community? Are social services available to them?

An additional contextual factor proposed by Collins and Collins (2005) is the ecosystem. From an ecosystemic perspective, clients should be considered within the context of their culture and ethnicity; family and extended family; friends; community affiliations such as church, school, workplace, and neighborhood; and formal social services at the institutional or society level.

FUNDAMENTALS OF WORKING WITH CRISIS CLIENTS

The underpinnings of working with clients in crisis begin with determining, based on assessment efforts, how best to approach them to deescalate the crisis. In other words, we need to assess whether the situation calls for us to be directive, nondirective, or collaborative (James, 2008).

Directive approaches call for us to "direct" or lead the person in crisis in a specific direction. Clients in crisis are typically scattered and unable to plan beyond their current situation. Therefore, providing some form of direction may help. For example, if someone is highly uncertain, spontaneous, or ambiguous and, at the same time, unable to get out of a crisis state, providing direction could provide immediate, though temporary, relief to feelings surrounding the crisis situation.

Nondirective approaches allow the person in crisis to come up with the directives while the crisis counselor facilitates that process. If the client is at a place where he or she can make rational decisions, even though he or she is still in a state of crisis, a nondirective approach may empower the client to make progress toward deescalation. For example, asking clients who were recently victimized by a flood "What might be of most help to you now?" allows them to respond with specifics, rather than having you guess what was needed. The thought process and response of such clients may also empower them to feel like they are regaining some control over their own lives.

A collaborative approach focuses on showing the person in crisis that you are there, with them, on the journey toward stabilization and normalcy. People in crisis need to know that there are others not only to provide help but also to decrease isolation and increase resource allocation. Collaborative approaches are considered a blending of directive and nondirective approaches—but with a flavor of togetherness. In other words, a collaborative approach provides support and a sense of working together toward a common goal.

Examples of directive, nondirective, and collaborative approaches in crisis situations follow. Discuss how each could be an appropriate statement in specific circumstances.

EXAMPLE 1

- I want you to put the gun down. (directive)
- Let's chat about how you feel about putting the gun down. (nondirective)
- I want to help, but knowing you have that gun in your hand scares me. Can you put the gun down for me so I can help you more? (collaborative)

EXAMPLE 2

- Calm down. (directive)
- How might you calm yourself down? (nondirective)
- Boy, I'm really upset. Let's try and calm down for a bit. (collaborative)

EXAMPLE 3

- I am calling the police. (directive)
- Would calling the police help? (nondirective)
- If I bring you the phone, would you call the police? (collaborative)

COMPLICATIONS OF INDIVIDUALS RESPONDING TO CRISIS

There is an old saying that exists in mental health treatment: "If you haven't had a client in crisis, then you haven't worked with clients long." Complications of working in crisis situations and with clients in crisis can take a physical, emotional, and professional toll on crisis counselors. It is important when reading the remainder of this text to consider how you might take care of yourself while helping others manage a crisis. Consider proactive ways to avoid burnout, manage your own emotional state during highly emotional crisis situations (e.g., when working with suicidal clients), and ensure that your physical, cognitive, and psychological self is up to working with clients in crisis. Working with others in a state of crisis is not easy. Crisis counselors need to stay abreast of their own well-being in order to help others.

Summary

A crisis is a situation in which there is a precipitating stressor event, a perception of that event that leads to distress, and diminished functioning when the distress is not relieved by familiar coping resources. Many individuals and families are resilient and benefit from having met the challenges of a crisis situation. How well an individual or family adapts following a crisis often is determined not only by the nature of the stressor event itself but also by the presence or absence of other stressors, the availability of tangible and intangible resources, and how the entire situation is perceived. Crises may be provoked by predictable events that occur during normal, developmental transitions during the lives of individuals and families or by situational events that often are sudden and unexpected.

Crisis intervention begins with assessment of the provoking event, reactions and responses to the provoking event, and other contextual variables that impact the situation. While there are times when a crisis counselor's response to a crisis appears indistinguishable from traditional counseling, crisis intervention generally is thought to be quite different from traditional counseling. Paraprofessionals and professionals from a variety of helping disciplines provide crisis intervention services, often working in teams where each helper may focus on a particular area of expertise. Working with clients in crisis places helpers at risk for vicarious trauma and burnout. The work is difficult, but the rewards are immeasurable.

2   Reacting in Crisis Situations

Charlotte Daughhetee and Mary Bartlett

PREVIEW

When responding to a crisis, counselors need to be able to act promptly; thus, crisis preparedness is essential to best practice during emergency situations. A brief overview of crisis planning guidelines and crisis counselor safety procedures is presented, along with a review of transcrisis issues, ethical considerations in crisis treatment, and counselor self-care concerns. While crisis planning can never be perfect, it does provide a framework for appropriate response and decision making in urgent situations. Prepared crisis counselors, well versed in crisis procedures and processes, will be able to provide ethical, skilled help in all types of crisis conditions.

SAFETY CONCERNS AND PRECAUTIONS

In addition to its emotional and psychological toll, a crisis event produces many safety and security concerns. Crisis planning and preparedness can facilitate a coordinated response among various crisis response units to mitigate further suffering for crisis survivors and to generate a safe environment for crisis workers. Basic safety precautions on the part of the crisis counselor when working with high-risk and/or dangerous clients can reduce the chances of harm to the counselor, the client, and other crisis workers. The ultimate success of crisis intervention, whether it involves responding to one suicidal client or to thousands of hurricane survivors, depends on planning and on the training and preparedness of team members.

Proactive Approaches

Some people are naturally inclined toward preparedness, and they plan for every reasonable contingency. However, most people might intend to get around to emergency planning, but they never seem to follow through with crisis planning and preparation. Schools, institutions, and communities do not have the luxury of putting off the development of a crisis plan. When a crisis event occurs, particularly a large-scale disaster that affects many people, crisis teams must be ready, with roles defined and each person trained in his or her role. McConnell and Drennan

ACTIVITY 2.1

In small groups, discuss the following. If a natural disaster such as a tornado or earthquake hits your area today, would you be prepared? Would you have enough food and water for at least three days, a battery-operated radio, flashlights, candles, extra batteries, and so on? Do you have cash and gas in the car in case you must evacuate? Are you prepared? Why or why not? What other aspects need to be taken into account in preparing for this type of disaster?

(2006) state, "[W]e need to give serious consideration to strong, well-resourced and forward thinking contingency planning if we want to tame and gain control over a crisis when it hits" (p. 59). However, crises, while having huge impacts on systems and communities, are usually a low-priority item with respect to planning and resources. The Federal Emergency Management Agency (FEMA, 2007) stresses that crisis planning is an ongoing cycle of planning, organizing, training, evaluating, and improving. An effective crisis team is one that coordinates and collaborates throughout both planning and crisis response.

Safety Issues

As part of a crisis team, counselors contribute to the success of crisis intervention through collaboration with other crisis workers. Ultimately, this collaborative spirit enhances public safety. Even as they are working to achieve public safety, crisis counselors must also be aware of their own safety and take proactive steps to ensure a secure counseling environment.

INTERACTION WITH LOCAL AUTHORITIES   A crisis team comprises workers from across the community who come together in response to a crisis event. Mental health providers are an essential component of any crisis team, and all members of a crisis response team should work together toward the same goal, which is to advance the recovery process following a disaster. Survivors of crises need access to medical care, food and water, shelter, mental health services, and basic safety; the realization of recovery is possible only when there is interagency cooperation. In the event of large-scale property damage, the safety and security of the area will be maintained by law enforcement, in some cases with the assistance of National Guard troops. Firefighters and medical personnel provide rescue and first aid assistance and collaborate with crisis counselors by referring clients in need of mental health evaluation services. It is important for crisis counselors to understand that during the initial impact of a crisis, the most critical needs correspond to Maslow's hierarchy of needs: shelter, food, water, and safety as well as the need to be connected with family. Mental health providers are used at this time to assess clients in order to prevent further personal crises stemming from the disaster, but specific clients often do not need the services of these mental health professionals until weeks or longer after the onset of the crisis.

It is imperative that crisis counselors be culturally sensitive and demonstrate cultural awareness, knowledge, and skills. Different cultures may react to crisis situations in different ways behaviorally, psychologically, and emotionally. Some cultural groups may distrust government agencies, which can complicate rapport building. Cultural stigmas may cause some clients to be reluctant to seek mental health care when they are in crisis. Additionally, socioeconomic status has a profound effect on crisis survivors, with low-income clients having few or no resources beyond immediate disaster aid. In order for effective crisis intervention to take place, multicultural factors must be considered in the triage and treatment of clients in crisis.

When a client is a danger to self and others, crisis counselors work in partnership with local authorities to ensure safety. Law enforcement is usually involved when a client presents a threat to public safety, as with high-threat homicidal and violent clients. Clients who pose a danger to self and others may need to be hospitalized (see Chapter 5 for information on voluntary and involuntary hospitalization). Crisis counselors should not transport such clients to the hospital but should instead enlist the client's family or friends if the client is low or moderate risk and is voluntarily entering an inpatient unit. A high-risk client who is being hospitalized involuntarily will likely need to be transported to the hospital by ambulance or by police. If a high-risk client suddenly leaves a counselor's office, the counselor should not attempt to physically stop the client but should notify law enforcement for assistance. Because crisis counselors work closely with hospitals and medical personnel during intervention and treatment of suicidal and homicidal clients, a strong working relationship between mental health providers and local authorities is essential to effective crisis intervention.

PHYSICAL SAFETY   Given that crisis counseling often takes place in the field, crisis counselors are likely to find themselves in hazardous surroundings and therefore must be aware of safety procedures for their own security and the well-being of their clients. Being knowledgeable about basic safety precautions is a must before crisis counselors enter disaster areas. Beyond the counselor's safety, survivors are sometimes reluctant to leave their property and may put their own lives at risk. Crisis counselors can offer information about disaster relief services and basic safety concerns. They must be aware of their surroundings, as it is easy to become complacent with the idea that "I am a helping professional and who would hurt a person trying to help someone else." The reality is that individuals who perceive they or someone they care for is being threatened (physically, mentally, spiritually) may go into "fight or flight" mode.

Clients in crisis, particularly suicidal and/or homicidal clients, present an increased risk for the counselor, particularly the sole practitioner in private practice. One of the most dangerous settings for a counselor is an isolated private practice. Despenser (2005) notes that sole private practitioners are vulnerable because their practices are secluded from others and there may not be an adequate prescreening process to indentify clients with borderline or psychotic disorders. Despenser stresses that the most dangerous setting is a counselor practicing alone in his or her home. Counselors who have solo practices in multipurpose buildings are also at risk, as the other occupants in the building may not be aware of calls for help.

Signs for concern in a client include a history of violent behavior, a psychiatric or forensic history, intoxication, erratic speech and behavior, and sexual posturing and insinuation. Whenever possible, counselors should get a thorough history, preferably from the referral source, before seeing a client. An alarm or other mechanism to call for help should be installed. Most importantly, counselors should pay attention to their own gut feelings of discomfort and uneasiness when screening a potential client. Twemlow (2001) also emphasizes the perils of an isolated practice and suggests that counselors should have an escape route that cannot be blocked by chairs or coffee tables, should install panic alarms, and may even consider carrying pepper spray. If a client becomes threatening, Twemlow emphasizes the need for the counselor to remain calm and attempt to redirect the client, thereby defusing the threatening situation.

Violent clients pose a very real threat to counselors, and some form of aggressive client behavior is likely to occur in every mental health provider's career (Tishler, Gordon, & Landry-Meyer, 2000). In a study of Georgia mental health providers, Arthur, Brende, and Quiroz (2003) found that 29% of the practitioners surveyed had feared for their lives at some point during their career and that 61% of the practitioners had suffered some type of physical or psychological assault during their careers. Arthur et al. suggest that mental health professionals working with clients at a high risk for violence (for example, those working on inpatient forensic units) exercise the following safety preparations: "securing wall frames, pictures, and diplomas on walls; identifying dangerous items that could easily be thrown; wearing proper clothing that cannot be grabbed by clients (e.g., ties, scarves); and installing a safety warning alarm" (pp. 40–41). Furthermore, Arthur et al. suggest that private practitioners and agency employees institute safety policies that include "office or body alarms and clue names or words that others would recognize when assistance is needed" (p. 40). Every counselor, regardless of setting, should institute safety rules and abide by them. To assume that violent client behavior "couldn't happen here" is to put oneself in peril.

Another danger faced by mental health providers is the threat of being stalked by a client. Purcell, Powell, and Mullen (2005) did a random survey of 1,750 psychologists and found that 19.5% had experienced stalking. The majority of stalking incidents involved male outpatient clients, and the majority of stalked psychologists were female. Most of the stalkers had a diagnosis of a personality disorder or psychotic disorder; however, some of the stalkers were diagnosed with substance abuse, major depression, or anxiety or had no previous mental disorder diagnosis. Purcell et al. found that clients who stalk were motivated by a need for intimacy, infatuation, resentment or revenge, or a misinterpretation of the therapeutic relationship as a friendship or romance. They stress that mental health providers must be very clear about the nature of the therapeutic relationship and set firm boundaries, preferably in writing. Setting boundaries should include not allowing contact between sessions, not extending session length, keeping personal information private (the counselor's home address and phone should be unlisted), and not placing personal objects such as family photographs in the office, which may give the client too much personal information or may create an atmosphere of familiarity. When clients cannot respect the nature of the therapeutic relationship and continually violate boundaries, the counseling relationship should be terminated and the client referred for a psychiatric evaluation. In extreme cases, the counselor may have to obtain a restraining order for self-protection. As always, counselors should seek supervision and consultation and should clearly document all events, actions, and decisions.

Some agencies offer in-home counseling, especially to low-income clients who may have difficulty finding transportation to counseling centers. Also, in the wake of a large-scale disaster, in-home counseling is a very common crisis intervention. In-home counseling is a highly effective service delivery method, but it brings with it increased safety concerns. In-home services should never be conducted alone; counselors should be accompanied by co-counselors or behavioral aides. Spencer and Munch (2003) emphasize that when conducting in-home counseling, counselors should familiarize themselves with the community and the environment. Where are the building exits? Is there adequate lighting? Also, they should be aware of other people who may be present at the home. If the counselor feels uneasy about the environment, he or she should leave the premises.

Many agencies do not allow counselors to provide transportation to clients. If an agency does allow client transportation, the counselor should obtain liability coverage from the agency for client transportation. The car should not contain weapons or loose objects that could be used as weapons, and car keys should remain in the possession of the counselor at all times (Spencer & Munch, 2003). Clients should be seated where the counselor can see them. When personal safety is in doubt, it is best to arrange for alternative transportation.

Mental health providers working in forensic inpatient units have an increased risk of harm from violent clients. Violent clients in inpatient units may be put in restraints, and staff at inpatient units must be trained in proper restraint methods. Sullivan et al. (2005) stress that staff training should focus on using therapeutic methods to deescalate a violent client and on empowering the client to take ownership of his or her treatment so that the need for restraint can be reduced. Inpatient mental health workers should be cognizant of the fact that federal policy requires that alternatives be attempted before restraints are used and that restraints be used only when absolutely necessary. Additionally, there must be a defined amount of time that a client will remain in restraints, and a restrained client must be assessed in a timely manner. Flannery and Stone (2001) suggest that inpatient facility staff be trained in early warning signs of violence and in the identification of high-risk clients. After violent incidents, staff should be debriefed and provided with support and training.

Remember, violence can occur in any and all counseling settings. Examine the safety of your setting, and consider these questions: Do you have a mechanism to call for help? Is your office set up with an escape route in the event of client violence? Do you have safety rules, and if so, do you abide by them? Crisis preparedness and adherence to basic safety precautions are essential factors for successful crisis intervention in immediate crisis situations and in transcrisis.

Handling Transcrisis in Long-Term Counseling

A crisis is generally recognized to be a time-limited cycle precipitated by an event that temporarily overloads the individual's ability to cope. The crisis is resolved when the individual's ability to cope expands, decreasing the subjective distress and returning functioning to the previous level (Kanel, 2007). There is a dearth of literature on transcrisis, but it is emerging as an important concept in the counseling field. Transcrisis is a variation on that cycle where the subjective distress is not fully mitigated by the expanding ability to cope; instead, the original event is submerged in the subconscious in such a way that it is triggered when subsequent events of a similar nature are encountered. It may arise at various junctures during long-term counseling, taking the client back to a pretherapeutic functioning—and quite often surprising both the client and the counselor. Therefore, even if the counselor has completed a thorough assessment, because the distress of the original event is buried in a person's subconscious, there is no way to predict when or how in long-term therapy it may present. However, when it does, both the client and the counselor must recognize it for what it is in order to work through the transcrisis effectively and return the client to a state of homeostasis or emotional balance (James, 2008). The nature, timing, and presentation of

CASE STUDY 2.1

Counselor Safety

Carol works as a college counselor at a small university counseling center that has one other counselor on staff. The counseling center is located in the basement of a campus office building that is vacant each day by 6:00 P.M. Carol and her colleague have an unwritten safety rule that they will not schedule appointments later than 4:30 P.M. Carol occasionally breaks this rule when she knows the client well. One day a married female student calls to inquire about marriage counseling; the student states that she and her husband are disagreeing about many issues and they want couples therapy to improve communication. Carol suggests several possible appointment times, but the student works and cannot possibly come in until 6:30 or 7:00 P.M. Since the case seems straight-forward, Carol agrees to meet the couple at 7:00 P.M. for an initial session.

When Carol unlocks the counseling center door and admits the couple she immediately feels anxious. The husband's appearance seems unkempt, and he does not make eye contact with Carol. Carol and the couple proceed to her office, fill out intake forms, and go over informed consent. The husband, while quiet, appears to be amenable to treatment, signing all documentation. Carol feels increasingly uneasy, and for the first time, she realizes that her office is arranged with the clients between her and the only door. The husband stares at the floor while the wife explains to Carol that she and her husband have been disagreeing because he has a diagnosis of paranoid schizophrenia and he refuses to take his medication. The wife hopes that through couples counseling, the husband will become more compliant with his medication and they can learn to communicate and interact more positively. Carol maintains an appearance of calm and listens to the wife (the husband remains silent). When Carol finds out from the wife that the husband is under the care of a psychiatrist, she explains to the couple that before any relationship work can be effective, it is necessary that all medical issues be addressed. She further explains that it would be inappropriate for her to work with the couple unless she was working collaboratively with the psychiatrist. The couple agrees to make an appointment with the psychiatrist the next day, and Carol has them both sign releases in case the psychiatrist wishes to speak with her. Carol escorts the couple from the counseling center and breathes a sigh of relief as she locks the door behind them.

Discussion Questions

What was Carol's initial mistake?

How could she have handled the situation differently?

What factors might have caused Carol's complacency with regard to safety?

What safety plan changes should Carol and her colleague institute?

---

transcrisis can be perplexing. Adding to the complexity of this concept is the fact that crisis counselors often assess a person's orientation to time, including whether a client is focused on the past, the present, or the future. According to Sue and Sue (1999), Asian Americans are primarily oriented toward the past or the present, so crisis events are likely to be interpreted from those perspectives. Given that a transcrisis is likely to be the result of a past event embedded in the subconscious and triggered by a present event, a transcrisis may be interpreted and understood similarly by both the crisis counselor and an Asian-American client. Contrast that, however, with Native Americans, who tend to experience crises primarily in the present. A transcrisis may be experienced by Native Americans in a different manner from Asian Americans or from other groups who maintain a focus other than one centered primarily on the present. Thus, a Native American client may be less likely to experience the psychological carryover of a previously experienced event (e.g., death of a parent) into a current crisis state (e.g., death of a child). Since transcrisis is an emerging concept that is not yet well understood or researched, it is important for crisis counselors to consistently consider the diversity of the people they serve and how various cultures may factor into the assessment of initial and subsequent reactions clients have while under treatment.

Developmental Transitions and Stressors

The terms *transcrisis states* and *transcrisis points* are used to describe characteristics of the development and resolution of the transcrisis cycle. An individual may be said to be in a transcrisis state when his or her behavior in the present moment is being affected by an unresolved or poorly resolved previous crisis (James, 2008). If the counselor is able to recognize the client's entry into a transcrisis state, then it becomes possible to begin to probe for the unresolved crisis and make progress toward resolving it; this can involve long-term treatment as the unresolved crisis is identified and explored and steps are taken to resolve it. A transcrisis point is a developmental stage encountered within a transcrisis state in which the individual achieves a step toward resolving the original transcrisis issue; transcrisis states do not necessarily occur in linear progression, but they often do occur in a smallest-step-to-largest-step fashion according to what the individual is capable of achieving. Transcrisis points may be thought of as benchmarks that must be achieved in order to completely resolve the original crisis and therefore break the transcrisis cycle.

Posttraumatic Stress Disorder

Transcrisis is often compared to Posttraumatic Stress Disorder (PTSD), which is an effect produced by experiencing or witnessing a traumatic event that threatened the person's life and in which the person experienced intense fear, horror, or a sense of helplessness (American Psychiatric Association, 2000). Transcrisis, however, generally exists only within a single category of stressor; for instance, if a woman is raped, then transcrisis may manifest itself as difficulty with subsequent intimate sexual relationships. If an individual has an insufficiently resolved crisis with a parent, transcrisis may manifest itself as difficulty with other authority figures whom the individual may encounter in the future (James, 2008). PTSD, on the other hand, typically affects the individual's behavior and ability to cope across a wide range of situations and circumstances (Collins & Collins, 2005). Transcrisis therefore may be thought of as a narrowed version of the much better known PTSD.

Regression, Mood Disorders, and Psychosis

Regression, mood disorders, anxiety disorders, and psychosis can be encountered in the treatment of individuals experiencing transcrisis, just as they are encountered during other modes of treatment. Clients struggling with the difficulty of proceeding through the transcrisis points necessary to resolve the underlying crisis may regress as a response to feeling overwhelmed; counselors may find that reassuring the client, breaking the overwhelming task into pieces, rehearsing, or using other normal techniques to move the client through difficult but necessary actions are effective in dealing with regression in those experiencing transcrisis. Clients with underlying mood disorders or psychoses may attempt to manipulate the transcrisis session, just as they may attempt to manipulate any session. Crisis counselors may find techniques such as establishing ground rules, setting and enforcing clear limits, working within a therapeutic structure

CASE STUDY 2.2

Julia

Julia is a 35-year-old married woman with three children. She grew up in a rural area and was raped when she was nine years old by a person she had never seen before and subsequently has never seen again. Julia never told her parents of the event, but the week following the rape she convinced her mother that she had the flu and was allowed to stay home from school; after a week in bed, she went on as if the incident never happened. The remainder of her childhood was relatively uneventful, and she married her high school sweetheart. Julia is a stay-at-home mother and volunteers two days a week at the school her children attend. A few years after she began her volunteer work at the school, Julia began experiencing low-grade panic attacks, so she began seeing a counselor to manage the attacks. The counselor has helped Julia learn how to manage the minor attacks quite strategically using solution-focused techniques. Last week the third-grade teacher of her oldest child asked Julia to assist on a field trip the class will be taking next month to the circus. Julia agrees to assist the teacher on the trip. You receive a call from Julia's husband, who explains Julia hasn't gotten out of bed in a week—since her last counseling appointment; she hasn't eaten, showered, dressed, or gone to help out on her normal days at the school. He has taken off from work to help out with the children, but he can see his wife is in severe distress. You ask him to get Julia dressed and bring her in for an appointment to explore what is happening to her and to determine how to proceed. He agrees.

Discussion Questions

What may be happening to Julia?

What do you need to explore with her, and what may you need to do with her?

How will you assist the family through this process?

What might you be thinking and feeling in response to Julia's behavior if you were her counselor?

designed to ensure counselor safety, confronting manipulative and maladaptive behavior, and acknowledging the source of the client's psychotic beliefs only as a means to achieve client safety useful in these situations (James, 2008).

Family System Considerations

A final consideration is the impact that transcrisis may have on the family system. There are typically two effects that are seen. The first is helping the family to understand that whatever progress a person makes, there is a risk of regression to pretherapeutic functioning and that the support of family members is essential to helping the person remain in the area where a therapeutic effect can be achieved. The second effect is the impact of the dysfunctionality of the family on the individual and the transcrisis experience. If dysfunctionality exceeds a critical level, then the counselor's role is to identify supports for the family to address and resolve these family members' own issues; this may be critical in assisting the client to move through the transcrisis episode and achieve improvement (James, 2008; Matsakis, 1998).

ETHICAL AND LEGAL ISSUES IN CRISIS COUNSELING

While crisis preparedness, personal safety, and knowledge of transcrisis are of vital importance in crisis counseling, ethical practice is central to appropriate crisis intervention. Crisis counselors need to be particularly aware of state and federal laws and professional ethics that govern and advise practice. This section will discuss the Health Insurance Portability and Accountability Act (HIPAA); the Family Educational Rights and Privacy Act (FERPA), also known as the Buckley Amendment; the *Tarasoff* decision; confidentiality; child abuse reporting; and termination issues.

The Health Insurance Portability and Accountability Act

The HIPAA is legislation implemented to address a number of perceived shortcomings in the management of information in the health care industry. Conceived in early 1990, the present legislation covers a wide range of areas that impact both the health care industry and patients.

WHAT IS HIPAA?   In the 1970s and 1980s, the American public perceived that health care information was not controlled and protected by the health care industry to the degree that it should be, in view of the increasing ability in those years for data to be compiled, manipulated, and used to negatively affect individuals and families. As a result of several high-profile cases and the resulting pressure on Congress, the legislative branch created health care information handling and protection standards of their own and communicated to the health care industry that these rather restrictive standards would be implemented if the health care industry did not solve the problem on its own.

The health care industry subsequently promulgated standards for information handling, management, and control that met Congress's desires, and Congress enacted these standards in HIPAA (Public Law 104-191). HIPAA, which went into effect on August 21, 1996, included four areas of legislation: privacy requirements, electronic transactions, security requirements, and national identifier requirements (Corey, Corey, & Callanan, 2007; Jensen, 2003; Remley & Herlihy, 2007; U.S. Department of Health and Human

Services). However, the version of HIPAA that became law in 1996 did not include privacy rules, and Congress instructed the U.S. Department of Health and Human Services (DHHS) to dictate privacy rules for the health care industry if Congress did not pass such rules in three years. The three-year period was provided in order to give the health care industry a chance to develop privacy rules, submit them to Congress, and get them passed. This did not occur, and in the absence of such legislation, DHHS followed the requirement of the 1996 act and implemented standards for privacy of individually identifiable health information, referred to as the Privacy Rule, the most recent of which became effective in April 2003. The Privacy Rule is still in effect and can be located at the HIPAA website of the DHHS Office for Civil Rights at www.hhs.gov/ocr/hipaa (Corey et al., 2007; Jensen, 2003; Remley & Herlihy, 2007; U.S. Department of Health and Human Services, 2002).

The Privacy Rule seeks to balance the concept of individual privacy against the need for medical professionals to have access to information in order to best do their jobs. It establishes that the right to privacy with regard to medical information is not absolute and therefore puts the onus on designated health care providers to protect the information they collect, use, and transmit. The Privacy Rule and other aspects of HIPAA govern information which contain personal identification; this type of information is defined as protected health information (PHI). The PHI must be treated according to the procedures established by HIPAA whenever it is created, transmitted, or received in any form whatsoever: electronic, paper-based, or by means of oral transmission. In short, if information contains individually identifiable material, it is considered PHI and is fully impacted by HIPAA (Horner & Wheeler, 2005; Remley & Herlihy, 2007).

Those who collect, use, or transmit PHI and who are covered under the requirements of HIPAA are referred to as covered entities. Terms such as *health care provider* and *health care* are sometimes used to refer to covered entities. The HIPAA legislation defines covered entities as those who are or who are employed by a health plan, a health clearinghouse, or a health care provider. *Health care provider* is further defined as "a person or organization who furnishes health care as a normal part of their business; who bills for health care, or who is paid by a third party to provide health care" (Horner & Wheeler, 2005, p. 10). In this way, HIPAA defines terms relating to the players in the health care arena and establishes standards through the Privacy Rule that define how these individuals or organizations are to collect, use, transmit, and handle information that contains individually identifiable material relating to health care.

THE IMPACT OF HIPAA   Over the intervening years, the health care industry sought to ensure that HIPAA-compliant operations were in place across the entire spectrum of health care providers, with various degrees of success. Part of the difficulty that has been experienced with HIPAA implementation is a result of the complexity of the regulations, combined with the various electronic information-handling systems that exist, the lack of standardization between them, and the continuing transition period between paper-based record keeping and the full electronic record-keeping goal of HIPAA. As systems become more standardized, dramatic cost -savings will be achieved when the transition to electronic records is completed. However, there is resistance, both on the individual provider level and institutionally, to many of the goals of the HIPAA legislation (Uses and Disclosures of Protected Health Information: General

Rules, 45 C.F.R. § 164.502, 2002). As a result, many health care providers are reluctant to share information fearing they will violate the standards and suffer penalties, which can range from fines to imprisonment, depending on the violation.

At the clinic level, one of the most dramatic impacts of HIPAA has been the requirement to perform and document a range of nonclinical, procedural actions to establish that the client has been informed of, understands, and agrees with a variety of requirements, rights, and privileges that HIPAA dictates. Since HIPAA puts the onus on the organization to show that it has complied with the requirements, counselors provide their clients with a written declaration of their rights under the HIPAA legislation, including the procedural practices regarding the clinic's collection, use, transmission, and handling of HIPAA-defined PHI. These procedural practices include, but are not limited to, what information clients can access, how they can access it, to whom their information is distributed, and how they can voice concerns regarding access to or dissemination of their private information; as a result, clinics require their clients to sign a statement indicating they have received and understand such information. Covered entities must also appoint a privacy officer who is responsible for ensuring that all staff handling PHI are trained and compliant with HIPAA (Remley & Herlihy, 2007).

HIPAA has also affected clinic operations through the establishment of the minimum necessary standard, which relates to the amount of information that can be released about a patient. Federal regulations establish that communications about a patient that involve PHI should consist only of that which is minimally necessary to achieve the purpose of the communication (45 C.F.R. § 164.502[b][1]). Interestingly, the minimum necessary standard does not apply to PHI when it is used for or disclosed in the process of medical treatment or payment for medical treatment or in the conduct of health care operations, when it is used by or disclosed to DHHS, or when it is used by or disclosed to the patient himself or herself (Horner & Wheeler, 2005).

HIPAA requirements have adversely affected research as a result of reliance on complicated consent forms and privacy protection materials that, while not specifically made necessary by HIPAA regulation, were felt by the organizations and institutions participating in the research to be a necessary protection against accusations of failure to implement the requirements of HIPAA. The requirements made organizations less willing to host research projects, while the forms that were felt necessary by the organizations to document their compliance with HIPAA were seen to decrease the number of people willing to participate in the research (Shen et al., 2006). Some organizations were hesitant to fully implement the electronic data interchange requirement of HIPAA for fear that such entirely electronic record-keeping methods might have a greater potential for unauthorized access, theft, or abuse than paper-based records, which were thought to be easier to segregate and control than electronic records would be (Chung, Chung, & Joo, 2006). HIPAA had less of an adverse impact on public health reporting, since it does not restrict the transmission and use of PHI when such transmission and use are made to public health agencies and as long as the source of the information complied with HIPAA requirements when it collected the information (Campos-Outcalt, 2004).

HOW HIPAA AFFECTS CRISIS COUNSELING   Crisis counseling differs from the kinds of services that are typically provided by health care workers. Crises such as hurricanes, tornadoes, and homicides typically occur quickly and often in unanticipated ways, so crisis counselors must respond quickly to stabilize and provide a way for people to move forward. There may be limited time to obtain HIPAA-required releases when critical care is needed, or it may be impossible to obtain such releases as a result of severe injury, unavailability of family members, or other unforeseen consequences of the disaster. According to the U.S. Department of Health and Human Services (2008a), HIPAA is not intended to interfere with the provision on emergency medical care associated with declared emergencies such as Hurricane Katrina, that covered health care providers may exercise their professional judgment and act, as long as such actions are in the best interests of the patient.

Actions permitted by health care workers may include disclosure of individually identifiable medical information to government officials at the local, state, or federal level; police; first responders; public health officials; or anyone whom the health care providers deem necessary to best serve the patient. And in any case, the federal government has the authority to waive sanctions and penalties associated with violations of the Privacy Rule, even in cases where a public health emergency is not declared (U.S. Department of Health and Human Services, 2008b).

For work with suicidal clients, the HIPAA Privacy Rule allows disclosure of PHI under the "Serious Threat to Health or Safety" provision. Release of information to anyone whom the health care provider reasonably believes may lessen the threat to health or safety (including the target of the threat) is allowed; however, in the case of a threat to health and safety, release of PHI to law enforcement is allowed only when the information is needed to identify or apprehend an escapee or a violent criminal (U.S. Department of Health and Human Services, 2003).

In cases where a crime has occurred or where law enforcement officials are investigating a suspected crime, disclosure of PHI is allowed under the "Law Enforcement Purposes" provision, which sets out various situations relating to law enforcement in which disclosure of protected information may—and, in fact, must—be made (U.S. Department of Health and Human Services, 2003).

Family Educational Rights and Privacy Act

In 1974, Congress passed the *Family Educational Rights and Privacy Act* (FERPA), also known as the Buckley Amendment. Sponsored by Senator John Buckley, the amendment was prompted by Buckley's concerns about privacy violations and about the inclusion in educational records of immaterial comments and personal opinions (Weeks, 2001).

WHAT IS FERPA? Essentially, FERPA protects privacy and gives records access to parents and to students over 18 years of age (known as eligible students). All schools, public or private, that receive federal funding must follow FERPA or face the loss of federal funds (Remley & Herlihy, 2007). According to the U.S. Department of Education (2008), a parent or an eligible student has the right to inspect and review the student's educational records. Additionally, the parent or eligible student who believes an educational record to be inaccurate may ask to amend the record. If a school refuses to amend an educational record, the parent or eligible student can request a formal hearing and may place in the record a statement about the information being contested.

Schools must obtain written permission to release information; however, FERPA allows the release of information in certain situations, as when a student transfers to another school, there is a legitimate educational interest, financial aid is being requested, a judicial order to that effect has been issued, or there is an emergency. Parents are to be notified when records are transferred to other schools and may receive copies of said records upon request (Remley & Herlihy, 2007). Under FERPA, colleges may release educational records, such as grades and financial records, to parents of college students claimed as dependents on parental tax forms. The release of student records to parents occurs either when the parent shows tax record proof that the student is a dependent or when the student signs a waiver allowing the release of records to parents (Weeks, 2001).

IMPACT OF FERPA   FERPA has had a major impact on the practice of record keeping in schools. With the advent of parental and student access to school records, school personnel had to be certain student records contained only essential and accurate information. Prior to FERPA, records might contain information about minor disciplinary actions and personal opinions, including derogatory remarks that could be damaging to students. Essex (2004) states that to abide by FERPA "school personnel must be certain that all information recorded in the student's educational file is accurate, necessary and based on reasonable grounds" (p. 111). FERPA ended the practice of untrained individuals entering psychological diagnoses into student records and also ended the inclusion of unsuitable negative remarks.

Before FERPA, educational institutions could be quite lax about how they communicated student information. In fact, Senator Buckley was motivated, in part, to introduce this legislation due to such abuses of confidential material (Weeks, 2001). Schools were known to reveal contents of student records to parties who had no educational interest or need to know. FERPA has served to advance professionalism in educational institutions, while at the same time securing students' rights to privacy and confidentiality.

FERPA contains a provision that exempts certain personal records. Records that are in the "sole possession of the maker" and are not revealed to others are excluded from FERPA (Russo & Mawdsley, 2004). This includes records made by school personnel such as crisis counselors who keep such records in their "sole possession." Due to this exemption, counseling case notes are not considered part of the educational record and do not have to be revealed (Remley & Herlihy, 2007).

HOW FERPA AFFECTS CRISIS COUNSELING   According to the U.S. Department of Education (2007), during emergency situations schools may release information from records in order to protect the health and safety of others. It is important to note that this exception is only for the time of the emergency and is not a blanket consent to release student information. The information may be released to appropriate individuals who are tasked with protecting health and safety such as law enforcement officials, medical personnel, and public officials. Law enforcement officials hired by schools are considered school officials and therefore have an "educational interest" and are permitted to view records. Threatening remarks made by a student and overheard by school personnel can be reported to appropriate officials because such remarks are not considered part of the educational record.

The aforementioned policies apply to higher education settings as well, with the following additions. Regarding disciplinary actions and rule violations, the final results of a disciplinary proceeding may be released to an alleged victim even if the perpetrator has not been found guilty of violating rules or policies (U.S. Department of Education, 2007). If a perpetrator has been found guilty of violating rules or policies, the institution may disclose the final results of a disciplinary hearing to anyone. Most colleges and universities have their own campus police; investigative records of campus law enforcement are not subject to FERPA and may be released to outside law enforcement without student consent.

In situations concerning health and safety, higher education institutions may disclose educational records to a parent if the student is involved in a health or safety issue or is under 21 years of age and has violated the school's drug and alcohol policies. Also, according to the U.S. Department of Education (2008), "a school official may generally share information with parents that is based on that official's personal knowledge or observation of the student." Therefore, in situations where a student's behavior involves the health and safety of self and others, school officials can communicate with parents. In fact, a school official may report concerns about student behavior to anyone, though it is wise to make such reports only to campus personnel who can intervene appropriately with the student, such as administrators, counselors, or campus police (Tribbensee & McDonald, 2007).

The interaction between HIPAA and FERPA can be very confusing. Rowe (2005) explains that HIPAA contains a FERPA exemption that excludes FERPA-covered records from HIPAA regulations; however, it must be remembered that treatment records such as counseling case files are exempt from FERPA but may be covered by HIPAA. The interplay between HIPAA and FERPA has yet to be fully understood, and currently, higher education institutions are interpreting HIPAA and FERPA in various ways. FERPA was never intended to block the information flow between institutions and others concerned about student health and safety; therefore, faculty, staff, and administrators who are troubled about the welfare of a student may contact the student's family or other entities and express general observations about health and psychological concerns, while protecting the privacy of medical or mental health records (Shuchman, 2007).

Tarasoff v. Regents of the University of California

In the *American Counseling Association (ACA) Code of Ethics* (2005), counselors are charged with recognizing trust as an important component of the counseling relationship and are obligated to facilitate a trusting relationship with clients through a series of mechanisms, including maintaining confidentiality. However, disclosure is required "to protect clients or identified others from serious and foreseeable harm or when legal requirements demand that confidential information must be revealed" (Standard B.2.a, p. 7). This standard was adopted as part of the counseling practice after the landmark case of *Tarasoff v. Regents of the University of California*.

In 1969, Prosenjit Poddar was seen by a psychologist on a voluntary outpatient basis at the university. Poddar confided his intent to kill a woman he claimed to be his girlfriend, a woman the psychologist surmised to be Tatiana Tarasoff, when she returned from Brazil. The psychologist, alarmed by the disclosure, contacted the campus police and then began proceedings to have Poddar committed for a psychiatric evaluation. In the interim, police picked Poddar up and questioned him. The police found Poddar to be rational. Poddar promised not to have contact with Tarasoff, so the police released him. The psychologist followed up on his concerns with a letter to the campus police chief in which he again expressed his concern; however, the supervisor of the psychologist requested that the letter be returned, ordered that all case notes destroyed, and ordered that no further action be taken. Poddar did not return to see the psychologist nor was he committed or evaluated further by anyone. Further, no one contacted Tarasoff or her family to alert them that a threat had been made against Tarasoff. Two months later Tarasoff was stabbed to death by Poddar, and her parents brought suit against the University of California Board of Regents (Cavaiola & Colford, 2006; Corey et al., 2007; Remley & Herlihy, 2007). Initially, a trial court ruled that the university wasn't liable because Tarasoff wasn't the patient in this case and therefore it had no duty of care toward her. Upon appeal, however, the California Supreme Court ruled there are some circumstances in which a therapist should break confidentiality, specifically when such a disclosure is necessary to avert danger to the client or others. This act of breaking confidentiality when disclosure is necessary to avert danger is known as the duty to warn (Melby, 2004).

WHAT WAS THE EFFECT OF *TARASOFF V. REGENTS*?   Part of what makes this case, and the duty to warn/protect, complicated is that there have been many interpretations of this case ruling. Melby (2004) points out that just how and when a counselor should break confidentiality differs depending on circumstances; and since many states depend on court rulings rather than statutes to guide the actions of a counselor, this issue is not black and white. He indicates that many legal experts are "unable to offer specific advice about when therapists should alert the police or potential victim about a threat to human life" (p. 4). While some courts have limited the application of the duty to warn to situations in which victims are identifiable, subsequent decisions have indicated that the duty to warn extends to unknown victims, which further complicates the matter. Another confusing part of this ruling is the terms *duty to warn* and *duty to protect*, which are often used interchangeably by professionals.

Legal definitions of the terms *duty to warn* and *duty to protect* are established by state legislation and state court rulings, so these definitions will vary from state to state. Counselors must be aware of the laws applicable to the states in which they are licensed and in which they intend to practice. Generally speaking, the duty to warn and the duty to protect represent degrees of what is essentially the same duty: first, the duty to inform someone of a danger or hazard with the idea that they will take action to protect himself or herself (this is the duty to warn) and second, the duty to protect someone by taking an action that reduces the danger or hazard to that person directly (this is the duty to protect). For example, when a counselor makes a telephone call to a family member whom a client has threatened, the counselor does so under the concept of duty to warn. If, on the other hand, the counselor arranges to have a client hospitalized who has threatened to harm himself, that action is taken under the concept of duty to protect, since it consists of a direct action (hospitalization) that makes it less likely that the client will execute the threat. In the *Tarasoff* case, the victim was not protected, and the appellate court ruled that the health care provider should have taken steps to protect the victim, and in *Gross v. Allen*, a 1994 California appellate court case, the court ruled that the *Tarasoff* concept applied not only to cases in which clients threaten homicide but also to cases in which clients threaten suicide, so reasonable measures are expected to be taken in cases of threatened suicide (Nugent & Jones, 2005; Simon, 2004).

The *Tarasoff* ruling, in fact, establishes a duty to protect and not just a duty to warn. The ruling and interpretation of the Tarasoff principle for counseling professional involves the awareness of the protective measure as a legal obligation to warn an intended victim of potential harm. For example, case outcomes have indicated that the duty to warn is extended to those who are foreseeably endangered by a client's conduct, including people who are unintentionally injured by the client, whole class of students that have been threatened by the client, bystanders who may be injured by the client's act, and individuals whose property is threatened by the client (Corey et al., 2007; McClarren, 1987; Melby, 2004; Remley & Herlihy, 2007). Further, in *Ewing v. Goldstein* (2004) the court ruled that in California a therapist could be held liable for failure to warn when the information regarding the client's potential to harm another person is obtained from family members who may be participating in counseling with the client. Additionally, Remley and Herlihy (2007) point out that the *Tarasoff* doctrine is not applied in every jurisdiction of the United States; specifically, Texas has rejected this doctrine.

When a decision is made that a client is a danger to another person or persons, the crisis counselor must then determine what the necessary steps are to prevent the harm from occurring. After notifying the potential victim and/or contacting appropriate authorities as needed to ensure the intended victim's safety, the counselor must take other steps to prevent harm, which can include continuing to work with the client on an outpatient basis. This uses the less restrictive action, whereas pursuing involuntary commitment would be considered a very restrictive option. These decisions are challenging for most counselors. Therefore, it is highly recommended that counselors seek supervision and consultation on a regular basis—but particularly whenever the issue of breaking confidentiality becomes a factor in practice. This is also known as the *duty to consult* principle and can assist crisis counselors in decreasing liability issues in similar cases. Counselors should not practice in isolation, should practice following reasonable standards, and should maintain accurate documentation to fall back on in order to verify when and why decisions regarding breaking confidentiality were made, particularly as they relate to the duty to warn (Knapp & VandeCreek, 1982).

Another consideration regarding confidentiality and the issue of duty to warn is how multicultural factors come into play. Perhaps the best way to preserve the counseling relationship, should the need to break confidentiality or to follow through on the duty to warn arise, is to assess how clients' cultural needs may influence your practice. This assessment should occur not only at the onset of the counseling relationship but also, as indicated in Sections B.1 and B.2 of the *ACA Code of Ethics* (2005), periodically throughout your work together. This is essential regardless of cultural context.

HOW *TARASOFF V. REGENTS* AFFECTS CRISIS COUNSELING   Collins and Collins (2005) identify three goals for a crisis worker dealing with a potentially violent individual: (1) ensure the client remains safe, reduce lethality, and stabilize the environment; (2) help the client to regain short-term control; and (3) connect the client with appropriate resources. The course of accomplishing these three goals, however, is balanced against the counselor's decision that a duty to warn exists and confidentiality must be broken in part to accomplish those very goals. Counselors working with people in crisis often encounter unique circumstances when a duty to warn or protect prevails; one particularly challenging circumstance is dealing with clients who are HIV and AIDS positive.

Interestingly, even though in Texas counselors may not break confidentiality to warn or protect a person whose life has been threatened by another, they are mandated to report suspected child abuse and have the option of reporting positive HIV results to various entities (Barbee, Ekleberry, & Villalobos, 2007). Likewise, the *ACA Code of Ethics* (2005) indicates that counselors are "justified in disclosing information to identifiable third parties, if they are known to be at demonstrable and high risk of contracting the disease" (Standard B.2.b). The *ACA Code of Ethics* further stipulates, however, that counselors must confirm the diagnosis and assess the client's intent to inform the third party about his or her disease or to participate in any behavior that may be harmful to an identifiable third party. The word *justified*, as compared to *required*, warrants consideration, and further, counselors are encouraged to evaluate their own thoughts about whether or not they will agree to work with, and how they will effectively work with, clients who are HIV positive. It is also important to keep in mind that not every exposure to HIV results in harm, thus making the process of determining how to proceed a grey area that a crisis counselor must navigate carefully. When dealing with this and other precarious issues of this sort, crisis counselors are wise to stay informed about specific statutes in their jurisdiction that have been passed regarding the duty to warn and third-party conversations and, of course, to review the guidelines of confidentiality periodically with clients, as well as seeking supervision and consultation as needed (Corey et al., 2007; Huprich, Fuller, & Schneider, 2003; Remley & Herlihy, 2007).

Negligence and Malpractice

Once a counselor and a client have entered into a professional relationship, the counselor has assumed a duty of care toward the client. A breach of duty owed to another is considered negligence; negligence that occurs in a professional setting is malpractice, also referred to as professional negligence. Malpractice is established "if the court finds that this duty was breached, through an act of omission or commission relative to the standard of care" (Berman, 2006, p. 171). The standard of care is care that does not depart from what "reasonable and prudent" counselors with similar training and in similar situations would carry out. To prove malpractice, four factors, the "4Ds"—"a dereliction (breach) of a duty (of care) that directly (proximately causes) damages (a compensable injury)"—must be present (Berman, 2006, p. 172). In the event of a lawsuit, a counselor's only defense is documentation in the case file that proves that the counselor conformed to the standard of care.

Documentation and Record Keeping

There is an old saying in the helping professions: "If it's not written down, it didn't happen." A counselor may have done everything right with a client, but failure to document means that no evidence exists of the counselor's actions and decisions. Documentation is an essential part of standard care and best practice. Appropriate professional documentation and record keeping display diligence and also reflect the promotion of client welfare (Cohen & Cohen, 1999). While client welfare is a counselor's main purpose, there is no denying that documentation can either help or hurt a counselor in legal cases. Mitchell (2001) asserts, "In a courtroom, your counseling records

CASE STUDY 2.3

Angela

Angela is a relatively new counselor; she has been practicing for just over a year since graduating with her master's degree in counseling. She likes the clinic she works at and overall has a positive working relationship with her supervisor, Gail. Angela has been working for a few months with Julio, a client who is struggling with his identity as a Puerto Rican gay man who recently came to the United States and is now living in a southern state. Recently, Angela has noticed that when she reviews the case each week during the treatment team meeting, Gail seems flustered and impatient with the discussion. Before Angela has a chance to discuss her observations with Gail during individual supervision, Julio discloses that he has tested positive for HIV; he would rather not tell his current partner about this discovery but prefers to just break up with him. Angela is uncertain about how to proceed but recognizes she needs guidance. When she discusses the case during individual supervision with Gail, Gail tells Angela that she should contact Julio's primary care physician, confirm that "the foreigner" is HIV positive, and then break confidentiality to notify Julio's partner.

Discussion Questions

How should Angela proceed?

What does Angela need to do to maintain a therapeutic alliance with Julio?

What multicultural considerations does Angela need to consider?

What ethical and legal issues are significant in this scenario?

How should Angela proceed with her supervisor, Gail?

What advice would you give to a counseling colleague facing a situation similar to Angela's?

What are your personal thoughts related to working with HIV- and AIDS-positive clients?

If you have not thought about it previously, how will you explore and determine your personal and professional position on the matter?

can be manipulated in ways you cannot imagine" (p. 7). This is particularly crucial in crisis situations such as suicide, homicide, or disaster relief where the risk of litigation increases.

Moline, Williams, and Austin (1998) state that records should at a minimum include "identifying data, background/historical data, diagnosis and prognosis, treatment plans, informed consent, progress notes, and termination summary (includes evaluation of all services client related)" (pp. 32–33). It is crucial that a risk assessment be conducted on every client. If the assessment produces any degree of lethality (either stated or observed), it is equally important to justify the actions taken and to follow up in subsequent case notes on the status of the risk. In addition, they note that certain material should not be included

ACTIVITY 2.2

Critique the following case note entries. What would improve them?

1. Client says she is doing better today.
2. Client's appearance is good.
3. Client went to doctor as requested.
4. Client began new medication last week.

in records. Inappropriate information is anything that is not treatment related and that could be problematic if viewed by others. Such information includes "personal opinions, discussion of a third party, sensitive information, [and] past criminal behavior" (p. 32).

Crisis counselors must keep documentation of their interventions with clients. Admittedly, crisis conditions (e.g., a disaster site) are not always conducive to writing case notes, but crisis counselors need to clearly document exact dates, pertinent details, assessments, and treatment decisions. It is important to remember that while case notes are succinct, they should never be vague. Case notes must be specific enough to demonstrate that the treatment reflected prevailing standards of care. The documentation must clearly illustrate the session with details that capture the essence of what occurred and validate treatment decisions. The need for client files to be in a locked and secured location applies during crisis events. Providing for locked and secure confidential file storage in crisis situations must be addressed in crisis planning.

Confidentiality

Gladding (2006) defines confidentiality as "[t]he professional, ethical, and legal obligation of counselors that they not disclose client information revealed during counseling without the client's written consent" (p. 34). The *ACA Code of Ethics* (2005) states, "Counselors do not share confidential information without client consent or without sound legal and ethical justification" (Standard B.1.c). In situations where a client is a danger to self or others or where the professional counselor is mandated by law to report abuse or is required by a court of law to disclose information, confidentiality can be legally breached. In situations other than these, a client must give consent for the release of information. Client records are confidential, and they must be kept in a secure and locked location for a specified time in accordance with professional ethical standards and the legal requirements of the state and HIPAA regulations.

Informed Consent

Clients enter counseling without much information about what will take place. They may, in fact, often have many misconceptions about the process of counseling and the nature of the counseling relationship. Clients must enter counseling freely and be fully informed of what is to be expected in the counseling relationship. Informed consent occurs when clients understand all the possible risks, benefits, and potential outcomes of counseling (Moline et al., 1998). The *ACA Code of Ethics* (2005) states, "Counselors have an obligation to review in writing and verbally with clients the rights and responsibilities of both the counselor and the client" (Standard A.2.a). The *ACA Code* further specifies that the counselor must explain to the client "the purposes, goals, techniques, procedures, limitations, potential risks, and benefits of services; the counselor's qualifications, credentials, and relevant experience; continuation of services upon incapacitation or death of a counselor; and other pertinent information" (Standard A.2.b). Informed consent forms should also include an explanation of office policies, fees, billing arrangements, record keeping, the right to refuse treatment, and the potential effect of refusal. Both the client and the counselor sign the informed consent form, and it becomes part of the counseling record.

Reporting and Intervening in Child Abuse

Crisis counselors in many settings encounter cases where children have been abused or neglected. The maltreatment of children occurs in all social contexts and the effects of childhood abuse and neglect are far-reaching, affecting the abused child's future and society as a whole. Professional counselors are change agents and advocates, and reporting and intervening in child abuse are an essential part of their responsibility as helpers.

CURRENT CHILD ABUSE   Mental health providers, health care professionals, school personnel, and members of law enforcement are mandated reporters, meaning they are required by law to report suspected child abuse and neglect (Collins & Collins, 2005). Laws regarding mandated reporting exist in all 50 states, and it is vital that counselors familiarize themselves with the specifics of their state's law and reporting procedures (Remley & Herlihy, 2007).

In most states, counselors who make "good faith" reports are protected from lawsuits (Sperry, 2007); therefore, fear of a lawsuit is not a defensible reason for failing to report abuse. Ford (2006) acknowledges that counselors are often uneasy about reporting child abuse and neglect. They may fear that reporting will increase the abuse suffered by the child or that the therapeutic relationship will be harmed or even terminated. Bryant and Milsom (2005) found that, while most suspected cases are reported, school counselors may experience reluctance to report abuse due to a lack of proof or fears that the state agency will not follow through on an investigation. It is important to remember that as mandated reporters, counselors are not required to prove abuse, but they must report suspected abuse. While in some areas the concerns about a lack of state agency follow-through are legitimate, not reporting abuse does nothing to protect the child and actually contributes to the problem. In these circumstances, counselors should advocate for better child protection laws and services. The Department of Child Protective Services in the state where the abuse took place should be contacted when any suspicion of child abuse is presented. The intake worker or other agency representative will determine if and how they will proceed.

According to the National Child Advocacy Center (2008), it is important that only trained forensic interviewers gather specific information related to the abuse. The forensic interview model uses narrative prompts to explore the most salient memories and allows children the opportunity to explain their experiences in their own words. Forensic interviews are taped and viewed by investigative teams and law enforcement, sparing the child repeated interviews. Most interview models begin with very general open-ended questions such as "Do you know why you are here today?" They then move on to more specific, but still nonleading, questions that are based on what the child has related: "Do you remember any more about the night you spent at Grandma's house?" Children are told up front that it is alright if they don't know an answer. Play therapy and anatomical dolls may also be used during the interview process, depending on the age of the child; however, Ferrara (2002) cautions that the use of anatomical dolls is controversial and has been challenged in court.

Mandated reporters who do not have training in forensic child abuse interviewing should refrain from asking leading questions that may serve only to confuse or retraumatize the child. It is important to remember that mandated reporters are charged with reporting suspected abuse, not investigating abuse. This is especially significant in school settings. Children reveal information to an adult with whom they feel comfortable. Forcing a child to repeat information to other school officials retraumatizes the child. The person to whom the child reported the abuse is the person who should contact Child Protective Services and make the report. Sparing a child the trauma of repeatedly telling the story is not the only reason school personnel should refrain from interviewing. In the event of a prosecution, the perpetrator's defense lawyer could subpoena all school personnel who questioned the child. Obviously, teachers and administrators are unlikely to have training in forensic interviewing. If various untrained adults interviewed the child prior to the forensic interview, the defense can imply that the child's testimony has been tainted, thus weakening the prosecution's case. Information about becoming a trained forensic interviewer is available from the National Child Advocacy Center.

As discussed above, it is important to document the call to Child Protective Services by including in your notes the name or identification number of the worker, date and time called, and status of the report (if available). Although not the norm, counselors should inquire as to whether a written confirmation will be sent to the counselor. If a parent or another person states that a report was previously made, but there is not a record in the client's file, the counselor should still contact Child Protective Services. In addition, most states outline a maximum time frame within which a mandated reporter who suspects abuse must contact Child Protective Services verbally, followed by a written report.

Children are afraid to report abuse, especially if the abuser is a family member. They may feel loyal to the perpetrator, or they may feel an obligation to keep the family together (Ferrara, 2002). The reluctance to breach family secrecy can extend into adulthood. According to the Child Welfare Information Gateway (2007), common signs of abuse include the following:

Signs of Physical Abuse

- Has unexplained burns, bites, bruises, broken bones, or black eyes.
- Has fading bruises or other marks noticeable after an absence from school.
- Seems frightened of parents and protests or cries when it is time to go home.
- Shrinks at the approach of adults.
- Reports injury by a parent or another adult caregiver.

Signs of Neglect

- Is frequently absent from school.
- Begs or steals food or money.
- Lacks needed medical or dental care, immunizations, or glasses.
- Is consistently dirty and has severe body odor.

- Lacks sufficient clothing for the weather.
- Abuses alcohol or other drugs.
- States that there is no one at home to provide care.

Signs of Sexual Abuse

- Has difficulty walking or sitting.
- Suddenly refuses to change for gym or to participate in physical activities.
- Reports nightmares or bed wetting.
- Experiences a sudden change in appetite.
- Demonstrates bizarre, sophisticated, or unusual sexual knowledge or behavior.
- Becomes pregnant or contracts a venereal disease, particularly if under 14 years of age.
- Runs away.
- Reports sexual abuse by a parent or other adult caregiver.

Signs of Emotional Abuse

- Shows extremes in behavior, such as overly compliant or demanding behavior, extreme passivity, or aggression.
- Is either inappropriately adult like (e.g., parenting other children) or inappropriately infantile (e.g., frequently rocking or banging his/her head).
- Has attempted suicide.
- Reports lack of attachment to the parent.

After a report, a case is investigated by trained forensic interviewers in accordance with state legal requirements. Whatever the legal outcome, it is essential that abused and neglected children receive treatment. Given the mistrust and fear that abused and neglected children feel, treatment must be supported by a strong therapeutic alliance (Capuzzi & Gross, 2004). The child must be able to openly tell his or her story and be believed by the counselor. Capuzzi and Gross stress that the process cannot be rushed and must proceed at the child's pace. According to the Child Welfare Information Gateway (2007), treatment of abuse must include building trust, protecting the child from future abuse (e.g., by removing the child from the home, treating the family), and dealing with emotional, cognitive, and behavioral symptoms to restore a child to healthy functioning. Individual, group, and family counseling modalities are all appropriate for treatment and can be effectively used simultaneously. Further discussion of physical and sexual abuse is found in Chapter 7.

Handling Past Reports of Child Sexual Abuse (Adult Survivors)

It is not uncommon for child sexual abuse victims to live with their pain without telling anyone, only revealing the abuse in adulthood. Memories of abuse may be suppressed or repressed and may emerge in later years during times of life stress (Ferrara, 2002). Warne and McAndrew (2005) report that adult memories of child sexual abuse have been associated with mood disorders, PTSD, Dissociative Disorders, substance abuse, psychosis, and low self-esteem.

Counseling goals for adult survivors should include bringing memories into conscious awareness, a painful emotional process that should occur at the client's pace

CASE STUDY 2.4

Child Sexual Abuse

Amelia is a quiet, withdrawn second-grade student. Her favorite subject is art, and she loves the art teacher. One day in art, the teacher notices that Amelia has drawn a picture of herself in the deep end of a pool surrounded by sharks. The art teacher leans down and says, "My, what a scary picture. Can you tell me about it?" Amelia's eyes fill with tears, and she says, "My Daddy does bad things to me at night in my bed. He touches my bottom, but I'm not supposed to tell anyone."

Discussion Questions

What should happen next?

(Ferrara, 2002). Colangelo (2007) expresses caution over the use of memory retrieval techniques such as age regression, guided imagery, and dream work. Colangelo notes that memory research indicates that while recovered memories do have accuracy, they may also contain inaccuracies that could result in harm to the client. It is critically important that counselors not ask leading questions about past abuse but rather let the client remember what the client needs to recall in order to heal. Ferrara (2002) states that over time the recall of abuse memories becomes less distressing; however, initially the client may experience dissociation during recall. It is important that the counselor build rapport and create an accepting supportive environment for the client, allowing the client to tell his or her story without coercion. Telling the story will let the client deal with the shame, anger, fear, and sadness that have been bottled up for many years. After recall, the client can begin to gain control over the emotional and psychological effects of sexual abuse, ultimately leading to healing and empowerment.

Bogar and Hulse-Killacky (2006) found a relationship between resiliency and recovery for female adult survivors of childhood sexual abuse. As a result of their research, they advocate a strength-based approach to working with adult survivors of child sexual abuse, focusing on constructive aspects of clients' lives and enhancing resiliency. Regarding forgiveness as a therapeutic strategy, Bogar and Hulse-Killacky note that there is a debate in the literature on the effectiveness and appropriateness of forgiveness as a therapeutic component of healing. It is important for counselors to remain sensitive to client needs with regard to forgiveness as a treatment option, as some clients may need to forgive as a part of their healing journey; however, clients must never be forced or pressured to forgive a perpetrator.

Reporting of adult survivor child sexual abuse differs according to the statute of limitations in each state; therefore, counselors and adult survivors should consult their state laws regarding reporting past abuse. Adult survivors may wish to pursue legal recourse against their perpetrators through the civil court system (Fairlie, 2000). While a civil lawsuit will not bring a perpetrator to justice, the perpetrator may have to pay restitution for damages, and the civil process may help the adult survivor find closure.

CASE STUDY 2.5

An Adult Survivor of Child Sexual Abuse

Kevin is a 28-year-old blue-collar worker. He has been referred to you through the Employee Assistance Program at his job site. He has suffered from depression for years and takes an antidepressant, but recently, his depression has worsened. Kevin responds well to treatment, and after several sessions, he opens up and tells you something he has never told anyone: that he was molested throughout his childhood by his grandfather who recently died. His grandfather was a highly respected member of the clergy and was loved and revered by his community and family. Kevin has never been able to reconcile his grandfather's abusive actions with the image that the rest of the family and the community hold of his grandfather. His grandfather's funeral was the precipitating event that led to Kevin's deepening depression and his referral to you.

Discussion Questions

Why do you think Kevin's grandfather's death worsened his depressive symptoms?

What role did the family system and community play in Kevin's reluctance to reveal his abuse until now?

How might you proceed from here?

Issues Related to Termination in Crisis Intervention

Because crisis intervention is generally brief and focused on immediate needs, crisis counselors must use appropriate termination skills with clients. Appropriate termination should not only bring closure for the crisis counseling relationship but also bolster the goals and plans laid out in the crisis counseling process.

TERMINATION AND ABANDONMENT Termination occurs when a counselor or a client decides to end the counseling relationship. According to Standard A.11.c of the *ACA Code of Ethics* (2005), professional counselors terminate cases when the treatment goals have been reached and the client no longer needs counseling, when the client isn't being helped by further counseling or might be harmed by further counseling, when the client or someone associated with the client poses harm to the counselor, or when the client does not pay counseling fees. In those circumstances where clients need further counseling services after termination, the counselor provides the client with referral information for other appropriate mental health providers. Unfortunately, lack of attention to termination documentation can lead to lawsuits based on abandonment (Mitchell, 2001). A final termination summary should be added to the client file. Mitchell (2001, pp. 70–71) recommends that this summary include (1) the reason for termination, (2) a summary of progress, (3) the final diagnostic impression, (4) a follow-up plan, and (5) other pertinent information.

When clients are neglected, deserted, or negligently terminated, the counselor has committed abandonment of the client. The *ACA Code of Ethics* (2005) prohibits abandonment; Standard A.11.a states, "Counselors do not abandon or neglect clients in counseling. Counselors assist in making appropriate arrangements for the continuation of treatment, when necessary, during interruptions such as vacations, illness and following termination."

Mitchell (2001) highlights circumstances that increase a counselor's risk of malpractice due to abandonment:

- A client comes to treatment erratically.
- Records do not verify outreach efforts to a client who breaks/misses appointments.
- High-risk clients drop out of treatment.
- A client is "fired" or refused treatment.
- A professional therapist and client have not discussed/agreed on closure.
- A client is not notified in writing that a case is being closed.
- The record indicates a failure to review/consult/refer.
- Staff notes do not verify that a plan is being followed. (p. 71)

Mitchell recommends that clients be given written information about the closure plan, including contact information for other counselors or resources. In the event that a client misses appointments and stops coming to counseling, the counselor should send a follow-up letter expressing interest in the client's welfare and asking the client to contact the counselor within a set period of time if the client wants to resume counseling. If a termination letter is to be sent to the home of the client, written consent to send

CASE STUDY 2.6

James

James is a new counselor working at his first job in a nonprofit agency that provides counseling to low-income clients. A major problem at the agency is clients who "no-show" for appointments. The agency policy is three no-shows and you're out, meaning that after three no-shows, the clients are terminated by letter. James is distressed to see that this policy is not included in the informed consent, and unless a counselor chooses to tell the client of the no-show policy, the client will not know that termination occurs after three no-shows. Furthermore, James is concerned that the termination letter does not contain any information about other counseling resources. At a staff meeting, James expresses these concerns regarding lack of informed consent and abandonment. He states that this policy is at odds with what he learned about ethical practice in his counseling program. The agency director makes a snide remark about counselor educators living in ivory towers, while another counselor on staff remarks, "Our clients are too stupid and too poor to ever sue us over abandonment, so we don't have to worry about that stuff."

Discussion Questions

What is your reaction to this situation and to the comments made by the director and the staff counselor?

What various ethical issues are being violated in this agency?

What should James do?

any information to that address should have been obtained during the informed consent process. Similarly, written consent to leave any information on a client's phone should have been obtained during intake. The consent should state the specific address or phone number for which the client has granted permission. The counselor should document all attempts to contact a client.

PROFESSIONAL SELF-ASSESSMENT

A major component of ethical practice is the ability of the counselor to monitor his or her own mental health and engage in self-care. This is particularly important for a counselor working in crisis situations. Self-assessment is the process whereby counselors self-monitor and maintain self-awareness of their reactions, behaviors, feelings, and thoughts, thereby recognizing how these internal processes affect their sense of self and their functioning as helping professionals. Self-assessment is crucial to effective crisis intervention. If a counselor is unable to attend to his or her internal state, that counselor is unlikely to be of much help to others. Self-care is fundamentally important to best practice.

Self-Assessment of the Counselor During Crises

Self-assessment and intentional self-care, while important for all counselors, are of particular importance to counselors who work with suicidal, homicidal, or other traumatized clients. Crises take an emotional, cognitive, and even physical toll, and crisis counselors should debrief with colleagues or supervisors and periodically do self check-ins to monitor for indications of reduced functioning. Since a lack of resiliency and health on the part of the counselor can hardly foster wellness in the client, crisis counselors have a responsibility to monitor their own mental health and seek supervision and counseling when needed. Failure to attend to self-assessment and restoration can lead to burnout, compassion fatigue, and vicarious trauma—and ultimately to counselor impairment. This is especially critical during crisis intervention circumstances when emotions are running high, the environment is charged with anxiety, and clients are suffering and in distress. Basically, commitment to assessment and maintenance of a healthy mind, body, and spirit is essential in the preservation of wellness and best practice. In our culturally diverse society, it is important to remember that self-assessment also includes regular evaluation of counselor values, which affect the care counselors give. Counselors are obligated to learn and consistently assess how their own cultural, ethnic, and racial identities affect their values and beliefs about the work they do. The way in which counselors perceive themselves and their own cultural context, as well as the cultural context of the clients they serve, can also affect their maintenance of a healthy mind and spirit (Sue & Sue, 1999).

Countertransference

Countertransference occurs when counselors ascribe characteristics of significant people and events in their past to their clients (James, 2008). Client emotions, behaviors, and issues may stir up unresolved or buried emotions within a counselor, who might then identify too closely with the client and use the counseling relationship to fulfill unmet needs. Dealing with one's own "stuff" is a vital aspect of good practice and healthy self-assessment. Exploring personal issues and increasing self-awareness underpin healthy practice and should be an ongoing part of counselor self-care and work. It is important for counselors to examine their internal reactions to clients. In cases that evoke unresolved issues, counselors should seek consultation, supervision, and personal counseling.

Burnout and Compassion Fatigue

Skovholt (2001) describes burnout as "a profound weariness and hemorrhaging of the self" (p. 107). Burnout occurs when counselors exhaust themselves both physically and emotionally through overwork and a lack of self-care. Counselors and other mental health professionals are at risk for burnout due to the emotionally intense nature of their jobs. Empathy, the quality that lies at the core of counselor efficacy, can also be the very factor that leads to counselor burnout (Lambie, 2006). Through empathy, counselors comprehend clients' circumstances and emotional responses. Empathic counselors communicate understanding and create a therapeutic environment for client healing. Most counselors enter the profession because they naturally possess empathic qualities and care about others; however, daily exposure to client trauma and pain can overwhelm counselors and lead to burnout. Sadly, burnout ultimately damages a counselor's capacity to experience empathy and function as a helper.

Counselor exposure to client pain and suffering can lead to suffering and a sense of being overwhelmed by client stories; this goes beyond burnout to a condition called *compassion fatigue*, also referred to as *secondary traumatic stress reaction*. Figley (2002) notes that compassion fatigue differs from burnout in that burnout is a state of exhaustion caused by the emotional nature of the counseling profession and overwork, whereas compassion fatigue is preoccupation with traumatic client cases and personal identification with this trauma. This overidentification with trauma creates symptoms within the counselor that are comparable to the symptoms of Posttraumatic Stress Disorder. Fortunately, self-care can be used to combat the exhaustion of mental and physical resources, the generalized stress of burnout, and the emotional exhaustion of compassion fatigue.

Vicarious Trauma

Counselors who work with traumatized clients may experience vicarious trauma. Vicarious trauma differs from burnout, compassion fatigue, and secondary traumatic stress in that, while all are similar constructs and all generate secondary trauma reactions, vicarious trauma additionally affects a counselor's worldview and sense of self (Trippany, White Kress, & Wilcoxon, 2004). Counselors who work with trauma clients are at a higher risk of vicarious trauma than are counselors working in other settings.

While burnout is a response to occupational stress, vicarious trauma involves a personal reaction within the counselor to a client's experience (Dunkley & Whelan, 2006). Essentially, exposure to the trauma stories of the client can trigger pervasive alterations in a counselor's cognitive schema; specifically, there are disruptions to the counselor's sense of safety, trust, esteem, control, and intimacy (McCann & Pearlman, 1990). In effect, the boundary between the client's trauma experience and the counselor's worldview is blurred, as the counselor begins to suffer trauma symptoms derived from hearing the client's story.

Trippany et al. (2004) developed the following guidelines for vicarious trauma prevention: (1) case management specifically limiting the number of trauma clients per week as much as possible; (2) peer supervision, which provides an avenue for debriefing and consultation; (3) agencies assuming responsibility to provide supervision, consultation, staffing, continuing education, and employee benefits, including personal counseling; (4) training and education on trauma work; (5) personal coping mechanisms, which include leisure activities and creative endeavors; and (6) spirituality to facilitate connection and meaning. While all counselors must be alert to signs of vicarious trauma, it is particularly important for counselors working with trauma clients to be intentional about self-care and self-awareness in their professional and personal lives.

Self-Care

It is imperative for crisis counselors to engage in restorative activities in order to regroup, revitalize, and avoid the effects of burnout, compassion fatigue, and vicarious trauma. Crisis counselor well-being is dependent on intentional choices to manage time, nurture personal and professional relationships, and grow as a professional (Meyer & Ponton, 2006). Grafanki et al. (2005) found that leisure activities, social support through connection with friends and family, spirituality and time in nature were important elements that served to counterbalance the effects of burnout in the mental health field. It is clear that crisis counselors have a personal and professional responsibility to engage in self-care. Monitoring one's own mental, physical, and spiritual health; managing time; nurturing relationships; and fostering professional growth are vital elements of self-care and best practice.

Death of Suicidal Clients and Counselor Care

As previously mentioned, it is well documented that the attempted or completed suicide is the most common and most challenging of clinical emergencies for mental health professionals (Ewalt, 1967; Knapp & VandeCreek, 1983; Shein, 1976). Losing a client to suicide is a traumatic event in the life of a counselor and, as such, deserves serious consideration. Foster and McAdams (1999) found that 23% of mental health counselors had a client commit suicide and 24% of that group consisted of counselors-in-training; yet few counselor education, psychology, or psychiatry programs train clinicians to deal with suicidal clients. Because it is likely that counselors will encounter suicidal clients and even experience the loss of a client to suicide, it is suggested that counselors consider this situation before it occurs. This proactive approach will help crisis counselors to better prepare for the work they must do with suicidal clients, to better prepare if they do experience a client who commits suicide, and hopefully to enable a less traumatic recovery for the counselor.

The loss of a client to suicide affects counseling providers not just on a professional level but also on a personal level and in ways they may not expect. This makes sense, given the oftentimes intense nature of the counseling relationship, particularly during a suicidal crisis. It is not uncommon for counselors to experience a wide range of feelings, including guilt, shame, anger, betrayal, loss of self-esteem, avoidance, intrusive thoughts, questioning of their competence, and fear related to the potential for litigation; some even give serious thought to leaving the profession (Foster & McAdams,

1999; Gitlin, 1999; Granello & Granello, 2007; Hendin, Lipschitz, Maltsberger, Haas, & Wynecoop, 2000; Simon, 2004).

Granello and Granello (2007) offer a list of suggestions a counselor might consider while working with a suicidal client and particularly after the experience of a client who commits suicide:

- Process the event with supervisors or professional mentors.
- Use peers and colleagues to help process feelings.
- Seek personal counseling to help resolve the remaining conflict.
- Recognize your own personal needs.
- Be cognizant of the personal stress that can result from working with suicidal clients.
- Recognize the limitations of the profession. (p. 290)

There is a bereavement process a counselor goes through when recovering from the experience of a client suicide, which is often complicated by the lack of resources available to them for support. The American Association of Suicidology Clinician Survivor Task Force was created to address these special needs. Various resources for clinician survivors—including relevant literature, vignettes of clinician survivors, and possible contacts to informally consult with task force members—are available through the American Association of Suicidology (Berman, 2006; Simon, 2004).

Additionally, Gutheil (1992) suggests there are both therapeutic and risk management benefits when the surviving counselor reaches out to the family members who are left following a suicide. She points out that the counselor and the family members are grieving a mutual loss and that family members oftentimes become suspicious if the

---

PERSONAL REFLECTION
Loss of a Client

I was on leave from work when I received a call from the manager at the clinic where I worked. She informed me that a client I had been working with for some time had shot and killed himself the previous night. The first thing I remember experiencing was classic denial when I responded with "No, that can't be!" After a brief pause, I asked for the details. The impact of that event and the days that followed remains in my heart as if it were just yesterday. I had dealt with suicide for many years, and while those memories still haunted me, this particular client had touched me so deeply because he had worked so hard and long to survive. I was honored to work, learn, and take the journey of recovery with this client and his family, who were also very connected and invested in his success. We had shared many tears and even laughs as he learned to manage his dual diagnosis. For months, I ruminated over what had gone wrong, what

I (and the treatment team as a whole) had missed, and what we could have done differently. I thought of many things and continued to agonize. I found myself unable to discuss his case specifically for a long time, which was challenging, given my area of specialization. Ever so slowly, I have turned his tragedy into hundreds of teaching moments, and when I feel myself losing patience with a high-risk client now, I reflect on this particular loss and am reminded of just how important this work is and how critical it is to be patient with both the client I am working with at that moment and myself.~*Mary Bartlett*

Discussion Questions

1. What do you think it would be like to lose a client to suicide?
2. What supports do you think you would need?
3. What would prevent you from accessing them?

counselor cuts off all contact with the family or refuses to respond to their requests for contact. There can be mutual gains when the surviving counselor reaches out to family members who share the loss; however, it is prudent for the counselor to consult with a lawyer before contacting the family to review what can and cannot be discussed and to be certain the counselor is not doing so based on guilt-driven feelings.

Marshall (1980) offered recommendations that can be initiated as a group process by the professional staff of an interdisciplinary team to help another staff member survive the loss of a client. Suggestions include (1) facilitating a supportive and nonblaming atmosphere to encourage safe expressions of feelings, (2) making a neutral individual group consultant available, and (3) following up with training to explore policies in place prior to the client suicide and changes that can be implemented thereafter. The process of recovery is challenging in the face of the counselor's own grief, but one thing is certain: Loss of a client to suicide can have a profound impact on the treating counselor, and support for the surviving counselor is critical not just at the time of the suicide but also well beyond the actual event.

Summary

Appropriate crisis intervention is built on proactive planning, training, and collaboration across the crisis response team. Crisis plans should be cooperatively developed and refined over time, integrating new knowledge gleaned from experience and current best practice. With good planning, a crisis team can more effectively address the safety, physical well-being, and mental health of survivors during response and recovery.

Crisis counselors must be cognizant of their own personal safety and well-being, particularly in crisis situations. Basic proactive safety precautions are a necessary aspect of good practice. Counselors practicing in isolation are particularly vulnerable, and they should have clear safety plans that are followed. Counselors who work with high-risk clients or in high-risk settings must be aware of safety rules and remain alert to their environment.

Awareness of developmental transitions and transcrisis issues will facilitate mental health intervention across time, as counselors are likely to encounter clients whose long-buried trauma symptoms from a previous crisis emerge unexpectedly and affect current functioning. These transcrisis states can be effectively treated and should be normalized as movement toward healing. Transcrisis points are developmental steps that clients must work through in order to heal from the original trauma. It is important for counselors to remember that healing from crisis is not a linear process but can occur over time.

Additionally, it is imperative that crisis counselors be well acquainted with legal and ethical obligations. Privacy laws like HIPAA and FERPA have provisions for crisis situations, but confidentiality is still central to ethical practice, even during times of crisis. Crisis counselors must be familiar with the particulars of HIPAA and FERPA and other legal requirements in their state. Ethical obligations, including the duty to warn, documentation, informed consent, mandatory reporting, referral, and termination, must be attended to whether the crisis counselor is working one on one with a client in crisis or intervening with many clients in a large-scale disaster. Planning, preparedness, and a commitment to ethical practice in all situations will ensure that crisis counselors maintain standards of care whatever the situation.

A critical aspect of crisis counseling is the need for crisis counselor self-assessment and self-care. Crisis and trauma clients can take a toll on crisis counselors, who may experience countertransference, burnout, compassion fatigue, and vicarious trauma. Crisis counselor self-care practices are a necessary component of effective crisis intervention.

3 Essential Crisis Intervention Skills

Joseph Cooper

PREVIEW

This chapter provides an overview of the fundamental skills for the provision of effective crisis intervention work. The skills in this chapter will focus on Ivey and Ivey's (2007) mircoskills hierarchy. At the heart of this hierarchy is the basic listening sequence, an interrelated set of skills that will not only foster the development of rapport with clients but also aid in the identification of interventions to help achieve a successful resolution to the client's crisis state. Examples of the skills in use, as well as practice exercises to foster individual skill development, are provided. Finally, a review of self-care strategies to deal with burnout and secondary trauma is included.

ESSENTIAL CRISIS INTERVENTION MICROSKILLS

The purpose of this chapter is to provide the basic foundational skills necessary for effective crisis intervention work. It is important to stress that these skills are indeed the foundational tools on which the success of interventions may depend. It is also important to stress that these skills will help to create the counselor–client relational conditions necessary for positive change. However, we also need to stress that the skills we cover in this chapter are *basic* counseling microskills applied to crisis situations. These basic skills form the foundation for the use of more advanced counseling skills.

These skills will provide the client with such alliance-building constructs as empathic understanding, genuineness, and acceptance and will greatly facilitate the development of a safe therapeutic environment (Rogers, 1951). These skills will also aid in establishing rapport with the client. Rapport can be understood as a harmonious or sympathetic relationship. In crisis intervention work, the development of rapport starts with the initial contact and continues throughout the process. The crisis counselor's primary concern should be fostering this rapport in order to develop a cohesive and supportive relationship with the client. How the crisis counselor conducts himself or herself is crucial, as this may be the client's first encounter with a counselor and this interaction may either encourage or discourage the client from seeking counseling in the future or from following up when a proposed crisis plan is developed.

The skills covered in this chapter focus on Ivey and Ivey's (2007) mircoskills hierarchy. The microskills represent a set of verbal and behavioral responses that facilitate the process of counseling and alliance formation regardless of the crisis counselor's theoretical orientation (Lambert & Ogles, 1997). For some, this chapter may be a review of the basic skills taught in a previous skills course, while for others it may be the first consideration of these skills. Either way, it is always important to continuously be aware of and practice effective skills, since this is the hallmark of effective crisis counseling. Ivey and Ivey present these skills as a hierarchy that is organized within a systematic framework. At the bottom of the hierarchy are the basic attending skills such as patterns of eye contact, body language, and tone of voice. A bit farther up the skills hierarchy is the basic listening sequence, which includes questioning, paraphrasing, summarizing, and reflecting feelings. In this chapter, each of these basic skills is reviewed, along with practical examples of the skills in use.

ATTENDING SKILLS

Good communication involves more than just verbal content, for crisis counselors communicate with more than just words. Much of our communication takes place nonverbally. The next time you are engaged in conversation with someone, take a moment to pay attention to all of the nonverbal cues your partner is giving you. What does his facial expression say to you? What is conveyed by the look in his eyes? Does he have a closed or open body stance? Although important in social relationships, these attending skills are even more important in the counseling relationship. In a recent study, Bedi (2006) surveyed clients who had received counseling and asked them to identify the specific counselor behaviors that most helped to form a working alliance. Following validation and education, clients ranked nonverbal gestures and presentation and body language as the most important alliance-building factors. These nonverbal attending behaviors communicate a counselor's interest, warmth, and understanding to the client and include such behaviors as eye contact, body position, and tone of voice.

Eye Contact

Maintaining good eye contact is how a crisis counselor conveys interest, confidence, and involvement in the client's story (Egan, 2002). Through eye contact, clients know a counselor is focusing on them and fully committed to the helping process. Moreover, for those clients who have difficulty with closeness, making eye contact can be an important vehicle of change (Vaillant, 1997). However, good eye contact is not the same as staring your client down. There should be natural breaks in eye contact; eye contact should be more of an "ebb and flow" as you collect your thoughts and listen to the client's story. Also, it is essential to be sensitive to differences in how eye contact is expressed across cultures. For example, whereas direct eye contact is usually interpreted as a sign of interest in the middle-class European-American culture, some Asian and

Native American groups believe direct eye contact is a sign of disrespect (Ivey & Ivey, 2007). Also, for clients who are overly fragile or under much stress and pressure, direct eye contact may increase their level of anxiety.

So how do you determine how much eye contact to maintain with your client? Unfortunately, there is no universal rule or criterion for what is considered either appropriate or inappropriate eye contact; as already noted, this varies among cultures. A good rule of thumb to follow is to maintain a moderate amount of eye contact while monitoring your client's level of comfort and to adjust your eye contact accordingly (Young, 2005). Also, it is helpful for you to become aware of your own attending behavior so you can understand how this behavior may affect the counseling relationship. Use Activities 3.1 and 3.2 to gain a deeper understanding of your own attending behaviors.

Body Position

As with eye contact, your body position should convey to the client your interest and involvement. Face the client and adopt an open, relaxed, and attentive body posture, as this will assist in putting your client at ease. Counselors should not cross arms and legs and should not sit behind a desk or other barrier. In addition, Egan (2002) recommends that the counselor lean slightly toward the client, as this communicates that the counselor is listening to the client and interested in what the client has to say. Slouching in the chair or leaning away from the client may be perceived by the client as lack of

ACTIVITY 3.1

In dyads, one person should be the listener, while the other (i.e., the speaker) talks about anything of interest for about five minutes. During this time, have each listener maintain the eye contact he or she would normally maintain in everyday conversation. After five minutes, take some time to process the experience. What feedback does the speaker have regarding the listener's level of eye contact? Was it too much? Darting? Too little? Empathic? What was most comfortable? Based on the feedback, do the exercise again, but this time have the listener try to incorporate some of the feedback received about his or her level of eye contact. Process the activity again, and then switch roles.

ACTIVITY 3.2

The purpose of this exercise is to become aware of how your clients might perceive your overall pattern of nonverbal communications. In this exercise, break up into pairs facing each other. One person will be the communicator, and the other will serve as the mirror. For the next five minutes, the communicator can talk about anything he or she wants, and throughout this time, the mirror is to nonverbally mirror each gesture, facial expression, eye contact, and movement of the communicator. It is important that the mirror not attempt to "interpret" the message that is being sent by the communicator but just mirror the perceived nonverbals. At the end of five minutes, process this experience with each other. What was it like to see your nonverbals mirrored back to you? Did you learn anything about how you come across to others? Is there anything you would want to change or to do more of?

interest or boredom on your part. Finally, the physical distance between counselor and client should be taken into consideration; getting too close can be overwhelming and uncomfortable, whereas too great a distance can make the counselor appear aloof and may be awkward for the client. Although in Western cultures the average physical distance for conversation is typically two to four feet, this "comfort zone" will vary from client to client (Young, 2005). When in doubt, a good idea is to let the client decide the distance by letting the client arrange the chairs at an individual comfort level. At the same time, the counselor should be aware of his or her personal space issues and set up personal space boundaries.

Vocal Tone

Have you ever had the experience where you are engaged in conversation with someone and you find yourself becoming increasingly anxious and tense regardless of the topic? The next time this happens pay attention to your partner's tone of voice, for you may be unconsciously responding to the emotional tone conveyed in your partner's voice. Emotions are frequently conveyed via tone of voice. The pitch, pacing, and volume can all have an effect on how a client responds emotionally to a crisis counselor. There is much to be said for a calm and soothing voice in times of distress, especially when the client is in a crisis situation. Do not underestimate the power of this attribute; your control and calmness may be among the greatest benefits to your client in crisis. Your voice can do much to help create a soothing and anxiety-regulating atmosphere for the client. Learn to use your voice as a therapeutic tool. For instance, if your client is overly agitated, it is often helpful to speak more slowly and in a soothing tone, as this will help your client to slow things down and begin to focus. Also, to convey a sense of empathic understanding, it can be helpful to give emphasis to the specific words used by your client. This technique of giving increased vocal emphasis to certain words or short phrases is called *verbal underlining* (Ivey & Ivey, 2007). For example, consider the difference between "You were very hurt by your husband's actions" and "You were *very* hurt by your husband's actions." In the latter sentence, the counselor places the emphasis on the word *very* to help reflect the intensity of the client's experience. Activity 3.3 will facilitate a greater awareness of the vocal subtleties in the spoken word.

ACTIVITY 3.3

In small groups, assign one person to be the speaker. Instruct the speaker to talk in a normal tone of voice for a few minutes about anything of interest. Have the other group members close their eyes as they listen to the speaker, paying close attention to the tone of voice, pacing, volume, and so on. After two or three minutes, stop and have the members give the speaker feedback on his or her voice. What was their reaction to the tone, volume, accent, rate of speech, and other characteristics? After this processing, repeat the exercise, but this time have the speaker make changes in voice tone, volume, or pacing to deliberately create different reactions. How do the members respond to the changes in vocal qualities? What were the members' emotional responses that corresponded with the various vocal qualities? Finally, have the members imagine themselves as a client in crisis. What types of vocal qualities would the listeners prefer to hear?

THE BASIC LISTENING SEQUENCE

The basic listening sequence represents a set of interrelated skills used to achieve three overarching goals: (1) to obtain an overall summary and understanding of the client's presenting issue, (2) to identify the key facts of the client's situation, and (3) to identify the core emotions and feelings the client is experiencing (Ivey & Ivey, 2007). In short, these skills allow you to understand the structure of your client's story. Through the use of these skills, not only will you convey empathy, respect, warmth, and congruence to your client, but also you will be laying the foundation for your understanding of the client's issues and the development of subsequent interventions to help achieve a successful resolution to his or her crisis state. The basic listening sequence involves the ability to ask open and closed questions as well as the reflecting skills—paraphrasing, reflecting feelings, and summarizing. An explanation and overview of these skills, examples of each skill in use, and some brief exercises to help you practice these basic listening skills follow.

Asking Open and Closed Questions

Questioning is a primary skill that allows crisis counselors to gather important and specific information about clients. Questions allow us to make an accurate assessment of our clients' issues and to guide and focus our clients so we can make the most effective use of the counseling session. However, the use of questioning can be a double-edged sword. Used inappropriately, questioning can impede communication and block client disclosure (Rosenbluh, 1981). Drilling clients with questions can give too much control to the crisis counselor. Moreover, bombarding clients with questions could confuse and frustrate them as well as increasing their level of anxiety. Crisis counselors definitely do not want counseling sessions to sound like an interrogation, although many of the initial intake questions are used to gather information and therefore necessary in crisis intervention. Counselors must be careful to appropriately pace the questions to guard against increasing clients' stress levels. Thus, crisis counselors need to be aware of how to use questions appropriately and pay close attention to the types of questions used to gather information. The two types of questions, open and closed questions, are examined next.

OPEN QUESTIONS   Open questions usually elicit fuller and more meaningful responses by encouraging the client to talk at greater length. Open questions typically begin with *what, how, could, would,* or *why* and are useful to help begin an interview, to help elaborate the client's story, and to help bring out specific details (Ivey & Ivey, 2007). With open questions, the client can choose the content and direction of the session and take more control. The following are examples of the use of open questions/statements:

1. *To begin an interview:*   "What would you like to talk about today?" "How can I be of help to you today?" "Tell me why you have come in today."
2. *To elicit details:*   "Give me an example." "What do you mean by 'just give up'?" "What do you usually do when you are feeling down?"
3. *To enrich and deepen:*   "Tell me more." "What were your feelings when that happened?" "What else is important for me to know?"

Finally, be careful when using *why* questions and questions that are leading in nature. Questions that begin with "Why" often cause the client to intellectualize and can lead to a discussion of reasons. In addition, *why* questions can cause the client to become defensive and to feel "put on the spot." When this happens, it is not uncommon for the client to become more guarded and to shut down. For example, think back to a time when you were younger and your parents asked the question "Why did you do that?" How did you feel and what was your reaction to them? Take a moment to consider the following: "Why do you hate yourself?" versus "You say you hate yourself. Help me understand that." Which of these approaches would you prefer your counselor to use?

Another roadblock to the use of effective questions involves questions that are leading in nature. Leading questions often contain a hidden agenda because the answer or expectation is already imbedded within the question. Although well intentioned, these types of questions place too much power in the hands of the crisis counselor and tend to push the client in a preconceived direction. Here are a couple of examples of leading questions: "You didn't really want do kill yourself, did you?" "Don't you think you will feel better if you stop drinking?" Try to guard against the use of these types of questions. Crisis counselors want to hear a client's story as he or she understands and experiences it. Open questions allow the counselor the opportunity to achieve this end without imposing values and expectations on the client.

CLOSED QUESTIONS   Closed questions can be used when crisis counselors need to obtain very specific, concrete information and get all the facts straight. Closed questions typically either elicit a "yes/no" response or provide specific factual information, such as the number of drinks a client consumes in a week or the age at which he or she began experiencing symptoms. In contrast to longer-term counseling, where information is gathered more slowly and the treatment plan develops over many weeks, crisis counseling often requires quick and focused responses. Thus, closed questions are very useful and in fact necessary in crisis counseling because the counselor must gather specific information to aid in the prompt assessment of the problem and development of a plan of action (James, 2008). Here are some examples of closed questions:

- "Are you thinking of killing yourself?"
- "When did these symptoms begin?"
- "Do you have a family member or friend to call on when you are feeling overwhelmed?"
- "How old were you when your parents divorced?"

As can be seen from the above examples, closed questions are good for obtaining the necessary details to aid in assessment and intervention. However, one must guard against the overuse of closed questions. Use of too many closed questions can cause the client to shut down and become passive because you are training the client to simply sit back and wait for the next question to answer. A good rule of thumb to follow is to move from the general to the specific in your assessment. In other words, begin with open (i.e., general) questions, and as you gather information and hear the client's story, move to more closed (i.e., specific) questions to obtain the details important for the assessment and subsequent development of an intervention plan.

The following dialogue provides a brief example of how the crisis counselor uses a blend of open and closed questions to obtain important information about Susan, who recently discovered her husband is having an affair and is planning on leaving her.

SUSAN: I've gotten to where I can't even sleep at night. My mind just races, and I can't stop thinking about everything.

COUNSELOR (C):   Tell me more about some of the thoughts you have been having as you lay in bed unable to sleep. (*open question to facilitate exploration and information gathering*)

SUSAN: That I will never be in a happy relationship again. That my husband never really cared about me and just used me. That this pain will never stop. I wonder how I can get my life back together without him.

C: You wonder if you will find peace again without him and want so much for this pain to go away. (*empathic paraphrase*) What are some of the feelings you have been experiencing? (*open question*)

SUSAN: Mainly down—angry and depressed. I feel this tremendous pain inside my chest, very hurt and sad I guess. I feel like he never really cared about me. He is so selfish.

C: You're feeling very hurt and betrayed. Susan, tell me when you began experiencing these symptoms? (*closed question to identify timeline of symptoms*)

SUSAN: I would say about three months ago, when I found out about his affair, but they have gotten much worse over the last month.

C: You say they have gotten worse over the last month. What do you make of that? (*open question to identify client's understanding of her progressing symptoms*)

SUSAN: Well, when I first found out about the affair, I would talk a lot with my friends and family, but I felt like they were getting sick of hearing me complain all the time. So lately I have just been trying to tough it out and deal with it on my own.

C: And is this the first time you have sought counseling for this?

SUSAN: Yes.

As this example demonstrates, the crisis worker began with open questions to encourage exploration and to help identify the client's thoughts (e.g., "I will never be in a happy relationship again") and feelings (e.g., anger, grief, and hurt) associated with the breakup of her marriage. The crisis worker then moved to closed questions to obtain more specific information regarding the duration of her symptoms and her experience in counseling.

OPEN VERSUS CLOSED QUESTIONS   As mentioned earlier, in crisis intervention work, crisis counselors often need to use closed questions to quickly identify and bring out specific details in order to seek the resolution of the crisis state. However, one can often obtain the same information by asking open questions, so try to refrain from moving too quickly into a closed questioning approach unless you are unable to obtain the information

ACTIVITY 3.4

Take a moment to practice changing these questions from closed to open questions.

1. Why did you quit your job?
2. Do you think you should stop using drugs?

3. Do you get eight hours of sleep a night?
4. Did you feel angry with him?
5. Don't you think there are other ways for you to cope with your anger?

otherwise. Consider these examples of closed questions and their open question counterparts:

Closed	Open
Were you afraid?	What feelings did you experience?
Are you concerned about what you will do if your husband returns?	How do you think you may react if your husband returns?
Do you see your drinking as a problem?	What concerns do you have about your drinking?

Notice in these examples that you can probably get all you need to know, and much more, by a subtle change in the wording of your questions to make them more open in nature. Now get some additional practice by completing Activity 3.4.

Reflecting Skills

Reflecting skills are a set of interventions used to help stimulate clients' exploration of their thoughts and feelings related to the presenting problems. Reflecting skills serve a number of important purposes. At the most basic level, reflecting skills are a form of active listening that convey to the client your interest in and understanding of what the client may be struggling with. Thus, reflecting skills allow you to convey empathy, genuineness, and acceptance to the client, and this in turn will facilitate the creation of a sense of safety. Moreover, reflecting skills will stimulate a deeper exploration and understanding of the problem so that the client can examine the issues more objectively. The reflecting skills covered in this chapter are paraphrasing, reflecting feelings, and summarizing.

PARAPHRASING   A paraphrase is how we feed back to the client the essence of what has just been spoken. By paraphrasing, we reflect the content and thoughts of the client's message. In other words, the crisis counselor is mirroring back to the client, in a nonjudgmental way, an accurate understanding of the client's communication and the implied meaning of that communication. Thus, paraphrasing is a reflecting skill used to convey empathic understanding and to facilitate the exploration and clarification of the client's problems (Ivey & Ivey, 2007). It is important for counselors to be sure the paraphrased information is accurate by checking with the client. Some clients in crisis may not feel they can refute what is being said, or their crisis state may impede their ability to completely follow the session; however, paraphrasing gives these clients permission to approve or disapprove the accuracy of the paraphrase and its implied meaning, thereby increasing their control. When the counselor paraphrases the client's information inaccurately and does not seek affirmation by the client, the counselor may then define the actual primary presenting problem inaccurately, which in turn may change the direction of the session and/or interfere with the development of the most appropriate treatment plan for the client. This is compounded when the client needs the counselor to use a more directive approach due to the severity of the crisis. Young (2005) proposed that reflecting skills are important because they provide the counselor a way to:

1. Communicate empathy.
2. Give feedback that enables the client to confirm or reject the impression he or she has been giving.
3. Stimulate further exploration of what the client has been experiencing.
4. Capture important aspects of the client's story that may have been overlooked or covert. (pp. 123–124)

As can be seen, paraphrasing, if used appropriately, is a powerful therapeutic tool. Appropriate use means crisis counselors must develop the ability to take the essence of the client's statement and reflect back those thoughts and facts in *their own words*. When the counselor uses paraphrasing accurately, the client will continue to explore and elaborate. On the other hand, the counselor should not "parrot" back to the client what has been said. Parroting back would be a simple word-for-word restatement, not a paraphrase. Consider this example:

SUSAN: I feel so put down and disrespected by my husband. He is just like my father in a lot of ways. He was verbally abusive and full of anger. I never really felt important to him. Why do I let men treat me this way?

C: You feel put down and disrespected by him.

As you can see from the above paraphrase, the crisis worker simply parrots back what the client has said, which adds little and keeps the focus superficial. A better response might be this:

C: Although you are trying to understand this pattern of hurt and disappointment you have experienced from the important men in your life, it sounds like you are blaming yourself for this.

To develop your paraphrasing skill, you may find it helpful to first identify the key words or content that captures the essence of your client's concern. Once you have the key content in mind, try to translate this into your own words. Following are some examples of a client's statements, the possible key themes or words, and the resulting paraphrase.

EXAMPLE 1

Client: "I am so fed up with my marriage. I try and try to get through to him, and he just shuts me out."

Possible key themes or words: *fed up, being shut out, failed efforts to connect.*

Paraphrase: "You are at your wit's end with this. In spite of your efforts to connect, you come up against a closed door. Is that correct?"

EXAMPLE 2

Client: "Exactly, and that is why I have been thinking about leaving him. I know I deserve much better, but I just keep going back to him. I can't seem to make that first move."

Possible key themes or words: *leaving her husband, being stuck, hesitation, self-worth.*

Paraphrase: "Although a part of you knows this is not the way you want to live your life, it is still difficult to break out of this cycle. Is that right?"

As you can see from the above examples, identifying the key words or themes can really aid in your ability to develop accurate paraphrases that convey the essence of your client's meaning without coming across as superficial. Use Activity 3.5 to practice your paraphrasing skills.

REFLECTING FEELINGS   A wealth of research attests to the usefulness of accessing and working with feelings and emotions in counseling (Greenberg & Pascual-Leone, 2006). Naming and identifying a client's feelings can serve a number of important functions (Young, 2005). By reflecting feelings, a crisis counselor can help the client to become aware of the emotions experienced in relation to the issue at hand. This awareness can then increase the client's overall level of self-awareness and deepen his or her self-disclosure. In addition, reflecting feelings can have a positive impact on the therapeutic relationship, and a convincing amount of research has shown the quality of the therapeutic relationship to be one of the strongest predictors of counseling outcomes (Horvath & Bedi, 2002). Moreover, it is not necessarily the specific theoretical approach of the helper but the strength of the therapeutic relationship that is associated with the successful achievement of your client's counseling goals (Nuttall, 2002). The therapeutic relationship should be characterized by an experience of mutual liking, trust, and respect between the client and the helper. In addition, such helper qualities as accurate empathy, unconditional positive regard, and genuineness greatly contribute to the development of the helping relationship (Rogers, 1951). Thus, the reflecting skills play an important role in the development of this vital working alliance by conveying these "relationship

---

ACTIVITY 3.5

Following are some client statements. Try to identify the key themes or words, and then, based on these key themes or words, develop a paraphrase of your client's statement.

1. "I don't know what to do with my life. I hate my job and everything seems so meaningless. I can barely muster the energy to get out of bed in the morning. Sometimes I just want to sleep for days."

2. "I am still in shock that my husband is having an affair. I really can't believe it. I thought we had the perfect marriage. How could I have been so stupid to not see this was happening? I feel like such a fool."

3. "I can't tell if I am coming or going. I can't sleep, I have nightmares, and I feel like a zombie throughout the day. I am so tense my body aches. No matter what I do, it just keeps getting worse."

enhancers" to your client (Young, 2005, p. 55). As with paraphrasing, reflecting feelings can promote the development of accurate empathy and help to create a safe environment for the client.

To reflect feelings one must be able to recognize and put words to those feeling states observed in the client. And what is the best way to practice this? One way is to work on becoming more aware of your own feelings and being able to accurately name these feelings. This in turn will really help you to accurately recognize and name the feelings clients may be experiencing. For example, in my counseling skills class, I will walk around the class and ask each student to tell me how he or she is feeling *right now*. The most common responses I receive are "fine," "good," and "ok." Notice, however, that these are not feelings and do not provide me with any understanding of what my students may be really feeling. Then I explain the importance of being able not only to correctly identify and name the core feelings we all experience as humans (e.g., anger, sadness, fear, surprise, joy, love, disgust) but also to accurately recognize and name our moment-to-moment feeling states that represent the finer shadings of those core emotions. For example, some of the finer shadings of anger are irritated, bitter, enraged, frustrated, and sore. By increasing your feelings awareness and feelings word vocabulary, you will be able to more easily and correctly identify and respond to a client's feelings.

How does a counselor identify the feelings in clients, especially if these feelings are not explicitly stated? When the client does not state his or her feelings directly, the counselor may still be able to infer these feelings either from the context of the client's communication or from the client's nonverbal behaviors (e.g., facial expression, posture). Thus, it is important to attend not only to what is being said but also to how it is being communicated. Here are a number of practical tips to aid in reflecting a client's feelings (Evans, Hearn, Uhlemann, & Ivey, 2008; Ivey & Ivey, 2007):

1. To aid in identifying a client's feelings:
   a. Pay attention to the affective component of the client's communication.
   b. Pay attention to the client's behavior (e.g., posture, tone of voice, facial expression).
   c. Use a broad range of words to correctly identify the client's emotions.
   d. Silently name the client's feeling(s) to yourself.

2. To aid in reflecting feelings to a client:
   a. Use an appropriate introductory phrase (e.g., *Sounds like. . . . Looks like. . . . You feel. . . . It seems. . . .*).
   b. Add a feeling word or emotional label to the stem (e.g., *Sounds like you are angry.*).
   c. Add a context or brief paraphrase to help anchor or broaden the reflection. This context should add the link or meaning for the perceived feeling (e.g., *Sounds like you are angry at your father's refusal to put you in his will.*).
   d. Pay attention to the tense. Present tense reflections can often be more powerful than past tense reflections (you *feel* angry versus you *felt* angry).
   e. Do not repeat the client's exact words (parroting).
   f. Reflect mixed emotions (e.g., *You are feeling both angry and hurt about your father's behavior toward you.*).
   g. Check out the accuracy of the reflection of feeling with the client (e.g. *Am I hearing you correctly? Is that close? Have I got that right?*).

Consider the following example:

SUSAN: I just sit around the house wondering what to do. We use to spend time with my husband's friends, but they know that we are no longer together. So there is no one for me to really spend time with. I really miss them, and my own friends seem so busy. I would hate to burden them with all of my problems.

C: You are feeling both sad and lonely right now, and you are concerned you may be just another burden on your own friends. Is that about right? (*reflection of feeling with check for accuracy*)

SUSAN: Yes, I don't want to bring everyone down with all my problems.

There is one last point to consider when reflecting feelings. Whereas in traditional psychotherapy the focus is often on uncovering feeling after feeling by attempting to unearth the "core" issue, in crisis intervention work the task is quite different. Thus, guard against going too far with uncovering feelings, as this could exacerbate the clients' crisis state by overwhelming them with emotion. Strive for a balance of skills to build rapport, and when you do reflect feelings, be sure to keep the focus directly related to the client's presenting concerns (James, 2008). Activity 3.6 will give you an opportunity to practice identifying feelings so you can develop accurate reflections of feelings.

SUMMARIZING   The final skill in the basic listening sequence is summarizing. By summarizing, a crisis counselor can begin to put together the key themes, feelings, and issues the client has presented. By distilling the key issues and themes and reflecting this back to the client, counselors can begin to help clients make sense of what may have originally seemed to be an overwhelming and confusing experience. In addition, when clients are feeling overwhelmed and are flooded with anxiety, they will often go on tangents in many directions, making it difficult for the crisis counselor to keep up. When this occurs, brief summaries are often a useful tool to help refocus the client and

---

ACTIVITY 3.6

Take a moment to read each vignette and to identify the feelings embedded within the client's communications. Once you have identified the feelings, come up with your own reflection of feelings.

1. "I don't know what to do. My husband keeps working late into the night, and I feel like I never get to see him. When we do get some time together, he is moody and reserved. To make matters worse, I saw a charge on our credit card statement to a local hotel. I think he might be having an affair."

2. "Ever since I was mugged I've been having a hard time. Because of the nightmares, I can't sleep at night and am exhausted all during the day. On top of that, I am panicky and nervous all the time. I worry I might be losing my mind."

3. "I can't believe what my father did. He stole all the money from the trust fund grandmother had willed to my brother and me. I have been calling him day and night, and he will not return my calls. I might have to get a lawyer, but I don't know how I am going to afford it. Why would he do this to us?"

reintroduce some structure into the session, which will help to modulate the client's (and the counselor's) anxiety. Thus, a summary not only is used to end a session or to begin a new session by recapping the previous session but also can be used periodical-ly throughout the session, helping to keep a focus and putting together the pertinent issues at hand for the client.

So when should a crisis counselor summarize? Although much will depend on the client and the content being discussed, Evans et al. (2008) offered a number of useful suggestions to help determine when a summary is in order: (1) when your client is ram-bling, confused, or overly lengthy in his or her comments; (2) when your client presents a number of unrelated ideas; (3) when you need to provide direction to the interview; (4) when you are ready to move the client from one phase of the interview to the next; (5) when you want to end the interview; and (6) when a summary of the prior interview will provide you an opening to the current interview.

When summarizing, you do not have to report back to the client every single detail he or she has disclosed. This would, of course, require a prodigious memory. The key is to capture the important elements, content, feelings, and issues and to reflect these back to the client in a concise manner. Following are three types of summaries relevant to crisis intervention counseling:

1. *Focusing summaries:*   These summaries are often used at the beginning of the session to pull together prior information the client has given and to provide a focus to the session. "Last time we met you were having trouble sleeping, and you were having nightmares and feeling panicky throughout the day. We identified some coping skills and relaxation exercises for you to use. Tell me how these have worked out for you so far."

2. *Signal summaries:*   These summaries are used to "signal" to the client that you have captured the essence of his or her topic and that the session can move on to the next area of concern. Signal summaries help to provide both structure and direction to the session. "So before we move on, let me make sure I am under-standing things correctly. You discovered your husband is having an affair. . . . "

3. *Planning summaries:*   These summaries help to provide closure and are used to recap the progress, plans, and any recommendations/agreements made. These summaries are good for ending the session on a positive note and for providing a sense of direction for the client. "Let's take a look at what we have covered today. Ever since you were mugged you have been having panic attacks and nightmares. We covered some coping techniques and relaxation exercises for you to practice between now and the next time we meet. . . . " (Young, 2005, pp. 161–163).

So, to put it all together, here is one more example of a summary statement: "Let me see if I understand you correctly. Yesterday you found out your son has been using cocaine for the last six months and has stolen money from you on a number of occa-sions. You are experiencing a mixture of feelings, especially shock and anger, and you are worried he might turn out to be an addict like your father was. However, you are determined to do all you can to not let that happen to him. How about discussing some possible directions we can go in from here." Note that this summary captures the key is-sues and feelings without being too wordy and offers a transition for the counselor and client to begin identifying some action steps to take. The following dialogue between

Susan and the crisis counselor demonstrates the skills of paraphrasing, reflecting feelings, and summarizing:

SUSAN: I really thought things were going well with my husband, so this came as a complete shock when I found out about the affair.

C: You were really blindsided by this. (*paraphrase*)

SUSAN: Exactly! And I have been trying to push away the pain, but I can't seem to stop thinking about it. I just want to strangle him for putting me through this.

C: Even though you want so much for the pain to go away, it is still there, especially your hurt and anger toward him. (*paraphrase with a reflection of feeling*)

SUSAN: Yes, and sometimes I can't tell which is worse, my anger or just the hurt I am going through. I sometimes lie in bed at night and wish something terrible would happen to him. I am not saying I want to kill him or anything, but I just want him to suffer like I am suffering.

C: And this reflects the intensity of your grief right now, wanting to see him suffer, too. (*reflection of feeling*)

SUSAN: Very true.

C: So, in essence, you never expected something like this to happen to you, and it has been difficult for you to tough it out and to push away the pain, grief, and anger that you have been feeling. Is that about right? (*summary with check for accuracy*)

BURNOUT AND SELF-CARE

Of the many challenges facing the crisis counselor, one of the most prominent is burnout. Crisis counselors face on a daily basis a wide array of individuals who present with severe psychological and traumatic problems. Such intense issues as physical and sexual abuse, suicidal ideations or gestures, physical assault, murder, and rape can wear down even the most optimistic and motivated helper. Because of the intense nature of this type of work, it is highly important for the crisis counselor to understand and to be aware of the symptoms of burnout and to have in place a self-care plan to manage such symptoms. Burnout is a serious matter, for we can only be helpful to others if we ourselves are psychologically healthy. In this section, we examine some of the symptoms of burnout and explore ways for you, the crisis counselor, to implement some self-care skills in your life.

Burnout has been defined as "a syndrome of emotional exhaustion, depersonalization, and reduced personal accomplishment" (Maslach, 1982, p. 3). Burnout is a state of emotional, physical, and mental exhaustion due to involvement in situations that are emotionally demanding and often long-standing. Unfortunately, burnout often causes counselors to treat their clients in detached and dehumanized ways. Moreover, the development of burnout can be insidious, often going unrecognized by the individual in the counseling setting. Common symptoms of burnout include feelings of helplessness and dissatisfaction, disillusionment, mental and physical exhaustion, emotional numbing, and psychological problems (Gilliland & James, 1997; Sprang, Clark, & Whitt-Woosley, 2007). In addition, those suffering from burnout may often develop a negative attitude toward their work, other people, and life itself.

Similar to the concept of burnout, compassion fatigue is often experienced by counselors who work with survivors of trauma (Stebnicki, 2007). It is hypothesized that crisis workers are more prone to compassion stress due to the repeated expression of empathy toward their clients' pain and suffering. In a way, a secondary traumatic stress, or vicarious traumatization, often develops in the helper due to the accumulation of traumatic stories (McCann & Pearlman, 1990). Like those with burnout, counselors with compassion fatigue often experience feelings of loss, grief, detachment, anxiety, and depression. They may feel helpless in the face of their clients' problems and come to believe that their interventions will have very little impact or be of any help (Stebnicki, 2007).

Research has found that workers with large caseloads of survivors of violent trauma and crisis situations are at greater risk of developing compassion fatigue (Sprang et al., 2007). Crisis workers often experience more negative effects from their job than do other human service workers, and the risk for developing compassion fatigue is much greater in crisis workers who work with long-term disasters (James, 2008). Although there have been few studies that have examined the epidemiology of compassion fatigue and burnout among various groups of helping professionals, research has consistently shown mental health workers to be at a much greater risk for developing compassion fatigue than are primary health care workers (e.g., Creamer & Liddle, 2005; Imai, Nakao, Tsuchiya, Kuroda, & Katon, 2004). For example, 64.7% of the crisis workers who responded to the Oklahoma City bombing reported experiencing significant traumatic stress.

Self-Care Strategies

Because of the nature of crisis counseling, crisis counselors need to be aware of the risk of developing burnout and compassion fatigue. Crisis counselors are simply more vulnerable to such stress as a result of both feeling and expressing empathy for the pain and suffering of clients. It would be safe to say that there are very few professionals who practice crisis intervention who are immune to burnout. Because of this, it is important that you begin to develop a self-care plan. To this end, some basic self-care guidelines will be offered to aid you in (1) developing a greater awareness of signs and symptoms of burnout and (2) implementing self-care strategies.

If one examines the literature on counselor self-care strategies, three basic themes emerge regarding the development and implementation of a self-care plan: (1) developing individual self-awareness, (2) identifying wellness and lifestyle approaches, and (3) creating and maintaining professional and interpersonal connections (Stebnicki, 2007).

INDIVIDUAL SELF-AWARENESS   To cope with burnout you must determine if you are experiencing any of its various symptoms. Although as mental health professionals we encourage self-awareness in our clients, it is often quite difficult to practice what we preach. Thus, the first step is simply to increase our own self-awareness and self-monitoring of any of the common symptoms of burnout. Table 3.1 contains a list of the common behavioral, physical, interpersonal, and attitudinal symptoms of burnout (James, 2008).

Obviously the list in Table 3.1 is not exhaustive. However, this should give you a good starting point in your self-assessment of potential symptoms of burnout.

TABLE 3.1 Symptoms of Burnout

Behavioral

- Abuse of alcohol and illicit drugs
- Difficulty coping with minor problems
- Loss of enjoyment
- Dread of work
- Increased irritability and impatience
- Losing things
- Suicidal or homicidal ideation/attempts
- Reduced work efficiency
- PTSD-like symptoms

Physical

- Chronic fatigue
- Insomnia
- Muscle tension
- Panic attacks
- Weakened immune system
- Flare-ups in preexisting medical conditions
- Weight gain or loss
- Changes in appetite

Interpersonal

- Withdrawal from family and friends
- Difficulty separating professional and personal life
- Decreased interest in physical or emotional intimacy
- Loss of trust
- Loneliness
- Allowing clients to abuse your professional boundaries
- Ending of long-lasting relationships
- Difficulty coping with minor interpersonal problems

Attitudinal

- Boredom
- Guilt
- Depression
- Pessimism
- Helplessness
- Survivor guilt
- Grandiosity
- Sense of meaninglessness
- Self-criticism

Self-awareness and self-monitoring are extremely important, as it is all too easy to experience burnout and yet continue to ignore the warning signs even as the symptoms continue to escalate.

WELLNESS AND LIFESTYLE APPROACHES   Much has been written regarding the importance of developing an individual wellness plan to promote a balanced mind, body, and spirit (e.g., Mahoney, 1997; Norcross, 2000; Schure, Christopher, & Christopher, 2008; Stebnicki, 2007). Some suggestions include using mindfulness exercises such as meditation and visualization and keeping a personal diary or reflective journal to aid in managing stress. Other techniques include a combination of mind and body approaches, such as yoga, Qigong, or Tai Chi. Physical exercise such as walking, running, biking, or swimming is also another healthy avenue for managing and relieving some of the day-to-day stresses from working with those in crisis.

PROFESSIONAL AND INTERPERSONAL CONNECTIONS   Crisis counseling is not a job to be done in isolation. Due to the intense nature of the clients' issues, it is important to maintain a healthy support system. By maintaining a healthy support system, you are more likely to keep a clear boundary between your work and your personal life. For example, maintaining consistent individual or peer group supervision is an important component to both your professional development and your personal wellness plan. Also, professional counseling organizations not only afford their members the opportunities for personal and professional growth but also can advocate for the identification and support of their members' mental, physical, and spiritual well-being (Stebnicki, 2007). In addition, developing a network of peers who do similar work on the local, state, and national levels can be an important part of your self-care plan. Finally, many counselors find leisure activities such as spending quality time with family and friends, taking vacations, and engaging in hobbies aid in keeping a balance between the demands of work and their emotional well-being (Bober & Regehr, 2006).

Summary

In this chapter, the basic counseling skills used in crisis intervention work were reviewed. The use of these skills will aid in the development of the counseling relationship with the client and will greatly facilitate the creation of a safe therapeutic environment. The nonverbal attending behaviors such as eye contact, body position, and tone of voice communicate interest, warmth, and understanding to the client. Be sure to face the client and adopt an open, relaxed, and attentive body posture, while maintaining culturally appropriate eye contact with the client. Tone of voice should be steady and clear and should be used to convey a sense of safety, warmth, and security for the client.

The skills covered in the basic listening sequence include asking open and closed questions, paraphrasing, reflecting feelings, and summarizing. The basic listening sequence allows the gathering of important information about the client's issues and the development of trust and rapport. Finally, the basic listening sequence allows the crisis counselor to pull together the key issues to begin the collaborative process of determining a plan of action for the client. Open and closed questions are used to gather information, to aid in assessment, and to provide focus and direction to the session. Paraphrasing is a reflective skill used to mirror back to the client, in a nonjudgmental way and in one's own words, an accurate understanding of the client's communication and the implied meaning of that communication. Like paraphrasing, reflecting feelings is a reflective skill used to convey to the client an understanding of the client's emotional experience. Through this awareness, the client can reach a higher level of overall self-awareness and deepen self-disclosure. Summarizing puts together the pieces, helping the client make sense of what may have originally seemed to be an overwhelming and confusing experience. Summarizing can also be used to keep the session focused, to provide direction to the interview, and to provide closure to the session by reviewing the progress, plans, and any recommendations/agreements made.

Finally, the phenomenon of burnout, its symptoms, and the strategies for self-care were examined. The importance of a good self-care plan for the crisis counselor cannot be stressed enough. The more we attend to our well-being, the better able we are to serve our clients in need. We believe that the basic skills and an appropriate self-care plan are fundamental for effective crisis intervention work. By using these skills appropriately, you create the necessary conditions for positive change.

4 Grief and Loss

Lourie W. Reichenberg

PREVIEW

This chapter covers approaches to crisis counseling with mourners, theories of grieving, and the variables that affect how a bereaved person mourns. Also addressed is how timing, the cause of death, and the role the relationship played in a person's life all mediate the mourning process, followed by a discussion that distinguishes between "normal grief" and complicated mourning. Finally, the chapter details how griefwork sometimes affects the crisis counselor through vicarious traumatization.

HISTORICAL PERSPECTIVES AND MODELS OF GRIEFWORK

Nearly two and a half million Americans die each year (Kung, Hoyert, Xu, & Murphy, 2008), leaving behind millions of husbands, wives, mothers, fathers, sisters, brothers, children, friends, co-workers, uncles, and aunts to mourn their losses. How the person died, whether it was sudden and unexpected or the result of a prolonged or chronic illness, affects the way the grieving process will unfold. So, too, does the cultural background of the bereaved; their temperaments, life circumstances, and previous experiences with death and loss; and the order of death (e.g., whether it is a grandparent at the end of a long life or a young person just starting out in life).

Of course, grief and loss reactions are not solely related to issues of death and dying. Feelings of loss may occur after many developmentally or situationally related changes. This chapter focuses on many of the different types of losses people encounter but does not address every type of loss specifically. Crises such as September 11, school shootings, and terrorist attacks are relatively rare. It is far more likely that a crisis counselor will work with a client or family experiencing a recent death or a situational or developmental loss that affects the individual or family.

Working with grieving clients is an important part of both crisis counseling and traditional counseling. Many people seek counseling specifically to help them cope with a recent loss.

CASE STUDY 4.1

My older sister, Susie, 53 years of age and in otherwise good health, had been diagnosed with a noncancerous tumor that was growing on her liver and causing excruciating pain. After obtaining opinions from three of the best medical centers in the country, it was determined that the tumor had to be removed. She decided to have the surgery at Northwestern in Chicago. Northwestern was chosen for its highly reputable liver transplant program (which she would not need, but that expertise was good to have just in case), and it was also where her daughter lived. This would allow family to visit and provide a place for her to recuperate from what we all knew would be a difficult surgery.

On the day of the surgery, my niece and I waited at the hospital, happily looking through her recent wedding photos to pass the time. Hours later a nurse led us into a small private room. The doctor, still in his scrubs, his shoes and pant legs covered with blood spatters, informed us that my sister was much sicker than he had realized. When he attempted to remove the tumor, she had "bled out," and despite transfusing 18 pints of blood, there was nothing he could do to control the bleeding. My sister had died in the operating room.

Immediately, my 30-year-old niece began to wail, keening back and forth in a state of disbelief. As I put my arms around her to comfort her, it felt surreal, as if I were watching the events unfold from a distance. It seemed as though someone had hit the slow motion button on my internal DVD and everything was proceeding in front of me like a movie, albeit at a slower, choppier pace. This feeling of numbness and unreality stayed with me for days as I went through the rituals of mourning—informing family members about Susie's death, helping to make funeral arrangements, comforting my elderly father, and delivering my sister's eulogy.

It seemed like I would catch conversations halfway through, as if my head had been underwater and I'd just come up for air. The symptoms were so obvious that my son thought I was doing it intentionally. Weeks after the funeral I sat at a University of Maryland football game and felt completely dissociated from the game, as if I weren't really there. For weeks, I would wake up each morning in peace, and within seconds, as the reality of what had happened came back to me, I had to stifle a visceral urge to scream. Eventually, as the shock and numbness wore off, I was able to allow the pain in and to mourn, with friends and family, my sister's untimely death.

Looking back, I see that the numbness and dissociation that I initially experienced were protective measures. It was my body's way of shielding me from feeling the full force of the shock of my sister's death. It was only as the numbness wore off and I was able to feel the pain that the healing process could begin. As I move on with my life, I will always feel sad at not being able to share memories or vacations or simply have an everyday conversation with my only sister. I have, however, integrated her death into my life, and I often imagine what she would say to me in any given situation. I am thankful for having had her in my life and for the continuing effect that she has on me. I often think of a quote attributed to Rose Kennedy: "Birds sing after a storm; why shouldn't people feel as free to delight in whatever sunlight remains to them?"

But far more frequently the client has been in counseling for a while for issues unrelated to death and then experiences the death of a family member or has memories of a previous death triggered by the counseling. At such points, what was previously career counseling or couples counseling may become crisis intervention as the crisis counselor helps the client through the initial impact of the death. For some clients, that will be all that is needed, and they will return to their previous treatment plan. However, for other clients, more extensive counseling may be necessary to help them cope with the loss.

In his work *Mourning and Melancholia* (1917), Freud proposed what was probably the first psychoanalytic theory of grieving. It was, of course, consistent with his drive theory. Mourning occurs when the libido psyche stubbornly hangs onto a lost object, refusing to give it up. Grieving ends, according to Freud, when the client lets go of attachment to the lost object and becomes free to devote his or her libido to another love object. Freud's writings on mourning provided the basis from which griefwork later evolved.

Lindemann's Approach

In what is perhaps the first research conducted on sudden death, Lindemann (1944) studied the Cocoanut Grove nightclub fire in Boston. Lindemann identified three tasks of mourners: (1) emancipation from the bond to the deceased, (2) readjustment to a life in which the deceased is missing, and (3) formation of new relationships (Berzoff & Silverman, 2004). Like Frankl's (1959) in his later work with concentration camp survivors, Lindemann observed feelings of intense guilt in many people who survived the fire.

Lindemann proposed that adjustment required letting go of the deceased. He believed that grief was resolved when the mourner severed the relationship with the deceased and moved on to form new attachments. For many years, Lindemann's work remained the main resource on bereavement.

The Death Awareness Movement: Kübler-Ross

Beginning in the 1960s, the work of Kübler-Ross was credited with creating the death awareness movement. Kübler-Ross's works, including *On Death and Dying* (1969) and *Death: The Final Stage of Growth* (1975), effected a core change in attitudes toward and education about the dying process and helped to reduce the taboo surrounding the discussion of death in the United States. Kübler-Ross was famous for her work with terminally ill patients, which led to her development of the five stages of dying: denial, rage and anger, bargaining, depression, and acceptance. Kübler-Ross later applied the stages of dying to grief.

Rather than proceeding through the stages as one would proceed from hole to hole on a golf course, people experience the stages of death and dying as more of a spiral, moving forward and then circling back over time. Kübler-Ross also warned that what people experience is far more than mere stages. It is not enough to identify the stages, she wrote. "It is not just about the life lost but also the life lived" (1969, p. 216).

Following are the five stages of death and dying developed by Kübler-Ross to give caregivers a framework to understand dying patients. Many crisis counselors base grief counseling on these early works on death and dying. They are presented here with the following caveats. Kübler-Ross's work does not apply to catastrophic or sudden death because there is no time to say good-bye and the dying person is not able to go through the stages of grieving. Nor did Kübler-Ross consider the stages to be concrete or contiguous; rather, her writings were based on observations of common emotions experienced by people in the midst of the dying process (1969, 1972, 1975).

- *Stage I: Denial.* "Not me." "I am not dying." "A miracle will happen." Such comments are typical reactions to being told of a terminal illness. According to Kübler-Ross, denial serves a protective function in the initial stages by cushioning the blow that death is inevitable.
- *Stage II: Rage and Anger.* "Why me?" The seemingly arbitrary nature of the news of one's impending death almost always causes one to erupt into anger and rage. Such anger is often targeted at those who are living and will survive as well as at God for handing down the death sentence. Kübler-Ross believed such feelings were not only acceptable but also inevitable.
- *Stage III: Bargaining.* "Yes me, but. . . ." In the bargaining stage, one begins to accept the inevitability of death. But one bargains for more time by offering to do good deeds or change in a specific way.
- *Stage IV: Depression.* "Yes, me." The depression stage is the beginning of acceptance. Initially, the person mourns previous regrets and losses, but this turns into an acceptance of the impending death and what Kübler-Ross refers to as "preparatory grief" (1975, p. 10). During this time, the dying person begins to face any unfinished business and prepares to "let go" peacefully.
- *Stage V: Acceptance.* "Death is very close now, and it's all right." Some people are able to cope with the news of a terminal illness and work through the anger and sadness to reach an emotional equilibrium that allows them to live out their final weeks and months with inner peace.

Research shows that a person's ability to cope with major life stressors in the past is predictive of the manner in which the person is likely to cope with chronic illness and face death. Other factors that facilitate the process of death acceptance include having lived a full life, harboring few regrets about the way in which one lived, being able to talk frankly about the terminal illness with family and medical personnel, holding hope for a life after death, having a close relationship with a significant other, and being concerned for one's children and close friends (Carey, 1975). Fear at the end of life seems to be mostly related to the actual process of dying: anxiety surrounding their pain and being able to cope with it, their desire not to become a burden to one's family, and their uncertainty about how loved ones will survive after they are gone.

Kübler-Ross did not believe that everyone reached the stage of acceptance of his or her own death, but she firmly believed in open communication, with supportive physicians and family members telling the person about the impending death and facilitating the process of emotional adjustment as much as possible. With terminally ill patients, adequate pain management can be the most frequent predictor of emotional adjustment at the end of life.

Multiple parallels exist between the stages of death and dying and the ways in which people adapt to other losses in life (e.g., ending a relationship, leaving a job, experiencing any other sudden crisis). In *On Grief and Grieving* (Kübler-Ross & Kessler, 2005), published after Kübler-Ross's death, the authors wrote specifically about the internal and external world of grief. Kübler-Ross wrote frankly about the nine years of anticipatory grief she experienced as she was waiting to die, following a series of strokes.

ACTIVITY 4.1
Your Feelings and the Grieving Process

Draw a circle and divide it into slices like a pie, based on your feelings about death (e.g., grief, regret, hope, sadness). The size of each slice should accurately depict the amount of that emotion you are feeling.

Kübler-Ross wrote that the stages of dying that she developed "apply equally to any significant change (e.g., retirement, moving to a new city, changing jobs, divorce) in a person's life" (1975, p. 145); these are commonly called developmental or situational changes. Further, Kübler-Ross believed that if people could accept the ultimate knowledge of their own death and integrate this knowledge into their lives, they could learn to face productively the challenges and losses that come their way and face death with peace and joy as the final stage of growth.

Over the years, a broader approach to death education has focused on the unique needs and perspectives of the individual. Workshops, support groups, and end-of-life planning, all serve to educate the individual about transitions at the end of life. Berzoff and Silverman (2004) categorized death education as prevention (i.e., preparing for the inevitable), intervention (i.e., dealing with the immediate), and postvention (i.e., understanding the crisis or experience). A good example of effective death education was that sponsored by a local church. The church offered a five-week workshop that examined the music of Brahms's *Requiem* along with Kübler-Ross's five stages of death and dying. Such workshops often help reduce death anxiety. Now assess your reaction to Kübler-Ross's perspectives on grief and loss by completing Activity 4.1.

Worden's Task Model of Grieving

Grieving "is not a state, but a process" (Lewis, 1961, p. 38). In a significant move away from stage theories, Worden (2008) proposed a task model of grieving that empowers the bereaved to accomplish the following four tasks:

1. *Accept the loss:* After a period of disbelief, the person must begin to accept that the death is real. A pervasive sense of shock, numbness, or unreality may be felt for a long time. A sudden death, or a death far away, makes it particularly difficult to grasp that death has occurred. As people begin to work through this task, they start to accept the reality of the facts surrounding the death of their loved one and the meaning behind the loss and to accept that the person is not coming back. People who remove pictures or otherwise avoid any reminders of their loss are hindering themselves from accepting the loss.

2. *Experience the pain:* Working through the pain of grief is the second task Worden believes people must undergo. Some people may dissociate from the pain, immersing themselves in work, cleaning, and any other manner of keeping busy. Still others may feel overwhelmed by their sorrow. But to move forward through the pain, rather than avoiding it, seems key to grieving successfully.

3. *Adjust to an environment without the person:* To accomplish this task people must learn to continue on despite the loss of a love object in their world. While it

is impossible to clearly delineate precisely what has been lost, the void of grief is often deep. Coming home to an empty house, missing the communication and companionship of a loved one, and celebrating special holidays, birthdays, and milestones in other people's lives can all serve to increase the pain associated with loss. To successfully work through this task, clients must learn to cope and adjust to the many different voids left after the loss of a loved one.

4. *Reinvest emotional energy in other relationships:* In Worden's fourth task, the person is called on to emotionally relocate the lost person and to move on with life, while still honoring their loved one (Toray, 2004). Worden (2008) considers it a "benchmark of a completed grief reaction" when the person is "able to think of the deceased without pain" (p. 46).

Worden (2008) believes that like a physical illness or wound, grief takes time to heal. He does not assign time periods to grief. Parkes's (2001) studies indicate that widows may take three or four years to move through the grief process and achieve stability in their lives. During that time, they are working to return to a level of equilibrium. Grieving requires effort, and those who do not take the time to work through the tasks of mourning will delay the grief process (Worden, 2008). Case Study 4.2 provides an example of a delayed grief process.

Attachment and Loss

Intimate attachments to other human beings are the hub around which a person's life revolves, not only when he is an infant or toddler or a schoolchild but throughout his adolescence and his years of maturity as well, and on into old age. From these intimate attachments a person draws his strength and enjoyment of life and, through what he contributes, he gives strength and enjoyment to others. (Bowlby, 1980, p. 442)

Drawing on the works of Ainsworth, Parkes, Winicott, Seligman, and others, Bowlby produced a three-volume series that became the seminal work on attachment and loss (1960, 1973, 1980). Bowlby (1980) noted four phases of the mourning process: (1) numbing, which lasts from a few hours to a week; (2) yearning or searching for the lost figure, lasting for months or even years; (3) disorganization or despair; and (4) some degree of reorganization. The numbing phase is often expressed as being stunned or shocked at the news of a death.

The yearning phase is seen by Bowlby as normal and may result in efforts by the bereaved to locate the lost person. Such searching may include motor restlessness or scanning the environment. The bereaved may develop a sense that the person is present with them or may construe sights or sounds to be an indication that their loved one is near. In a study of widows, Parkes (1975) found that half of the widows felt drawn toward objects they had associated with their husbands, and many located a person in a specific portion of the environment (e.g., the chair he used to sit in). Many continued to talk to their spouses one, two, and even three years after they had died.

Disorganization or despair often takes the form of irritability or bitterness. In most cases in which there is a target of the anger, it may be clergy, doctors, or surviving family members. Self-reproach is also common and can be intense and unrelenting. Anger associated with grief must be discussed. Anger falls along a continuum from anger to rage to

CASE STUDY 4.2

An Example of Delayed Grieving

I once had an aunt whom I loved and treasured no less than my biological mother until she was taken away from me by the devastating, disturbing disease of breast cancer. I spent most of my childhood at her house. She was the one who taught me how to walk, ride a bicycle, cook, and differentiate right from wrong. The day I lost her I was in denial and refused to accept the fact that she was gone and that I would never see her again. I was not able to go to her funeral because she was in Ethiopia when she passed away.

Ever since her death, I had panic attacks whenever I passed by a cemetery, and it became my biggest fear. Two years after her death my best friend's mother passed away, and I was not able to attend her funeral. I was hurt and frustrated by the fact that I couldn't face my fears. I spent the entire day crying and started thinking how I would feel if my best friend did the same thing to me.

Seven years after my aunt's death I had an opportunity to return to Ethiopia, but I refused to go because I knew I would have to face her grave once I got there. It was not something that I was ready to do. I spoke with my friends about the struggle I was facing, and each of them tried to help me. They told me that death was a part of life and that I just had to accept it and move on. The feedback they gave me made me realize that I still had not accepted my aunt's death and that it was playing a huge part in my fear.

Earlier this year I had another opportunity to go back home. At this point, it had been almost 10 years since my aunt passed away and more than 12 years since I had been in Ethiopia. I told myself I would just have to find someone to help me. I decided to talk with someone. He told me that facing my aunt's grave would give me closure to her death. He also talked to me about where my aunt could be now and helped me to slowly try to process it. I started looking at old pictures and even videos. When I watched, I noticed that she is in a better place. She struggled with and suffered from cancer. It was killing her while she was still alive.

I boarded the airplane to Ethiopia. During my 18-hour flight, I remember processing what I had learned about aunt's death. My teacher told me to go visit her grave first so that I could enjoy the rest of my visit home. When I got there, I was ready to face the reality. I rested for two days and then went to visit her grave on the third day. The closer I got, the more nervous I became. My body was shaking, and I actually had such a hard time walking that my cousin had to help me. But once I got to her, I let all of my emotions out, asking her why she had to go. I realized she was in a better place. I remembered what my teacher had told me. His words gave me strength and helped me to overcome my fear. I prayed and told my aunt how much I had missed her and asked her to keep looking over me. My experience was overwhelming to my cousins because they could not believe that I was still in denial over my aunt's death. For them, it was something that happened a long time ago. It had become a part of their lives, and they had moved on. I now feel okay—and happy with the fact that I have faced her grave.

violence. Anger that is externalized, spoken, and processed is less likely to manifest itself in negative behaviors, which can mask the underlying feelings of grief and loss.

Bowlby noted that in most instances of disordered mourning, the loss was almost always of an immediate family member—most notably, a parent, child, or spouse. In other words, the strength of the attachment bond and the closeness of the relationship are important variables that profoundly affect the grieving process. Earlier Lindemann (1944) noted that severe reactions seemed to occur in mothers who had lost young children.

Bowlby saw mourning as a time of transition during which mourners adapt to the loss, reorganize their lives, and find new roles for themselves. During this period, it is necessary for the bereaved to experience sadness and despair. Lewis wrote extensively about the loss of connection following the death of his wife, expressing not only his deep feelings but also the loss of cognitions and actions that were formerly shared and now must be reworked. "So many roads once; now so many culs-de-sac" (1961, p. 59). During the period of reorganization, so much work must be done by the bereaved. Where one previously defined oneself as part of a couple, he or she is now single. Those once connected to a mother as a child now see themselves as orphans. Bowlby notes that this redefinition of self is a painful but necessary process. The bereaved can reestablish themselves and develop plans for the future only when they have recognized that their loved one will not return.

Pathology tends to result when people do not take the time to grieve or do not grieve properly, resulting in devolution of the natural process of mourning into clinical depression. Loss can be a provoking agent that increases the risk of a disorder developing, or the person may have a preexisting vulnerability that increases his or her sensitivity to loss. Either can result in a pattern of disorganized mourning.

Bowlby noted that depression-prone individuals deal with death differently than do those who do not become depressed. Numbness, for example, is common to all mourners. After an initial few days or a week of numbness, however, the healthy mourner may begin to talk about the pain and suffering of the deceased and express frustration at not having been able to do more to help. In contrast, depression-prone mourners may experience numbness that lasts indefinitely and may dissociate themselves from feelings of grief. When thoughts of the deceased do arise, they may focus on self-centered ruminations about their own loss, rather than expressing sadness at the loss of their loved one. Bowlby (1980) noted that "depression-prone individuals possess cognitive schemas having certain unusual but characteristic features which result in their construing events in their lives" in idiosyncratic ways (p. 249). Seligman (1973) wrote that such people have often failed to solve problems in their lives and, when confronted with loss, revive the cycle of "learned helplessness."

UNDERSTANDING GRIEF

In the *Diagnostic and Statistical Manual of Mental Disorders* (*DSM–IV–TR*; American Psychiatric Association, 2000), bereavement has been narrowly defined as the loss of a loved one. More expansive (and historically accurate) definitions are likely to embrace the concept that *any* negative life event serious enough to affect a person's thoughts, emotions, or important areas of life can be considered a loss. Even changes in role or position, such as the birth of a baby, relocation, or retirement, can trigger feelings of loss or grief. Life is filled with "little deaths" of what we give up and what we learn (Kübler-Ross, 1969). Grief is a natural and universal reaction to those developmental or situational losses.

Even though there are many similarities, every grief experience is different. Grief is an intensely personal experience that affects not only the individual but also the entire family system and in some situations (e.g., September 11, natural disasters, school shootings) the entire community. Grief reactions vary by culture, individual, and relationship to the deceased. All of these factors should be considered as mediators of the mourning process and will be discussed in greater detail.

Cultural Similarities in Grieving

Grief is a uniquely personal experience, yet similarities in how we grieve have been identified. In a study of 78 different cultures, Rosenblatt, Walsh, and Jackson (1976) found that people in all cultures express grief through tears, depressed affect, anger, disorganization, and difficulty performing normal activities.

Each culture has its own way of marking death that is consistent with their beliefs and values and that may include prescribed rituals and ceremonies. For example, bereavement, known as "sorry business," is a very important part of Aboriginal culture. Funerals can involve entire communities, and the expression of grief can include self-injury. The grieving relatives may live in a specially designated area, the sorry camp, for a period of time. The relatives may also cut off their hair or wear white pigment on their faces. The community refrains from using the name of the deceased but can refer to him or her by the name *Kwementyaye*. People with the same name as the deceased should also be called *Kwementyaye*. Photographs or videos of the deceased have to be destroyed. It is important for the interviewer to realize that asking about the self-injury (sorry cuts) or other physical manifestations of the grieving will cause embarrassment. Mentioning the name of the deceased or asking 'Who has died?' will also cause distress—perhaps even a renewal of the wailing (Australian Academy of Medicine, 2008).

Guilt is not always a part of loss but is more common in suicide, sudden death, or other situations in which people have not been able to say good-bye, have left something unsaid, or feel that they somehow could have done something to change the outcome (Hooyman & Kramer, 2006). Recent and ongoing research distinguishes between normal (or uncomplicated) grief and complicated mourning, which may require additional griefwork or additional steps before the griefwork can begin.

Delayed or masked grief reactions can complicate the mourning process. According to Worden (2008), grief that is repressed or denied can result in aberrant behavior or can cause physical symptoms. He notes that pain can be a symptom of repressed grief and that many people who are treated for Somatoform Disorders are really experiencing the pain of loss. This is particularly noticeable if the physical symptoms are similar to those experienced by the deceased. Similarly, unexplained depression, acting-out behavior on the part of adolescents, and overly intense grief reactions that occur after seemingly minor losses can all be indications of repressed grief. Thorough assessment and clinical skills are required to identify the problem. Complicated grief will be discussed later in this chapter.

Continuing Bonds

"Death ends a life, but it does not end a relationship" (Anderson, 1974, p. 71). Past history and current research indicate that most mourners do not believe that the relationship ends with the death of their loved one. This is contrary to the medical view of grief, in which mourning is a phase from which people should recover. The distinction between normal grief and clinical depression is important and will be discussed in depth later in this chapter. For most people, grief is an accepted and normal part of the life cycle, from which they eventually return to their previous level of equilibrium.

Ambiguous Loss and Disenfranchised Grief

Doka (2002) and Boss (2004, 2006) expanded the concept of grief to include loss that is ambiguous or disenfranchised. Included in this definition are relationships that are not recognized (e.g., lovers, friends, co-workers), loss that is not recognized (e.g., perinatal loss, abortion, pet loss), grievers who are not recognized (e.g., the very old, the very young, persons with developmental disabilities), and disenfranchised death (e.g., murder, suicide, AIDS). Coping with a loss that is an experience rather than the actual death of a person, such as children who are kidnapped, family members who disappear, or soldiers who are missing in action, can also be considered an ambiguous loss. As Boss noted, one of the primary tasks of a family is to come together to grieve the loss of a family member. Not knowing whether the person is dead or alive prevents any type of grieving from beginning. The person is physically gone from their lives, but little support is available, and in many instances, friends and family do not understand the depth of the loss or know what to say.

Boss (2004) noted that in such situations the primary mission of the therapist is to understand the stress of the situation, the ambiguity surrounding decision-making processes, and the manner in which this stress and ambiguity affect the family relationships and then to help the family develop resilience. Long-term effects of living with ambiguous loss can include depression, anxiety, guilt, ambivalence, and interpersonal conflicts. Everyone heals at his or her own pace. After an ambiguous loss, the client may take years, even decades, to develop the perspective necessary to become centered again and to create a healthy and fulfilling life. During that time within a couples relationship, the partnership is at risk. It is not uncommon for couples to initially reach out to each other in their pain, but since each spouse is apt to grieve differently and at a different pace, the couple may begin to find fault and blame each other. During infertility treatments, after a miscarriage, or after the loss of child, couples should seek couples counseling. An example of an ambiguous loss through miscarriage and infertility is provided in Case Study 4.3, which poignantly reflects the experience of a young woman who desperately wanted to have a baby and was told she never would.

When helping clients adjust to an ambiguous loss, the first step is to acknowledge the depth of the loss, not to minimize the pain. Find out exactly what having a baby meant to each partner. In the case study, Aisha felt isolated because none of her friends knew what to say. There are no greeting cards expressing sorrow for infertility. None of the men in her life was comfortable talking about reproduction. In addition to her grief over the loss of the future she had envisioned and over her inability to provide a child for her husband, Aisha felt depressed and hopeless about her future. When hope is gone, the risk of suicide increases.

Whether childless by choice or happenstance, at midlife, women who chose a lifestyle of childlessness may feel a resurgence of ambivalence surrounding not having had children. While friends are discussing the "empty nest," those without children have difficulty relating. As one woman said, "How can you discuss the empty nest

CASE STUDY 4.3

Miscarriage and Infertility: Ambiguous Losses

The thin, pale woman with matted hair and her arm in a plaster cast sat in my office as if melted into the chair. It was our first counseling session. "I know it wasn't right," she said, "but the night after the doctor told me I was not a good candidate for IVF [in vitro fertilization], I took a bottle of sleeping pills."

"I knew right away it was the wrong thing to do," she continued, wincing with pain as she used her broken arm to brush the hair out of her eyes. "Right away I picked up the phone and called my mother and told her what I had done."

What followed for Aisha was a self-described "week of hell"—the emergency room trip, a stomach pump, the technicians laughing that so much volume could come out of her childlike frame of barely 100 pounds. This humiliation preceded commitment in a private mental hospital, a court hearing to determine her sanity, and the requirement that, before leaving the hospital, Aisha schedule an appointment with a counselor. That's how she found me.

Despite her childlike appearance, the woman in front of me was no stranger to pain. At 37 years, she had been through every fertility test and procedure until a recent MRI of her uterus revealed tumors that would need to be biopsied for possible malignancy. The doctor gave her the news that further fertility treatments were out of the question. Aisha and her husband of three years were facing not only the reality of never giving birth to their own children but also the possibility of a diagnosis of cancer.

It was too much to bear, and after a day spent drinking with her husband and friends to calm down, Aisha gave in to the volcanic fire of emotions that seared inside her. She went home and "tore the kitchen apart," broke her arm against the wall, swallowed the bottle of antianxiety medication the doctor had given her, and then called her mother. She sat down to wait for the emotional help she so desperately needed.

In my office, Aisha reported, "No one understands. Not the nurse in the E.R. who rebuked me, 'You tried to kill yourself. You don't deserve sympathy.'" Not the psychiatrist who saw Aisha for 15 minutes and prescribed medication for depression. Not even the counselor in the hospital who told her, "Don't worry. You can always have another child." When Aisha explained that, no, she couldn't have another child and that was why she wanted to end her own life, the counselor replied dismissively, "Well, you can always adopt."

No one was listening to Aisha. No one had grasped the totality of her pain. "I just want someone who can understand what I am going through," she cried.

From the moment she learned she could never bear a child, Aisha was grieving the loss of future plans that would never be realized. She would never be a mother, never hold her infant, never have a family. All of those holidays, birthdays, years stretching out ahead of her, alone and barren.

Her husband, a kind man with a calm, logical attitude toward life, would never be a father. And it was her fault. Would he leave her? Would he find someone younger? Prettier? A healthier woman who could bear his offspring and complete his family?

How could she look at children again without being reminded of her loss? Life was so unfair. All she had ever wanted was to be married and raise a family. Now that dream was shattered, and worse, she had lost her job as a result of the depression. She no longer cared about the uterine tumors or her future health. It was all she could do to get out of bed in the morning and come to my office.

How to go on? Why go on? The existential questions stretched like open fields for miles in front of her—questions that were not easily answered by the meaningless mantra of well-meaning friends and relatives: "You can adopt," or "Relax, you'll get pregnant."

More than losing her footing, Aisha had had the neatly woven, homey rug she had been spinning in her mind for most of her adult life yanked right out from under her in one horrible afternoon. She needed time just to accept the reality of her loss before she could even start to think about the future. It was months before she came to terms with the loss and was able, at her husband's gentle urging, to schedule a biopsy for her tumors. It was even longer before Aisha could start to dream again about the color, the texture, and the design she would weave into the rug of her new life.

When working with women who have recently miscarried or are coping, like Aisha, with infertility, hollow reassurances and suggestions about the future are ineffective. They cannot think about adopting or fostering a future baby until they have fully grieved their loss. Only the professional who fully understands and helps these women cope with the loss will be capable of moving the grieving process forward.

The loss of the ability to have children is similar to the loss of your future. In Aisha's case, the professionals failed her. A nurse shamed her suicide attempt. A psychiatrist and a counselor gave her platitudes instead of helping her to come to the terms with and process her loss. Even the physician who gave Aisha the bad news failed to ensure she received adequate counseling. He focused on saving her body but ignored how she felt about the prospect of living life without children. Once Aisha was able to define the loss she was feeling—the need to nurture a baby—we were able to help her find an appropriate outlet by volunteering at the hospital to rock babies in the nursery. Years later she was able to see that there were actually benefits of not having children of her own. She and her husband loved to travel, and they were able to take trips their friends could only dream of. Her husband was able to fill his parenting need by coaching a boy's basketball team. The couple ruled out adoption but was able to build a fulfilling life that included friends and nurturing others' children.

---

when your nest was never feathered?" As others take pleasure at the birth of grandchildren, those without children may feel further isolated and begin to doubt their place in life. "It didn't occur to me," one woman told me, "that they live on through their children and their children's children, for generations. But my life stops with me."

Coping with this type of loss involves helping people to clarify the missing role and then find other outlets and activities that provide a meaningful substitute. Those who feel isolated could be referred to Resolve, the national infertility association (www .resolve.org), to find information, research, and support groups for people working through infertility. Online support is also available for women who experience loss through a miscarriage. BellaOnline (bellaonline.com) provides a clearinghouse of information and online blogs and support groups.

ACTIVITY 4.2
Looking for Death

In American culture, death is frequently hidden. Look for personal and cultural images of death in the media and your immediate environment. Discuss your findings with the class or a peer.

Someone who feels isolated and alone, for example, may benefit from adopting or rescuing a dog. Those who feel they have much to give to children may find meaning by volunteering at an elementary school, becoming a foster grandparent, or tutoring children after school. Younger men or women who are missing children in their lives can be encouraged to become a special aunt or uncle to a niece or nephew, become a Big Brother or Big Sister, become foster parents, or house an exchange student from another country. Activity 4.2 will help you become more sensitized to the way grief and coping with grief are hidden in American culture.

MEDIATORS OF THE MOURNING PROCESS

Bowlby (1980) notes five conditions that affect the course of grieving that may be used in the crisis intervention assessment: (1) the role of the person who died, (2) the age and gender of the bereaved person, (3) the cause and circumstances surrounding the death, (4) the social and psychological circumstances affecting the bereaved at that time of loss, and (5) the personality of the bereaved, especially as it relates to his or her capacity for making attachments and for coping with stressful situations. The role of the person who died (number 1 above) and the circumstances surrounding the death (number 3 above) are examined in the sections that follow. Readers are encouraged also to take into consideration other conditions that may affect the bereaved (e.g., numbers 2, 4, and 5 above).

Relationship: The Role of the Person Who Died

Just as every relationship in a person's life is unique, so, too, is every death. The closeness of the relationship, whether the person who died was a spouse of 30 years or a distant uncle, is a key ingredient in how the death is perceived and mourned and what the length of the grieving process is. It is important to define the unique attachment or loss associated with the death so that if a referral is needed, this information can be transferred as well.

Some of the most difficult deaths to accept are those of people we are the closest to: our children, our parents (especially if the death is experienced by a child), and our spouses or life partners. The death of a sibling, too, can have a tremendous impact on a family. Each of these relationships is discussed in more detail below. Readers are encouraged to consider other deaths that may be particularly difficult to accept, such as the loss of a family pet.

DEATH OF A CHILD   The death of a child reverses the natural generational order of death and can have a devastating impact on the entire family. Children play multiple roles in their parents' lives—socially, psychologically, and genetically. So the death of a child disrupts the parents' attachment not only to the child in the moment but also to their dreams and expectations for the future as well as to the child's place in the generational structure of the family.

"The death of an only child, only son or daughter, or the last of a generation leaves a particular void" (Walsh & McGoldrick, 2004, p. 20). Epidemiological studies have found that the death of a child leaves parents more susceptible to depression, illness, and premature death due to changes in the immune system.

Many authors write of the differences in grief responses between men and women, with a focus on the impact of grief on a woman's continuing relationship with her surviving children (Walsh & McGoldrick, 2004; Wang, 2007). Unfortunately, little research is available that is specific to fathers. In general, men are less likely to express their grief by verbalizing or by expressing their emotions; rather, they tend to stay busy and become task oriented (Wang, 2007).

When there is a death in the family, parents are not the only grievers. Siblings, too, may be distraught by the loss and experience survivor guilt. Often, a parent's coping response may be functional for him or her but may have a negative impact on his or her partner or surviving children. Sometimes a parent's behavior toward surviving children may change. The research indicates that the grieving process is determined to a large extent by the quality of the parents' relationship. Maternal depression, marital discord, and separation are likely to result in additional psychological fallout for the remaining children. Previously well-adjusted siblings commonly develop symptoms of anxiety, school refusal, depression, and severe separation anxiety (Bowlby, 1980). Some parents may withdraw from their surviving children, while others may turn to another child as a stand-in for the deceased. Both coping styles are fraught with problems. A stable, secure environment in which both parents nurture each other as they go from one stage of mourning to the next, while also helping their surviving children to express and cope with their own feelings, seems likely to foster the best outcome.

Only 10% of adults over 60 years of age experience the death of an adult child, severing the lifelong relationship between parent and child. Parents who lose a child in their later years are at a significant disadvantage; since it is rare, very few other people can empathize with their loss. In addition, these parents experience a sense of failure; it does not seem natural to them to bury their own children (Bryant, 2003).

DEATH OF A PARENT   Children mourn differently than adults do. The way in which children mourn depends on their age, level of cognition, emotional development, relationship to the deceased, and the quality of the support network available to them. Clinicians working with children need to take these factors into account when developing individualized treatment programs for bereaved children or adolescents. Five- to seven-year-olds are especially vulnerable due to their lack of cognitive ability to understand fully the concept and permanence of death. Complications may result, and these children may develop a fear of losing the other parent. Preadolescents and adolescents are strongly influenced by their peers and the need to belong. They may feel isolated and different from their friends who have not experienced the death of a parent. Particularly vulnerable are teenage daughters who lose their mothers.

SIBLING LOSS   Losing a sibling at any age or stage of life is difficult. But often the loss of a brother or sister is a silent loss. When a sibling dies, parents or children are often viewed as the primary mourners, and sibling grief is often forgotten. In fact, when a sibling dies, one loses more than the relationship; one loses a part of oneself. A 60-year-old client whose brother had recently died said, "It was like losing my hard drive," because no one else shared her childhood memories and experiences, nor was there anyone she could talk to about her parents, family history, and other childhood recollections.

The effect of sibling loss is complicated by factors such as the age of the child, the inability to accept death, and the inability to discuss emotions. Eighty-three percent of children who die leave behind at least one sibling (Doka, 2000). The death of a child can disrupt the entire family system. Ultimately, it is the manner in which the parents cope with the death that is the most relevant to the surviving children's ability to cope. Whenever there is a question of whether a child should be referred for therapy or not, err on the side of caution and seek professional help with someone experienced in child psychology and grief.

Charles and Charles (2006) note the importance of working with families who have lost a child to help them develop coping skills that allow them to facilitate the grieving process in their other children. Even young adolescents and teens who appear on the surface to be coping well may really be presenting a façade. This failure to grieve can have a deleterious effect on normal childhood and adolescent development and may even affect future generations. "Without intervention unresolved trauma tends to be passed along from generation to generation" (Charles & Charles, 2006, p. 86). Somatic symptoms are particularly common in children experiencing grief and loss. Stomachaches, headaches, and loss of appetite are common. It is also common for young children to regress to an earlier form of behavior during this time. Sleep disturbances, nightmares, and enuresis may occur, as might a drop in school performance, lack of concentration, and school refusal. Adolescents may begin using alcohol or drugs as a way of self-medicating their feelings. Professional help should be sought for substance abuse problems as well as for any grief that turns into severe depression or is accompanied by hopelessness or suicidal ideation. Additionally, Fox (1988) identifies the following four indications for referral of a child for grief counseling: (1) children who have a life-threatening or serious illness themselves, (2) children who have previously been identified as emotionally disturbed, (3) children who have a developmental disability and may not understand the concept of death, and (4) children who remain "stuck" in grief or shock after others have moved on.

LOSS OF A SPOUSE The loss of a spouse can be devastating. The effect is compounded when the person is elderly. Seventy-five percent of deaths occur in the over-65 age bracket. The death of a spouse therefore frequently occurs at a time when losses associated with health, retirement, and decreased independence and mobility have a cumulative effect. When a spouse dies, the surviving spouse is at increased risk for heart attack or stroke.

Guilt over "what could have been" in the relationship, as well as guilt about surviving when one's loved one died, is a normal part of the grieving process. When we consider that four out of every five widowers are women and that the average age of women who lose their husbands is 53 years of age, we can see that many women are living alone long after the death of their spouses (Rock & Rock, 2004). For most of these women, making meaning of the rest of their lives becomes a primary focus.

The need to make sense of the death of a loved one has been considered one of the necessary conditions for adjustment or recovery (Neimeyer, 2001). However, recent studies have shown that a widow who lost a spouse and had not found meaning in the death by 5 months was not likely to have found meaning at 18 months (Carnelley, Wortman, Bolger, & Burke, 2006). Especially at the end of life when losses are frequent, a bereaved person may not have enough time to work through the death of a loved one before another loss occurs. Such back-to-back losses are called *grief overload*.

THE LOSS OF ANIMAL COMPANIONS   Pets can play important roles in people's lives by reducing loneliness and isolation for the elderly, providing a purpose in life, and even replacing the loss of a human social contact. For some people, losing a pet can be as difficult as losing a family member. For these reasons, pet loss is included in this discussion of grief and loss.

More than 50% of American households and 70% of families with children live with pets (Toray, 2004). Pets have become so common in this country that more people now live with a pet than living with children (American Pet Products Association, 2008). Toray (2004) notes that some people—particularly those who live by themselves, have no children in the household, and are socially isolated—may be at higher risk for prolonged or intense grief. Grief over the loss of a pet can be magnified due to lack of support by society for the loss of a pet.

For children, however, the loss of a pet is frequently their first experience with death. If handled sensitively, the loss of a pet can provide a valuable opportunity to learn about death and to be involved in the grieving process. Children may express anger at their parents or the veterinarian for not being able to save their pet. They may also express fear and concern that others may be taken from them as well. Burial or other rituals are particularly important for children and help them feel involved in the grieving process.

Elderly people who live alone may become especially distraught after the death of a pet. Companion animals provide unconditional love and help owners maintain a daily schedule. It is critical to take such losses seriously and to help seniors cope with their loss and begin to find a new sense of purpose.

According to Toray (2004), the optimal pet loss counselor is one who recognizes the human–animal attachment and is skilled in bereavement and grief counseling. As with other types of loss, the primary goal of therapy is to validate the person's loss; reduce the pain, regret, guilt, and sadness that follow the death of a pet; and help the person resume a healthy level of functioning. Some people may decide to get another pet, while others may take the time to reassess the commitment necessary to raise another pet.

Cause of Death

It seems to be human nature to scan the obituaries looking for causes of death. An immediate flurry of questions results when someone dies. How did he die? When? How long did he know? What did he do to prevent it? What happened? By gathering the details associated with the cause of death, questioners are distancing themselves from death and assessing the potential likelihood of the same type of death happening to them. Such distancing does nothing to help the bereaved and often leaves them feeling alienated and alone. By blaming the victim for his or her own demise (e.g., "He smoked cigarettes," "She didn't wear a seat belt," "He had a family history of heart disease") or projecting blame onto others, people are actually reassuring themselves: "This will never happen to me." The effect of this reaction is to leave the bereaved feeling alone in their grief. To be supportive, crisis counselors should acknowledge that the death could have happened to any one of us.

TERMINAL ILLNESS   When the dying process has been prolonged by treatment for a chronic, long-term illness, families may have to grapple with difficult financial, legal, religious, and ethical decisions about treatment. Questions about who makes the final decision, what the patient would want, how long to continue life support, and other ethical issues may arise. An extended illness can deplete a family's financial as well as emotional resources. A sense of ambivalence can result from the juxtaposition of relief that the person is not suffering any more and feelings of guilt that he or she has died. Crisis counselors can help families share their feelings about the complicated situation, consider different options, and eventually come to terms with the loss. They may also be instrumental in helping family members deal with any guilt or regrets over their actions.

SUDDEN DEATH   Sudden death creates special problems for survivors. Unlike a death following a prolonged illness, sudden death denies family members the opportunity to come to terms with unfinished business, to prepare for the loss, and to say good-bye. According to Doka (1996), sudden loss often leads to intensified grief. The world as the survivor knew it has been shattered. Concurrent crises and secondary losses such as lost income, a lost home, or even the loss of spiritual beliefs may also occur. Doka listed several factors that should be taken into consideration when working with survivors of sudden loss: (1) natural versus human-made losses (e.g., heart attacks and tsunamis are examples of natural causes; hostile actions and bombings are human made), (2) the degree of intentionality (e.g., accident versus drunk driving), and (3) how preventable the death was.

SUICIDE   More than 30,000 suicides occur in the United States each year, making it the 11th leading cause of death nationwide (Kung et al., 2008). Although the elderly are only 13% of the population of the United States, they make up 19% of the country's suicides (American Association of Suicidology, 2008). Suicide is all too often a way in which the elderly cope with bodily deterioration, reduced vitality, the fear of dying, and the innumerable losses that occur during life's final stage. Biological aging, chronic disease, loss of autonomy, and loss of financial security all affect the lifestyle of the aging adult. These role decrements begin to occur during the decade between the mid-60s and mid-70s. Retirement, loss of a social network, and loss of couple status due to the death of a spouse are difficult to bear, sometimes leading to clinical depression or even suicide (American Association of Suicidology, 2008).

For the terminally ill patient in late adulthood, suicide can be perceived as offering an escape from intolerable pain and a method for being remembered by family members as he or she is. If death is inevitable, and for the elderly death's shadow is never far from sight, suicide may be a way of choosing how one dies, free from expensive medical care and without placing the burden for caregiving on the family.

Suicide in the elderly can take many forms, including (1) passive suicide, in which the individual chooses to stop treatment for a terminal illness, resulting eventually in death; and (2) "subintentional deaths," which occur as a result of indirect self-destructive behaviors (ISDBs), such as failure to take medications, refusal to cooperate with doctors, drug or alcohol abuse, hyperobesity, and auto accidents (Langner, 2002). Factors that increase the risk of suicide among the elderly include being diagnosed with clinical depression, having access to a firearm, being a white male over 65 years of age, and having experienced significant loss (American Association of Suicidology, 2008).

HOMICIDE   A violent death is devastating to a family and can be especially traumatic if loved ones have witnessed the murder. When death is the result of homicide, the grief process is circumvented by forces outside the survivor's control. Oftentimes the media, detectives, forensics experts, and others in the criminal justice system may require their attention. Prolonged investigations may result in deferred funerals, delays in accessing the home if it was the location where the crime took place, and other necessary intrusions that may interrupt the grieving process.

Violent death is predictive of prolonged grief and depression as well as the development of PTSD symptoms in as many as 23% of family members (Amick-McMullen, Kilpatrick, & Resnick, 1989; Kaltman & Bonanno, 2003). At particular risk are family members who witnessed the violent death or who later found the body.

The suddenness of such deaths and the inability to say good-bye often cause family members to desire to see the body as a way to gain some type of closure. Depending on the cause of death and the condition of the corpse, this may not be the best decision. In such cases, the police officer, chaplain, or crisis counselor who is involved in the event should be prepared to describe to the family exactly what they will see (e.g., trauma, blood, dismemberment) to prevent additional crises and allow family members to make their own choices as to whether to view their loved one's body or not.

Some family members will choose to go the morgue or the medical examiner's office before the funeral home. Others may want to accompany the body to the crematorium and bear witness to the cremation. Again, they should be informed in advance exactly what to expect and what they will see. According to Lord (1997), family members need to talk about what happened to the body. Pictures may be requested from officers or paramedics. Sometimes the reality of the photos is easier than what is created in the imagination. This may be their last look at their loved one and may help them to come to terms with the death and be able to move on.

Homicide survivors may feel that their grief cannot be completed until the murderer is found, the trial is held, and the perpetrator is brought to justice. While necessary, such proceedings may prolong the mourning process by months or even years. Survivors may put grief off until these issues have been resolved. Survivors of homicide, like survivors of suicide or AIDs, may feel powerless, abandoned, and alone in their grief. If left untreated, grief reactions to murder may lead to psychopathology. According to Walsh (1998), "families of murder victims are in need of ongoing support and advocacy" (p. 190). The goal of counseling should be to work to prevent dysfunction and restore balance to life.

COMMUNITY LOSSES: SCHOOL SHOOTINGS, TERRORIST ATTACKS, AND NATURAL DISASTERS
Traumatic loss of any type can lead to special needs and problems in the process of grieving. Normal sources of support such as family, friends, and community may be affected by the traumatic event as well and may not be able to provide the necessary support. In the case of natural disasters, entire infrastructures may be wiped out, and

those who survive may be focused in the initial stages on seeking medical help, food, and shelter. People may have seen images and events of such catastrophic magnitude that they have a hard time purging them from their mind's eye.

Bonanno and Mancini (2008) report that after traumatic events such as school shootings, natural disasters, terrorist attacks, and sudden bereavement, four outcomes are possible: recovery, resilience, chronic dysfunction, and delayed reactions. Surprisingly, as many as 50% of adults and children are able to carry through resiliently. Factors that contribute to such resilience include male gender (more women than men develop PTSD), older age, higher education, and personal variables such as temperament and coping skills. Relationships and community support are also buttressing factors. Based on this research, Bonanno and Mancini recommend that treatment be reserved for those who need it most.

Parkes (2005) noted that if a person continues to see disturbing images—whether appearing in recurring nightmares or triggered by reminders of the loss such as loud noises—and tends to dissociate from the loss—sequestering himself/herself at home, keeping busy with frantic activity, or avoiding talking about the trauma—that person may be experiencing PTSD. In the wake of the tsunami that struck Southeast Asia in December 2004, Parkes (2005) developed a handbook to help people affected by natural disasters, terrorist attacks, and other traumatic losses. Following are recommendations for working with trauma survivors:

1. Survivors should seek help for PTSD. Treatment has improved over the years as our knowledge of posttraumatic stress has increased. Eye movement desensitization and reprocessing (EMDR), medications, and psychotherapy have been shown to be effective at reducing the images and helping people to move on with the grieving process.
2. Anger is a commonly held feeling after experiencing a traumatic event as people attempt to comprehend the loss, search for a reason, and find someone or something to blame. Frequently, people begin to blame themselves and believe that if they had only done or said something differently, the disaster would not have happened. Such anger, if left unfocused, can lead to outbursts or be directed inappropriately and lead to violence. Parkes (2005) recommends helping people find a way to channel their anger and creatively use their grief "to bring something good out of the bad that has happened" (p. 5).
3. We tend to go through life with a sense of security and safety in the world as we know it. But then a traumatic event such as September 11, 2001, occurs and we have no point of reference—no secure, safe base—from which to move forward. This leads to problems of changing. In effect, our security has been jarred, and we may begin waiting for the next disaster. Physical symptoms of fear (e.g., heart palpitations, headaches, panic, stomach problems) may occur at this point. Parkes (2005) noted that during World War II this phenomenon was called the "Near-Miss Phenomenon." It eventually lessened but was frequently found in those whose illusion of invulnerability was shattered by the trauma of bombings.
4. Victims must seek to regain meaning in life. Parkes (2005) writes:

   When faced with a disaster of this magnitude we must realise that it takes time and hard work to adjust. It is rather like learning to cope with the loss of a limb. For a while we will feel crippled, mutilated, as if a part of ourselves is missing. . . . But take heart, all is not lost. Now is the time to take stock of our lives, to ask ourselves what really matters? When we do that we may be surprised to find that many of the things that made sense of our lives when the lost person was with us continue to make sense of our lives now that they are away. (pp. 6–7)

Normal Versus Complicated Bereavement

The *DSM–IV–TR* (American Psychiatric Association, 2000) distinguishes between uncomplicated bereavement, which is considered a normal response to the death of a loved one, and complicated bereavement, which includes symptoms of unusual duration or severity that interfere with life activities. Both of these conditions are defined and addressed below.

NORMAL BEREAVEMENT   Bereavement, according to the *DSM–IV–TR*, is the normal reaction to the death of a loved one, lasts no longer than two months, and includes some symptoms of a Major Depressive Episode such as sadness or somatic symptoms; the symptoms and duration can be expected to vary across cultures. In general, "the bereaved individual typically regards the depressed mood as 'normal,' although the person may seek professional help for relief of associated symptoms such as insomnia or anorexia" (American Psychiatric Association, 2000, p. 740).

Classic somatic symptoms that a mourner may experience include interrupted sleep, lack of energy, and appetite disturbances. These symptoms are also found in depression, and yet clinical depression differs from the sadness of grief in several important ways. First, any guilt associated with grief tends to be very specific to the loss and does not permeate all areas of life, as depression does. Neither does grieving generally lower the bereaved's self-esteem.

Depression may co-occur with bereavement, particularly if the person has a previous history of clinical depression. Worden (2008) notes that in such cases the person should be referred for medication management, along with continuation of grief counseling. Antidepressants will lift the depression but will not be effective in helping the person come to terms with the attachment loss (Seligman & Reichenberg, 2007); therefore, referral for medical treatment should be done only when the loss affects the normal functioning of the individual and the loss is perceived as exceeding the current coping skills or resources. Crisis counselors are extremely crucial when assessing and referring individuals in their immediate grief. The grief process is a normal process, and often individuals do not want to feel the normal reaction to their loss. However, in order to move forward in the healing process, it is important to experience the feelings associated with the loss and not to deaden the feelings through medication. This will only prolong or delay the grief process.

COMPLICATED BEREAVEMENT   Although most bereavement reactions fall into the "normal" category and will resolve and the bereaved will soon return to previous levels of functioning, 10 to 15% of people will go on to experience more enduring grief reactions (Bonanno et al., 2007). Grief that is comorbid with depression, anxiety, or other, more severe symptoms is diagnosed as a more serious disorder (e.g., Mood Disorder, Anxiety Disorder, Adjustment Disorder, PTSD).

Individuals displaying symptoms of normal bereavement may subsequently be diagnosed as having a Major Depressive Disorder if the symptoms are long-standing (i.e., last more than two months), cause severe impairment, and include such signs of a major depression as strong feelings of guilt and worthlessness, suicidal ideation and preoccupation with death, psychomotor retardation, and loss of contact with reality (other than seeing or hearing the deceased). PTSD may be diagnosed following a violent death by homicide or suicide if the survivor was present at the death or following a natural disaster or terrorist attack (Bonanno et al., 2007). People with few support systems and those with coexisting medical problems are at particularly high risk for severe reactions to a death (Seligman & Reichenberg, 2007).

According to Worden (2008), diagnosing complicated grief is done in one of two ways: Either the client comes into therapy with problems related to the process of grieving a death or the client is completely unaware that what he or she is struggling with is the result of a loss. Worden suggests "clues" that may indicate unresolved grief: (1) The person cannot speak of the deceased without become distressed, (2) a relatively minor event may trigger an exaggerated grief reaction, (3) themes of loss may repeatedly come up in therapy, (4) the person may be unable to let go of any of the possessions of the deceased, or (5) the person may develop physical symptoms similar to those experienced by the deceased before he or she died. Imitation of the dead person may also indicate an inability to grieve. A good example here would be a 36-year-old single woman who, after her mother's death, took to wearing her mother's outdated shoes and clothes. She joined her mother's garden club, and for months, her only form of social activity was entertaining her elderly neighbors. Clearly, she was not grieving well. Other symptoms—such as isolating oneself from friends and family members, becoming phobic about illnesses (especially the illness that killed the deceased), engaging in self-harming behaviors and suicidal ideation, and developing subclinical depression or intense guilt—indicate that the person should be referred for treatment (Worden, 2008).

According to the literature, clients with symptoms of complicated grief may benefit from earlier intervention, as these symptoms portend a less favorable outcome (Boelen, van den Bout, & deKeijser, 2003; Doka, 2005). Future editions of the *DSM* may include a separate category for complicated grief. Additional research will be necessary to determine the exact symptoms and diagnostic criteria for complicated grief. As we have already discussed, different relationships, different causes of death, and other mediators can increase the length of time for and complicate the bereavement process. For example, a married woman who loses her spouse of 50 years can be expected to experience bereavement for years. Or a father who lost his only son in a tragic school shooting may not recover his equilibrium in the two months considered "normal" by *DSM* standards.

Other losses in life can result in symptoms similar to "normal" bereavement. Losing a marriage through separation or divorce or being fired from a job after 20 years can lead to loss of meaning in life. Horwitz and Wakefield (2007) suggested that as many as 25% of people who are diagnosed as having a Major Depressive Disorder could actually be experiencing "normal" sadness reactions to a major loss.

Until additional research is conducted and better definitions of bereavement and complicated bereavement are established, clinicians must carefully assess the symptoms of their bereaved patients to distinguish between the normal sadness reactions to death and other losses and the more prolonged symptoms of Adjustment Disorder, Major Depressive Disorder, or PTSD.

INTERVENTIONS FOR GRIEF AND LOSS

In the past decade, growing controversy over the effectiveness of griefwork has necessitated taking a closer look at the empirical evidence related to such work. Several articles published in notable journals have suggested that griefwork, especially with normal bereavement, could actually do more harm than good. Larson and Hoyt (2007) investigated such claims and found no evidence to support a harmful effect of bereavement counseling. Rather, they noted that previous claims of harm were actually based on misrepresentations of several meta-analyses and subsequent republication of erroneous results. While a complete discussion of the controversy is beyond the scope of this chapter, readers should be aware that working with bereaved clients not only can be a positive and fulfilling mission for crisis counselors but also can and does provide positive outcomes with no evidence to suggest a harmful effect. Readers are referred to Larson and Hoyt (2007) for additional supporting information.

Despite limited research on effective interventions for the grieving process, it has become fairly common practice to help clients "work through" their grief. This is not to suggest that there is a linear, preferred method or manner in which to do this; rather, as memories and thoughts come up, the bereaved client addresses the feelings, accepts them, and moves on.

Worden (2008) notes that one of the most important benefits of grief counseling is educating the client about the dynamics of the grieving process. Crisis counselors should help clients understand that there is no set period of time for the mourning process, that sadness and grief are normal, and that the process is not linear but rather comes and goes like waves. Specifically, holidays, birthdays, and the first-year anniversary may be particularly difficult. Some people may also experience increased sadness during the change of the seasons and may not feel appreciably better until an entire year has gone by and anniversary dates begin to include new memories of life after the loss of their loved one. An effective intervention is to help the person realize that such times may be difficult and to plan ahead for additional support during holidays, birthdays, and anniversaries of the death.

When working with bereaved clients, Wang (2007) underscores the need for the crisis counselor to join with the client empathically and "from the utmost genuine spot" (p. 77). To quote Rogers (1980): "I find that when I am closest to my inner, intuitive self, when I am somehow in touch with the unknown in me, when perhaps I am in a slightly altered state of consciousness, then whatever I do seems to be full of healing. Then, simply my presence is releasing and helpful to the other" (p. 129). By practicing the necessary conditions of unconditional positive regard, genuineness, and empathy first set forth by Rogers, the benefits are twofold: First, the client feels heard and no longer alone; second, the crisis counselor, who cannot do anything to solve the client's grief or bring the loved one back, *can* do the one thing available—be there in an empathic, genuine, respectful, and honest way.

Grief is an individual, subjective experience (Neimeyer, 1999) with many mediators. There is no single model for all people because any model of grief therapy must consider the importance of culture, background, and family history as well as the individual qualities, circumstances, and personalities of the mourner. Helping people focus on re-creating a meaningful existence becomes the most important function of the grieving process.

Doka (2005) identified a continuum of grieving styles ranging from intuitive to instrumental. People who are intuitive respond to grief affectively, while instrumental grievers are more likely to react cognitively or behaviorally. By taking into account individual grieving styles, crisis counselors can tailor appropriate interventions.

Doka (2005) suggested that recovery from a loss may not be possible or desirable and instead described amelioration of grief, a return to similar (or better) levels of functioning with diminished pain. The bereaved maintain connections to the deceased through memory, biography, legacy, and spirituality. Crisis counselors face the challenge of helping the bereaved to celebrate connections, while avoiding potential problems, such as an inability to grow or move forward.

The emotional impact of the loss of a family member, especially the death of a spouse, can linger for years, even decades, depending on circumstances, age and cause of death, social support, and other mediators. Because loss of a family member can have detrimental effects on the health and mental health of survivors, a thorough assessment that includes the physical, psychological, cognitive, and spiritual effects of the loss should be conducted with these clients.

Crisis counselors should routinely ask how their clients found out about the death. Especially in sudden loss including suicide, the survivors should be encouraged to talk about what happened as often as possible, to have their reactions validated and believed, and to be with others who have been through similar experiences. What is not helpful is to be told that they need medication or that they shouldn't think about it or to be referred to support groups prematurely (Lord, 1997). Grassroots organizations such as Compassionate Friends, Parents of Murdered Children, and Mothers Against Drunk Driving can offer support and information for survivors.

For the treatment of complicated grief, cognitive behavior therapy has been found to be more effective than other types of therapy. Boelen, de Keijser, van den Hout, and van den Bout (2007) found that cognitive distortions and maladaptive behaviors not only are common in complicated grieving but also actually contribute to its creation. In one study, they compared cognitive behavior therapy with supportive counseling. The results indicate that six sessions of pure cognitive restructuring combined with six sessions of exposure therapy were more effective than supportive counseling. Since avoidance and negative thinking are central to the creation of complicated grief, Boelen et al. (2007) concluded that "encouraging patients to confront and work through the loss is important to treating complicated grief and more helpful than targeting thinking patterns" (p. 283). In general, the mourning process concludes when the person feels more hopeful, experiences a renewed interest in life, is able to discuss his or her loss without extreme emotion, and responds to condolences with gratitude, rather than avoidance.

Group Support

Short-term bereavement support groups can sometimes provide a positive adjunct to individual griefwork, especially when the type of loss results in feelings of isolation (e.g., suicide, homicide, HIV, miscarriage, infertility). As with all therapeutic groups, clients should be screened prior to participation to ensure that they are appropriate for the group. Parents who have lost a child should not be put in groups with those who have miscarried. People who have lost a grandparent should not be grouped with people who have lost a spouse or a child. As much as possible, the makeup of support groups should be homogeneous. Shayna, from Case Study 4.4, which follows later in the chapter, felt comfortable in a support group for young adults (aged 23–29 years) who had lost a spouse, fiancé, sibling, or parent. During each week of the six-week group, they were asked to process a different aspect of their loss. In week one, clients were asked to talk about the person they lost. In week two, attendees were asked what surprised them most about the grieving process. In week three, they had a type of "show and tell," with each person bringing in an object and explaining its relationship to the person. Week four was devoted to rituals, and each person in turn lit a candle as he or she spoke of rituals that had proved helpful. During the final two sessions, the group members processed their feelings toward one another and the connection they had made, vowing to continue meeting outside of the hospice environment. As with all other groups, it is important to screen clients beforehand for readiness for the group experience. In general, most people will not be ready to join a support group in the first month after a loss.

Support groups for survivors of suicide should help members focus on the unique elements of their loss. Many survivors are eager to know why their loved one ended his or her life, so reconstructing the final days, looking for clues, and talking about their last telephone call may be integral to the grieving process. Absolving guilt is another important aspect. Processing these feelings together as a group helps normalize the feelings so that the guilt frequently begins to dissipate. Another distinctive goal of survivor support groups is to prevent future suicides. The research shows that family members and friends of a person who has completed a suicide are more likely to attempt suicide themselves. The reason is unclear, but it may be that once the taboo of suicide has been breached, it becomes an acceptable alternative to life. Another possibility is that the survivor empathizes with the other's despair. Whatever the reason, interventions with survivors of suicide have been shown to prevent future suicides.

Working With Children

According to Worden (2008), "the same tasks of grieving that apply to the adult obviously apply to the child" (p. 235). But such tasks have to be modified to meet the social, cognitive, emotional, and developmental stages of the child. Preparing children, first-time funeral goers, or people from cultures not familiar with the concept of viewings and funerals in traditional American society for what to expect can help decrease additional crisis or anxiety. A child attending a funeral for the first time may have extreme reactions to specific funeral customs (e.g., open caskets, touching the dead body, graveside burial), but if explained appropriately, these customs can help the healing process.

Following the death of a parent, children need support, continuity, and nurturance. In a two-year study of 125 schoolchildren who experienced the loss of a parent, Worden (2001) found that 80% were coping well by the first or second anniversary of their parent's death. The stability of the remaining parent was the greatest predictor of the level of a child's adjustment to a parent's death. Based on the study, the following needs of bereaved children were identified:

1. Bereaved children need to have their questions answered in an age-appropriate way. They need to know that they were not responsible in any way for their parent's death. Frequently asked questions on children's minds include the circumstances

surrounding the death: "How did my mother [or father] die?" "Where is my dad [or mom] now?" If the parent died from disease or cancer, the concept of contagion may need to be explained to children who think they might contract their parent's illness: "Will it happen to me?"

2. Children need to feel involved. Developing a ritual, allowing children to be involved in the funeral, and including them in decision making are important. For example, having a child place a memento in the casket, light a candle, or decide which dress mommy will wear allows a child of any age to be included in the rituals of mourning.

3. Children's routines should be kept as consistent as possible. This can be difficult for the grieving parent, but research has shown that children do better when they know what to expect, can rely on the remaining parent for support and nurturance, and have families that exhibit an active rather than a passive coping style. Families in which the surviving parent is not coping well, is young, is the father, becomes depressed, or begins dating within one year of the spouse's death are likely to have children who have more anxiety, lower self-esteem, and less self-efficacy and who exhibit more acting-out behavior.

4. Children need a way to remember the deceased. Photographs, scrapbooks, and memory books filled with stories or pictures of the deceased can all help the children remember. Such books may be referred to again and again as they grow older.

Due to their limited life experiences and coping skills, children may have more difficulty mourning than adults do. Children's reality is often formed through fantasy and play. They are likely to fill in the blanks with assumptions or partial truths suited to their developmental age. They have a limited understanding of the world around them; therefore, they need playtime to act out their feelings of anger, anxiety, or fear. If a child regresses or participates in acting-out behavior, a thorough assessment may be in order. A screening instrument for identifying bereaved children who are at increased risk can be found in Worden's book *Children and Grief: When a Parent Dies* (2001).

Mourning may be a lifelong process for children who lose a parent. Feelings may be reactivated during adulthood when life events (e.g., weddings, other deaths or losses, reaching the same age as the parent who died) trigger the memory of loss. Recognition of these potentially vulnerable times allows people to actively plan their griefwork.

Family Interventions

Walsh and McGoldrick (2004) recommend that a systems approach be taken with the loss of any family member. This approach views the interactions among relationships, family processes, and the extended family as key to understanding how the death has affected the entire family system. Connectedness, communication, and mutual support and respect among members of the family seem the most likely to engender a balanced response to the loss. Two extremes run the risk of developing dysfunctional patterns: (1) families in which grief is avoided and pain is hidden and (2) families that cannot eventually work together to pick up the pieces and begin to form new attachments. Such patterns can impact the family for generations to come.

Finding meaning in the loss can help family members begin to heal. For example, those who have lost a loved one to suicide might invite crisis counselors or crisis line workers to attend the funeral, pass out literature delineating the warning signs of suicide, and offer grief counseling for those who need it. In this way, families can find a purpose and begin to create something good out of a traumatic experience.

DIFFICULTIES IN GRIEF COUNSELING

Withdrawal

When the survivor feels that no one understands or when the circumstances of the death or loss are so rare that no one in the survivor's social network has experienced such a loss before, the result can be withdrawal and isolation. This loss of empathy and connection leaves the person to withdraw into himself/herself to make sense of the tragedy. The person may be overwhelmed with feelings of loss, guilt, anger, shame, or vulnerability. And yet no one in the person's support network can share in his or her specific form of loss. The person feels alone and, in this aloneness, may lose faith in all he or she believed to be true. An example of withdrawal is provided in Case Study 4.4.

CASE STUDY 4.4

Shayna

Shayna, a woman in her mid-20s, presented for counseling several months after the death of her fiancé from a rare viral infection. While hospitalized for the virus, her fiancé had a heart attack, lapsed into a coma, and died several days later. He was 25 years old. Shayna was distraught, as was the fiancé's family. The death was completely unexpected—and making sense of the death was deferred for months as they awaited autopsy results. It was only on autopsy that they discovered that a rare and fatal virus had crystallized in his organs, and one by one, his organs failed. Even then, the cause of death was not fully comprehensible. It did not make sense. His mother and father were in their 40s; his younger brothers and sisters still lived at home. His death was out of chronological order. Shayna was sad and could not stop searching for answers. She sought out her minister and a psychic, and she even attended new age healing sessions in her efforts to make sense of the tragedy. She had a large support network of college friends and co-workers of her own age. While initially supportive of her grief, many of her friends had never experienced the death of a loved one, and one by one, they stopped asking about her loss and began to focus instead on their latest career moves, graduate school plans, and other day-to-day activities. Shayna stopped returning their calls. She began to isolate herself from friends and family and, other than going to work, did not leave her house. She reported, "No one can understand what I am going through." She could no longer relate to the trivial matters that made up the drama of her young friends' lives. "Only someone who has experienced death can appreciate the fragility of life," Shayna said.

Discussion Questions

What symptoms of grief did Shayna exhibit?

What facts surrounding the death of her fiancé made recovery more difficult?

What other questions would you ask about Shayna's life to help in your clinical decision making?

What type of treatment would you recommend?

In our sessions together, we worked to help Shayna build a bridge back to this life. At first, her days were filled with yearning to have her boyfriend back, while at night she dreamed about him but could not communicate with him. Each morning she awoke sad and frustrated. We discussed the dreams' meaning to her as well as the importance of rituals. Shayna decided to honor her fiancé by lighting a candle each night and talking to his picture. This gave her comfort and the communication she was missing. We also talked about the goals she and her fiancé had for the future. She decided to continue on the same path for awhile and to move ahead with one of their goals—to get a dog. The puppy proved to be source of solace and support over the days and months.

Shayna continued to go to work as an accountant, although in the beginning her concentration was poor. Gradually, she began to confide in two co-workers who checked in with her regularly and helped reschedule meetings and run interference when necessary. The trust and support she found in these two women helped her begin to integrate the trauma into her life and begin to reconnect with the community. When she was ready, she participated in a support group, run by a local hospice, specifically for young people who were widowed or had lost siblings or significant others. Finally, she found a group of people of her own age who could relate to her, and she began to tell her story in an empathic, supportive environment. "I no longer feel like I'm a freak," she said. "I looked at the men and women in that room and realized that every person has baggage. Everyone has some trauma or some deep dark secret that they're living with. I'm not alone."

Counseling the Crisis Counselor

Working with grieving clients can raise some of our own issues surrounding grief, loss, and mortality. Walsh (1998) wrote: "There is no safe boundary between clients and therapists; we all must experience and come to terms with our own losses and mortality. Forming caring and therapeutic bonds in the face of loss deepens our humanity and offers a model to clients of living and loving beyond loss" (p. 206). However, to avoid secondary traumatization or compassion fatigue, therapists learn to establish healthy boundaries, seek supervision, and recognize transference. Appropriate self-care is particularly important for crisis counselors, as we have seen in Chapter 2.

When working with grieving clients, Worden (2008) warns against cutting therapy short because of the therapist's own frustration or anger. He counsels that nothing is more frustrating for a crisis counselor than not being able to help a client, and yet, in the case of the death of a loved one, there is nothing a counselor can do. Participating in a client's grieving process has a profound effect on crisis counselors, who must make sure that their own issues do not get in the way. Worden is particularly concerned about three areas that might affect a crisis counselor's ability to be helpful: (1) counselors who have had a similar loss that they have not worked through, (2) counselors working with a client's loss when they fear a similar loss of their own (such as the death of a parent or child), and (3) existential fears resulting from the counselor's failure to come to terms

ACTIVITY 4.3
A Clinician Death Awareness Exercise

Worden (2008) recommends that all counselors, prior to working with grieving clients, take an honest look at their own histories of loss. Grief counseling is not the place for counselors to work out their own unresolved issues, and those who find themselves in acute grief should first seek their own counseling before trying to help others. However, people who have worked through their own grief successfully can be instrumental in helping others work through their grief. Think back on your earliest experience with death. How old were you? How did you feel? What helped you to cope with the loss? Now think of a more recent loss you experienced. Again, what coping skills did you develop? Look into your future. What do you expect will be the most difficult death for you to accept? How will you cope? What thoughts arise when you think about your own death?

with his or her own mortality. The last issue, according to Worden, can be addressed if clinicians are willing to explore their own history of loss and fine-tune their death awareness. An exercise to facilitate this process within the counselor is included in Activity 4.3.

Clinicians working with dying patients frequently have difficulty with one or more types of death. Perhaps one of the most important traits for crisis counselors to possess is knowledge of their own limitations and recognition of their own unresolved issues. By recognizing that not every counselor can work with every issue, we are better prepared to help those we can help and provide appropriate referrals for those we can't. Worden (2008) further suggested that counselors who do griefwork or who work with dying clients should (1) recognize their own limitations, (2) work to prevent burnout by practicing active grieving, and (3) know how to ask for help when necessary.

Anticipatory Grief: Helping Clients Face Their Own Deaths

Creating a personal narrative as one approaches the last stage of life can help to give life meaning and can provide a valuable integration of the totality of one's life. Butler (1963) was the first to describe the universal occurrence of life review in older people. Butler noted that the "looking-back process" was set in motion by the nearness of death, coupled with the additional time available for self-reflection that is a by-product of retirement. He noted that dreams and thoughts of death and of the past are reported to increase in the seventh and eighth decades of life.

Congruent with Erikson's (1980, 1997) crisis of stage eight (i.e., integrity versus despair), Butler found that, depending on the environment and the individual's character, life review can increase reminiscences and mild nostalgia, which can result in adaptive and positive integration of one's life, or it can result in increased anxiety, depression, and despair. Those who cannot integrate, comprehend, and realistically accept their lives as adequate run the risk of inner turmoil, increased rumination, depression, and possibly suicide. The research suggested that it is not the process of life review but the achievement of integrity that promotes successful aging (Butler, 1963). Counselors may have to assist in providing crisis intervention for clients with end-of-life issues. This can be a crucial but often emotional task. Clients may need to work through unfinished business, forgive themselves or others, arrange for last rites, finalize legal documents, and/or make

---

ACTIVITY 4.4

Draw a Lifeline

═══

Beginning with your birth date and ending with your projected death date, draw a lifeline that documents significant life events. Include both positive events (e.g., starting school, graduation, marriage) and losses (e.g., pets, grandparents, friends, family). Continue the lifeline out until your anticipated death. Discuss your lifeline with the class or a peer.

---

personal funeral arrangements. All of these issues can help clients accept the reality of their death and gain more peace and tranquility in having some power and control over the process. Although this can be difficult for crisis counselors, their gift of organization, peace, and reduction of anxiety can be a major benefit to those whose death is imminent.

In her book *Promoting a Fighting Spirit: Psychotherapy for Cancer Patients, Survivors, and Their Families* (1996), Seligman suggests that crisis counselors must walk a fine line between helping terminally ill clients prepare for death and encouraging them to be "realistically optimistic." Therapists can help clients hope for the best, while simultaneously preparing for the worst. Such an attitude will help people to write wills and make important decisions that must be made, while also appreciating the meaning in their lives. Crisis counselors can help people talk about death, discuss their deepest fears, and come to terms with their own impending deaths.

Crisis counselors face the same anticipatory process about their own deaths as other people do, and this is an emerging area of the literature. Both Yalom (2008) and Kübler-Ross (Kübler-Ross & Kessler, 2005) addressed issues of anticipatory grief over their own eventual demise. Yalom described his thoughts of death and various death encounters across his lifetime, beginning with the death of his cat Stripy when Yalom was five or six years old. It was these encounters with others' deaths, Yalom notes, that prompted him to always strive to fulfill his own potential. Indeed, the research indicates that therapists who have not come to terms with their own mortality are more likely to become overly involved with terminally ill clients or to maintain an inappropriate emotional detachment (Rolland, 2004). Crisis counselors should strive to develop a level of comfort with their own mortality. Now construct a personal lifeline by completing Activity 4.4.

Summary

In this chapter on grief and loss, several different psychological theories of grief were reviewed, including Freud's original drive theory, Kübler-Ross's groundbreaking work on death and dying, and the task model put forth by Worden. The importance of attachment across the lifespan was discussed in relation to the work of Bowlby and Ainsworth on the role of attachment and loss. More recently, Walsh and McGoldrick have added a family systems perspective, illuminating the intergenerational layers involved in the grieving process.

We are all born the same way, but each of us dies differently. Death can come peacefully at the end of a life well lived, or it can be untimely, traumatic, or life-changing for the bereaved. As in the case of infertility, Alzheimer's, or missing persons, loss can also be ambiguous. It is not possible in this space to create specific interventions for every possible grief experience; an extensive list of references is included for readers to conduct additional research. Rather, the goal is to help professionals learn about grief, be able to identify the nuances between normal and complicated grief, and understand and address any continuing issues of their own concerning death and dying.

Type of relationship, attachment, cause of death, and timing are unique to each situation and require individually tailored responses. Professionals who work with crisis intervention, and particularly death and dying, would do well to follow the basics set forth by Rogers: to be fully present and responsive to the needs of the bereaved, to be open to familial and cultural adaptations to loss, and to encourage strength and resilience, which offer hope even in the midst of the deepest despair. The ultimate goal should be to provide appropriate and timely interventions during times of crisis so that people can experience and process their grief in a healthy manner and not become stuck in patterns that lead to depression or result in more serious pathology. If successful, we will have helped our clients forge a path through their grief and find strength in what remains.

5 Intervention With Clients: Suicide and Homicide

Mary Bartlett and Charlotte Daughhetee

PREVIEW

Suicide and homicide continue to play increasingly important roles in American society and on the world stage. The variables associated with the end of life are no longer confined to a violent or desperate fringe but have at least the capability to affect us personally as we, family members, friends, and those in extended social networks struggle with the ever-increasing challenges of modern life. It is well documented that humans are equipped with an automatic fight-or-flight response to stress, and when these options are less available, stress can manifest itself in highly destructive ways. Individual options for response to the increasingly stressful demands of a Western lifestyle are amplified by technological advances that put unprecedented power, for good or for harm, into the hands of ordinary, often confused, sometimes poorly educated people who may have only a rudimentary awareness and understanding of themselves. As personal liberty has increased, the chance for violent response to stressful situations has increased. While no one expects suicide or homicide to have a personal impact, the chance of being personally affected by a suicide or homicide over one's lifetime is no longer remote, if it ever was. The effectiveness of the care given by professional emergency first responders, as well as the effectiveness of ordinary people responding to their own crises and the crises of those about whom they care, is improved by background knowledge involving current trends in and treatments for suicide and homicide impulses.

SUICIDE INTERVENTION

Suicide is a crisis situation that all crisis counselors, regardless of setting, must learn to assess and treat because of its prevalence in society. Yet it continues to be an aspect of counseling in which professionals are undertrained (Farrow, 2002; Granello & Granello, 2007; Jobes & Berman, 1993; Maltsberger, 1991; Neimeyer, 2000; Neimeyer & Pfeiffer, 1994; Range et al., 2002). Assessing and treating suicidal clients is the most common and most challenging of clinical emergencies for mental health professionals regardless of setting. It is consistently

ACTIVITY 5.1

In groups of three of four, discuss what you are aware of feeling when you say the word *suicide*. What has your experience with suicide been, both personally and professionally? Further, consider what you do and do not know about working with a suicidal client in crisis and what you want and feel the need to know before you step into a session with a client who is suicidal.

rated by counselors as a highly stressful experience, has a significant emotional impact on the treating clinician, and has become a frequent basis for malpractice suits against counselors over the past 15 years. It is imperative for crisis counselors to understand how to work with suicidal clients, since there is little way of avoiding this clinical crisis in the professional setting (Berman & Cohen-Sandler, 1983; Bongar & Harmatz, 1989; Chemtob, Hamada, Bauer, Torigoe, & Kinney, 1988; Deutsch, 1984; Ewalt, 1967; Farber, 1983; Granello & Granello, 2007; Jobes & Berman, 1993; Knapp & VandeCreek, 1983; Reid, 2004; Shein, 1976).

All too often, counselors focus on their own anxiety associated with having a suicidal client before them and for various reasons are unable or unwilling to complete a comprehensive assessment that best protects the client and themselves. Simon (2004) identified a series of common intervention obstacles, including counselor fear and anger, counselor and client dynamics, paradigm problems, lack of resources, inadequate assessment, poor treatment planning, inappropriate management of care, and failure to document. When counselors do not complete periodic self-examinations of their own response to suicide, it is not uncommon for them to begin experiencing the expressed thoughts and behaviors of their suicidal clients as attention seeking rather than help seeking, which is what they often are. It is clear that when counselors have done the work necessary to understand and manage their own reactions to the suicidal crisis, they are better prepared to respond with empathy, genuine concern, and positive regard and to use the strategic methods necessary to complete a comprehensive assessment and appropriate referral (Assey, 1985; Chiles & Strosahl, 1995; Sethi & Uppal, 2006). It is well understood that the client–counselor relationship is an important factor in the ongoing assessment and therapy of a suicidal client and that a well-established relationship increases the counselor's ability to obtain information from the client in order to increase treatment options as well as to assist the client through a painful period when no other sources of emotional support appear evident (Dulit & Michels, 1992; Kleespies, Deleppo, Gallagher, & Niles, 1999; Maltsberger, 1986; Mothersole, 1996; Motto, 1979).

Among the many things that make working with suicidal clients challenging is the lack of consistent standards of care for their assessment, treatment, and management; standards of care in this area remain ambiguous (Berman & Cohen-Sandler, 1983; Bongar, Maris, Berman, & Litman, 1998; Bongar, Peterson, Harris, & Aissis, 1989; Wettstein, 1989). Standard of care is defined as the reliable and appropriate implementation of interventions or precautions that a reasonably prudent person or professional should exercise in the same or similar circumstances and is based on foreseeability. Foreseeability is the reasonable and comprehensive assessment of risk. It is not predictability or preventability. Standards of care vary based on the degree to which a counselor understands, practices, and documents risk. Decisions are determined by the information gathered by the counselor, and failure to obtain as much data as possible through the range of means available falls below the standard of care. This requires, then, that crisis counselors remain informed about the ever-changing assessment strategies that continue to be researched and are demonstrated to be empirically useful. Since counselors across the range of therapeutic practice areas are susceptible to having a suicidal client, the principles of risk management for and appropriate response to the suicidal client apply to all counselors regardless of the setting in which they work (Black, 1979; Bongar et al., 1998; Jobes & Berman, 1993; Simon, 1988).

While this chapter examines the many risk management challenges that crisis counselors encounter when working with suicidal individuals, it is also important to examine some of the inherent challenges in working with suicidal people. Much of the work a crisis counselor will do with a suicidal person occurs within the first 24 hours of contact, when the person is likely in an immediate state of chaos and despair. This makes it more challenging for the counselor to assess the functional impairment and impulse control of the person he or she is assessing. At this crucial time, the crisis counselor must not only gauge his or her own internal reactions to the situation but also balance the art of asking necessary and often personally intrusive questions with the degree to which the suicidal person is capable of responding honestly and accurately (Kleespies, 1998; Shea, 2002).

People in suicidal crisis may present as resistant when, in fact, they are confused and disoriented and highly focused on one outcome, which is to end their psychological pain. This may lead to an adversarial standoff at a time when it is most critical for the crisis counselor to align with the suicidal thinker and empathize with that person's emotional pain. If a crisis counselor is unable to understand the functional purpose of suicidality to the client, maintain a nonjudgmental and supportive stance, and voice authentic concern and a true desire to help the person who is suicidal, that counselor may not be able to illicit the information needed to make the necessary assessment that drives the outcome of the treatment (Shea, 2002; Suicide Prevention Resource Center, 2006).

A difference in paradigms, such as treating the suicidal person as a member of a statistical group rather than as one individual case among many, is an obstacle to the interview process. At a time when they must remain most calm internally, counselors may feel their own anxiety increasing and focus on the multitude of tasks they must tend to, thus complicating the process. Differences in clinical opinion among mental health disciplines, supervisors, and departments may interfere. A lack of resources is another inherent complication. When the person being assessed and treated lacks insurance, when there are too few providers or too few hospital beds to be able to refer and place the distressed person, or when necessary assessment tools are not available or accessible to the crisis worker, the process of interviewing and assisting the suicidal person becomes inherently more challenging (Simon, 2004). All these matters need to be considered before the suicidal client comes to the crisis counselor so that one can consider and identify what is happening and how to navigate and proceed most effectively during the process as well as understanding what to address afterward during a review of the treatment that was provided. Having a clear understanding of risk management procedures may help the crisis counselor to better handle the inherent challenges identified in working with suicidal crises.

Overview of Suicidal Crises

Suicide is the act of taking one's own life voluntarily and intentionally and is at an all-time epidemic rate both within the United States and across the world. According to the World Health Organization (2007), over the past 45 years completed suicides have increased by 60%, with suicide attempts occurring more than 20 times more frequently than completed suicides among the general population. Worldwide, the prevention of suicide has not been adequately addressed and remains a taboo topic. Only a few countries have included prevention of suicide among their priorities, and inaccurate and insufficient reporting remains a problem worldwide. Many experts in the field of suicide agree that suicide prevention requires input from multisocial and increased government involvement. Within the United States, more than 32,000 people died by suicide in 2005, and more than 800,000 suicide attempts were documented that same year. Additionally, it is estimated that for each suicide, an average of six people are affected and left behind to deal with the aftermath of this emotional tragedy. A fact most people are not aware of is that more people die by suicide each year than by homicide; suicide is ranked as the 11th leading cause of death among Americans, whereas homicide is ranked 15th (American Association of Suicidology, 2006a; Suicide Prevention Action Network USA, 2008).

Suicide significantly affects youth in this country and is the third leading cause of death for young adults between 15 and 24 years of age. In fact, over the past 60 years, suicide rates have quadrupled for males in this age category and doubled for females. It is estimated that each day there are approximately 12 youth suicides and that for every completed suicide there are between 100 and 200 attempts made. This suggests that at its lowest rate 1,200 young people attempt suicide each day (American Association of Suicidology, 2006b; Centers for Disease Control and Prevention, 2007). Therefore, counselors working with children a nd teens in school and other clinical settings must be prepared to deal with this emotional crisis as it relates to the younger population. Counselors must know what to look for, be prepared to discuss the topic of suicide and be comfortable when doing so, have a current protocol to use to address the issue, and know how to adequately document their work. Further, they must understand the myriad legal and ethical issues related to the Health Insurance Portability and Accountability Act (HIPAA) and the Family Educational Rights and Privacy Act (FERPA), which, if not complied with, can lead to poor decision making that fails to serve the younger suicidal client, his or her family, the counselor, and the organization in which the counselor works. Additionally, failure to comply with HIPAA and FERPA requirements can result in potentially disastrous legal complications (Berman, Jobes, & Silverman, 2006).

Suicide rates increase with age and are the highest among Caucasian men over age 60, although suicide reaches across all cultural domains and socioeconomic levels. Information about various cultural groups can be found in the literature, and, in fact, suicidology research seems to focus on specific cultures without examining commonalities across cultures. Therefore, future research needs to explore and understand the universal aspects of suicide as well as the cultural specificity of suicidal behavior. Even given the limited research into the universal aspects of suicide, it is, nonetheless, important for crisis counselors to understand specific risk and protective factors that seem to span cultural contexts. Protective factors are situations or circumstances that reduce the risk of a person considering or engaging in suicidal behavior, such as family cohesion, an extended support network, and good problem-solving and conflict resolution skills, among others. Protective factors for people across various cultures are important considerations (American Association of Suicidology, 2006b; Mishara, 2006; Sue & Sue, 2003).

Regardless of how long the interaction is between the crisis counselor and the client, counseling professionals are often uncertain and challenged regarding how to properly assess this clinical crisis. New counselors should avoid working in isolation, and actively request consultation with supervisors, colleagues, and experts in this field. New counselors, and even experienced counselors, are often apprehensive about admitting their limited knowledge about working with this client population. It is advised that crisis counselors acknowledge their level of expertise, whatever it may be, and seek the assistance they need, rather than failing to provide competent services, which could result in a disastrous outcome for both clients and crisis counselors.

Crisis workers have short-term contact, perhaps only one session, with clients who present as suicidal. Crisis workers who work on crisis intervention hotlines have a similar time restriction. In these cases, Collins and Collins (2005) indicate there are three primary goals for the initial session: (1) ensuring client safety, (2) assisting the client to

CASE STUDY 5.1

Holly

Holly is a recently licensed counselor at a local community agency working with children and teens. She received no orientation regarding the protocol for handling suicidal clients in crisis at the agency and has limited training and experience working with suicidal clients. Holly recognized that this area of her training was weak and intended to ask the agency for guidance in this area. Before she could do so, she met with a 15-year-old girl who was clear and definite about her plan to commit suicide. During the counseling session, Holly realized she was undertrained in this area and asked her supervisor for assistance. Together, Holly and the supervisor assessed and referred the client appropriately. This experience influenced Holly to become more proficient in crisis intervention work.

Discussion Questions

What can counselors do to ensure they have adequate training to deal with this high-risk population?

What can counselor educators do to adequately train students to work with this population?

What should clinical supervisors consider when preparing their supervisees to serve high-risk clients?

How do these factors vary based on the setting one is practicing in?

How can you best prepare yourself to work effectively with suicidal clients?

achieve immediate short-term mastery of himself or herself and the situation, and (3) connecting the client to formal and informal supports. A six-step process is outlined to help crisis workers in this scenario achieve these three goals:

- Supportively and empathetically join with the client.
- Intervene to create safety, stabilize the situation, and handle the client's immediate needs.
- Explore and assess the dimensions of the crisis and the client's reaction to the crisis, encouraging ventilation.
- Identify and examine alternative actions and develop options.
- Help the client mobilize personal and social resources.
- Anticipate the future and arrange follow-up contact. (Collins & Collins, 2005, pp. 126–130)

However, the work of many counselors trained in crisis intervention may span a period of time longer than one session, and these counselors must know not only how to complete an immediate assessment but also how to work with these clients through the entire crisis experience. In this scenario, there are several approaches to assessing suicide that are applicable to both short-term and longer-term work; a few are described here for your consideration.

Joiner, Walker, Rudd, and Jobes (1999) provide a framework from which to assess suicide risk that emphasized the history of past attempts and current symptoms. They delineated seven domains relevant to suicide risk that a counselor should explore: "previous suicidal behavior; the nature of current suicidal symptoms; precipitant stressors; general symptomatic presentation including the presence of hopelessness; impulsivity and self-control; other predispositions; and protective factors" (p. 447).

Jobes (2006) offers a comprehensive approach to assessing and managing suicidal risk using that he calls the *Collaborative Assessment and Management of Suicidality (CAMS)* approach. The CAMS approach has three phases—initial assessment and treatment planning, clinical tracking, and clinical outcomes—and uses a core multipurpose tool, the *Suicide Status Form (SSF)*, as a road map to guide the crisis counselor through the three stages. The goals of this approach are to give the process a therapeutic structure, to keep the client out of the hospital, and to help the client become actively engaged in personal safety and stability. This novel clinical protocol identifies and engages suicidal outpatients as a part of their own clinical care. It emphasizes an initial assessment of the patient's suicidality and then calls for the implementation of a treatment plan co-written by the clinician and the client. With an emphasis on problem solving, this approach implements a therapeutic alliance to achieve an effective treatment trajectory (Jobes & Drozd, 2004). In the CAMS approach, a series of forms are provided to assist the crisis counselor in tracking the suicidality of a client until improvement is noted. The forms not only make this often complex process collaborative but also ensure that assessment occurs early in the interview process and that documentation is completed. So often counselors note that suicidality exists and that an initial assessment was completed, but they fail to demonstrate that follow-up was effectively conducted. Using the CAMS approach assures that assessment is documented from the session in which suicidality was initially expressed to completion.

The *Chronological Assessment of Suicide Events (CASE)* approach provides an in-depth interviewing strategy for eliciting suicidal ideation (Shea, 2002). It emphasizes that how questions are phrased and the sequence in which they are asked affect the information that is obtained; this approach is generally applicable regardless of setting. It is an excellent resource, providing a multitude of specific questions that a crisis counselor can use.

Another approach to assessing suicidal emergencies is *Question, Persuade, and Refer (QPR)*. This is a three-step process used as an emergency mental health intervention by first responders who are professionally qualified to engage with suicidal persons. These first responders include such service providers as crisis line workers, clergy, hospice workers, case managers, law enforcement officials, school counselors and teachers, and correctional personnel who respond to people at risk for suicide.

The question step of the QPR model involves asking a series of questions to make an adequate assessment of the suicidal state. Questions might include "Are you feeling suicidal?" and "Do you have a plan to kill yourself?" If the assessor, called the gatekeeper in the QPR model, determines that there is a legitimate risk of suicide, then the model transitions to the next step, the persuade step. The persuade step of the QPR model consists of a process designed both to stop or at least delay the suicidal act and to convince the person to seek help. This step is personalized from a menu-like range of alternatives provided by the QPR model. The refer step of the QPR model includes finding an appropriate caregiver for the person at risk to see, making an appointment, and following up to ensure that the person at risk receives the treatment needed to prevent the suicide event (Quinnett & Stover, 2007). This model offers a specific process for asking questions in order to persuade and refer the suicidal person; it emphasizes the appropriateness of training a wider variety of first responders who serve as gatekeepers beyond trained clinical and mental health providers (Quinnett & Stover, 2007).

Simon's (2004) assessment approach suggests the following:

- Identify suicide risk factors unique to the individual.
- Identify acute suicide risk factors.
- Identify protective factors.
- Evaluate the status of the therapeutic alliance.
- Obtain treatment team information.
- Interview the patient's family or significant others.
- Speak with the current or prior treatment providers.
- Review the patient's daily hospital record (depending on the setting).

In the triage model approach, a set of behaviors and impressions is established, and then an assessment of suicide risk is made in an orderly fashion, relying on a predetermined benchmark of behaviors and impressions to define various degrees of risk. It is not a perfect science, since much of what is used to assess requires some degree of subjective judgment. However, individuals who are considering suicide as an option have characteristics that can be recognized, and an assessment of risk can be made on the basis of these characteristics. The triage model includes characteristics in the categories of affect, behavior, and cognition. By focusing attention on and evaluating the client's verbal and nonverbal communication in terms of what the client is feeling, doing, and thinking, the assessing professional is able to make an accurate judgment about the suicide risk that the client represents (American Association of Suicidology, 2006a; Collins & Collins, 2005).

From the above, it is apparent that a variety of models can be used to approach the issue of suicide risk assessment. Regardless of which assessment model a crisis counselor uses, it is wise for the counselor to ensure that the approach is well grounded and researched, as are those offered above. In malpractice cases involving suicide, the courts recognize that mental health professionals cannot predict the act of suicide in clients; however, risk assessment must be demonstrated to establish a reasonable standard of care (Chiles & Strosahl, 1995; Gutheil, 1992; Jobes & Berman, 1993; Kleespies et al., 1999; Mahrer & Bongar, 1993; Maltsberger, 1986). While various aspects of the information-gathering process in risk assessment are subjective, and courts recognize this, risk management protocols are offered, and sufficient empirically based assessment tools exist that it is unnecessary for counselors to rely on tools that are not yet empirically confirmed (Knapp & VandeCreek, 1983; Range et al., 2002).

It might be tempting for crisis workers to consider using what is called a no-suicide contract—that is, a written agreement between the counselor and the client that the client will refrain from attempting suicide. While some research has shown that the no-suicide contract may have some therapeutic value when used in long-term counseling relationships, no-suicide contracts should not be used during emergency situations when no therapeutic relationship can be established, or when clients are actively abusing substances, or when clients are psychotic or severely agitated (Assey, 1985; Davidson, Wagner, & Range, 1995; Drew, 1999; Fine & Sansome, 1990; Hipple & Cimbolic, 1979; Miller, 1999; Mothersole, 1996; Range et al., 2002; Simon, 1991; Stanford, Goetz, & Bloom, 1994; Weiss, 2001). This, combined with the fact that there is little empirical evidence to confirm the usefulness of no-suicide contracts in helping to reduce suicidal impulses among clients, makes their use less desirable when compared to the many empirically based assessment tools a crisis counselor can use (Bartlett, 2006; Davidson et al., 1995; Kelly & Knudson, 2000; Lee & Bartlett, 2005; Maltsberger, 1991; Stanford et al., 1994; Weiss, 2001). Instead of using a no-suicide contract, Jobes (2006) suggests creating a plan to keep the client safe, which focuses on what that client will do to remain safe rather than on what the client will not do, in addition to keeping the client active and engaged in the process. Even in cases of low lethality, the traditional no-suicide contract is not demonstrated to be effective and has drawbacks that may interfere with the assessment process. Therefore, an approach like that Jobes suggests is preferred for both low- and moderate-risk clients (Bartlett, 2006). High-risk clients will most likely require at least a short hospital stay to assess and stabilize.

SUICIDE RISK FACTORS

As indicated previously, the evaluation of risk factors is an important component of the suicide assessment process. The American Association of Suicidology indicates that risk factors are traits, characteristics, or circumstances that are associated with an increased risk for considering or engaging in suicide across the lifespan and include age; gender; ethnicity; psychiatric illness (e.g., depression, schizophrenia, alcoholism, personality disorders, anxiety disorders); physical illness; relationship instability; family history of suicide, psychiatric hospitalizations, or diagnosis of major depression; perceptions of suicide; poor support system; substance abuse; loss (e.g., divorce, separation, death of a loved one, loss of a job, loss of a pet); childhood trauma (e.g., sexual abuse); existence and severity of previous attempts; risk-taking behavior; impulsivity; feelings of hopelessness; and suicide rehearsal (i.e., the process of acting out the suicide). A correlation between some psychiatric disorders and suicide has been identified. According to the American Foundation for Suicide Prevention (2008), 90% of all people who die by suicide have a diagnosable psychiatric disorder at the time of their death. A more in-depth discussion of the complex interplay of the two is covered in Chapter 8.

Crisis counselors working with children and teens must also become proficient in recognizing risk factors that are specific to this younger client base, such as a poor self-view, parental psychopathology, and sexual orientation issues. Dozens of books have been written to guide counselors in this regard, and their content is beyond the scope of this one chapter; however, information to best prepare crisis counselors for working with suicidal youth is readily available on the websites of organizations such as the American Association of Suicidology, the Suicide Prevention Resource Center, and the Jason Foundation (American Association of Suicidology, 2006b; Berman et al., 2006; Granello & Granello, 2007; James, 2008).

In addition to assessing for the presence of these risk factors, the crisis counselor also should assess to determine if warning signs are present. Warning signs are indicators that the client may be in imminent danger and require an immediate referral for hospitalization. Warning signs include

- Quiet and withdrawn behavior,
- Changes in behavior and/or moods,
- Symptomatic statements (e.g., "I would be better off dead"),
- Symptomatic acts (e.g., giving away personal possessions and getting personal affairs in order),
- The presence of a suicide plan, and
- Feelings of hopelessness and helplessness. (American Association of Suicidology, 2006b)

The American Association of Suicidology (2006b) offers an easy mnemonic method to remember these warning signs of suicide while a crisis counselor is asking questions and making observations during the assessment process: IS PATH WARM or Ideation, Substance abuse, Purposelessness, Anxiety, Trapped, Hopelessness, Withdrawal, Anger, Recklessness, and Mood change. A mnemonic to assist crisis counselors in remembering major areas to cover during a suicide risk assessment interview is SLAP or Specific details, Lethality of plan, Availability of method of choice, and Proximity to getting help. These informal assessment techniques are useful and should be considered along with more formal standardized assessments such as the Positive and Negative Suicide Ideation Inventory, the Beck Scale for Suicide Ideation, and the Scale for Suicide Ideation—Worst. The kind of formal assessment tool that crisis counselors use is dependent on their training and the setting in which they work (Granello & Granello, 2007; James, 2008; Jobes, 2007).

The Positive and Negative Suicide Ideation Inventory is a 20-item self-report measure of positive and negative thoughts related to suicide. Items include statements such as "I am in control of my life" and "I think about killing myself"—to which clients respond on a 1- to 5-point Likert-type scale. This instrument is intended for use with adults and has been used as an informal screening device for high school students. The instrument is a simple and relatively easy assessment for crisis counselors to use. The Beck Scale for Suicide Ideation is a self-administered, 10-minute instrument that evaluates a client's thoughts, plans, and intentions to commit suicide. It includes items such as "I have made plans to commit suicide" and "I have access to lethal means." The Scale for Suicide Ideation—Worst is a 19-item interviewer-administered rating scale. This instrument is unique in that it asks the client to recall the time when he or she felt most suicidal and answer the questions from that perspective. It includes items such as "I was ____ % decided to commit suicide" and "I have only felt that suicidal ____ number of times" (Granello & Granello, 2007).

In exploring assessment tools used within the United States, none has been identified that has empirically assessed cultural appropriateness for use with various multicultural populations. Rather, leaders in suicide research seem to be in agreement that culturally sensitive assessment of suicidal behavior has more to do with the actual assessment process as opposed to a specific instrument (Alan Berman, personal communication, August 20, 2007). Effective assessment procedures, regardless of culture, appear to include the following elements: phrasing questions effectively to elicit the most information about suicidal thoughts; specifically sequencing or structuring questions about suicide; sequencing questions about specific aspects of suicidal thoughts, plans, and behaviors; and collecting information from collateral sources to best determine how to proceed. Additionally, how a counselor phrases and sequences assessment questions should be considered in context of specific cultures (American Psychiatric Association, 2003; International Association for Suicide Prevention, 2000; Shea, 2002).

Suicide Protective Factors

In contrast to risk factors are suicide protective factors; these are also traits, characteristics, and circumstances, but they are associated with a decreased risk for suicide across the lifespan. These factors will help the crisis counselor to gain a more comprehensive picture of the situation and to determine the client's level of risk. Suicide protective factors include family cohesion, religiosity/spirituality, optimistic outlook, problem-solving skills, and conflict resolution skills (American Association of Suicidology, 2006a; Suicide Prevention Resource Center, 2006).

Levels of Risk

Once a crisis counselor has assessed the components already outlined, the next task is to determine the client's level of risk. Although risk assessment is a professional judgment, crisis counselors must be prepared to justify and document the rationale for the conclusion reached. Assessing suicide risk level is not a one-time event; it is an ongoing process that continues from the time the client is met, through the period of time the client expresses suicidal thoughts, and periodically after that. The decision as to risk level will directly affect referral and treatment recommendations. Levels of risk can range anywhere from none, to mild, moderate, and severe (Bongar, 1991; Granello & Granello, 2007, Kanel, 2007; Shea, 2002; Simon, 2004). It has been pointed out that the most common suicidal client a crisis worker will see is the moderate-client, but regardless of the client's risk level, the crisis worker must make quick, decisive, and justifiable decisions during a suicidal crisis (Kanel, 2007). The Crisis Center, Inc. (2008), offers a quick, at-a-glance assessment protocol to gauge lethality that includes an examination of the plan to commit suicide, the chance for intervention, the level of intoxication, the degree of ambivalence, and acute versus chronic symptoms. Keep in mind, however, that this grid is simply a guide; all risk factors need to be considered on an individual basis and within a culturally competent framework. This Crisis Center, Inc., guide identifies a client's risk level according to the following grid:

- *Low Risk:* There is no plan, or it is vague; the method under consideration is slower (e.g., pills); the means to carry out the plan are not available; the person is contemplating suicide within the next 48 hours or more; others are present or nearby and could easily intervene; the person has not been drinking and readily acknowledges a desire to live; and the problems are (or the ideation is) chronic.
- *Moderate Risk:* There are some specifics to the plan; the method is quicker (e.g., drugs, alcohol, or a car wreck); the person has easy access to the means to carry out the plan; the person is contemplating suicide within the next 18 to 24 hours; others are available or expected to arrive; there is limited use of alcohol; the person has some desire to live; and the problems are chronic.
- *High Risk:* The plan is very specific, and the person can describe when, where, and how in detail; the method is swift (such as a gun, hanging, or jumping); the person has the method in hand; the person intends to complete the suicide within next 24 hours; no one is nearby (the person is alone and isolated); there has been heavy drinking, combined with drugs: the person shows little ambivalence—the decision is made; and there has been a precipitating event or acute trauma as defined by the person.

Documentation

Documentation of this clinical emergency is an aspect crisis counselors routinely struggle with and continue to be poorly informed about. Remley and Herlihy (2007) point out that if counselors are not well prepared in their graduate program to handle crisis situations, they are responsible for overcoming that deficit by completing additional reading, attending workshops, completing advanced courses, and obtaining supervision. As mentioned previously, the process of working with suicidal clients is not static—it is ever changing; therefore, crisis counselors must remain current on all aspects of working with suicidal clients, including how to document the interventions that are applied.

According to Berman (1990), "Given the war zone of the courtroom, it is nothing short of playing Russian roulette with your professional life should you not document your decisions, your rationale for your judgments, and for the procedures you choose to employ. This is not defensive practice, it is reasonable, prudent and competent practice" (p. 39). He went on to explain that while a counselor does not have to conform to any one strategy of assessment and treatment because there is no universally agreed on and accepted mode, the best and only defense for any particular practice is documentation. The only way for a counselor to establish that he or she acted competently, again, regardless of setting, is by keeping adequate session notes and client records, which unfortunately many caregivers fail to do.

According to Jobes (2006), a model documentation package, meaning the overall content of a client file, includes informed consent, information from bio-psycho-social perspectives, formulation of risk and rationale, the treatment and services plan, evidence of case management, interaction with professional colleagues, and progress and outcomes.

CASE STUDY 5.2

A Sample Documentation Package

Paul has a thriving private practice and tends to work with clients with a high risk of suicide. He begins working with a new client, Betty, who indicates during the initial assessment that she is feeling suicidal and has a history of feeling suicidal. Paul has already collected a comprehensive informed consent and spends a larger amount of time collecting information about factors that might affect her suicidality, such as biological, psychological, and social components. He determines that while Betty is currently feeling suicidal, she is low risk and can be treated on an outpatient basis. Paul follows the Jobes model and completes a plan of safety for Betty, which includes an initial appointment schedule of twice-a-week sessions, involvement of family members in the treatment, identification of skills that Betty can use between sessions to self-soothe, and a referral to see a psychiatrist with whom Paul works closely. Paul obtains her previous treatment records, and then weekly over the course of the next three months, he continues to assess and document the treatment, Betty's progress, and Paul's interaction with supervisors, Betty's family, and the treating psychiatrist.

Discussion Questions

Why is Paul's treatment of this client likely to be effective?

What client factors has Paul failed to consider as a part of the treatment, if any?

What additional steps might Paul take if the client fails to respond to the course of treatment outlined above?

According to VandeCreek, Knapp, and Hezog (1987), a model risk-benefit note, meaning the form that documents a specific call or session and reviews the content of the interaction, contains the following:

- A description of the comprehensive assessment of risk,
- Information obtained alerting the counselor to the risk,
- Indication of which high-risk factors are present,
- Indication of which low-risk factors are present,
- What questions were asked and what responses were given,
- How compiled information directed the action of the counselor, and
- Why other actions were rejected.

Referral

The information a crisis counselor obtains through the assessment process assists the professional in determining an appropriate referral. As noted, assessment can be a somewhat complex process to navigate and is done in an effort to determine the kind of referral that is required and the treatment method that will be most prudent for the client at that point of the suicidal crisis (Bongar, 1991; Bongar et al., 1998; Granello & Granello, 2007; Simon, 2004).

CASE STUDY 5.3

A Model Risk-Benefit Note

Jane has been treating Jody for nine months with no indication of suicide. Jody returns for a biweekly appointment, and Jane suspects that Jody is feeling suicidal. Jane makes an entry for the appointment as follows:

> Client alert and oriented times four; mood and affect depressed as evidenced by self-report, slowed speech, disheveled appearance, and teariness throughout session. Client reported that her boyfriend broke up with her last week and she hasn't returned for college classes since then. Client was asked, "On a scale of 1 to 10, how depressed are you?"; client responded "Seven." Client was asked, "Are you feeling suicidal?"; client answered "Yes, I don't know how to get over this." Client was asked, "Have you ever felt suicidal after a breakup before?"; client responded, "Yes." Client was asked if she attempted after previous breakup; answer "No." Client was asked, "Do you think you will attempt suicide now?"; client responded, "I'm not sure." Client was asked how she recovered from those previous suicidal feelings; answer: "I relied on family and friends." Client agreed to counselor's request to contact family and to identify how family could be of assistance to her and was given a same-day referral to see the clinic psychiatrist. A plan for proceeding was determined based on the outcome of the meeting with the psychiatrist and included a referral to a partial hospitalization program, which she would begin the next morning. Parents were contacted and agreed to let Jody stay with them until she is discharged from the partial hospitalization program; the parents will dispense medications provided during treatment. Inpatient hospitalization was rejected for this client because she had no immediate suicide plan or means; however, her level of hopelessness was severe enough to warrant daily counseling interaction during the crisis period.

Discussion Questions

What questions did Jane ask to determine the level of risk?

What high-risk and low-risk factors did Jane note?

Based on the client's responses to the questions Jane asked, how would you have proceeded?

TREATMENT OPTIONS

While referrals to inpatient units are appropriate and necessary in order to protect clients who are a clear and immediate threat to themselves (Drew, 1999; Kreitman, 1986; Robins, Murphy, Wilkinson, Gassner, & Kayes, 1996), it is also recognized that mental health providers need to be trained to understand how to effectively treat clients whose conditions do not warrant such a referral. Making a decision regarding a particular treatment option is no small task; it depends on several factors, including the level of suicidal crisis, the client's willingness to participate, and available resources as well as legal and ethical matters (Bongar, 2002; Maltsberger, 1994; Rudd & Joiner, 1998). Keeping these factors in mind, crisis counselors choose between three primary treatment options, which are presented next for consideration in the order of most restrictive to least restrictive.

Inpatient Hospitalization

When it is determined that a client's condition warrants a referral for inpatient hospitalization, the issue of client willingness to be hospitalized arises. In cases where the client recognizes the problem and agrees to inpatient hospitalization, the probability of successful treatment and recovery is generally good; however, many clients will present with difficulties that prevent them from seeing the value of inpatient treatment, so they may resist this kind of treatment. In these cases, an involuntary hospitalization may be necessary. Voluntary hospitalization is hospitalization that is entered into with the client's consent and cooperation, whereas involuntary hospitalization is imposed on an unwilling client; involuntary hospitalization is one of the few instances in which a person's liberty can be denied if a health care provider believes the client is an immediate danger to self or others. Standards for involuntary hospitalization vary not only from state to state but also from locality to locality within a state, with counties, cities, and other government organizations instituting codes that affect the level of impairment necessary before an involuntary confinement can be imposed; the crisis counselor must become familiar with the laws within the jurisdiction of practice to best protect the counselor and the client (Bongar, 1991).

Generally, there are three primary goals when referring a client for inpatient treatment: (1) to ensure the client is watched and kept safe, (2) to reduce or eliminate the suicidal intent, and (3) to provide immediate medication management and restabilization (Bongar, 2002; Jobes, 2007; Klott & Jongsma, 2004). When a decision is made that there is imminent risk that a client is a potential threat to self, then a referral for inpatient hospitalization is warranted. Additional considerations for this referral include but are not limited to who will remain with the client until arrangements for transportation can be made (under no circumstances should the suicidal person be left alone); who will transport the client (a counselor should never drive a highly suicidal client to the hospital) and how; the civil commitment requirements specific to the client's location, as those requirements often differ for both voluntary and involuntary commitments specific to the organization one works in and the hospital the client is being referred to; client insurance coverage, as this will influence decisions about where to send the client and the potential length of stay the client may have; what diagnostic and assessment information may need to accompany the client with the referral to ensure the client is successfully admitted; what the counselor's involvement may be with the client while the client is hospitalized; and what the counselor will do to best prepare to receive the client back if the client is not admitted or if the counselor expects the client will return upon discharge (Bongar, 1991; Bongar et al., 1998; Granello & Granello, 2007; Jobes, 2007; Simon, 2004).

The role of the referring crisis counselor begins before a call is made to secure the inpatient placement and is not completed simply by picking up the phone and making the referral. Documentation and collaboration among the referring crisis counselor, the

CASE STUDY 5.4

Becky

Becky works as a counselor at an outpatient counseling clinic. She assesses that a client she has been working with for more than six months has become highly suicidal, and she successfully gets her client admitted into a local inpatient psychiatric facility. Becky expects that once stabilized, the client will return and continue counseling with her. As the client is being escorted out of Becky's office by a family member who is taking the client to the hospital for admission, the client asks Becky to visit her during her stay.

Discussion Questions

What should Becky say and do?

What are the legal, ethical, and therapeutic factors Becky must consider in this situation?

Examine your thoughts and feelings about visiting clients you have referred for inpatient services.

family or significant others identified by the client, possibly law enforcement agencies, and the receiving hospital staff are necessary. Given all the considerations that occur in the process of the referral for inpatient hospitalization, it is highly recommended that a predetermined set of steps be established to best guide the crisis counselor. When agencies are not proactive in this regard, and many are not, it can negatively affect the crisis counselor's ability to make clinically sound decisions during this often stressful emergency crisis referral process (Kleespies et al., 1999). States differ in their process for involuntary hospitalizations. Some states permit counselors to execute emergency petitions, which require law enforcement to transport the client based on the clinical judgment of the counselor. In other states, not all counselors can execute an emergency petition, and those that cannot must refer the client to a crisis board review where they will be assessed by a professional certified by the state. Crisis counselors should become aware of the practice of their state before a suicide situation is presented.

Partial Hospitalization Programs

Partial hospitalization programs (PHPs), also commonly referred to as day treatment, are designed as an alternative when the situation may not require overnight hospitalization but may be such that routine outpatient counseling is inadequate. Participation in a PHP allows clients to reach stabilization in a less restrictive manner than does inpatient hospitalization. Comprehensive treatment is provided using multiple modalities, including individual and family counseling, group therapy, education, and medication management by a physician. A PHP uses a coordinated treatment team approach to provide intensive treatment and achieve short-term stabilization of the immediate crisis. A client referred to a PHP must have already been ruled out as an immediate danger to self or others and must have been assessed as needing a level of treatment that cannot be provided by regular outpatient counseling sessions (Bongar et al., 1998; Granello & Granello, 2007; Munson Healthcare Organization, 2008; Psychiatric Solutions, 2008; Simon, 2004).

This treatment method is time limited, generally running five days a week, several hours a day, over the course of weeks to months. Participants in a PHP return home in the evening; however, it is important that the client have a structured and safe environment to return to each day, or this approach may not be effective. Progress is monitored daily, and treatment is concluded when the client's immediate presenting problem is stabilized or resolved and his or her target goals for improved coping are realized. Even though the structure of the PHP is consistent, the therapeutic interventions are designed to meet the individual needs of clients, recognizing that people have differing issues and needs. Often, PHPs are used as a step-down from hospitalization. Local departments of mental health and mental retardation can provide a list of hospitals and counseling agencies with approved PHPs (Bongar et al., 1998; Granello & Granello, 2007; Munson Healthcare Organization, 2008; Psychiatric Solutions, 2008; Simon, 2004).

Outpatient Care

As managed care systems grow in an effort to reduce the cost of medical care, the number of seriously ill and seriously suicidal clients who receive their care on an outpatient basis has increased. Therefore, counselors in all settings must be educated, informed, and prepared to work with these often high-risk clients. Jobes and Berman (1993) offered a comprehensive clinical risk management plan for the outpatient setting that consists of the following: (1) making sure that all practicing counselors know and understand the applicable statutes relevant to suicide, confidentiality, and informed consent; protocols for involuntary confinement; and ethical guidelines for working with suicidal clients; (2) having a detailed written policy specifying risk assessment, treatment, and referral guidelines; (3) assuring the clinical competency of staff members, including training for novice counselors and continuing education opportunities for experienced counselors; (4) maintaining thorough and detailed written documentation of assessments and treatments by using ongoing progress notes or by using forms that are specific to suicidal clients, including assessments used in the existing record; (5) implementing a formal tracking system throughout the course of a client's treatment, which, while cumbersome, forces counselors to remain clinically responsible for ongoing assessment and care; and (6) establishing and maintaining relevant resources for staff, including external clinical consultation relationships with other counseling professionals and legal contacts; understanding malpractice coverage terms; developing a resource library; and maintaining current lists of outpatient, inpatient, and emergency resources.

Specific techniques for working with these high-risk clients on an outpatient basis can be categorized into broad themes of clinical practice, client involvement, education, and family involvement. Among the techniques in the clinical category are the ever-present issues of adequate documentation, treatment planning, and professional collaboration. It is critical that this work not only addresses the presenting issues but also complies with the complicated and often changing standards of care. Failure to adequately plan treatments, document them, and collaborate with related professionals can lead to terrible legal and personal problems for crisis counselors.

Techniques of treatment in the client involvement category might include creating an alliance with the client, discussing with the client problems and potential solutions, identifying with the client alternatives for destructive behaviors, and exploring with the client ways to strengthen his or her personal support system. Often, these techniques succeed or fail according to the degree of participation and commitment that can be gained from the client, but a large part of the success can also be attributed to the crisis counselor's ability to achieve a therapeutic alliance.

Treatment techniques in the education category can include helping the client to understand his or her issues or problems cognitively, if the client is capable of a cognitive approach; helping the client to identify alternatives to destructive behaviors; helping the client to develop techniques to use to address emotional sadness, loneliness, and pain; and helping the client to practice newly learned self-help techniques.

Family involvement treatment techniques can be a critical source of improvement for the client and include soliciting support from family members, helping them learn effective ways to address and resolve the client's issues and problems, and demonstrating practical methods by which they can help within the scope of what can be done by nonprofessional but caring persons.

If crisis counselors are working with children and teens, strategies might also include sitting on the same level with them (e.g., perhaps on the floor in the case of a child client); talking on their level (e.g., speaking more slowly and using words they can relate to); using a wide variety of play therapy techniques to help them explore and express inner feelings related to their experiences, thoughts, and feelings of suicide; using assessments that are age appropriate; and educating, working with, and counseling their parents and significant others involved in helping them to effectively work through the suicidal crisis (Berman et al., 2006; Dass-Brailsford, 2007; Granello & Granello, 2007).

While suicide remains a predominantly Caucasian phenomenon based on the overall number of completed suicides, Granello and Granello (2007) point out that it is dangerous and unwise to ignore suicide risk among other ethnic groups; "[y]et little information is available on suicide in a multicultural context" (p. 86). An overview of prevention and interventions in four selected multicultural populations follows:

- *Latino Americans:* Integrate family and religious values into the counseling discussion; involve extended family members, friends, and church members as a source of support.
- *African Americans:* Screen for affective disorders (e.g., depression, hopelessness, PTSD, anxiety disorders) and substance use disorders; assess whether mental health services are available and ensure they are utilized; screen for suicidal ideation and previous attempts even though the presenting concern is not relevant to suicide, given the negative view of suicide among members of this population.
- *Native Americans:* Assess cultural beliefs, values, and customs with regard to death as a natural extension of the life cycle; infuse life skills into each counseling session to reduce suicide risk, including knowledge about preventing suicide, managing depression or stress or anger, improving communication, increasing goal setting, and increasing the ability to refer a potentially suicidal friend for help; assist in the development of cultural identity with an emphasis on tribal

values and rituals; emphasize community empowerment; assess whether mental health services are available; and ensure they are used.

- *Asian Americans:* Assess access to health insurance; assess the level of acculturation; facilitate English language skills or access to a translator; have accurate mental health information on various Asian groups (e.g., the myth of model minority); encourage an improved social status for women; treat the symptoms of PTSD for those who immigrated as refugees (Granello & Granello, 2007; Leong & Lau, 2001; Leong & Leach, 2008).

As always, crisis counselors are encouraged to remain abreast of new theories, research, and practice among racial and ethnic minority groups.

Following a suicide attempt, it is not uncommon for family members and friends to experience conflicting feelings with regard to the person who tried to take his or her own life. Feelings of anger, embarrassment, confusion, disappointment, and guilt are common. If left unaddressed, these feelings can lead to relational conflict. A crisis counselor can assist family members and friends by explaining how they can care for themselves and the loved one who attempted. This begins during the triage process. At this time, it helps for family members to know that the information they can provide about the person who attempted, or the events leading up to the attempt, can often greatly assist the medical staff as the triage process is completed and more long-term treatment is planned. If the person who attempted is admitted to the hospital, the family may be invited to participate in that treatment. Family members should be encouraged to participate, and most families are willing to do so because they recognize that their loved one needs treatment to address the underlying causes of the attempt. In cases where family members are unwilling to participate, the crisis counselor can encourage them to consider supporting the treatment by pointing out the advantages of familial support and the disadvantages of a lack of family involvement. Through participation, family members have the opportunity to explore their own reactions to the attempt and any relational conflict that existed or resulted (U.S. Department of Health and Human Services, 2006).

Crisis counselors can also help family members identify questions to ask their loved one: "Are you comfortable with the discharge plan?" "What can I do to assist you after leaving the emergency room?" "When is your follow-up appointment?" These questions reflect a concern for the attempter but do not include assignments of blame that family members might be inclined to engage in, particularly when the triage process has been completed and their loved one is stabilized. Crisis counselors can also guide family members regarding questions to ask the team that treated their loved one: "What is my role as a family member in the treatment?" "How will we know if he or she needs to return to the emergency room?" "What local resources or providers are available?" Crisis counselors can also assist family members in determining how to reduce risks at their loved one's home, such as removing firearms, potent drugs, and other lethal means and promoting communication in the relationship as they move beyond the crisis experience (U.S. Department of Health and Human Services, 2006).

While it is a confusing and challenging experience for family and friends when a person they love attempts suicide, family members' lives are dramatically changed when a loved one completes a suicide. A survivor can be described as a person who has some close association with someone who has died by suicide. Sometimes family and friends who have lost a loved one to suicide are referred to as survivors of suicide loss (Jordan & Harpel, 2007; Smith, 2006). A crisis counselor can begin assisting a survivor of suicide by emphasizing that the survivor is not alone; there are millions of survivors who are trying to cope with this heartbreaking loss, and about 200,000 are added to these rolls every year (Granello & Granello, 2007). Survivors may experience feelings similar to those of people whose loved ones have attempted; however, survivors' feelings may also include shock, depression, and relief. These feelings usually diminish over time as survivors learn to cope with the loss and begin to heal (American Foundation for Suicide Prevention, 2008).

Survivors have identified the following suggestions to help a new survivor cope, and crisis counselors are wise to share these suggestions with new survivors with whom they are working: It is best to acknowledge that the loved one died by suicide when people ask; reach out to family and friends, share feelings as desired, and ask for help even if they are hesitant to do so because they are afraid to talk about suicide; maintain contact with people even though this may be difficult during the initial stress-filled months following the suicide; address the question of why the suicide occurred; find a personalized way to grieve; set a timeline for healing and move at your own pace. Holidays, birthdays, and anniversaries can be difficult, so survivors should consider maintaining past traditions or creating new ones, talking to a trusted member of the clergy or engaging in spiritual activities if that is comfortable, keeping a journal of the healing process, and maintaining their own wellness by visiting a doctor for necessary checkups and support. It is normal to expect setbacks, so the survivor might be well advised to delay major decisions until the initial coping period is over, consider joining a support group, and entertain the notion of enjoying life again without viewing this as a betrayal of the person who died by suicide. An interest in enjoyable activities is a sign of healing in these circumstances (American Foundation for Suicide Prevention, 2008). There are a growing number of organizations and websites to which survivors can be referred. Referral resources are an area that is constantly changing; the best approach is to use any of the many search engines such as Yahoo! or Google to locate resources in your area.

For many family survivors, the stigma of suicide may seem overwhelming. It is not unusual for survivors to feel ashamed and to feel as if the suicide was somehow their fault. This experience can be isolating, particularly since in American society bereavement is seen to be temporary. Survivors may feel pressure to either find closure for the experience or be abandoned by friends and family who don't understand the experience or who even place blame on them. It is important for survivors to locate a place where they can share their experiences and feel understood. For many survivors, locating and becoming part of a support group can be critical. Support groups can help reduce the loneliness survivors feel, provide reassurance that healing is possible, allow survivors to grieve safely and to feel understood and validated, and offer an opportunity to learn from other survivors who may be further along in the healing process (Jordan & Harpel, 2007). Crisis counselors can assist survivors of suicide loss by helping them to locate a suicide bereavement support group in their local area. Often, family and friends who have lost a loved one may have to drive great distances to participate in a support group but find it worth the time and commitment to be in the company of others who truly understand their experience.

HOMICIDE

While most counselors are aware that they are likely to encounter suicidal clients in their counseling practice (Laux, 2002), they may underestimate the need for expertise in assessment and intervention skills with homicidal clients. There is a general assumption that clients with homicidal ideation are found primarily within the domain of forensic mental health and therefore are not a concern for most counselors. Obviously, clients with a history of mental disorders and violent offenses do present an elevated risk to the public, and mental health professionals working with violent offenders endeavor to balance public safety and client rights (Carroll, Lyall, & Forrester, 2004), but violent client behavior is documented in both inpatient and outpatient treatment facilities and therefore ought to be of concern for all mental health practitioners (Tishler, Gordon, & Landry-Meyer, 2000). One need to only read the newspaper to grasp that the potential for violence and homicide exists in families, schools, colleges, the workplace, and across all communities. Accordingly, it is essential that counselors in all practice settings be equipped to assess the lethality of clients with homicidal ideation and be capable of making decisions regarding the referral and treatment of dangerous clients. Additionally, counselors in all settings may be called on to provide services to homicide survivors. A homicidal crisis is intense and has long-lasting repercussions for individuals and communities who are left struggling to make sense of their traumatic loss and complicated grief (Currier, Holland, & Neimeyer, 2006).

Homicide, or murder, is the willful killing of one person by another person, and in 2006, there were 17,034 people murdered in the United States (Federal Bureau of Investigation [FBI], 2008). The overall homicide rate has been trending down since reaching an all-time high in the early 1990s; however, the rate of adolescent homicide has increased (Bureau of Justice Statistics, 2007), and the need for homicide prevention and intervention continues.

"I could just kill him!" That is not an uncommon declaration from a client venting anger at a difficult partner, peer, or work colleague. Such threats of harm toward another usually transpire when a client is experiencing extreme psychological suffering and is attempting to resolve feelings of distress (James, 2008). The counselor is then tasked with determining whether such pronouncements are simply common idiomatic expressions of anger or are legitimate lethal threats. Fortunately, in most instances, clients are merely indulging in hyperbole to give voice to intense anger or frustration; however, counselors must be prepared to recognize and assess potential lethality in cases where resentment and infuriation have escalated into homicidal ideation and possible violent actions.

Working with potentially violent clients presents a challenge to crisis counselors as they attempt to provide treatment, assess possible violent behavior, and protect would-be victims (Collins & Collins, 2005). When counseling a violent client, the protection of the public is always on the table. The noteworthy case of *Tarasoff v. Board of Regents of the University of California* clarified that the duty under California law to warn individuals who are in peril is of greater importance than the preservation of client confidentiality (Cohen & Cohen, 1999). Thus, counselors must assess the threat of lethality toward others and warn possible victims of harm. While all other states mandate the duty to warn, it is a good idea for crisis counselors to become familiar with the particular details of their own state laws regarding the duty to warn, as these issues are constantly being addressed by legislators at the state and national levels. Additionally, crisis counselors should be cognizant of their own safety and implement appropriate precautions, as discussed in Chapter 2.

Assessment of Homicide: Homicide Risk Factors

There are some basic indicators and risk factors that tend to be associated with homicide and violence. However, a word of caution: While these risk factors may assist crisis counselors in assessment, it is important to remember that the existence of risk factors does not mean the client will become violent, and conversely, the absence of risk factors does not indicate a lack of homicidal intention. Remember, each case must be evaluated on its own terms.

In most instances, homicide appears to be fueled by interpersonal discord. According to the FBI (2008), in 2006, 78.9% of victims were killed by someone known to them, such as a family member, a friend, or an acquaintance, and 32% of women victims were killed by their husbands or boyfriends. Most often, homicide motives were relational and included romantic triangles, disputes over money or property, and arguments fueled by substance abuse. The majority of murders were perpetrated by men, and firearms were the most common killing method. Obviously, heightened emotions, substance-induced impulsivity, and easy access to firearms cultivate a context for rash, violent actions, sometimes resulting in death.

Klott and Jongsma (2004) note that, among other behaviors, homicidal males tend to exhibit impulsivity and have a history of mental illness, family violence, job instability, and overall insecurity. They usually have a need to control intimate relationships and may exhibit possessiveness and rage. The need to control others is most clearly demonstrated in domestic violence cases where batterers control their partners through threats, physical violence, isolation from friends and family, and limited access to money (Collins & Collins, 2005). Every year there are approximately 2,000 domestic violence homicides, around 500 of which are cases of women who have killed their partners after years of battering and trauma (Roberts, 2006).

Alarmingly, in the midst of a decade-long downward trend in overall homicide rates, the adolescent homicide rate increased (Braga, 2003). Darby, Allan, Kashani, Hartke, and Reid (1998) found that male adolescent offenders are likely to have the following characteristics: a history of academic difficulties, substance abuse problems, and involvement with the juvenile justice system. Family of origin disruption and violence, parental endorsement of violent and abusive conduct, and the availability of guns were also found to be significant influences on male adolescent homicidal behavior. Loeber et al. (2005) studied risk factors in youth homicide and identified long-term risk factors, including a childhood diagnosis of conduct disorder and family poverty as well as contextual factors such as peer delinquency, drug abuse, and access to weapons. According to Roe-Sepowitz (2007), female adolescent murderers tended to have a history of substance abuse, prior involvement with the juvenile justice system, and very little parental supervision. Peers exert a powerful influence on adolescents, and the peers of female adolescent homicide offenders were prone to be substance abusers and also to have had previous involvement with the juvenile justice system. In addition, adolescent female offenders had indications of mood disorders and exhibited difficulty with anger management. These risk factors speak to the need for early intervention with at-risk children and adolescents, as well as their families, through the school and the juvenile justice system.

School Homicide and Violence

Columbine High School; Pearl, Mississippi; Virginia Tech; and Northern Illinois University are just a few of the names that remind us that K–12 schools and higher education settings are vulnerable to heinous acts of violence. As with violent incidents in other settings, school shootings are precipitated by a complex interplay of personal issues and environmental circumstances. Again, it is important to note that the presence of certain traits cannot predict actual violent acts, but since most violent students communicate their intentions, ongoing threat assessment can help school officials prevent violence and provide intervention to troubled students (Cornell, 2007). O'Toole (2000) recommends that evaluation of a potential school shooter's level of threat be approached with a four-pronged assessment model that includes investigation of (1) the student's personality, behavior, and traits; (2) family dynamics, familial violence, and family attitude toward violence; (3) school dynamics, culture, and climate; and (4) social dynamics, peer network, and community culture. The more areas in which a student has difficulty, the more the student's threat should be taken seriously. Serious threats will necessitate the notification of school officials and possibly law enforcement.

Leary, Kowalski, Smith, and Phillips (2003) examined 15 K–12 school shooting incidents that occurred between 1995 and 2001. The shooters ranged from 11 to 18 years of age. In all but two of the events, the primary motivation was interpersonal rejection—mainly bullying, teasing, and ostracism—and in half of the events, the perpetrators had experienced a specific rejection, such as a romantic breakup. Most of the perpetrators had exhibited previous psychological symptoms and were known in the school as troubled individuals. Other indicators included a fascination with guns and explosives, which was evident in six of the incidents, and an interest in death, darkly themed music, and sinister belief systems, which was manifested in four of the incidents. Violence in school is usually planned, and school staff and faculty need to be attentive to signs and symptoms of violence as well as being alert to school environmental factors that give rise to bullying, rejection, and the promotion of violence (Miller et al., 2000).

In general, college campuses are safe environments, and there is a lower rate of crime on college campuses than off campus (Carr, 2005; Cornell, 2007). Horrific shootings on college campuses are more reflective of problems with mental health access and compliance than of problems with campus safety (Cornell, 2007). Colleges and universities should combat violent incidents through training for faculty, staff, and even students. The implementation of threat assessment and prevention programs on campus and campuswide warning systems could provide the means to thwart future acts of violence and protect student lives.

Workplace Homicide

According to the U.S. Department of Labor (2008), in 2005 there were 5,702 fatal work injuries, and 564 of these were workplace homicides. Law enforcement officers are at the greatest risk for workplace homicide. The FBI's National Center for the Analysis of Violent Crime (NCAVC, 2001) categorizes workplace violence as follows: (1) violence from criminals who have entered the workplace to commit a crime, (2) violence from customers, clients, patients, and the like, directed toward workers who are providing services, (3) violence against supervisors or co-workers from current or former employees, and (4) violence from an outside person who has a personal relationship with an employee. Prevention of violence from an outside person is nearly impossible, though safety measures can be established to improve workplace security. Violent acts on the part of employees cannot be specifically predicted, but the following indicators can be used for threat assessment in the workplace: personality conflicts on the job; mishandled termination or disciplinary action; family or relationship problems; legal or financial problems; emotional disturbance; increasing belligerence; ominous increasing threats; heightened sensitivity to criticism; acquisition of and fascination with weapons; obsession with supervisor, co-worker, or employee grievance; preoccupation with violent themes; interest in recent publicized violent events; outbursts of anger; extreme disorganization; noticeable changes in behavior; and homicidal/suicidal comments or threats (FBI, 2001, pp. 21–22).

The risk of workplace violence and homicide increases during times of extreme job stress. Understaffed job sites, overworked employees, and times of downsizing or labor disputes will create a tense and potentially dangerous context for the development of violent behavior. Additionally, poor management, a high number of grievances, and the lack of employee access to counseling can contribute to violence and homicidal threat in the workplace (FBI, 2001). It is essential that workplaces, particularly high-pressure workplaces or ones undergoing turmoil, be mindful of the need for ongoing threat assessment and be proactive by providing support to employees.

Threat Level Assessment

When a client has overtly indicated an intent to harm others or has indirectly exhibited predictors or behaviors of violence and harm to others, the counselor must assess the level of threat. Threat level assessment is critically important to ensure the safety of others and to appropriately guide treatment decisions. While most threateners are unlikely to carry out a violent action, all threats must be taken seriously and evaluated (O'Toole, 2000). Threat assessment is the evaluation of the lethality of a threat through an examination of motive, risk factors, intent, and the means and ability to enact the threat. When evaluating lethal intent, the NCAVC provides specific guidance on areas for evaluation. O'Toole (2000) explains that threat assessment should involve the exploration of the following: What are the details of the threat? Are the victims identified? Are the details logical, plausible, and spelled out in a specific manner (time of day, method)? Does the client have the means to carry out the threat? What is the emotional state of the client? While emotionality does not specifically indicate lethality, knowing the affective condition of the client provides important assessment and diagnostic information. Are there stressors or triggers that might predispose a client to violence? And finally, what is the level of threat: low, medium, or high? NCAVC delineates threat levels as follows:

Low Level of Threat: A threat that poses a minimal risk to victim and public safety.

- The threat is vague and indirect.
- Information contained within the threat is inconsistent.
- The threat lacks realism.
- The content of the threat suggests the person is unlikely to carry it out.

Medium Level of Threat: A threat that could be carried out, although it may not appear to be entirely realistic.

- The threat is more direct and more concrete than a low-level threat.
- The wording in the threat suggests that the threatener has given some thought to how the act will be carried out.
- There may be a general indication of a possible place and time (though these signs still fall well short of a detailed plan).
- There is no strong indication that the threatener has taken preparatory steps, although there may be veiled reference or ambiguous or inconclusive evidence pointing to that possibility—an allusion to a book or movie that shows planning of a violent act or a vague general statement seeking to convey that the threat is not empty: "I'm serious!" or "I really mean this!"

High Level of Threat: A threat that appears to pose an imminent and serious danger to the safety of others.

- The threat is direct, specific, and plausible.
- The threat suggests that concrete steps have been taken toward carrying it out—for example, statements indicating that the threatener has acquired or practiced with a weapon or has had the victim under surveillance. (O'Toole, 2000, pp. 8–9)

The process of threat assessment must be conducted in an environment that will calm the client, facilitate the deescalation of intense emotions, and assist in the attainment of precise information regarding the level of threat intent. Tishler et al. (2000) note that the assessment of violence is similar to the assessment of other symptoms in that the client's history of violence, family and medical history, mental status, and drug use must be investigated. They also emphasize that a calm demeanor and basic rapport-building communication skills are necessary to create a constructive environment for assessment. Crisis counselors should avoid quick movements and be mindful of personal space when assessing an agitated, potentially homicidal client. Once the client has calmed down, the counselor can delve into precise questions to obtain detailed information about the intent of the client to harm another, the extent and intrusiveness of the homicidal thoughts, and the ability of the client to acquire the means to implement homicide plans. When dealing with a client expressing homicidal intent, crisis counselors must always keep the ethical obligation of public safety and the duty to warn at the forefront of their minds, even with low-threat clients.

CASE STUDY 5.5

Charlene

Charlene is a 14-year-old girl who was brought to counseling by her mother for "behavior issues" at school. After working with the counselor for three sessions, Charlene commented, "I'm just sick and tired of those three girls always poking fun at me. They think they are better than me and they're not. I'm going to shoot them when I go to school tomorrow—that will show them."

Discussion Questions

What does the counselor need to do?

How should she proceed?

If she assesses that Charlene will follow through on the threat, how should the counselor proceed?

What are the legal, ethical, and administrative steps the counselor must take in this scenario?

Referral

Because of the danger to others and the possible existence of mental disorders in homicidal clients, crisis counselors usually refer to or work collaboratively with other mental health providers, particularly psychiatrists, when treating clients who pose a threat to others. Violent clients often need the help of specialists in forensic mental health, and it is a good idea for crisis counselors to be familiar with forensic specialists in their local area.

Clinical assessment of low-threat-level clients may reveal the need for psychiatric evaluation and treatment with psychotropic medication; however, it is imperative that clients with homicidal ideation who are assessed at the high and medium threat level be referred for psychiatric evaluation and possible treatment with medications. Because of imminent danger to others, high-threat-level clients require immediate law enforcement involvement and probable voluntary or involuntary commitment (O'Toole, 2000). Medium-threat-level clients need to be monitored closely and may need to be hospitalized. In instances with out-of-control and impulsive clients, homicidal and suicidal ideation may coexist, and therefore, such a client poses a threat to both self and others. The procedures for voluntary and involuntary commitment discussed previously in this chapter in relation to suicide should be followed for homicide cases, with the inclusion of law enforcement in high-threat-level situations. Personal safety of the crisis counselor should always be a priority. A counselor should never attempt to physically stop a resistant client from leaving. If the client is intent on leaving, it is best to get as much information as possible about the client and request law enforcement to intervene.

What is the relationship between mental illness and homicide? Individuals with diagnosed mental disorders are at a higher risk than the general population for violent or homicidal behavior (Laajasalo & Hakkanen, 2004). It should be noted, however, that this risk is not present across the board and that an elevated threat to others is mainly associated with certain diagnoses (Eronen, Angermeyer, & Schulze, 1998). An increased risk of violent behavior has been found with diagnoses of Schizophrenia and other psychotic disorders, but the highest risk of violent and homicidal behavior has been found in individuals with a dual diagnosis of Antisocial Personality Disorder and Substance Abuse Disorder. Substance abuse repeatedly emerges as a major risk factor for violent behavior and homicide; the comorbidity of substance abuse and any mental disorder will increase the likelihood of violence and should be taken into account when assessing and treating violent clients.

Treatment Options

The establishment of a strong therapeutic alliance through counseling microskills is essential in all counseling relationships and is discussed thoroughly in Chapter 3. A therapeutic alliance is particularly imperative with potential homicide offenders, since client investment in treatment compliance is necessary for public safety. Tishler et al. (2000) note that mental health providers may struggle with achieving empathy and may experience fear when working with homicidal clients. While such reactions are understandable, it is important to remember that homicidal behaviors are symptoms of a client's illness and that open displays of fear and distaste will undermine rapport building and impair treatment outcomes.

Once the immediate homicidal crisis has been dealt with, the safety of others has been assured, and appropriate medical treatment has begun, long-term treatment planning can proceed. Ongoing assessment of the client is crucial to both treatment outcomes and public safety; therefore, assessment must remain foremost in the crisis counselor's mind. One concern in assessment is the tendency for violent offenders to be less than forthright about the facts surrounding violent acts (Carroll et al., 2004; Towl & Crighton, 1997). Crisis counselors should thoroughly examine client history and obtain external substantiation of client facts. Hillbrand (2001) cautions that suicidal ideation and homicidal ideation often co-occur and stresses the importance of assessing the risk of both suicide and homicide in clients who have thoughts of harm to self or others.

In addition to ongoing assessment, homicidal and violent client treatment plans typically include anger and stress management, medication, substance abuse treatment (when indicated), and limitation of access to weapons (Hillbrand, 2001). Treatment should also include the identification of factors that increase and decrease violent ideation. Brems (2000) discusses several aggression-motivating and -mitigating factors that should be assessed and addressed during treatment of violent clients:

- *Habit Strength:* Assessment of the degree to which past violence has worked for the client indicates whether this type of behavior has been reinforced. Clients who have gotten their way through aggression and violence in the past are more likely to use these behaviors in the future.
- *Inhibitions:* A client without inhibitions will be more likely to become aggressive; however, inhibitions may act to moderate aggressive acting out. Examples of inhibiting factors include personal morality and values, impulse control, fear of being caught, and fear of negative consequences. By exploring past times when the client did not resort to violence, a crisis counselor can identify inhibiting factors that can be integrated into treatment.

- *Situational Factors:* Exploration of context can yield important data for treatment. If a client is more likely to engage in violent action in certain circumstances, the treatment plan can include avoidance of triggering settings.

By understanding how aggression may have been reinforced in the client's past and by exploring any inhibiting factors and situational contexts, crisis counselors and clients can identify thoughts and behaviors that may lessen violent behavior in the future. The client can begin to learn other ways to cope with anger and aggression.

Klott and Jongsma (2004) suggested the following long-term treatment goals for assaultive/homicidal males:

- Terminate the use of violence to meet social, psychological, and environmental needs.
- Enhance access to emotions and a capacity for empathy toward the needs, feelings, and desires of others.
- Develop adaptive coping strategies and problem-solving skills.
- Enhance personal resiliency, flexibility, and a capacity to manage crises and failures.
- Develop a supportive social network and the ability to engage in intimate relationships based on mutuality.
- Develop a sense of self-acceptance and the capacity for self-affirmation. (p. 324)

In addition to these goals, Klott and Jongsma suggest a goal of impulse resolution for males with both homicidal ideation and suicidal ideation.

Compliance with treatment—in particular, compliance with medication—must be stressed with homicidal clients. Nordstrom, Dahlgren, and Kullgren (2006) studied convicted homicide offenders who had been diagnosed with Schizophrenia. The majority of offenders were found to have been noncompliant with medication and treatment at the time of their crimes, resulting in active hallucinations and delusions during the homicidal crisis. Therefore, it is essential that crisis counselors conduct ongoing evaluations of medication compliance throughout treatment.

Family involvement in the treatment of homicidal clients is critical as a support for ongoing treatment compliance. Families can communicate to counselors if clients stop taking medication and can also report observed behaviors of concern that might indicate elevated risk (Carroll et al., 2004). Additionally, families provide a social network foundation that can facilitate client coping. In some instances, family members need to be given information to ensure their own safety. Family members and friends, rather than strangers, were the most frequent victims of homicide offenders with a diagnosis of Schizophrenia (Laajasalo & Hakkanen, 2004). This fact highlights the need for families to be an active part of collaborative treatment and ongoing evaluation of homicidal clients.

Early environmental factors influence the development of mental disorders and violent behavior; thus, early intervention with children at risk and their families may deter the development of future antisocial behavior, including homicide (Laajasalo & Hakkanen, 2004). Schools provide the first opportunity for intervention with children who are exhibiting behavioral problems and struggling with academics, both of which are associated with violence. Farmer, Farmer, Estell, and Hutchins (2007) recommend a service delivery structure that supports intervention and prevention in order to

CASE STUDY 5.6

Judy

Judy is a 43-year-old single woman who has been placed on two weeks' administrative leave from her job as a research and development technician at a chemical company. Over the years, she has had many personality conflicts with other workers, but her expertise is valuable, and these conflicts have always been smoothed over and worked out. Recently, she "lost it" with her boss and flew into a rage when she was denied time off in compensation for working late the previous week; this incident was the basis for her administrative leave. Her family doctor has prescribed antidepressants for her and has referred her to you for counseling. Judy expresses anger and a sense of hopelessness about her situation. She is distraught and has to drink wine every night just to go to sleep. Judy is convinced that she will be fired and that the boss is using these two weeks to build a case against her. She expresses to you how valuable she is to the company and how much knowledge she has, including her knowledge of tasteless but deadly poisons. She states, "Just one minute in the break room is all someone would need; just slip it in the coffee and they wouldn't know what hit them."

Discussion Questions

What level of threat is indicated in this case?

Are there factors that increase the homicide risk in this client?

What actions should you take?

promote academic achievement and social skills, intervention with at-risk youth, and developmental systemic prevention strategies. It should be noted that such a delivery structure can be achieved by the full implementation of *The ASCA National Model* (American School Counselor Association [ASCA], 2005).

Homicide Survivor Needs

In the aftermath of a homicide, the family, friends, and sometimes even the community of the victim experience impediments to healing as the mourning process is complicated by the brutality and abruptness of their loss. Hatton (2003) estimates that there are at least 50,000 bereaved homicide survivors every year in the United States. Unfortunately, homicide survivors may underutilize available services and may also have their grief and trauma compounded during subsequent crime investigations and legal proceedings (Horne, 2003). Homicide survivors often find themselves isolated as members of their social network withdraw due to distress and uneasiness over the terrible circumstances surrounding the loss (Currier et al., 2006) or due to stigmatizing circumstances surrounding the death (Hatton, 2003). This lack of community support can be thought of as a secondary victimization that further complicates the grief process. Collins and Collins (2005) point out that the common grief and loss reactions—such as anger, guilt, and self-blame—are amplified in homicide survivor cases.

Homicide is a violent loss, and survivor grief is complicated and multifaceted (Currier et al., 2006). In essence, violent death rocks the foundations of a survivor's worldview and impedes the ability to make sense of the death or to find meaning within the loss. The bereavement experienced after loss to homicide or suicide usually falls within the category of complicated grief. Complicated grief can occur when a death is sudden, developmentally unexpected, or violent. According to the Mayo Clinic (2008), symptoms of complicated grief can include

- Extreme focus on the loss and reminders of the loved one,
- Intense longing or pining for the deceased,
- Problems accepting the death,
- Preoccupation with your sorrow,
- Bitterness about your loss,
- Inability to enjoy life,
- Depression or deep sadness,
- Difficulty moving on with life,
- Trouble carrying out a normal routine,
- Withdrawing from social activities,
- Feeling that life holds no meaning or purpose,
- Irritability or agitation, and
- Lack of trust in others.

Homicide survivors are almost certain to experience complicated grief. Asaro (2001) recommends the following treatment interventions for homicide survivors: (1) Promote feelings of safety within the counseling, (2) discuss the specifics of the murder and allow the client to review the murder as needed, (3) address any co-occurring conditions (e.g., substance abuse), (4) normalize and reframe the myriad feelings the client is experiencing, and (5) refer the client to support groups or other resources.

Armour (2005) promotes a constructivist, meaning-making approach to working with homicide survivors. To heal from violent loss, survivors need to feel able to openly express what has happened to them and to fight for change in a system where they have felt injustice. It is also important that survivors find meaning in the death of their loved one by working to benefit others experiencing similar circumstances; this gives meaning to the loss as well as purpose to the survivor.

The support experienced in group counseling is especially healing for homicide survivors and cannot be underestimated as a treatment modality (Piper, Ogrodniczuk, McCollum, & Rosie, 2002). Hatton (2003) found that homicide survivors found support group counseling to be one of the most helpful interventions in the bereavement process. Support groups give the participants an opportunity to express their feelings without the fear of alienation and stigmatization. Participants can openly talk about their experiences with others who have shared similar experiences and can offer informed support. The U.S. Department of Justice's Office for Victims of Crime (OVC, 2006) has links to support organizations and resources across the nation at www.ojp .usdoj.gov/ovc/help/hv.htm.

Crisis counselors responding to the crisis of homicide should be prepared for complex and varied reactions and symptoms from individual survivors. Not just individuals but also entire communities can be altered by homicide. At college campuses where homicide has taken place, students no longer feel safe, and the stress and anxiety affect

CASE STUDY 5.7

Debbie

Debbie, a 19-year-old college freshman, didn't show up for classes or for her job one day. When she didn't answer her cell phone or come home that night, her roommate was worried and contacted Debbie's family, who reported her as a missing person. After three weeks of searching and televised pleas for her return, Debbie's decomposing body was found in a wooded area 30 miles from her apartment. She had been sexually assaulted and strangled. DNA found on her body was a match with DNA from a man out on parole from a previous rape conviction. He was accused in Debbie's murder. The killer claimed that he had consensual sex with Debbie in his car and that she was fine when he dropped her off at campus. Debbie's parents were appalled when the killer's defense team attempted to portray Debbie as a wild, out-of-control college student who partied too much, had multiple sex partners, and put herself at risk. The trial ended with a hung jury, and there is uncertainty about when there will be a new trial. Debbie's parents have come to you for grief counseling.

Discussion Questions

What factors contribute to the parents' complicated grief?

What emotions and reactions might you expect from the parents in this case?

What treatment goals and interventions are called for in this case?

---

their academic achievement (Carr, 2005). Communities touched by homicide are altered by the brutal reality of murder within their midst; a coordinated community counseling response and activation of resources will serve to facilitate healing. Additionally, crisis counselors should be sensitive to cultural differences in grief expression. Clients from expressive cultures will show more outward signs of grieving. A lack of outward grief expression may be indicative of a more emotionally restrictive culture, and crisis counselors should not underestimate the inner grief state of less expressive clients (Cavaiola & Colford, 2006).

Summary

Suicide and homicide are both crisis situations that counselors who are emergency firstresponders and who provide more long-term treatment are almost certain to be called on to address. These are critical incidents across the span of a professional career. Suicide rates are increasing among all segments of our population, and this trend is expected to continue despite the elaborate prevention efforts ongoing at school, local, state, and national levels.

In the treatment of suicide as a crisis, counselors and other response-oriented personnel may find that their own anxiety surrounding this topic affects their approach to helping clients resolve their own situations. Periodic self-examination is therefore necessary to maintain an adequate degree of separation from the client's crisis, to prevent transference of the crisis counselor's anxieties onto the client, and to avoid damaging the potential for a positive counselor–client relationship.

No universally recognized standard of care is in place with regard to response to suicide and suicide attempts and to treatment of those with suicidal ideation, but professional concepts of foreseeability and assessment of risk have been established to guide and protect crisis counselors as they work with this population.

Three primary goals are presented for the crisis responder to set in dealing with crises of suicide or homicide: to ensure client safety, to assist the client in achieving immediate short-term mastery of self and situation, and to connect the client to formal and informal supports. There are a variety of models presented to help the crisis responder achieve these goals. When the intervention spans more than one contact, as it often does for counselors, additional tools, such as Jobes's Collaborative Assessment and Management of Suicidality (CAMS) approach, have been demonstrated to be an effective way to achieve meaningful and maintainable client improvement and progress. A knowledge of suicide risk factors, warning signs, and protective factors is essential for the crisis counselor to make a justifiable assessment of suicide risk in clients who are struggling with this issue. Once the client is assessed, the counselor makes a decision regarding level of risk and actively monitors the client as he or she makes progress or subsequent events affect the client's disposition. Documentation of the entire process is an increasingly important part of the assessment and treatment cycle; it is emphasized that documentation is the single most important factor in justifying and defending a particular course of treatment action.

A variety of treatment options are in place to respond to those struggling with the issue of suicide, including inpatient hospitalization, partial hospitalization programs, and outpatient care. As managed care operations become the norm in American mental health treatment protocols, a comprehensive risk management plan becomes an essential part of cost-effective and medically justifiable care. The risk management plan typically consists of six components: ensuring that all the included professionals understand the statutes relevant to suicide treatment, confidentiality, and informed consent; having a detailed risk management policy; ensuring clinical competency of staff members; maintaining adequate documentation of treatment; implementing a tracking system for follow-up actions; and establishing and maintaining relevant resources.

Responding to incidents of homicide presents many of the same kinds of challenges as responding to suicide incidents does, although many crisis counselors underestimate the need for readiness to respond to homicide. But since instances where homicide must be responded to in the counseling setting are becoming more frequent, crisis counselors must prepare themselves to engage with this crisis in a professional, defensible way. Crisis counselors may find themselves in a position of potential influence over those who might become capable of homicide, so the *Tarasoff v. Board of Regents of the University of California* case, which clarified the duty to warn individuals who may be in peril, applies to counselors; it is critical that crisis counselors be aware of their legal duties in these situations.

Just as with suicide risk assessment and management, homicide risk factors are presented, and violence capable of escalating to homicide is examined in the educational arena and in the workplace. Crisis counselors must use a threat-level assessment to gauge the need for treatment and implement an appropriate treatment option that includes ongoing assessment of risk.

Homicide survivors usually experience complicated grief. They may feel stigmatized, isolated, and retraumatized by the legal system. Treatment of survivors should address their complicated grief issues and help them find resolution and meaning. Support groups for homicide survivors have been found to be a highly effective method of treatment.

6 Intimate Partner Violence

Amy L. McLeod, John Muldoon, and Danica G. Hays

PREVIEW

Intimate partner violence (IPV) is the infliction of physical, sexual, and/or emotional harm to a person by a current or former partner or spouse with the intent of establishing power and control over the abused partner. IPV is a major public health concern, and it is imperative that crisis counselors be able to recognize and respond to IPV survivors competently. This chapter provides an overview of the facts and figures associated with IPV, discusses the cycle of violence commonly experienced in abusive relationships, and explores various perspectives on survivors who stay in relationships with abusive partners. Common crisis issues experienced by IPV survivors, including dealing with physical injury, establishing immediate safety, and reporting IPV to the police, are also highlighted. In addition, this chapter explores special considerations regarding IPV in lesbian, gay, bisexual, and transgender (LGBT) relationships, relationships characterized by female-to-male violence, abusive relationships in racial and ethnic minority populations, and abusive dating relationships among adolescents and young adults. Guidelines for crisis counselors on conducting IPV assessment, responding to IPV disclosure, planning for safety, and addressing the emotional impact of IPV are provided. Finally, the goals, theories, and challenges associated with IPV offender intervention are discussed.

INTIMATE PARTNER VIOLENCE

IPV is the infliction of physical, sexual, and/or emotional harm to a person by a current or former partner or spouse with the intention of establishing power and control over the abused partner (Centers for Disease Control and Prevention, 2005a; Family Violence Prevention Fund, 1999). IPV is an inclusive term that can be used to describe violence among heterosexual couples as well as LGBT couples. The term *intimate* does not imply that the couple is necessarily sexually intimate (Centers for Disease Control and Prevention, 2005a). IPV can occur in dating relationships as well as in marital relationships.

CASE STUDY 6.1

Casey and Jamie

For days, Casey had taken extra precautions to make sure that nothing upset Jamie. Casey kept the house extra clean, had Jamie's favorite meals prepared for dinner every night, and tried to seem cheerful and upbeat. Still Casey couldn't get rid of the uneasy feeling that trouble was brewing with Jamie. It was eight o'clock, and Jamie still wasn't home from work. Casey was concerned. When Jamie walked in the door, Casey smelled whiskey. "Where have you been? I was so worried!" Casey exclaimed. Jamie's eyes narrowed. In a low, angry voice, Jamie growled, "I'll go where I damn well please" and knocked Casey into the wall. Casey immediately apologized to Jamie, but it was too late. "You constantly nag me," Jamie yelled and hit Casey hard across the face. Casey fell to the ground and sobbed. Jamie walked into the kitchen and said, "I'm hungry." Not wanting to make matters worse, Casey got up, walked into the kitchen, and started to warm up dinner. Casey's mind was racing, "I can't believe this is happening again. Jamie promised never again after the last time. Jamie promised!"

Questions

Take out a piece of paper and answer the following questions as quickly as possible:

Is Casey a female or male?

Is Jamie a female or male?

What do Casey and Jamie look like?

What is Casey's racial/ethnic background?

What is Jamie's racial/ethnic background?

Are Casey and Jamie heterosexual, homosexual, or bisexual?

Are they married?

Does either Casey or Jamie have a disability?

Are Casey and Jamie religious?

What does Jamie do for a living?

What does Casey do for a living?

Are Casey and Jamie upper, middle, or lower socioeconomic status (SES)?

Whom do you blame for the violence in this relationship?

How do your answers to these questions reflect your biases about IPV?

How may this influence your work with clients?

Statistics regarding IPV vary due to the range of IPV definitions and methods of data collection used by researchers. It is also important to note that most instances of IPV are never reported, so the available facts and figures are likely an underestimation of the extent of the IPV crisis. Regardless of which statistical estimates are consulted, it is clear that IPV is a major public health concern and a common cause of injury that disproportionately affects women. An estimated 95% of victims of IPV are female, and approximately 30% of women experience IPV during their lifetime (Berry, 2000; Centers for Disease Control, 2006). In the United States, approximately 5.3 million and 3.2 million incidents of IPV are experienced by women and men each year, respectively (Tjaden & Thoennes, 2000). An estimated 1.5 million women and 800,000 men are raped or physically assaulted by an intimate partner annually. IPV affects women and men in all racial, ethnic, socioeconomic, and religious groups; however, individuals who are members of multiple oppressed groups (e.g., lower-SES women of color) are at increased risk of harm due to IPV because of their multiple oppressed social positions (Sokoloff & Dupont, 2005).

The tremendous emotional, social, and physical consequences of IPV for survivors are well documented. For example, IPV results in more injuries to women than do automobile accidents, muggings, and rapes combined (Keller, 1996), totaling nearly 2 million injuries and 1,300 deaths in the United States each year (Centers for Disease Control and Prevention, 2003). Annual health care and lost productivity costs of IPV against women exceed $8.3 billion. Additionally, 11% of homicide victims from 1976 to 2002 were murdered by a current or former partner or spouse (Fox & Zawitz, 2004). The magnitude of the consequences of IPV calls for a greater understanding of the dynamics of IPV and the experiences of survivors of abuse. Increased understanding can assist crisis counselors in using more effective and appropriate interventions when working with IPV survivors (Hays, Green, Orr, & Flowers, 2007).

CYCLE OF VIOLENCE THEORY

The cycle of violence theory was developed by Walker (1979), a psychologist who based her theory on interviews with hundreds of women who experienced IPV. Walker noted that the violence described by women in her research typically followed a three-phase pattern: the tension-building phase, the explosion or acute battering incident, and the honeymoon phase of kindness and contrite, loving behavior (Figure 6.1). Each phase varies in time and intensity during each cycle of violence for the same couple and between different couples.

Phase One: The Tension-Building Phase

The tension-building phase of the cycle of violence is characterized by mounting pressure and strain in the relationship. The abused partner "walks on eggshells" around the abusive partner, becoming compliant, nurturing, or whatever it takes to keep the abusive partner's anger from escalating. The tension-building phase also involves minor battering incidents (Walker, 1979). Minor battering incidents include insults, threats, or even actions such as throwing a dinner on to the floor and blaming the abused partner

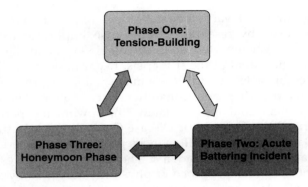

FIGURE 6.1 The Cycle of Violence.

for overcooking the food. During the tension-building phase, the abused partner may cope with the minor battering incidents by denying anger about the incident, rationalizing the abuse to himself or herself (e.g., thinking that he or she did something to deserve this), or making excuses for the abuser. Following each minor battering incident, the tension and stress in the relationship build.

Phase Two: The Acute Battering Incident

The second phase of the cycle of violence occurs when tensions build to the point of explosion in an acute battering incident. The acute battering incident is characterized by unpredictability, uncontrollable rage, brutality, and seriously damaging consequences (Walker, 1979). The acute battering incident is typically triggered by an external event (e.g., stress at work) or the abusive partner's internal state and can last for a number of hours to a number of days. During an acute battering incident, survivors have reported dissociative experiences, such as feeling as though they are outside their own bodies and watching themselves be thrown into a wall, choked, or raped. Following an acute battering incident, many survivors enter a state of shock and disbelief. Both partners may make attempts to rationalize the violence.

Phase Three: The Honeymoon Phase

The third phase in the cycle of violence is characterized by loving and repentant behavior from the abusive partner. The abuser may shower the IPV survivor with gifts, beg for forgiveness, and promise never to be violent again. During the honeymoon phase, the abusive partner may also attempt to guilt the survivor into staying in the relationship with statements such as "I would be lost without you" and "Don't make our kids grow up without me in their lives." The honeymoon phase results in the IPV survivor feeling needed and loved, leading to a renewed commitment to the relationship. The length of the contrite, loving phase varies, although it is typically shorter than the tension-building phase and longer than the acute battering incident (Walker, 1979). After repeated cycles of violence, the honeymoon phase may shorten or eventually be eliminated. The IPV survivor who has experienced numerous cycles of violence may experience increased shame and humiliation during the honeymoon phase due to the realization that the abuse will almost certainly reoccur, despite the batterer's promises, which the IPV survivor now recognizes as empty.

Educating IPV survivors about the cycle of violence can help in naming experiences as abusive. For example, some clients may not define their relationships as abusive because violence doesn't occur frequently. Other clients may see the batterer's apologies and gifts as a unique indication of how special their relationship is until learning that the honeymoon phase is typical during a cycle of violence (McLeod, Hays, & Chang, in press).

LEARNED HELPLESSNESS THEORY

The concept of learned helplessness originates from the research of Seligman (1975) in which dogs were locked in a cage and administered random electric shocks. The dogs quickly learned that none of their responses and attempts to escape was successful in eliminating the unwanted stimulus and therefore submitted passively to the shocks. Later the cages were opened, providing the dogs with an opportunity to escape, yet the dogs did not attempt to do so. In other words, the dogs learned to believe they were not in control of their situation so even when they actually had the opportunity to control their situation (i.e., avoid shocks by leaving the cage), the dogs responded with learned helplessness.

Learned helplessness theory has been used to explain why IPV survivors remain in abusive relationships. During the tension-building phase of the cycle of violence, the abused partner behaves in an accommodating manner in an attempt to avoid escalating the abusive partner's anger. Eventually, the tension builds to an explosive battering incident, and the survivor learns that his or her attempts to control the situation were unsuccessful. An IPV survivor may reach out for help from family, friends, or the police, yet the battering still continues. Again, the survivor receives the message that efforts to control the situation are ineffective. Repeated incidents of uncontrollable violence diminish the survivor's motivation to respond, leading to passivity and learned helplessness (Walker, 1979).

ALTERNATIVES TO LEARNED HELPLESSNESS THEORY

Opponents of the application of learned helplessness theory to IPV survivors argue that the theory pathologizes the survivor, places the responsibility for ending abuse on the survivor while ignoring the larger sociocultural context, and implies that leaving the relationship ensures the survivor's safety (Humphreys & Thiara, 2003; Peled, Eisikovits, Enosh, & Winstok, 2000; Werner-Wilson, Zimmerman, & Whalen, 2000). Ecological theory offers an alternative explanation for why the IPV survivor stays in a relationship with an abusive partner and states that the sociocultural system (i.e., the ideological and institutional patterns of a culture), the institutional-organizational system (e.g., agencies, policies, programs, professional groups), the interpersonal system (i.e., the survivor's direct interactions with the abusive partner, children, family, and friends), and the individual system (i.e., the survivor's perceptions, meanings, and actions) all play roles in the survivor's decision (Peled et al., 2000). Further, constructivist theorists argue that the decision to stay with an abusive partner could result from a rational decision-making process based on weighing the costs and benefits of ending

ACTIVITY 6.1

IPV in the Movies

Watch and critique a movie that depicts IPV. You may choose a movie from the following list or select a movie of your choice as long as IPV is a central issue in the film. Movies depicting IPV include *A Streetcar Named Desire* (1951), *Petulia* (1968), *The Burning Bed* (1984), *Crimes of the Heart* (1986), *Sleeping with the Enemy* (1991), *What's Love Got to Do with It* (1993), and *Enough* (2002). How does the movie you chose portray the abusive partner and the IPV survivor? Is the cycle of violence evident in the film? What stereotypes or myths are perpetuated by the film? What messages does the film send about staying in an abusive relationship? What positive or awareness-raising messages about IPV, if any, are present in the film? What was your reaction to watching the movie from a personal perspective? What was your reaction to watching the movie from a counseling perspective?

the relationship. The survivor who decides to stay in the relationship, instead of being viewed as powerless and helpless, is viewed as choosing to confront violence from within the relationship. In addition, researchers have rejected the notion that the survivor who stays in the relationship is helpless and have focused on the inner resources (e.g., resilience, sense of humor, hope, spirituality) and survival strategies of the IPV survivor who chooses to stay with an abusive partner (Davis, 2002; Werner-Wilson et al., 2000). Crisis counselors are advised to consider how their interventions with survivors and perpetrators of IPV may be influenced by their beliefs about IPV and why women stay in abusive relationships.

COMMON CRISIS ISSUES

The intense emotional and physical stress caused by IPV can often exceed the perceived coping resources of the abused partner. As a crisis counselor responding to an IPV crisis, the goal is to empower survivors to solve problem effectively. Crisis counselors should conduct a triage assessment in order to determine which aspects of the situation require immediate intervention. Additionally, crisis counselors should work with IPV survivors in crisis to increase perceived options, mobilize resources, and identify sources of continued support after the crisis is stabilized (Greenstone & Leviton, 2002). Common crisis issues when working with IPV survivors include attending to physical injury, establishing immediate safety, and deciding whether or not to report IPV to the police.

Attending to Physical Injury

Many IPV survivors receive treatment in emergency rooms and doctors' offices for injuries inflicted by an intimate partner; yet health care providers often fail to assess the cause of the injuries they are treating (L. E. Tower, 2006; M. Tower, 2007). Just as it is imperative for health care providers to screen for IPV, it is also essential that crisis counselors ask about physical injuries and facilitate medical care when necessary. Physical injury resulting from IPV can range from scrapes and bruises to permanent disfigurement, disability, and death (Kramer, Lorenzon, & Mueller, 2004). Emergency medical treatment may be required before any further counseling intervention can occur; therefore, crisis counselors should be prepared to refer and arrange transportation to appropriate medical facilities. Crisis counselors should be aware of free and low-cost medical resources, since survivors may not have health insurance. In addition, since IPV can take the form of sexual assault and rape, crisis counselors should be aware of medical facilities that specialize in rape. Advising the survivor of what to expect during use of a rape kit can help reduce anxiety and allow the survivor to make an informed decision about consenting to the procedure (Walker, 1994). Also, when a referral to a medical facility is necessary, crisis counselors should ensure continuity of care by communicating that they are not abandoning the survivor, checking to make sure that the survivor arrives at the medical facility safely, and advising the survivor that counseling is available for continued support once medical needs are addressed.

Establishing Immediate Safety

During an IPV crisis, establishing physical safety and preventing further harm to the survivor are paramount. Time is of the essence, and crisis counselors must gain thorough and accurate information quickly by conducting a detailed assessment of the situation, including violence severity, available resources, and barriers to accessing resources (McCloskey & Grigsby, 2005; Walker, 1994). The crisis counselor must also directly assess for suicide and homicide risk and be prepared to take protective measures if needed (e.g., to act on the duty to warn, to arrange for involuntary psychiatric hospitalization of the survivor or perpetrator in severe cases). In some situations, the survivor may not be able to return home safely, so the crisis counselor must arrange for emergency shelter. Provisions for children and pets at risk of harm may also be necessary (Walker, 1994). A detailed description of how to construct a safety plan is provided later in the chapter.

Reporting IPV to the Police

The decision about whether or not to report an IPV incident to the police is complex. It is clear that the majority of IPV incidents are not reported to the police (France, 2002; Fugate, Landis, Riordan, Naureckas, & Engel, 2005; Walker, 1979). A survivor may choose not to contact the police due to the belief that the abuse was not serious enough to require police intervention, that the police will not be helpful, and that if the police are called, the relationship with the abusive partner will need to end (Fugate et al., 2005). In addition, survivors may fear the consequences of contacting the police, such as the loss of housing or the involvement of child protective services (Fugate et al., 2005; Liang, Goodman, Tummala-Narra, & Weintraub, 2005). For members of minority groups (e.g., gay, lesbian, and bisexual individuals; racial and ethnic minorities; immigrants), the decision to call the police may be further complicated by other factors discussed in greater detail later in this chapter. Survivors may also fear that calling the police will increase the risk of further harm from their abusers (Humphreys & Thiara, 2003; Walker, 1979). Unless suicidality, homicidality, or child abuse is disclosed, crisis counselors are not required to report IPV incidents and should support the choice the survivor makes regarding police notification (Chang et al., 2005; France, 2002). The

ACTIVITY 6.2

Self-Awareness Assessment: What Are Your Values and Beliefs About IPV?

Read the following statements and honestly evaluate whether you agree or disagree with each one:

- IPV is a personal matter. People outside the relationship should not interfere.
- Women who stay in abusive relationships are partially at fault for the treatment they receive because someone can only treat you as bad as you let them.
- You cannot be raped by your spouse or partner.
- It is okay to get a divorce if you have been emotionally, physically, or sexually abused by your partner.

- It is justifiable to resort to physical violence if you find out your significant other has been unfaithful to you.
- It is okay to be physically violent in self-defense.
- It is never okay to hit a woman.

What has shaped your responses to these questions (e.g., messages from your family of origin, religious/spiritual teachings, the media)? In addition to the statements listed above, what other messages have you received about IPV? How may your beliefs and values affect your work with clients?

crisis counselor should discuss the pros and cons of police intervention with the survivor and then respect the survivor's autonomy as much as possible.

IPV IN SPECIAL POPULATIONS

Culture is important to consider in understanding and treating IPV. Culture guides how clients define, view, experience, and respond to IPV. Crisis counselors responding to IPV should attend to cultural dimensions such as gender, race, ethnicity, socioeconomic status, level of acculturation, language, religiosity, sexual orientation, ability status, and age. With the increased acknowledgment that IPV is a global problem, the social and cultural contexts of IPV are gaining much needed attention. Unfortunately, the impact of culture on the IPV experience, including the reporting of IPV and help-seeking behaviors, has been largely ignored in the counseling literature. The following sections highlight some of the social and cultural considerations relevant to the conceptualization, prevalence, and presentation of IPV. These include (1) racial and ethnic minority concerns and the intersection of gender, social class, immigration status, and religiosity; (2) female-to-male violence; (3) LGBT concerns; (4) IPV and disability status; and (5) dating violence among adolescent and young adult populations.

Race and Ethnicity

Race and ethnicity are important considerations in understanding and intervening in IPV. There seems to be very little difference between White women and women identified as members of racial and ethnic minorities (i.e., African-American, Native American, Asian/Pacific Islander, and multiracial women) in terms of the prevalence of rape, physical assault, or stalking: 17.7% and 19.8% of White and racial and ethnic minority women, respectively, report they have experienced a completed or attempted rape at some time in their life; 51.3% and 54% of White and racial and ethnic minority women, respectively, report they have been physically assaulted; and 8.2% of both White and racial and ethnic minority women report they have been stalked at some

ACTIVITY 6.3

Identifying Abusive Acts Against Women

Review this list of intentional acts. Circle the acts you would consider abusive toward females, adding more acts to the list as appropriate.

Scratching	Pulling hair	Disrupting sleep
Using physical restraint	Biting	Slapping
Throwing objects	Burning with cigarette	Humiliating in front of others
Pushing	Grabbing	Forcing sex
Calling names	Withholding sex	Committing adultery
Threatening to leave	Threatening to kill self	Threatening to kill others
Poisoning	Kicking	Choking
Destroying property	Using jealousy	Isolating from others
Deciding how a partner dresses	Controlling a schedule	Punishing for no sex
Killing partner	Disrupting meals	Wounding with a knife

Review the list. Would your choices be different if you were considering IPV among racial and ethnic minorities? Toward a male? Toward someone from a more religious background? Toward someone with a disability? Toward someone identifying as LGBT?

Discuss how the behaviors you consider abusive may depend on the cultural makeup of the client.

time in their life. However, a closer look at prevalence rates for specific racial groups reveals significantly different rates of victimization (see Table 6.1). There are significant differences in rape victimization between White and Native American women, between African-American and Native American women, and between White and multiracial women. That is, Native American and multiracial women may be more likely than White and African-American women to report they were raped. Further, there are significant differences in victimization by stalking between Native American women and White and African-American women (Tjaden & Thoennes, 2000). Unfortunately, the small number of Asian/Pacific Islander women who reported they were raped and stalked made it difficult to accurately test for statistically significant differences between them and women from other racial backgrounds. Data from this survey demonstrate that examining violence victimization for racial minority groups as a whole may diminish or mask important differences between groups. Additionally, African Americans and Native Americans may experience more severe injuries and greater mental health consequences (Lee, Thompson, & Mechanic, 2002). Table 6.2 provides prevalence data by ethnicity. Those identifying as Hispanic (any race) report significantly less rape than do non-Hispanics, although there may be concerns of underreporting. While the survey data described in Tables 6.1 and 6.2 provide important information, they do not distinguish rates for IPV specifically or highlight complexities in within-group variation of violence victimization.

Other studies provide somewhat mixed findings regarding IPV prevalence by racial/ethnic group. In one study, African-American women reported IPV at a rate 35%

TABLE 6.1 Lifetime Victimization Rates (in Percentages) of Rape, Physical Assault, and Stalking by Race

	Total (n = 7,850)	White (n = 6,742)	African-American (n = 780)	Asian/Pacific Islander (n = 133)	Native American (n = 88)	Multiracial (n = 397)
Rape	18.3	17.7	18.8	6.8	34.1	24.4
Physical assault	51.8	51.3	52.1	49.6	61.4	57.7
Stalking	8.2	8.2	6.5	4.5	17.0	10.6

Source: From *Full Report of the Prevalence, Incidence and Consequences of Violence Against Women: Findings from the National Violence Against Women Survey*, by P. Tjaden and N. Thoennes, 2000, Washington, DC: U.S. Department of Justice.

TABLE 6.2 Lifetime Victimization Rates (in Percentages) of Rape, Physical Assault, and Stalking by Ethnicity

	Total (n = 7,945)	Hispanic (n = 628)	Non-Hispanic (n = 7,317)
Rape	18.1	14.6	18.4
Physical assault	51.9	53.2	51.8
Stalking	8.1	7.6	5.2

Source: From *Full Report of the Prevalence, Incidence and Consequences of Violence Against Women: Findings from the National Violence Against Women Survey*, by P. Tjaden and N. Thoennes, 2000, Washington, DC: U.S. Department of Justice.

higher than that of White women and about 2.5 times that of women of other races (Rennison, 2002). Other findings show that White and African-American women report more IPV than do Hispanic women (McFarlane, Groff, O'Brien, & Watson, 2005). However, the prevalence of IPV victimization among African Americans and Hispanics were similar in one study (14% and 10%, respectively), while African Americans were approximately twice as likely to report IPV perpetration (Lipsky, Caetano, Field, & Bazargan, 2005). Finally, Asian and Pacific Islander women have reported lower rates of physical assault and rape (12.8% and 3.8%, respectively), although other studies show lifetime rates for physical and/or sexual abuse as high as 41–60%, depending on the amount of time subgroups have resided in the United States (Asian and Pacific Islander Institute on Domestic Violence, 2008). The prevalence of IPV, as indicated by these data, can differ depending on the study; hence, reported data may not accurately indicate actual prevalence. This may occur for several reasons. First, some of these rates may be underreported due to cultural values or social factors, as discussed shortly. Second, there are flaws in reporting as individuals get "lumped" into larger racial and ethnic groups, ignoring great variation within each racial or ethnic group. Third, information is self-report data obtained from samples of convenience, samples that vary significantly depending on the setting in which they are obtained.

IPV reporting trends may be associated with community services sought by different racial/ethnic minority groups. For example, non-Hispanic Whites and African Americans are more likely than other racial groups to use housing assistance and emergency department services. African Americans were more likely to use police assistance compared to Hispanic women in some studies (Kaukinen, 2004; Lipsky, Caetano, Field, & Larkin, 2006; McFarlane, Soeken, Reel, Parker, & Silva, 1997; West, Kanter, & Jasinski, 1998). However, African-American and Hispanic women were more likely to use police than White women in another study (Pearlman, Zierler, Gjelsvik, & Verhoek-Oftedahl, 2003). Further, there seems to be an underuse of IPV mental health services by African Americans but a comparable use of shelters and medical personnel (Coley & Beckett, 1988). With the exception of seeking police assistance, the underuse of community resources may be highest by Hispanics (McFarlane et al., 1997; West et al., 1998).

Several factors should be considered as we examine cultural variations in IPV. Differences in reporting trends and help-seeking behaviors among racial/ethnic groups may occur for several reasons. First, IPV may be defined differently across groups and thus be tolerated differentially. For many cultures, the concept of IPV is unknown, partly due to a lack of terminology. For example, there is no term for *domestic violence* in many Asian languages (Lemberg, 2002); further, *domestic violence* was known in Japan as children's violence toward their parents (Kozu, 1999). Another example is that there are no terms synonymous with *batterer* or *rape* in Russian (Horne, 1999). In Chile, IPV is called *private violence* (McWhirter, 1999). Even with increased attention to IPV, having to consider IPV a crime makes it difficult for many racial/ethnic minority women to report the abuse, often leading them to report only severe cases of abuse.

Second, cultural issues may influence the timing, presentation, and sequencing of reporting. These might include cultural solidarity, family structure, gender role socialization, socioeconomic status, and religiosity, to name a few. Cultural factors such as social isolation, language barriers, economic barriers, dedication to family, shame, and a cultural stigma of divorce also influence IPV reporting. Immigrants and refugees may also experience fear of deportation or may be familiar only with their home country's cultural mores surrounding IPV (see Table 6.3 for examples).

Finally, IPV-related resources may be unavailable in certain lower SES communities of color, affecting reporting and help-seeking trends (Lee et al., 2002). Various forms of oppression such as racism, heterosexism, classism, and ableism may intersect to further prohibit a sense of safety to report. Alternatively, the degree of cultural solidarity may perpetuate IPV. Strong cultural ties, particularly in smaller communities, may isolate women from outside resources, promote greater acceptance of gender inequities, and result in a stronger tradition of family secrecy. For example, cultural norms, particularly those in non-Western cultures, may restrict survivors from seeking legal or medical attention for IPV.

Regardless of the differences in IPV prevalence rates by race and ethnicity, there seem to be similar reasons for remaining in violent relationships. However, there are cultural subtleties in how IPV is recognized and addressed that affect reporting trends across racial and ethnic groups. The interrelated factors include patriarchal family structure, socioeconomic status, immigrant status, and religiosity.

PATRIARCHAL FAMILY STRUCTURE Patriarchy denotes clear gender role assignments based on patrilineal descent. Feminists view patriarchy as the most important cause of

---

TABLE 6.3 Examples of IPV from Around the World

Jordan: In a review of 89 criminal records for homicides in 1995, 38 were homicides involving women, with 23 reported as "honor crimes" (i.e., violence against a female by a male relative for alleged sexual misconduct that "violated the honor of the family"). This may be supported by Article 340 of the Jordanian Penal Code, which states:

1. He who catches his wife, or one of his (female) unlawfuls, committing adultery with another, and he kills, wounds, or injures them, is exempt from penalty.

2. He who catches his wife, or one of his (female) ascendants or descendants or sisters, with another in an unlawful bed, and he kills, wounds, or injures one or both of them, benefits from a reduction of penalty.

Russia: Some common Russian proverbs that seem to support IPV include these: "If he beats you, it means he loves you" and "Beat the wife for better cabbage soup." Additionally, a common joke stated by males is "If I could think of a reason, I would kill you" (Horne, 1999).

Japan: It is commonly understood that internal family life is free from legal intervention in Japan. Further, one Japanese proverb roughly translates to illustrate the tradition of family secrecy and honor that perpetuates IPV: "A nail that sticks out will get struck down" (Kozu, 1999).

Chile: Until 1989, the Civil Code of Chile called for wives to obey their husbands and for a husband to have authority over a wife's possessions and person. Unfortunately, much resistance to the dissolution of the Civil Code still remains today. Also, Chile is the only country in the Western world in which divorce is illegal (McWhirter, 1999).

IPV because there is a power imbalance between males and females and abuse is used as a source of control. In patrilineal societies, where male honor is measured by female chastity and fidelity, IPV could be higher, since any male member of the patriline may be violent toward any female member of the patriline. Patriarchal societies oftentimes create violent environments for women and increased tolerance of IPV.

Traditional gender roles are characteristic of patriarchal family structure, creating cultural pressure to remain in violent relationships. For example, *marianismo* in Latin cultures is the value of having females be economically dependent on males, maintain the family unit above their own personal needs, and respect males as decision makers (Mattson & Rodriguez, 1999). Further, African-American women are often socialized to be strong and may avoid the impression of "victim" (Sleutel, 1998). Japanese women may view sexual acts with shame and embarrassment and thus tend to underreport sexual abuse (Kozu, 1999).

A final example illustrates practices in Arab cultures. The concepts of family honor (*sharaf*) and shame (*ird, ayb*) promote "manliness" of male members, sexual purity of females, and fidelity of a wife or mother. This in turn creates norms and practices that shape social and sexual behavior among males and females and in some instances promote IPV without criminal prosecution (Kulwicki, 2002). In Arab cultures, violence from husbands is often legitimized and accepted by women as occupational or domestic stress, with women tolerating some forms of IPV. For example, between 14% and 69% of Palestinian women support wife beating on "certain occasions" (e.g., when the wife refuses to have sex, disobeys the husband, or challenges the husband's manhood) (Haj-Yahia, 1998); 86% of Egyptian women, ever or currently married, agreed that wife beating is appropriate under certain circumstances (e.g., when the wife burns food, neglects the children, disobeys the husband, wastes money, refuses to have sex, or talks to other men) (El-Zanaty, Hussein, Shawky, Way, & Kishor, 1996); and some Jordanian women justified wife beating in cases where the wife commits sexual infidelity, challenges the husband's manhood, or insults the husband in front of others (Haj-Yahia, 2002).

SOCIOECONOMIC STATUS The role of lower SES has been examined in relation to IPV. While accurate data may be difficult to obtain, poor women are more likely to be victims of IPV. Poverty is inextricably linked to limited resources, substance abuse, social isolation, pregnancy, and unemployment. These variables collectively create unhealthy environments that both initiate and perpetuate IPV. Some argue that it may be income or social inequality rather than poverty that is associated with IPV. That is, the wider the gap between the "haves" and "have nots," the greater the violence victimization of those with lower SESs. For example, violence has increased with the widening SES gap among women, racial/ethnic minorities, and minority and majority communities in general (Hines & Malley-Morrison, 2005).

IMMIGRANT STATUS IPV is common among immigrants and refugees, as migration from one country to another often creates isolation that facilitates IPV. On a global level, 17–38% of the world's women have been physically assaulted by a partner, with as many as 60% of women in developing countries experiencing IPV (United Nations, 1995). For women not highly acculturated to the U.S. culture, there is an overall decrease in the use of social and health care services (Lipsky et al., 2006; Mattson & Rodriguez, 1999). Language barriers often prevent women in abusive relationships from seeking assistance. In addition, dissonance with gender roles may perpetuate IPV, as women often become the primary breadwinner in the family due to more restricted employment opportunities for male immigrants (Mattson & Ruiz, 2005). With many immigrant and refugee women entering the United States each year, it is imperative that crisis counselors acknowledge the prevalence and consequences of IPV in this population.

RELIGIOSITY Religion may perpetuate IPV, although the prevalence of violence across religious groups is not known. Some examples of how more conservative religious beliefs and practices may perpetuate IPV include the following: male domination, superior male morality, the value of suffering, references in biblical text to "submission" to husbands, and the importance of marital reconciliation in Christianity (Foss & Warnke, 2003; Sleutel, 1998); reference to husbands as *shujin* (meaning "master") and to the need to put aside work to care for a husband's elderly parents in Confucianism (Kozu, 1999); and Koran passages that highlight obedience and respect for the husband as a wife's duty (Haj-Yahia, 2002). Thus, religious texts have been used (and misused) to promote violence in intimate partnerships.

Religion may also serve as a protective factor against IPV and as a coping mechanism in recovering from its consequences. For example, increased religiosity may be associated with decreased IPV (Elliott, 1994) or decreased severity of violence (Bowker, 1988). In the African-American community, prayer is used significantly for coping with IPV consequences (El-Khoury et al., 2004).

Female-to-Male Violence

All reviews of IPV statistics reveal that women are significantly more likely to report IPV than are men, no matter the type of abuse (e.g., rape, physical assault, stalking, verbal assault). Additionally, there is no doubt in the literature that women are more likely to experience IPV, and particularly the more severe forms of abuse, than are men. Therefore, female-to-male violence, sometimes referred to as husband abuse, has received minimal attention in the counseling literature and is probably underreported. Some common methods of female-to-male violence involve burning, inflicting gunshot wounds, hitting with objects, poisoning, and threatening to withhold sex (Hines & Malley-Morrison, 2005). The prevalence of physical assault ranges from 7.4% to 16%, with rape/sexual assault estimated at 1.3 per 1,000 males aged 12 years and older (Tjaden & Thoennes, 2000). Additionally, estimates indicate that 50–90% of males experience emotional abuse (Hines & Malley-Morrison, 2005).

Why might female-to-male violence be underreported? Gender norms may prevent males who suffer emotional, physical, or sexual abuse from reporting, as disclosure might "emasculate" them. For example, males may be less likely to report sexual abuse (typically occurring through female persuasion rather than force or threat) because of societal fears of homosexuality and rigid definitions of gender roles. There are gender differences in defining aggression and thus in reporting IPV. While women tend to report both intentional and unintentional violent acts, men are more likely to report only intentional acts of aggression or violence (Walker, 1999). For example, while females may report jealousy, pushing, or grabbing as aggressive, males may be more inclined to report only more severe forms of violence, such as throwing objects or attempting to poison, as abusive.

Why has female-to-male violence not received much attention? Some advocates for preventing and intervening in IPV toward females assert that attending to female-to-male violence draws attention away from the depth and scope of female victimization, limiting resources available to those who may need it more. Others claim that female-to-male violence does not exist, stating that gender norms do not allow for such. Instead, they explain that women are participating in mutual battering, which involves IPV between both partners typically as an effort by females to defend against IPV or retaliate to control the timing of IPV. The concept of mutual battering justifies female-to-male violence as the fault of the male partner. That is, violence against males by females is acceptable because it limits or prevents violence toward females. Another argument is that women are often unable to cause serious injury and males are better able to escape violent situations; that is, the problem of female-to-male violence cannot become as serious as male-to-female violence is.

Some studies have found evidence to dispel the feminist rationale behind mutual battering. For example, contrary to traditional findings, mutual abuse practices have been found to involve primarily female-to-male abuse, and clinical abuse (i.e., severe injury leading to intervention) was equal among males and females for community samples of couples (Ehrensaft, Moffitt, & Caspi, 2004). Further, qualitative findings for 68 families indicated the self-defense rationale for mutual battering may be unfounded (Sarrantakos, 2004). Thus, there is some question whether mutual battering is truly a self-defense tactic or masks unprovoked violence toward male partners. Clearly, the behaviors and rationale surrounding female-to-male violence are complex. Crisis counselors are encouraged to thoroughly assess male clients for risk of violence, gain insight into how male clients may be defining aggression and violence, and assess for mutual battering and its potential causes and consequences.

LGBT Violence

The prevalence of IPV for LGBT individuals is similar to or greater than that in hetero-sexual couples (Peterman & Dixon, 2003; Potoczniak, Mourot, Crosbie-Burnett, & Potoczniak, 2003). Approximately one in three gay and lesbian individuals experiences LGBT violence in intimate partnerships, although this figure may be an underestima-tion, since most research involves White, higher-SES samples (Griffin, 2008). Considering data on lifetime victimization of IPV, 50–90% of lesbians experience physi-cal and/or emotional abuse, 12–30% of lesbians experience sexual abuse, and 12–33% of gay men experience sexual abuse (Hines & Malley-Morrison, 2005). Further, there may be increased violence for females in both lesbian and bisexual relationships compared with females in only lesbian relationships. Comparing rates among lesbians, gay men, and bisexual men and women, lesbians experience more physical abuse than do gay men, and bisexual women experience more abuse than do lesbians or gay men. Prevalence in the transgender community is harder to estimate, yet the problem seems to be more pervasive. While accounting for only 4% of LGBT cases, we see approxi-mately 50% rape and physical assault victimization rates for transgender individuals (National Coalition of Anti-Violence Programs, 2003). These figures should be reviewed with caution, as national figures on LGBT violence are difficult to obtain due to the dis-proportionate clustering of LGBT individuals in select U.S. regions.

Estimating the prevalence of LGBT violence presents difficulties similar to those encountered in estimating violence among racial/ethnic minorities and against males. Among the systems affecting LGBT disclosure of IPV are family and friends, mutual friends of the abused and abuser in the LGBT community, LGBT-affirmative shelters and crisis counselors, the legal system (i.e., attorneys, jurors, judges, laws), public policy, and societal myths based in gender norms, homophobia, and heterosexism (Potoczniak et al., 2003).

Is IPV a gendered problem, as many feminists assert? Can men be victims and women be batters? Feminists' notion that IPV is caused by traditional gender role social-ization in a patriarchal family structure often does not fit LGBT relationships. If IPV is explained as a result of patriarchy, gay and bisexual men cannot be abused, and lesbian and bisexual women cannot be abusive. Thus, feminist theory may leave those working with LGBT couples with little information about the causes of IPV. Additionally, there is not a uniform definition of same-sex violence (Potoczniak et al., 2003).

Homophobia, the prejudice and discrimination toward LGBT individuals and their culture, may be another reason IPV is minimized in the LGBT community, which pre-cludes many from seeking help from traditional IPV resources (e.g., shelters, community agencies, the legal system). These attitudes and behaviors are often based in heterosex-ism, the idea that heterosexuality is normative and thus superior to homosexuality. LGBT couples may internalize heterosexist ideas and thus feel responsible for protecting one another due to societal oppression and the resulting social isolation. When one part-ner is being abused, it is difficult to report for several reasons: (1) the abuser may threaten to "out" the abused if he or she discloses the IPV to anyone; (2) the abused may be fearful of disclosing sexual orientation in the process of disclosing the abuse; (3) the abusive partner may be the only source of support; (4) the abusive partner may share the same friends as the abused partner, and embarrassing the abuser may result in potentially losing the community in which the abused partner feels accepted for his or her sexual orientation; (5) the process of disclosure may reinforce or strengthen internalized homophobia in the abused partner; and (6) the desire to maintain the LGBT community's reputation for offering safety and advocating for equal rights (e.g., marriage, adoption) may outweigh the desire to assert there is "something wrong" in the community, such as IPV (Peterman & Dixon, 2003).

Taken together, these factors have contributed to a lack of resources for LGBT individuals. Lesbians seek help from friends, crisis counselors, relatives, police, religious advisors, and hotline/shelters in that order; heterosexual women rate shelters as the primary resource (Renzetti, 1992). Gay and bisexual men may have fewer resources than do lesbian and bisexual women. Few shelters accept gay and bisexual men due to the propensity toward aggression and homophobia of other male batterers who may be living in the shelter. Further, IPV survivors seeking services may be revictimized if their relationship is viewed as not being "real" or if they are subjected to other forms of homophobia and heterosexism. Those providing community resources are often placed in a difficult position: Since LGBT violence goes against the typical view of the causes and course of IPV, they are left to decide "who to believe" and thus who should receive assistance and who should be reprimanded. This creates many situations where victims are ignored, abusers are unintentionally allowed into similar shelters as those they abuse, and abusers are not prosecuted.

Further, the lack of a uniform definition of LGBT violence leads to the lack of legal protection. For example, Vermont is the only state with an IPV statute to protect same-sex couples. Approximately 12 states preclude gays and lesbians from legal protection, with 2 directly stating so. Sodomy laws in approximately 12 states prevent disclosure for many gay men because raising IPV essentially forces them to admit to a criminality (Peterman & Dixon, 2003). Additionally, abused lesbian women may feel it is difficult to hold violent women accountable and thus opt to keep the IPV secret (Griffin, 2008).

Disability Status

Another special population that has received some attention is women with physical, cognitive, or emotional disabilities. Controlling for race, ethnicity, age, and SES, women with disabilities are physically or sexually assaulted at a rate double that of those without disability (Fiduccia & Wolfe, 1999). A disability in either the victim or the perpetrator can be a risk factor for IPV, or the disability may be a result of IPV toward the individual.

Vulnerability and powerlessness are prevalent for this population, as they often depend on their intimate partners to assist them with activities of daily living, such as providing medication, bathing, dressing, and running errands. Thus, a partner could be considered abusive if he removes a battery from a wheelchair, withholds medication, demands a kiss or verbal expression of appreciation before a task, or engages in an unwanted sexual touch during bathing or dressing (Hassouneh-Phillips & Curry, 2002). Able-bodied women might not readily consider many of these acts abusive, as they do not experience them. Thus, women with disabilities are concerned not just with typical forms of abuse but also with those specific to disability accommodations.

Unfortunately, women with disabilities experience a higher risk of victimization than do able-bodied women. The risk of victimization increases if individuals experience multiple oppressions from racism and classism. When women with disabilities seek support, they often find there are inaccessible or insufficient shelters or other community services. Crisis counselors are strongly encouraged to ensure that agencies in which they work are prepared adequately for women with disabilities; this may include having physical items such as wheelchairs readily available or making referrals for physical health needs.

Dating Violence Among Adolescents and Young Adults

IPV begins early for many—sometimes with their first dating experiences. During the transition from adolescence to young adulthood, approximately 30% of adolescents experience some form of victimization (Halpern, Oslak, Young, Martin, & Kupper, 2001). Adolescents often witness and/or experience some form of domestic violence at home. They learn from these experiences that violence is a normal and "appropriate" outlet for conflict within intimate relationships, since the abuser seldom gets punished. By the time adolescents enter their first romantic relationship, ideas related to interpersonal skills, expectations, partner selection, pace of intimacy, and sexual behavior are well established. Thus, adolescents and young adults may be simultaneously witnessing IPV within the home and being abused in dating relationships, creating minimal outlets for support and making them less likely to report the victimization to others.

According to the national Youth Risk Behavior Survey, physical violence is similar across genders. Approximately 9.0% of male students and 9.3% of female students report experiencing dating violence in the form of being slapped, hit, or physically hurt by a partner (Centers for Disease Control and Prevention, 2005b). In a study of 2,320 high school students, a similar proportion of males and females reporting having been subjected to physical aggression by their dating partners (Cascardi, Avery-Leaf, O'Leary, & Slep, 1999). By early adulthood, many similarities between the genders disappear, with males becoming more physically aggressive than females. Approximately 33% of females in grades 10–12 and 20–30% of female college students report at least one incident of physical or sexual abuse (Berry, 2000).

The consequences of dating violence are great and include higher rates of eating disorders, substance abuse, depression, anxiety, somatization, and suicidal thoughts and

---

ACTIVITY 6.4
Raising Awareness About Adolescent Dating Violence

Unfortunately, dating violence is a problem that affects many individuals at an early age. When first beginning to explore dating relationships, many adolescents are unaware of what a healthy or unhealthy dating relationship looks like. Work individually or in groups to develop an awareness-raising brochure or poster that is developmentally appropriate for adolescents. Include information such as facts and figures on dating violence, how to recognize warning signs that a dating relationship may be unhealthy, and how to ask for help if they experience dating violence. Consider how you may use the brochure or poster you developed in your future counseling practice.

attempts (Ackard & Neumark-Sztainer, 2002; Amar & Gennaro, 2005; Holt & Espelage, 2005) as well as poor academic performance (Hanson, 2002). In addition, adolescent and young adult females who experience dating violence are more likely to be revictimized and experience marital violence. Both male and female dating violence survivors are more likely to engage in delinquent or risky behaviors (Giordano, Millhollin, Cernkovich, Pugh, & Rudolph, 1999; Hanson, 2002; Howard, Wang, & Yan, 2007).

THE CRISIS COUNSELOR'S RESPONSE TO IPV

Screening for IPV

Due to the prevalence of IPV, it is generally agreed that IPV screening should be universal. Just as crisis counselors assess for suicidal and homicidal ideation with every client, they should ask all clients, particularly female clients, directly about IPV. Most research on IPV screening focuses on assessment in doctors' offices and emergency rooms, since many IPV survivors require medical treatment for physical injury inflicted by an intimate partner but may not necessarily seek counseling to address the effects of IPV. Nevertheless, these studies provide important information for crisis counselors.

While acknowledging the need for intervention with IPV survivors, most health care providers fail to routinely screen for IPV (L. E. Tower, 2006; M. Tower, 2007). A primary barrier to universal IPV screening is the lack of knowledge of and training on how to ask about IPV, how to recognize symptoms that may indicate an individual is experiencing abuse, and how to respond if IPV is disclosed (Gerbert et al., 2000; L. E. Tower, 2006; M. Tower, 2007). Personal variables may also prevent health care professionals and crisis counselors from asking about IPV. For example, clinicians may have negative attitudes toward IPV survivors stemming from personal experiences with IPV or have prejudicial attitudes including racism, classism, ageism, and homophobia (L. E. Tower, 2006; M. Tower, 2007). Health care workers may also avoid screening for IPV due to fear for their own safety, fear of offending their patient, or perhaps because they do not view intervention in domestic affairs to be part of their health care responsibilities (M. Tower, 2007; Gerbert et al., 2000). Institutional and professional barriers to IPV screening, such as the perception of powerlessness to help IPV survivors due to insufficient community resources and the fear of marginalization by colleagues, are also important variables to consider (L. E. Tower, 2006). However, the multitude of reasons for not asking about IPV do not outweigh the argument for IPV screening. Screening can help prevent injury and literally help save the lives of individuals who suffer from partner abuse.

The first step in screening for IPV is to create a safe environment that is conducive to disclosure. Disclosing IPV can be a very difficult and painful process for survivors due to shame, embarrassment, and fear of being judged. Survivors may also fear losing their children or being further abused by their partner as a result of IPV disclosure (Kramer et al., 2004; Lutenbacher, Cohen, & Mitzel, 2003). Crisis counselors can indicate that it is safe to talk about IPV by placing posters and other IPV awareness materials in their office (Chang et al., 2005). The crisis counselor's interpersonal style can also help to create a safe atmosphere. For example, IPV survivors report that crisis counselors who smile, demonstrate care through empowering statements, reduce the power differential by using personal self-disclosure, don't appear to be rushed, are easily accessible, and are easier to trust and to talk about IPV (Battaglia, Finley, & Liebschutz, 2003;

Chang et al., 2005; Kramer et al., 2004). The single most important thing to remember about IPV screening is that crisis counselors should never ask about abuse in the presence of the client's partner; doing so may greatly increase the risk of harm to the client (Chang et al., 2005; Keller, 1996; Kramer et al., 2004; McCloskey & Grigsby, 2005).

Once you establish a safe atmosphere and develop rapport with your client, you should ask directly about IPV, gathering as many concrete and specific details as possible. During initial screening, you can ask the potential survivor if anyone is hurting them, who is hurting them, how arguments usually begin, details of the most recent incident of violence, how long the most recent incident lasted, and what happened when the incident was over (Keller, 1996; McCloskey & Grigsby, 2005). The client's IPV history is important as well, including the first and worst incidents of violence, past attempts at intervention by others (e.g., family, friends, neighbors, police, the legal system), and the role of mental health and substance abuse issues in the IPV (McCloskey & Grigsby, 2005). Crisis counselors are also advised to complete a lethality assessment whenever IPV is disclosed in order to determine the degree of urgency necessary in responding to the crisis, which may range from developing a safety plan with the survivor to seeking immediate police intervention and hospitalization. A lethality assessment includes questions about the severity of violence, other criminal behaviors of the abuser (e.g., assaults or harassment of others, previous criminal charges), failed past interventions (e.g., multiple calls made to 911; abuser ignores court orders; family, friends, and neighbors have tried to intervene, yet violence continues), obsessive or stalking behaviors, psychological risk factors (e.g., previous homicidal or suicidal threats or attempts, substance abuse issues, external life stressors, severe depression), perceived threats to the relationship (e.g., survivor planning to leave, separation or divorce, infidelity), access to weapons, and behaviors that prevent the survivor from accessing emergency resources. Throughout the process of IPV assessment, be mindful of the phrasing of IPV screening questions, and take care to ensure that you are not inadvertently conveying judgment or blame. Also, remember that survivors may initially deny that they are experiencing abuse. If this occurs, make sure to revisit questions about IPV in later sessions.

Response to IPV Disclosure

Since nearly all counselors will work with an IPV survivor at some point, you must be prepared to respond when a client reports being abused by a partner. Immediately following an IPV disclosure, it is critical for the crisis counselor to validate the survivor's experience and communicate that the survivor is not to blame for the abuse (Dienemann, Glass, & Hyman, 2005; Gerbert et al., 2000; Keller, 1996). Documentation that the client is experiencing IPV is also important. IPV survivors indicate that it is helpful for crisis counselors or health care workers to make notes about the disclosure of IPV and take pictures of physical injuries (Dienemann et al., 2005), which could later be used in court if the survivor chooses to take legal action.

Providing the survivor with resources and protection is another essential component of responding to an IPV crisis. Crisis counselors should have an extensive list of IPV resources available, including options for emergency shelter, transportation, food, child care, medical needs, mental health care, and legal aid. Crisis counselors may also consider providing a list of IPV resources to clients whether or not IPV is disclosed.

Some agencies place small cards printed with IPV crisis resources in the restroom so that survivors may anonymously take the information and hide it if necessary (Chang et al., 2005).

While crisis intervention is typically more directive than traditional counseling, crisis counselors should strive to empower IPV survivors by giving them as much control over their situations as possible (Dienemann et al., 2005). Finally, survivors indicate that it is helpful to be informed that even if they initially choose not to access IPV resources, they can return to the agency and receive assistance if they ever decide to do so.

Safety Planning

Safety planning involves working with an IPV survivor to create a strategy for establishing physical and emotional safety that incorporates available resources and existing barriers. The safety plan is tailored to the unique situation of each IPV survivor; therefore, gaining concrete and specific information about the survivor's experiences is essential. It is also important to emphasize that a safety plan in no way guarantees the safety of the IPV survivor (McCloskey & Grigsby, 2005).

Safety plans can be developed for clients who do not intend to leave the abusive partner as well as for clients who are seeking to leave the relationship. Crisis counselors should be careful not to recommend ending the relationship as the only way to establish safety. In fact, the risk of harm to an IPV survivor may increase following separation from an abusive partner. Postseparation violence involves the batterer's attempts to regain control over the abused partner and may include physical assault, rape, stalking, harassment, and even homicide (Humphreys & Thiara, 2003). Research on nonlethal postseparation

---

Intimate Partner Violence Shelters: Opportunities and Challenges

IPV shelters provide a safe haven for many abused women and their children. Not only do IPV shelters protect survivors from additional physical harm, but also they may be a place where emotional healing can begin. Shelter residents are often able to deeply connect with one another around their shared experiences. Shelter staff may provide much needed support and encouragement to survivors. Many IPV shelters also offer counseling services and provide survivors with comprehensive resources, including legal aid and assistance finding long-term housing and employment.

While IPV shelters are invaluable resources for many survivors, life in a shelter is certainly not stress free. Living in a shelter requires adherence to programmatic rules and regulations that may infringe on a survivor's sense of autonomy. In addition, survivors may not feel ready to address the emotional impact of their abuse, yet may be required to do so as part of the shelter program (Madsen, Blitz, McCorkle, & Panzer, 2003). Adjusting to a shared living environment may also present difficulty, particularly for survivors from cultural minority groups (Few, 2005). Finally, as a result of their traumatic experiences, some IPV survivors struggle with self-regulation and engage in behaviors such as verbal or physical altercations with shelter staff and residents or substance abuse (Madsen et al., 2003).

Working as a crisis counselor in an IPV shelter can also be stressful. For example, crisis counselors may experience secondary traumatization from exposure to survivors' experiences. Crisis counselors must be sure to practice self-care in order to avoid burning out or taking a blaming attitude toward survivors. Crisis counselors may also experience the stress of dual roles (Madsen et al., 2003). For example, a counselor may deeply empathize with a survivor during an individual or group session and then later be required to enforce shelter rules (e.g., imposing a penalty for not completing a required chore, dismissing from the shelter for substance abuse).

ACTIVITY 6.5
Create an IPV Resource Manual

Work individually or in groups to compile a list of IPV resources that are available in your community. Consider the multitude of needs of someone who is leaving an abusive partner (e.g., shelter, food, transportation, clothing, child care, employment assistance, legal aid, medical care) as well as the barriers to accessing resources that a survivor may encounter (e.g., having no Internet access, having to sneak out of the house to go to counseling, having limited financial resources). Gather specific information about how to access these community resources (e.g., hours of operation, cost of services, criteria for assistance). If possible, obtain written materials or brochures from community organizations that could be provided to IPV survivors. What was your experience like when trying to gather information? Were resources hard to identify? Were the agencies that you contacted helpful? How might your experiences identifying resources be similar to or different from those of an IPV survivor in crisis?

violence among heterosexual married couples indicates that the prevalence of IPV is nine times greater among women who are separated from their abusive husbands than among women who are still living with their husbands; IPV is four times more prevalent among divorced women than among women who are still married (Brownridge et al., 2008). Other research indicates that an estimated 76% of women experience some form of post-separation violence (Humphreys & Thiara, 2003) and that women are at the greatest risk of being killed by an abusive partner at the point of separation or after leaving the abusive partner (Wilson & Daly, 1992).

In order for the survivor to leave the abusive partner as safely as possible, the crisis counselor and the survivor should work together to ensure that adequate personal and community resources are in place to provide protection and safety for the survivor. For clients who are not ready or who do not plan to leave the abusive partner, the goal of safety planning is harm reduction. For example, the IPV survivor may strategize to avoid rooms with no outside doors that contain weapons (e.g., bathrooms, kitchens) when they anticipate violence (McCloskey & Grigsby, 2005). Other ideas for safety planning include developing a code word or signal to let friends and neighbors know when they need help, creating a signal for children when they need to stay in their bedrooms or flee to a neighbor's house for safety, and hiding a bag filled with essential items (e.g., clothes, cash, documents, extra sets of keys) in case the survivor needs to leave the house hurriedly.

Safety plans may also include self-care techniques that can help relieve some of the emotional pain caused by the abuse. For example, survivors report taking a quiet walk, listening to music, and reading self-care books helped in coping with IPV (McLeod et al., in press). The key to safety planning is creativity in mobilizing community and personal resources.

Addressing the Emotional Impact of IPV

The emotional consequences of IPV are equally as devastating as the physical consequences. High rates of depression and low self-esteem are common among IPV survivors (Holtzworth-Munroe, Bates, Smultzer, & Sandin, 1997), and IPV is a major predictor of female drug and alcohol abuse (Clark & Foy, 2000). Many IPV survivors experience symptoms of Posttraumatic Stress Disorder (PTSD), including a reexperiencing of the trauma (e.g., intrusive recollections, nightmares, flashbacks), avoidance/numbing (e.g., restricted range of affect, anhedonia, social withdrawal, inability to recall aspects of the trauma), and increased arousal (e.g., hypervigilance, exaggerated startle response, difficult falling or staying asleep) (Riger, Raja, & Camacho, 2002; Walker, 2006). Walker (2006) argues that, in addition to the symptoms traditionally associated with PTSD, IPV survivors often experience a cluster of symptoms referred to as battered woman syndrome, which includes disrupted interpersonal relationships, difficulties with body image/somatic concerns, and sexual or intimacy problems.

When working with IPV survivors, it is essential to consider their trauma history in constructing a treatment plan or making a diagnosis. Unfortunately, many survivors are misdiagnosed and prescribed inappropriate medications by mental health care providers who fail to account for the effects of IPV. Survivors may be empowered by learning that the symptoms they are experiencing are a normal response to a traumatic event (McLeod et al., in press).

CASE STUDY 6.2

Counseling an IPV Survivor: Melinda's Journey

Melinda, a 25-year-old, middle-class, African-American female, first came to counseling for depression. During the initial intake interview, Melinda reported experiencing difficulty sleeping, frequent crying spells, low self-esteem, and feelings of hopelessness. Melinda's counselor, Candace, screened for suicidal ideation, homicidal ideation, and IPV as a routine part of the initial interview. Melinda denied suicidal and homicidal ideation and said that she had never been abused by her current boyfriend. At the end of the initial session, Candace provided Melinda with a packet of materials that she distributes to all new clients, which included a pamphlet on IPV.

Over the next two sessions, Melinda and Candace developed a strong rapport. During her third session, Melinda tearfully disclosed that her live-in boyfriend sometimes pushes or hits her when he has been drinking. Candace listened empathically to Melinda and let her know that the abuse was not her fault and that she believed her. After Melinda's disclosure, Candace asked for more information about the abuse, including how arguments usually begin, details of the most recent incident of violence, and Melinda's history of experience with IPV. Melinda reported that the last time her boyfriend hit her was a week ago, when he came home drunk from a party. Melinda sustained a split lip but did not require stitches.

Candace also completed a lethality assessment and determined that Melinda's boyfriend had never threatened to kill her, did not have a criminal record, and did not have a gun in the house. Melinda stated that she had never feared for her life when her boyfriend became abusive. She indicated that she did not want to break up with her boyfriend and that she did not think the abuse was serious enough to report to the police. Candace respected Melinda's autonomy and provided her with additional educational materials about IPV and information on 24-hour IPV crisis resources that Melinda could use in case of an emergency. Since Melinda reported that her boyfriend typically drank every weekend, Candace scheduled another appointment with Melinda before the upcoming weekend in order to develop a safety plan. Melinda and Candace collaboratively developed the following safety plan in order to minimize the risk and impact of IPV:

1. Plan to be away from the house when boyfriend comes home drunk.
2. If boyfriend comes home drunk unexpectedly, stay away from the bathroom and kitchen.
3. Pack and hide an emergency bag with clothes, cash, and an extra set of keys in case of the need to flee the house quickly.
4. Program IPV crisis hotline number into cell phone.

Melinda and Candace also discussed ideas for building coping resources, including engaging in self-care activities like reading empowerment books and joining a women's support group at church.

Over the next several months, Candace and Melinda met once a week for counseling. They continued to discuss and evaluate Melinda's safety. Despite her efforts to avoid physical violence from her boyfriend, the incidents of abuse became more frequent over time. Melinda had now sustained several injuries, including a broken arm and a broken rib. A turning point occurred when Melinda learned that she was eight weeks' pregnant with her first child. Melinda decided that she did not want to raise a child in an abusive home. She was ready to leave. Candace and Melinda discussed the risks associated with leaving an abusive partner and tips for ensuring a safe escape. Together, they decided that an IPV shelter was the best option, since Melinda had no trusted family or friends in the area. Candace arranged for transportation to the shelter straight from her office and waited with Melinda until help arrived.

BATTERER INTERVENTION

IPV response has two aspects, survivor advocacy and batterer intervention; both are valid attempts to end partner abuse. One model of attending to the needs of both IPV survivors and batterers is a coordinated community response, which involves the collaboration of local organizations in developing a method of addressing IPV incidents. Response teams are formed from representatives of local businesses, churches, law enforcement agencies, and mental health care professionals. These teams meet periodically to refine and process responses to IPV crises, sponsor training sessions, and develop protocols for IPV intervention. These response teams strive to create an infrastructure that will facilitate systems-level and ultimately societal-level change (Salazar, Emshoff, Baker, & Crowley, 2007). In addition to the efforts of community organizations, many states have developed standards to ensure that batterer intervention programs hire qualified staff, follow a structured curriculum, and have policies and procedures for referral, admission, and dismissal of program participants.

Batterer intervention programs have three primary goals: ensuring the safety of IPV survivors, stopping future acts of partner violence, and increasing offenders' accountability for their behavior. In addition, batterer intervention programs strive to

ACTIVITY 6.6
Crisis Counselor Self-Care

Working with survivors of IPV can vicariously traumatize crisis counselors; therefore, self-care is essential. Start practicing self-care now. Make a list of self-care activities that you find personally renewing. Plan to incorporate at least one self-care activity into each day of the upcoming week. Keep a brief journal about your self-care experiences.

help offenders increase healthy expression of emotions, improve communication and anger management skills, decrease control in relationships, recognize the dynamics of abuse and the effects of violence on children, and understand social factors that condone power and control (Domestic Abuse Project, 1993).

Safety

The primary goal of batterer intervention programs is to ensure the safety of the abused partner and any children who may be involved. Steps to ensuring safety include assessment of the resources that are available to IPV survivors, assessment of the severity and repetition of violent incidents, and assessment of the impact on children who were exposed to IPV. Depending on the aforementioned factors, offenders may need to reside separately from the survivors. If law enforcement has been notified and an arrest has been made, incarceration of the offender may provide temporary safety.

Cessation of Violence

A second goal of batterer intervention programs is stopping all forms of violence, including verbal, emotional, physical, and sexual abuses. One of the first steps toward this goal is acknowledgment of one's violent behavior. Such an acknowledgment means discarding denial (e.g., "I did not do it"), minimizing (e.g., "I only hit her"), and blaming (e.g., "She should have been home on time"). It also means accepting that threats, coercion, and emotional abuses—the types of violence where there is no physical contact—qualify as IPV.

Researchers have investigated which aspects of batterer intervention programs are most helpful in stopping violence. In one study, participants reported that developing supportive relationships with other program participants and the facilitators of the batterer intervention group enabled them to successfully address their violence. In addition, participants reported that learning specific strategies for violence cessation (e.g., taking a time-out, sharing feelings rather than holding feelings inside) was helpful (Rosenberg, 2003). Research also indicates that participation in a pro-feminist, cognitive-behavioral batterer intervention group may lead to a positive change in attitudes toward women and abusive behavior (Schmidt et al., 2007). For example, batterers who participated in this program were less likely to endorse statements in support of IPV (e.g., "Smashing things is not abusive, just venting") and more likely to endorse statements in support of nonviolent relationships (e.g., "I cannot be provoked into being violent").

Accountability

The third goal of batterer intervention is increasing individual accountability for IPV in the form of accepting responsibility for one's behavior. Simply saying "I'm sorry," especially if that's been said on multiple occasions, is not enough. Developing alternatives to battering is an essential component of increasing accountability. One alternative strategy involves understanding and subsequently changing negative self-talk to positive self-talk. Negative self-talk involves destructive comments made when challenged with an uncomfortable or threatening situation. For example, a batterer might say, "I am so mad that my partner does not have dinner ready." The idea is to change this statement to something more constructive, such as "Dinner is not ready yet; perhaps I can help." A second task in becoming accountable is to learn to recognize triggers or cues leading to violent behavior. Triggers can be words, phrases, or statements that either the individual or his/her partner uses (e.g., profanity, degrading comments); situations that typically create arguments (e.g., payday, drinking/drug use); and physiological changes (e.g., muscle tension, headaches, increased blood pressure/pulse). The identification of triggers enables IPV offenders to be responsible for initiating behaviors that will decrease their level of anxiety, frustration, and anger and thereby prevent any further acts of IPV.

THEORIES/APPROACHES TO BATTERER TREATMENT

Counselors who work with IPV perpetrators may use a wide variety of counseling theories and approaches. Some of the theories most commonly applied to batterer intervention include power and control theory (Domestic Abuse Project, 1993), moral development theory (Kohlberg, 1984), and feminist-informed cognitive-behavioral theories.

Power and Control Theory

The predominant model that influences both survivor and offender services is the power and control theory (Domestic Abuse Project, 1993). Essentially, this theory states that IPV occurs when individuals in intimate relationships influence their partner's behavior by controlling them with violence or the use of power. Violence may include verbal taunts or threats, psychologically demeaning statements or actions, physical assaults, and sexual violence.

VIOLENCE IS A LEARNED BEHAVIOR According to power and control theory, violence is a learned behavior. There is no genetic predisposition for violence or existence of a violence gene; instead, people learn violence from many sources, including the media and community dysfunction but primarily from parents or guardians.

VIOLENCE IS A CHOICE A second principle of power and control theory is that people choose to be violent. Violence occurs because people are aware of a situation, understand potential rewards and consequences, and then choose to be violent. Sometimes people choose violent behavior because they are not aware of other behavioral options. Similarly, people might be unconsciously aware of behavioral alternatives but are not able to access these behaviors in a crisis situation. To that end, one can choose to "unlearn" violence through training in recognizing pending violence and in replacing violent behaviors with positive coping strategies.

ENDING VIOLENCE IS A PROCESS   Power and control theory also asserts that when the generational cycle of violence is understood and paired with nonviolent alternative behaviors, violence can be stopped. People who are seeking to end their violent behavior eventually begin to comprehend that learning to be nonviolent is a process. An individual does not awake one morning and vow to be nonviolent. There are occasional setbacks that require additional learning.

Moral Development Theory

Some batterer intervention programs apply Kohlberg's (1976) theory of moral reasoning to individuals that batter. According to Kohlberg, moral development occurs over time and in stages, moving from simple to higher-order moral reasoning. Kohlberg's (1984) moral development model is organized into three levels: preconventional, conventional, and postconventional.

PRECONVENTIONAL LEVEL   The majority of children under nine years of age, some adolescents, and most juvenile and adult criminal offenders operate at the preconventional level, which is characterized by moral decision making based on being afraid of authority, avoiding punishment, or satisfying personal needs. An IPV offender at the preconventional level of development may attend IPV treatment to avoid going to jail.

CONVENTIONAL LEVEL   The majority of adolescents and adults function at the conventional level of moral development, at which people behave so as to win approval and meet the expectations of their immediate group or to uphold laws for their own sake. Right behavior is equated with doing one's duty and abiding by the social order (Rich & DeVitis, 1985). A batterer at the conventional level of moral development may make statements such as these: "I don't argue with my wife because she'll get upset" (abiding by the conduct of the social order) or "I admit I hit her because she was cheating; I have to accept the penalties just as anyone else" (taking responsibility for a wrong act).

POSTCONVENTIONAL LEVEL   A minority of adults reach the postconventional level of development, which is characterized by a belief in equality and mutual obligation within the democratic order and by comprehension of the relativism of personal values. In group settings, procedural rules are followed in reaching consensus. Individual principles of conscience are comprehensive and universal, and rightness is determined by conscience in accord with ethical principles (Rich & DeVitis, 1985). A statement such as "I am speaking to groups of adolescents about how to treat a partner with respect; I encourage other men to seek help when they are mistreating their partners" would be characteristic of an IPV offender who has reached the postconventional level of moral reasoning.

Empirical evidence suggests that moral development is universal among people of diverse cultural backgrounds (Kohlberg, 1984), and moral education programs have shown to be effective in raising levels of moral reasoning (Buttell, 2001; Rest & Navarez,

1994), which may result in reduced criminal activity (Kohlberg & Candee, 1984; MacPhail, 1989). Batterer intervention programs using a moral education approach do not focus solely on Kohlberg's theory but may educate participants about the levels of moral development, present them with moral dilemmas, and structure discussions that allow them to challenge one another. For example, a participant would be challenged if he described himself to the members of the group as being contrite about his abusive behaviors and wanting to reconcile with his partner (a conventional level of moral development response), but then told them he was there because his probation officer told him to attend (a preconventional response).

Attachment Theory

According to attachment theory, excessive interpersonal dependency among abusive men is a consequence of insecure attachment in childhood (Dutton, 1995; Holtzworth-Monroe et al., 1997). In brief, attachment theory proposes that the overall quality of the infant-caretaker relationship during infancy and early childhood is both the primary determinant of dependent traits in adulthood (Ainsworth, 1969) and a model for later interpersonal relationships (Bowlby, 1980). Regarding the development of excessive interpersonal dependency among batterers, Dutton has argued that battered mothers cannot adequately attend to the demands of the attachment process, while simultaneously attempting to negotiate a hostile and dangerous home environment. Consequently, children in this situation become insecurely attached and in adulthood exhibit excessive dependency on their partners (Dutton, 1995; Holtzworth-Monroe et al., 1997; Murphy, Meyer, & O'Leary, 1994). In addition, people with battering issues have difficulty initiating and maintaining an emotionally supportive relationship. As a result, they desire closeness with their partners but, given their inability to achieve emotional closeness, engage in violent and controlling behaviors to ensure physical closeness instead (Murphy et al., 1994). Similar to moral development batterer intervention programs, a batterer program based on attachment theory does not focus entirely on attachment issues. However, some sessions teach participants about attachment theory and the short- and long-term effects of insecure attachment.

Feminist-Informed Cognitive-Behavioral Theory

Most treatment programs for batterers employ a feminist-informed cognitive-behavioral treatment approach (Bennett & Williams, 2001). Feminist theory asserts that IPV involves a wide range of behaviors aimed at maintaining an imbalance of power in a relationship, IPV is a violation of human rights, and IPV is supported and maintained by sexism and homophobia (Schmidt et al., 2007). Many types of cognitive and behavioral therapies (e.g., Ellis's (1962) rational emotive behavior therapy, Glasser's (1965) reality therapy) operate under the tenets of feminist theory used in batterer intervention.

CHALLENGES IN BATTERER INTERVENTION

Counselors who work with IPV perpetrators encounter numerous challenges, including the underreporting of IPV incidents, the need to distinguish batterer intervention programs from anger management programs, and limited financial resources.

PERSONAL REFLECTION
Working in Batterer Intervention

I was the director of a batterer intervention program for almost seven years. While my body sometimes cringed at statements men would make, I also saw the trauma that some male offenders experienced as a result of growing up with inappropriate or absent male role models and the interconnection of substance use and IPV. My experiences raised my awareness about the lack of equality inherent in batterer intervention. Many of the batterers that chose to attend our program in order to avoid incarceration were either unemployed or working in blue-collar jobs. IPV offenders with higher income levels were often able to hire an attorney to dispute the criminal charges at the time of the incident. I also saw the lack of consistency from one jurisdiction to another and even from one judge or probation officer to another in terms of willingness to understand the general mission of batterer programs and to collaborate with our program. To this end, I know there are pockets of places that are committed to seeing that something is being done to end IPV. Overall, there is much work that still needs to be done regarding educating people about IPV, which is a social crisis that is greatly unknown and misunderstood, except to those who experience it. ~ *John Muldoon*

Underreporting of IPV Incidents

One of the biggest challenges regarding batterer intervention is that most program participants are court mandated. In order for a judge or probation officer to refer an IPV offender to treatment, someone must first report an IPV incident. Survivors may choose not to report IPV or not to seek community-based assistance for many reasons, including feelings of shame and embarrassment, a desire to protect the abusive partner and preserve the relationship (Dutton, Goodman, & Bennett, 1999; Gondolf & Fisher, 1988), the belief that assistance is not needed or is not useful (Fugate et al., 2005; Gondolf, 2002), a lack of resources (e.g., money, transportation, child care, insurance) (Fugate et al., 2005; Gondolf, 2002), and fear of retaliation from the abusive partner (Fugate et al., 2005). Although many of these reasons are valid, if an IPV incident is not reported, batterer intervention is nearly impossible.

IPV and Anger Management

The misconception that anger management problems and IPV are synonymous terms is another challenge to batterer intervention. Persons with an anger management problem are unable to control their temper regardless of whom or what they become angry at or when they become angry. Persons with a battering problem are able to control their anger when it is advantageous to do so, and then they impose that anger on an intimate partner. For example, consider the person who becomes angry at his supervisor at work for not receiving a deserved promotion. If he has an anger problem, he will probably express his anger inappropriately to his supervisor at that time. If he has a battering problem, he will withhold his anger in the moment and later direct that anger at his intimate partner.

The distinction between anger management programs and batterer programs is important when marketing a batterer program. Generally, it would be better to market batterer programs to look more like anger management programs because anger management programs are more socially acceptable. Many participants are reticent to enroll in a batterer program, believing it implies that they are chronic offenders who leave bruises on their partners or beat their partners to the point of requiring medical attention. Similarly, donors might not want to give money to a batterer program, believing it could reflect negatively on the organization or business. The distinction between anger management programs and batterer intervention programs is also important because some states and jurisdictions refer offenders specifically to batterer intervention programs and others do not. If there is not a specific referral, individuals are highly likely to enroll in an anger management program that they believe can be completed in less time, costs less money, and may be covered by insurance. However, it is doubtful that traditional anger management programs cover the IPV issues that need to be addressed to prevent the reoccurrence of partner abuse.

Financial Resources

The financial aspect of batterer intervention is also a challenge. A significant number of batterer programs charge fees for services in order to sustain the program's existence. Most federal and state monies for IPV go to battered women's programs—and rightly so. However, if we do not intervene with batterers and reeducate them, IPV will likely never end. Therefore, it is left to the batterer program staff to solicit referrals from judges and probation officers. Unfortunately, potential referral sources often refuse to make appropriate referrals to batterer intervention programs due to their cost. Some judges and probation officers do not want to require someone to attend a program for a minimum of 26 weeks (or sometimes less in some states) and pay money (generally $20 to $30 per session) because of one reported incident of IPV. Ironically, many IPV offenders are bailed out of jail for about as much money as it would cost to attend a batterer intervention program.

CASE STUDY 6.3

An Ethical Dilemma

Imagine you are a counselor who is leading groups in a batterer intervention program for men. One afternoon a woman whose partner is enrolled in the program calls to ask what the program is teaching about violence. During the course of your conversation, the woman discloses that her partner, the program's client, threatened her the night before. Consult the *ACA Code of Ethics* (American Counseling Association, 2005) and discuss the dilemma.

Discussion Questions

What additional questions do you ask?

What referrals do you offer?

What, if anything, do you do with this information, knowing that confronting your client might cause additional violence to the partner?

Summary

IPV is a crisis all too commonly experienced. As a result, crisis counselors must be prepared to respond to the needs of IPV survivors. Understanding the cycle of violence is a critical first step for crisis counselors. The cycle of violence consists of the tension-building phase, the acute battering incident, and the honeymoon phase which is characterized by contrite, loving behavior. It is also important for crisis counselors to examine their beliefs about why IPV survivors stay in relationships with abusive partners. In this chapter, two explanations for staying with an abusive partner were offered: learned helplessness theory and the ecological theory of IPV.

Common crisis issues for IPV survivors were highlighted, including attending to physical injury, establishing immediate safety, and deciding whether or not to report the IPV to the police. When addressing IPV crises, crisis counselors should strive to empower survivors to problem solve effectively and respect survivors' autonomy as much as possible. When addressing IPV in racial and ethnic minority and LGBT communities, crisis counselors must be aware of the compounded effects of IPV on these populations due to oppression stemming from racism, classism, and homophobia. In addition, issues specific to female-to-male violence, dating violence, and violence against a disabled partner must also be considered.

This chapter discussed barriers to IPV screening and argued that due to the prevalence of IPV, universal screening is necessary. IPV screening includes gathering concrete and specific details about the client's IPV history and conducting a lethality assessment in order to determine the degree of urgency that is required in responding to the IPV crisis. When IPV is disclosed, the crisis counselor should validate the survivor's experience, document that IPV is occurring, and provide resources and continued support to the survivor. A specific component of IPV response is safety planning, which involves constructing a detailed strategy for reducing harm caused by the abusive partner based on the resources available to the survivor and the barriers to accessing these resources. Finally, when responding to IPV, the crisis counselor should consider the emotional consequences of abuse and be careful not to pathologize a normal response to the trauma of IPV.

Lastly, various aspects of batterer intervention were discussed. The goals of batterer intervention programs include ensuring the safety of IPV survivors, stopping future violence, and increasing the batterers' accountability for their behavior. Batterer intervention programs are based on power and control theory, moral development theory, attachment theory, and feminist-informed cognitive-behavioral theories. Common challenges encountered in batterer intervention include the underreporting of IPV, the confusion surrounding the differences in anger management problems and battering behavior, and limited financial resources.

7 Sexual Assault and Sexual Abuse

Carrie Wachter and Robin Lee

PREVIEW

Sexual assault and child sexual abuse are two of the most underreported crimes, with survivors facing a number of potential physical, psychological, cognitive, behavioral, and emotional consequences. Crisis counselors who work with survivors of sexual assault and child sexual abuse need to be aware of the multitude of challenges these individuals face, best practices for treatment, and support services available in the local community. In this chapter, sexual assault and child sexual abuse will be defined, signs and symptoms described, treatment interventions discussed, and guidelines for working with law enforcement and child protective services personnel provided. In addition, the final portion of this chapter addresses sexual offenders, their patterns of behavior, and common treatment options.

SEXUAL ASSAULT

According to the Rape, Abuse, and Incest National Network (RAINN, 2008b), a sexual assault occurs every two minutes in the United States. Within one year, slightly more than 230,000 people are victims of rape, attempted rape, or sexual assault. According to the Federal Bureau of Investigation (FBI), in 2005 approximately 93,000 forcible rapes were reported, which constitutes 6% of all violent crimes (i.e., murder and nonnegligent manslaughter, forcible rape, robbery, and aggravated assault) reported. Although instances of rape and sexual assault have declined by more than 60% since 1993, rape and sexual assault are still the most underreported crimes, with more than half of all instances not reported.

The women's movement was responsible for first drawing attention to sexual assault in the late 1960s and early 1970s (Largen, 1985). Women began to gather in informal consciousness-raising groups in communities to discuss problems they were facing, including experiences with sexual assault. Because these women had remained mostly silent until this point, it became evident that this was a problem that needed attention. In the 1970s, the National Organization for Women (NOW) drew attention to the issue of sexual assault by developing rape task forces, which were designed to investigate and document the problems rape victims experienced in their communities. Based on this documentation, these task forces began advocating for change in public policies and for change in social institutions, including court systems, public education, and law enforcement agencies.

In the 1970s, a network of NOW, the National Organization for Victim Assistance (NOVA), was also formed, which led to the development of the National Coalition Against Sexual Assault (NCASA). In 1975, Brownmiller published *Against Our Will*, which also brought attention to the issue of rape and sexual assault. Later, in the 1980s, attention was given to acquaintance rape after an article on campus sexual assault was published in *Ms.* magazine (Warshaw, 1988). This article, based on research conducted by Koss, challenged the myth that stranger rape was the most common form of sexual assault. In 1994, the *Violence Against Women Act* (VAWA) was passed. VAWA was the first federal legislation that focused specifically on violent crimes (including sexual assault) specifically committed against women and children (Roe, 2004). VAWA was reauthorized in 1999 and more recently in 2005.

PREVALENCE OF SEXUAL ASSAULT

In the United States, 1 in 6 women and 1 in 33 men are victims of sexual assault (Tjaden & Thoennes, 2000). According to RAINN (2008a), over 17 million women have been victims of rape or sexual assault. It is estimated that between 14% and 20% of women are at risk of being a victim of a sexual assault in a lifetime (Kilpatrick & Resnick, 1993; Koss, 1993; Tjaden & Thoennes, 2000). According to the 2003 National Crime Victimization Survey (U.S. Department of Justice, Bureau of Justice Statistics [USDOJBJS], 2008), 90% of rape survivors were female. In addition, women with a history of rape before the age of 18 years were two times as likely to be raped when they were adults.

Statistics reveal little difference between Whites and persons of color in prevalence of rape or sexual assault (Tjaden & Thoennes, 2000). However, when the statistics of the sexual assaults of people of color are examined more closely, they reveal that American Indian and Alaska Native women were more likely to report having experienced rape, sexual assault, or stalking than were Caucasian, African-American, Hispanic-American, Asian-American, or Pacific Islander women.

DEFINITIONS AND TERMS RELATED TO SEXUAL ASSAULT

According to the U.S. Department of Justice (USDOJBJS, 2008), sexual assault is defined as an attack or attempted attack involving unwanted sexual contact, either forcibly or nonforcibly. An attack does not have to be completed in order to be considered a sexual assault. Also, a sexual assault consists of both forcible attacks and attacks where consent is not or cannot be given (e.g., due to intoxication, being below the age of legal consent, being mentally incapacitated). A forcible sexual assault may be violent. Forcible sexual assaults are frequently reported in the media and are easily identified and agreed on. However, nonforcible sexual assault is less understood and identifiable. Nonforcible sexual assault occurs when the person attacked lacks the capacity to give consent. Individuals who may lack the capacity to give consent include minors, people with mental disabilities, and people who may be incapacitated due to intoxication. In such cases, the diminished capacity of the individual makes consent impossible. A final factor in defining sexual assault is the types of contact that can occur, which can include grabbing, fondling, exhibitionism, verbal threats, and penetration.

Rape is often considered a specific category of sexual assault. Rape is defined as forcible sexual intercourse, perpetrated by either psychological coercion or physical force (USDOJBJS, 2008). In many states, penetration is an act that distinguishes rape from other types of sexual assault. Penetration can occur vaginally, anally, or orally with either a person's body part or an object. While these definitions are typically standard, terms may vary from state to state.

Definitions and Types of Rape

In the following sections, different types of rape are discussed. First, acquaintance rape is presented, followed by a discussion of three types of rape defined by Groth (2001).

ACQUAINTANCE RAPE   One of the most prevalent acts within the area of sexual assault and rape is acquaintance rape. This term has evolved over the past several decades from what was once described as date rape. This semantic change helps distinguish sexual assault and/or rape that occurs between people who are in an intimate or dating relationship from sexual assault and/or rape that occurs between people who are not (see Chapter 6, Intimate Partner Violence). The term *acquaintance* indicates that while the victim may know the assailant, the victim is not necessarily in an intimate relationship with the perpetrator. Although acquaintance rape occurs within the general population, it is most prevalent on college campuses. According to RAINN (2008a), females in early adulthood are four times more likely to be sexually assaulted than females in other age groups. Shockingly, few of these rapes are reported. According to a report published by the National Institute of Justice, fewer than 5% of rapes, either completed or attempted, that occurred among college-aged females were reported to law enforcement (Fisher, Cullen, & Turner, 2000). This report, *The Sexual Victimization of College Women*, found that more than half of college-aged females surveyed limit the people they share these experiences with to friends, often not reporting the experiences to family members or campus officials. Koss, Gidycz, and Wisniewski (1987) found that 42% of college-aged rape victims had not revealed the assault to anyone. Fisher et al. also found that 9 in 10 women knew their attackers, who included boyfriends, ex-boyfriends, classmates, friends, co-workers, or other acquaintances. Four main factors emerged that increased the risk of college-aged women being a victim of a sexual assault and/or rape: (1) frequent intoxication to the point of incapacitation, (2) single status, (3) previous sexual victimizations, and (4) residing on campus.

When addressing acquaintance rape on college campuses, education is a primary focus. According to Franiuk (2007), college students had difficulty identifying situations as sexual assaults, even when these assaults met legal definitions. In this study, students were more likely to label the incident as a sexual assault when physical force was present or the victim was drugged. When consent was at issue, including incidents involving self-intoxication, however, students had more difficulty identifying incidents of sexual assault. In order to address college students' inability to correctly identify ambiguous situations as sexual assault, many college campuses conduct awareness weeks aimed at providing education on the subject. For detailed guidelines on conducting a campuswide prevention campaign, see Lee, Caruso, Goins, and Southerland (2003).

Groth (2001) defines rape as a "pseudosexual act, complex and multidetermined, but addressing issues of hostility (anger) and control (power) more than passion (sexuality)" (p. 2). Sex is present in a rape but becomes the method by which aggression is expressed. Groth developed three basic patterns of rape: (1) power rape, (2) anger rape, and (3) sadistic rape. Power rapes account for the majority of rapes committed (55%), while anger rapes account for 40%, and sadistic rapes account for 5%.

POWER RAPE   The power rape, the most common type of rape, is one in which "sexuality becomes an expression of conquest" (Groth, 2001, p. 13). Power is the ultimate form of gratification for the rapist. Victims are viewed as possessions that are obtained through sex. Having sexual intercourse with the victim is the goal rather than only achieving power and control. Unlike anger or sadistic rapists, the power rapist may use only the amount of force necessary to subdue his victim. Methods used to subdue the victim may include verbal threats (telling the victim that she will be hurt if she does not cooperate), intimidation using a weapon, and brief physical violence when the victim does not cooperate. Victims may often be kidnapped and held captive, subjected to repeated assaults.

ANGER RAPE   In the anger rape, the sexual encounter is considered a hostile act, often leading to physical brutality (Groth, 2001). The force used in the rape may exceed what is necessary to subdue the victim and achieve the goal of sexual penetration. The perpetrator attacks the victim, often exhibiting strong forms of violence (e.g., grabbing, hitting, beating, tearing clothes). This type of attack may take two forms: (1) a surprise attack on the victim, catching the victim off guard, and (2) a manipulated approach during which the perpetrator demonstrates a charisma and confidence to make the victim feel secure, only to change, suddenly becoming angry and aggressive. Anger rapes are typically short in nature, with the primary objectives of hurting, humiliating, and demeaning the victim.

SADISTIC RAPE   The sadistic rape, the most brutal and least common of the types identified by Groth (2001), is an act in which anger and power are eroticized. This type of rape integrates sexuality and aggression to form a "single psychological experience known as sadism" (p. 44). The main goal of the sadistic rapist is to achieve sexual gratification through inflicting pain. The assault may be a bizarre encounter, often including bondage or types of ritualistic incidents such as washing her body, dressing a certain way, burning, or biting. Parts of the victim's body other than the sex organs may become the focus of injury by the rapist, and foreign objects may be used to penetrate the victim. Homicide may be the end result of the encounter, even leading to necrophilia (i.e., sex with dead bodies). Victims' bodies may be mutilated either during the act or after they are dead. Sadistic rapes are typically premeditated, with the rapist often preying on victims regarded as promiscuous.

ACTIVITY 7.2

Interviewing Activity

Determine if your community has an agency that specifically deals with victims of sexual assault. Request an interview with an agency official to obtain answers to these questions: What services are provided to victims in the community? Who provides these services? How can victims access these services?

Rape Myths

One reason sexual assault is one of the most underreported crimes may be the social stigma of being a sexual assault victim. For many years, myths about sexual assault were commonly accepted, but with continued research and awareness raising, many of these myths have been dispelled. Some of the more common myths about rape and sexual assault include the following:

- *Myth #1: Rape is about sex.* Rape is typically about the perpetrator's need to exert power and control over another individual, with sex as the weapon of choice.
- *Myth #2: Victims of rape deserve to be raped due to their appearance or their neglect of safety issues.* Although sexual assault and rape awareness have improved over the years, many individuals still believe that victims are to blame for their assault. Some may believe that victims incite a rapist because of provocative dress, appearance, or behavior. Others may blame the victim if they perceive that the victim did not take appropriate safety precautions to guard against an attack. As discussed later in this chapter, sexual predators will often rape someone with little or no cause to do so—regardless of how a person dresses or behaves.
- *Myth #3: Victims of sexual assault often make false reports based on revenge.* According to statistics from the FBI's Uniform Crime Reporting Program (2005), just under 5,000 of the 90,518 forcible rapes reported in the United States in 2006 were determined to be unfounded—either false or baseless complaints. This constitutes 5.4% of forcible rapes reported in 2006.
- *Myth #4: Only strangers lurking in dark alleys commit sexual assaults.* According to the U.S. Department of Justice (USDOJBJS, 2008), approximately 65% of all sexual assaults and/or rapes were committed by nonstrangers; 35% were committed by strangers. Sexual perpetrators are no longer thought of as mentally ill sociopaths who victimize strangers. Those who sexually assault others come from diverse socioeconomic, racial, geographic, and educational backgrounds.

EFFECTS OF SEXUAL ASSAULT

In 1974, Burgess and Holmstrom first coined the term *rape trauma syndrome* to describe the cluster of symptoms reported (see Table 7.1) by women who were raped (Burgess, 1985). Burgess, a psychiatric nurse, and Holmstrom, a sociologist, conducted research with women who presented in the emergency room after having experienced a rape. Burgess and Holmstrom described two distinct phases of women's response to sexual assault: the acute phase and the reorganization phase. During the acute phase, the survivor experienced a heightened stress level, lasting from several days to multiple weeks.

TABLE 7.1 Symptoms of Rape Trauma Syndrome

- Continuing anxiety
- Severe mood swings
- Sense of helplessness
- Persistent fear or phobia
- Depression
- Rage
- Difficulty sleeping (nightmares, insomnia, etc.)
- Eating difficulties (nausea, vomiting, compulsive eating, etc.)
- Denial
- Withdrawal from friends, family, activities
- Hypervigilance
- Reluctance to leave the house and/or go places that remind the individual of the sexual assault or perpetrator
- Sexual problems
- Difficulty concentrating
- Flashbacks

Source: From *National Sexual Assault Hotline,* Rape, Abuse & Incest National Network, 2008a. Retrieved March 21, 2008, from www.rainn.org/get-help/national-sexual-assault-hotline.

The reorganization phase was a longer-term process of integration, during which the victim regained a sense of control over her life. In conceptualizing rape trauma syndrome, Burgess and Holmstrom found commonalities consistent with Posttraumatic Stress Disorder (PTSD), including a significant stressor, intrusive thoughts about the sexual assault, and decreased involvement in their environment (e.g., feeling emotionally numb), as well as various other symptoms such as sleep disturbances, hypervigilance, guilt, impaired memory, and fears about reoccurrence of the sexual assault.

Physical Effects of Sexual Assault

Physical reactions to sexual assault can manifest in varying somatic complaints including sleep disturbances, hyperalertness, and impaired memory. Sleep disturbances may range from sleeplessness or frequent waking to excessive amounts of sleeping. Victims may deal with other physical issues as a result of the sexual assault, including headaches, pregnancy, sexually transmitted infections (STIs) contracted during the assault, or permanent physical injuries sustained during the attack (Burgess & Holmstrom, 1985).

Emotional/Psychological Effects of Sexual Assault

Emotional and psychological reactions to a sexual assault may be either expressed or controlled (Burgess & Holmstrom, 1985). Victims who demonstrate more expressed reactions openly show emotions by crying, screaming, yelling, or even laughing. Those who demonstrate more controlled reactions may show little outward emotion or remain completely silent. Victims may experience a wide range of emotions, including (1) guilt about surviving the attack, (2) self-blame about not being able to stop the attack, (3) shame if they chose not to report the assault, (4) humiliation with family and friends, (5) anxiety about another attack, and (6) depression that manifests as an inability to return to normal functioning in daily life. Victims may report feeling emotionally numb and being unable to reconnect with the world around them.

Cognitive/Behavioral Effects of Sexual Assault

Victims also may experience cognitive or behavioral problems. They may have impaired memory and/or concentration, including memory loss or the inability to recall certain details in their lives. They may have a marked inability to concentrate on work tasks and other activities of daily living. Victims of sexual assaults may change addresses or telephone numbers to try to ensure safety. They may find themselves in a state of hyperalertness, which can manifest as paranoia (e.g., feeling as if they are being followed), compulsive behaviors (e.g., constantly checking the house for intruders), or displaying an imaginary audience (e.g., thinking that others can tell they were sexually assaulted by looking at them).

INTERVENTIONS WITH SURVIVORS OF SEXUAL ASSAULT

Early evaluation and intervention are vital for victims of sexual assault. There are typically two facilities that provide intervention and evaluation services for victims of sexual assault. Many victims of sexual assault first present in local emergency rooms, having been physically injured during an attack. Once victims enter the health care system, they are treated for a variety of possible health concerns (e.g., pregnancy, STIs, HIV/AIDS, Hepatitis B). A second treatment facility for victims of sexual assault is the crisis center, which is typically in a different location from the local medical facility and can be a self-contained unit, providing all services on-site. The majority of these crisis centers have 24-hour crisis telephone services through which victims can make initial contact. Often, if a victim of sexual assault presents to a law enforcement facility, she will be taken to either an emergency room or a crisis center, depending on which facility typically handles these types of cases in the local community. Services that are provided at emergency rooms or crisis centers may include (1) evidence collection, (2) medical interventions to treat possible health concerns, and (3) examinations by Sexual Assault Nurse Examiners (SANE nurses), who are specially trained to work with victims of sexual assault. The crisis center may use trained volunteers, who are often on call both during and after hours, to assist victims of sexual assault when they present at the crisis center, police department, or emergency room. Crisis counselors may participate in this volunteer program, often by providing the services during regular hours and by preparing, supporting, and supervising volunteer workers. The most important function of these volunteers is to support victims during the process of reporting and help prepare them for future steps. Crisis counselors and volunteers help victims understand the medical examination and evidence collection process, anticipate legal requirements, and develop safety plans. The crisis center may also offer additional services, including short-term or long-term counseling, education, and legal assistance.

Medical examinations are a crucial crisis intervention strategy when dealing with sexual assault. The medical exam, however, can be both uncomfortable and overwhelming to a victim. Victims have experienced a violation that is both physically and psychologically intrusive, and many of them may fear that the medical exam required to collect evidence may lead to reliving the trauma they experienced.

It is important for crisis counselors to become familiar with the medical exam process to help victims understand and prepare for the exam. The U.S. Department of Justice, Office of Violence Against Women (USDOJOVW, 2004) developed a national protocol for sexual assault forensic exams (SAFEs) to recognize the sensitive needs of sexual assault victims and preserve evidence vital to the successful prosecution of offenders. Once a victim presents to an emergency room or crisis center, a SAFE is conducted by a trained medical professional such as a SANE nurse. The SAFE typically takes about four hours to complete and involves collecting biological samples, including blood, urine, hair, and saliva, and obtaining oral, vaginal, and anal swabs and smears that may be used for DNA analysis and comparison. Urine samples help to determine if victims were drugged during the sexual assault. Clothing and any foreign materials on the body are collected, and many crisis centers provide donated clothing to victims once their clothing has been collected for evidence. For evidence preservation purposes, it is important for victims not to bathe, wash their hands, or brush their teeth; crisis counselors should be knowledgeable about the need for collecting urine samples in case victims are unable to wait until the forensic examiner arrives. A final aspect of the medical exam involves treating any potential medical conditions that occur due to the sexual assault (e.g., pregnancy, STIs, HIV/AIDS, Hepatitis B). These conditions are treated with oral medications during the exam. The Centers for Disease Control (CDC) recommends follow-up testing for STIs 1 to 2 weeks after the assault and for syphilis and HIV 6, 12, and 24 weeks after the assault (USDOJOVW, 2004).

Because law enforcement may be an entry point for some victims of sexual assault, many police departments have begun offering specific training and specialized units for working with survivors of sexual assaults. The first step for many departments is to train personnel to understand the dynamics of rape and sexual assault. This training may range from a basic one-day training to a more extensive course to help officers develop a deeper understanding of how to handle sexual assaults. Training should include understanding the victims they will encounter, common reactions and responses victims may have, types of violence that may occur during assaults, and patterns of perpetrators. Officers need to be aware of services available to victims and how to help people who have been sexually assaulted access those services.

Once the first responders have connected sexual assault victims to the health care system, the next step for law enforcement officials is the investigation, which may be handled by specialized units. These units are trained in investigating sexual assaults, including procedures for interviewing survivors and collecting evidence. After the conclusion of the investigation, the case may be turned over to the local prosecutor's office, which will then develop a case to present to a judge and/or jury. Victims may be referred to a victims' assistance program to help deal with the personal impact of the trial. These programs can help victims understand their rights regarding the court case. In 2004, President George W. Bush signed the *Justice for All Act*, which allows for victim impact statements (U.S. Department of Justice, Office for Victims of Crime, 2006), which may be one of the first steps toward empowerment for victims of sexual assault or abuse. According to the National Center for Victims of Crimes (2009), a victim impact statement allows the victim of a crime to share the effect(s) of the crime. Statements typically focus on the harm the offense caused, including physical, emotional, and financial harm as well as harm to family and other significant relationships. Statements are most often given in either written or oral forms and used at sentencing.

TREATMENT OF SURVIVORS OF SEXUAL ASSAULT

As discussed earlier, rape trauma syndrome is an adaptation of PTSD used to understand symptoms experienced by survivors of sexual assault. Because there are significant similarities between rape trauma syndrome and PTSD, crisis counselors should familiarize themselves with both. PTSD, Acute Stress Disorder, and other related diagnoses are discussed in more depth in Chapter 1.

After victims have survived the immediate aftereffects of the attack (e.g., medical interventions), long-term counseling services should be considered. Crisis counselors should perform a thorough evaluation to determine the most appropriate treatment plan (Foa & Rothbaum, 1998). Several assessments exist that may be helpful when collecting information related to the assault, including the Assault Information and History Interview (AIHI; Foa & Rothbaum, 1998), the Clinician-Administered PTSD Scale (Blake et al., 1995), and the PTSD Symptom Scale (Foa, Riggs, Dancu, & Rothbaum, 1993). Self-report measures include the Impact of Event Scale (Horowitz, Wilner, & Alvarez, 1979) and the Rape Aftermath Symptom Test (Kilpatrick, 1988).

A second consideration is the length of the treatment program. While survivors have already experienced short-term interventions (e.g., medical examinations, involvement with law enforcement), longer-term counseling may help them to deal with effects that occur long after the sexual assault. Foa and Rothbaum (1998) offer these suggestions to crisis counselors when working with survivors: (1) provide support to the survivor for other issues she is dealing with (involvement in the legal system, family considerations, job stress, etc.), (2) take and maintain a nonjudgmental attitude; (3) show a level of comfort with the traumatic events described; (4) demonstrate competence with rape trauma syndrome; (5) feel confident about the treatments chosen; (6) focus on personal resources; and (7) normalize the response to the assault.

When making treatment choices for survivors of sexual assault, mental health professionals should consider several cognitive-behavioral treatment options because cognitive-behavioral approaches are well researched and have been shown to have positive results for survivors of sexual assault (e.g., Bryant, Harvey, Dang, Sackville, & Basten, 1998; Foa, Hearst-Ikeda, & Perry, 1995; Foa & Rothbaum, 1998; Foa, Rothbaum, Riggs, & Murdock, 1991; Kubany, 1998; Muran & DiGiuseppe, 1994; Resick & Schnicke, 1992). Foa et al. (1995) conducted a study to examine the use of brief prevention programs designed to treat PTSD symptoms with sexual assault survivors. This program, like many abuse-focused cognitive-behavioral therapies (CBTs), included techniques such as exposure, relaxation training, and cognitive restructuring. Treatments for sexual assault survivors, including exposure therapy, anxiety management programs, and psychoeducation, are discussed in the following sections.

Exposure Therapy

According to Foa and Rothbaum (1998), exposure therapy is considered the most appropriate treatment for PTSD symptoms related to sexual assault. It is a form of systematic desensitization that calls for repeated exposure to a traumatic event in order to reduce the fear, anxiety, and pathology associated with the event. During exposure therapy, clients, with eyes closed, are encouraged to recall the traumatic event in the safety of a counselor's office. These sessions are often audiotaped to allow the client to review them at home in order to continue the repeated exposure to the memories, with the intent of continuing to lessen the fear and anxiety associated with the event. Although this treatment may be stressful, it is considered the most effective intervention for treating sexual assault survivors. Another form of exposure therapy, in vivo therapy, involves repeated exposure to real-life situations and/or places that remind the survivor of the event in order to restore feelings of safety.

Anxiety Management Programs

There are several anxiety management training (AMT) programs that are effective for treating the PTSD symptoms following a sexual assault. AMT programs are designed to help equip clients with tools to better handle anxiety (Foa & Rothbaum, 1998). AMT treatments that have been found to be most successful working with sexual assault survivors include stress inoculation training and relaxation training.

STRESS INOCULATION TRAINING   Stress inoculation training (SIT) was developed by Meichenbaum (1996) as a treatment to help clients deal with a stressful event and prevent or "inoculate" them against future stressors. According to Meichenbaum, SIT has three phases: (1) conceptualization, (2) skills acquisition and rehearsal, and (3) application and follow-through. In the conceptualization phase, the counseling relationship is developed, stressors are evaluated to determine severity, problem-solving methods are employed to determine stressors that can be changed, and goals are set. In the acquisition and rehearsal phase, coping skills are taught and rehearsed in the clinical setting so they can be applied in stressful situations. These coping skills include emotional regulation, self-soothing, relaxation training, problem-solving skills, communication tools, and social support networks. In the application and follow-through phase, the client applies the coping skills developed through modeling and role playing. In this final phase, ways to prevent relapse are discussed.

RELAXATION TRAINING   Relaxation techniques can be incorporated in any treatment plan when working with survivors of sexual assault. Crisis counselors can train sexual assault survivors so that they know how and when to use relaxation techniques. These techniques include deep breathing, deep muscle relaxation, and cue-controlled relaxation which involves teaching the client to recognize body tension, using it as a cue for employing relaxation techniques (Foa & Rothbaum, 1998).

Psychoeducation and Other Treatments

During the process of recovery, survivors must learn many things relating to sexual assault. They may need help to understand the myths that surround sexual assault. Survivors need to be educated about negative thoughts they may experience and any triggers associated with the assault. Common reactions to sexual assault—including (1) fear and anxiety, (2) reexperiencing the trauma through nightmares or flashbacks, (3) increased arousal such as impatience or irritability, (4) avoidance of situations that remind the client of the assault, (5) numbness, (6) anger, (7) guilt and shame, (8) depression, (9) negative self-image, and (10) problems with intimate relationships including issues with sexual pleasure—should be discussed. Other longer-term treatments to help clients deal with sexual assault trauma may include eye movement desensitization and reprocessing (EMDR) and pharmacological interventions.

ETHICAL AND LEGAL ISSUES REGARDING SEXUAL ASSAULT

Ethical and legal issues regarding sexual assault include confidentiality, release of information, counselor competence, and personal values. When working with victims of sexual assault, a crisis counselor may experience ethical dilemmas related to confidentiality, which may conflict with his or her personal values. It may be quite obvious to the crisis counselor that reporting the assault may be in the best interest of the client. However, the crisis counselor is both ethically and legally obligated to maintain confidentiality even if it is counterintuitive to the client's needs. In addition, the crisis counselor is ethically obligated to avoid imposing personal values on the client (American Counseling Association, 2005). The crisis counselor must not persuade clients to report sexual assaults or endure forensic examinations against their will. Particularly after something as intrusive as a sexual assault, empowering clients to make decisions about what happens to their bodies is important.

According the *ACA Code of Ethics* (American Counseling Association, 2005), crisis counselors "practice only within the boundaries of their competence, based on their education, training, supervised experience, state and national professional credentials, and appropriate professional experience" (p. 9). Although working with survivors of sexual assault is not considered a specialty area, crisis counselors must develop knowledge and skills specific to dealing with sexual assault survivors to help these clients improve through counseling. Counselors should gain competence in treatment modalities applicable to sexual assault issues (e.g., cognitive-behavioral approaches, exposure therapy, anxiety management programs) and develop skills related to rape trauma syndrome and PTSD prior to working with this population. Competence can be gained by attending workshops, seminars, or training sessions on working with sexual assault survivors. Crisis counselors can choose to read literature about sexual assault or conduct conjoint counseling with another counselor who is experienced in working with sexual assault survivors.

Because many sexual assault survivors are involved in the legal system, it is important to recognize that they may be particularly sensitive to having their information disclosed. Voluntary release of information forms should be in place to allow crisis counselors to share information with attorneys, medical personnel, and law enforcement. If a survivor chooses not to sign these documents, information cannot be revealed unless the crisis counselor is legally required to do so (i.e., by subpoena or court order). It is important to recognize that just because a counselor receives a subpoena does not mean that information is automatically shared. Many subpoenas are not considered official subpoenas. Crisis counselors are encouraged to seek legal counsel in any situation in which the legal system is involved. Legal representatives can help crisis counselors prepare for possible court testimony and become familiar with state laws pertaining to crisis counseling.

CASE STUDY 7.1

Sexual Assault

Imagine you are a counselor for the university counseling center. Cindy is an 18-year-old college student who recently began seeing you for problems she is having in her classes. She reports that she is failing most of her classes. She recently took her midterm exams and did not pass any of the tests she took. In addition, she did not even take two of the exams. She graduated at the top of her high school class, even receiving an academic scholarship covering the majority of her tuition. She reports that she is in jeopardy of losing her scholarship. She is also concerned because her grades will be sent home to her parents in the next few weeks. They have always expected her to excel in school, and she feels they will be very disappointed with her, possibly even insisting she return home to her small rural town, which she was trying to escape.

At your first meeting with Cindy, she also reports that she is having trouble going to class because she is sleeping through most of them. She reports wanting to sleep all the time, having a depressed mood, and avoiding her friends, who have ultimately convinced her to attend counseling. Cindy's appearance is disheveled, and she appears to have dressed in dirty clothes.

During the first two sessions, Cindy cries frequently and rarely shares information. Finally, she reveals to you that one month ago she attended a party at an off-campus apartment. The apartment belonged to the man who is dating Cindy's best friend. Although Cindy reports not being a big drinker, while at the party she had a few drinks with a guy from her sociology class, whom she has been interested in dating since the beginning of the semester. They were having a great time, talking and laughing, until she felt dizzy. She reported that the next thing she remembered was waking up in this guy's bed with no clothes on, feeling sore in her "private area," and bleeding slightly. She quickly put her clothes on while the guy was in the bathroom and ran out of the apartment. She told no one what happened. She has not been back to the sociology class that she has with the guy.

Discussion Questions

Does this case meet the legal definition of sexual assault?

In this situation, how would you proceed with your work with Cindy?

What are the legal and ethical guidelines that will drive your work with Cindy?

CHILD SEXUAL ABUSE

Child sexual abuse (CSA) affects children, families, and communities worldwide (Krug, Dahlberg, Mercy, Zwi, & Lozano, 2002). Despite national efforts in the United States (i.e., the National Child Abuse and Neglect Data System [NCANDS] and the National Incidence System [NIS]), exact statistics regarding the number of children and families affected by CSA are difficult to derive (e.g., Berliner & Elliott, 2002; Johnson, 2008). Estimates of annual CSA cases range from 83,810 (U.S. Department of Health & Human Services, 2007) to 300,200 (Sedlak & Broadhurst, 1996), and even these reports are thought to be underestimates. NCANDS data include only the reports of state Child

Protective Services (CPS) workers, while the NIS contains data from CPS agencies and community professionals from nationally representative, randomly sampled counties. The NIS–3, which is thought to be the most comprehensive collection of child abuse and neglect data, does not include incidences of sexual abuse by perpetrators who are not in parental or caregiving roles. Although most of the sexual abuse cases that come to the attention of CPS involve intrafamilial relationships, it should be noted that on average only about one-third of CSA cases involve family members, with the remainder involving nonfamily (extrafamilial) individuals known to the child or strangers (U.S. Department of Health & Human Services, 2007). Of the extrafamilial CSA incidences, only 5–15% are perpetrated by strangers (Berliner & Elliott, 2002), meaning that the vast majority of extrafamilial CSA occurs at the hands of individual(s) whom the child or adolescent knows. Thus, many CSA cases would not fall into the definitions used for data collection of these national samples, leading to an underestimate of CSA incidents.

In addition to those victims who do not meet an agency definition, children who fail to come to the attention of these agencies and individuals are not included in estimates. Children and adolescents who have been sexually abused but have not disclosed the abuse, those who have disclosed the abuse but have not had that disclosure come to the attention of CPS, and those who have disclosed the abuse but have not had it substantiated are not included in the official count. Keeping in mind that studies have found that typically only about one-third of those who reported being sexually abused as children disclosed that abuse (Arata, 1998), the incidence rates of CSA reported by government agencies are likely to be significantly lower than the true incidence rate. Also, it should be noted that although the average percentage of substantiated child maltreatment cases that involved CSA was only 9.3%, state reports of substantiated cases of CSA ranged from 2.7% to 62.5% of all substantiated child maltreatment cases (U.S. Department of Health and Human Services, 2005). This suggests a wide variability of substantiation among states and perhaps points to an underlying variability in the veracity with which these charges are pursued.

Prevalence of CSA by Gender, Age, and Race

Females are the victims of CSA at nearly three times the rate of males (Sedlak & Broadhurst, 1996). This appears to be consistent over time, with multiple iterations of the NIS reporting similar rates and retrospective studies underscoring a differential in rates, suggesting that, in the United States, at least 20% of females and between 5% and 10% of males have experienced sexual abuse as children (Finkelhor, 1994). When considering gender of victims, however, it is also important to keep in mind that males are less likely to disclose CSA than are females (Finkelhor, 1981), and therefore, the statistics may not represent the true differential in rates of victimization.

Reports of average ages of victimization vary, with sources reporting the mean age of onset at between 7 and 12 years of age (Berliner & Elliott, 2002; Finkelhor, 1993; Trickett, 2006), but national statistics indicate higher rates of substantiated abuse at higher ages—for example,12–15 years of age (U.S. Department of Health & Human Services, 2005)—or, conversely, consistent rates from 3 through 18 years of age (Sedlak & Broadhurst, 1996). Therefore, it appears that individuals may be at risk for CSA across their childhood and adolescent years.

Unlike gender and (potentially) age, race does not appear to be a differentiating characteristic in CSA, with consistent rates of CSA victimization in children of all races (e.g., Sedlak & Broadhurst, 1996). Caucasian children, however, had a slightly higher proportion of sexual abuse at the hands of biological parents than did children of other racial backgrounds. This could be due to higher incidence rates, but it could also be linked to factors such as a greater distrust of the systems involved in child protection or a reliance on less formalized support systems to address issues of CSA.

DEFINITION OF CSA AND RELATED TERMS

In addition to the difficulty in tracking children and adolescents who have been sexually abused, there is no agreed-on definition of CSA (Haugaard, 2000). Further complicating the process of defining CSA is how to distinguish it from statutory rape. In this section, CSA and statutory rape are defined, with an explanation of the distinction between statutory rape and CSA and how statutory rape may be handled differently.

Child Sexual Abuse

There is no set definition of child sexual abuse, with definitions varying from state to state and from one research project to the next. Some broader definitions include "any sexual activity or contact with a child where consent is not or cannot [for reasons of age or power differential] be given" (Berliner & Elliott, 2002, p. 55). More-narrow definitions used by some states or research groups may include only specific sexual behaviors (e.g., penetration), specific perpetrator groups (e.g., intrafamilial), or specific ages or age differences (e.g., an age difference of four years) and refer to other sexual acts (e.g., showing pornography to a child, exposing one's genitalia to a child) or perpetrator groups (e.g., neighbors, acquaintances, strangers) in categories like child exploitation, child molestation, or statutory rape. In the *Child Abuse Prevention and Treatment Act* (CAPTA; Public Law No. 93-247), child abuse and neglect is limited to "a parent or caretaker" (p. 44), and CSA is defined as

> the employment, use, persuasion, inducement, enticement, or coercion of any child to engage in, or assist any other person to engage in, any sexually explicit conduct or simulation of such conduct for the purpose of producing a visual depiction of such conduct; or . . . the rape, and in cases of caretaker or interfamilial relationships, statutory rape, molestation, prostitution, or other form of sexual exploitation of children, or incest with children. . . . (p. 44)

CAPTA specifies that "child" is specific to all individuals under the age of 18 years for sexual abuse.

Although CAPTA does give a definition of CSA, age of consent differs from state to state, and even within the same state, ages of consent may differ for heterosexual and homosexual relationships and for males and females. It is important for clinicians working with children and adolescents to be aware of the most recent legislation for the state(s) within which they practice regarding CSA and age of consent and with mandatory reporting laws regarding sexual behaviors and relationships involving individuals under the age of consent. For the purposes of this chapter, CSA is defined as any sexual contact, behavior, or exposure for the purposes of sexual gratification of another individual that involves a child who is unable or unwilling to give consent.

ACTIVITY 7.3

Internet Activity

Find the legislation for three different states, including the one in which you hope to practice, regarding CSA, statutory rape, and the age of consent for opposite and same-sex relationships for males and for females.

Statutory Rape

Complicating the definition of CSA further is the delineation between CSA and statutory rape. Legally, CSA usually includes only those individuals who are in parental or care-taking roles (e.g., babysitter, teacher, coach) with the child or adolescent. Statutory rape, however, refers primarily to a relationship "between a juvenile and an adult that is illegal under age of consent statutes, but that does not involve the degree of coercion or manipulation sufficient to qualify under criminal statutes as a forcible sex crime" (Hines & Finkelhor, 2007, p. 302). Just as age of consent statutes may vary from state to state, legal definitions and terminology for statutory rape also vary between states (Mitchell & Rogers, 2003).

CYCLE OF CHILD SEXUAL ABUSE

CSA typically develops through a cycle of behavior (see Lanning, 2001). This process begins when a perpetrator identifies a child who may be an easy target, due to some sort of neediness, passivity, or suggestibility. Once a child has been identified, the perpetrator will begin "grooming" the child for sexual abuse by starting with nonsexual contact and behavior and progressing slowly to more sexual activity and behavior, which the perpetrator normalizes. Through a system of reinforcement (e.g., toys, candy, ice cream, attention) and punishment (e.g., anger, threats against the child or the child's loved ones), the child is coerced into entering into and remaining in a sexually exploitive relationship with the perpetrator and keeping the relationship hidden from others.

SIGNS AND SYMPTOMS OF CHILD SEXUAL ABUSE

Children and adolescents who have experienced CSA may respond and react in a variety of ways, ranging from nonresponse to more severe reactions, including PTSD symptomology (e.g., Kendall-Tackett, Meyer Williams, & Finkelhor, 1993; Miller-Perrin & Perrin, 2007). Given this range, it is important to view children or adolescents in the context of developmentally appropriate behavior patterns, giving special attention to significant deviations from those norms and from typical developmental behaviors and milestones. For example, a kindergarten-age boy who touches his penis in class or a four-year-old girl who lifts up her dress in a grocery store may be exhibiting developmentally normal behavior. If that kindergarten boy, however, accompanies the touching of his penis with moaning or thrusting behaviors or if the four-year-old girl lifts up her dress and rubs up against another individual in a seductive manner, those behaviors are not developmentally appropriate and may signify that those children have witnessed sexual behaviors or been the victims of CSA. Table 7.2 provides summaries of cues that may indicate child sexual abuse.

TABLE 7.2 Cues That May Indicate Child Sexual Abuse

Behavioral cues

- Difficulty in walking or sitting
- Frequent vomiting
- Sexually explicit drawings or writings
- Sexual interaction with other people
- In-depth sexual play with peers
- Sexual interactions involving animals or toys
- Exceptionally secretive behavior
- Extreme compliance or withdrawal
- Overt aggression
- Extremely seductive behavior
- Sudden nonparticipation in school activities
- Crying without provocation
- Regression behaviors (e.g., sucking thumb, clinging, separation anxiety)
- A sudden onset of wetting or soiling of pants
- Sudden phobic behavior
- Talks about being damaged
- Suicide attempts
- Attempting to run away
- Cruelty to animals (especially those that would normally be pets)
- Fire-setting
- Eating disordered behavior
- Self-injurious behavior
- Masturbation if
  - Child masturbates to the point of injury
  - Child masturbates numerous times a day
  - Child cannot stop masturbating
  - Child makes groaning or moaning sounds while masturbating
  - Child engages in thrusting motions while masturbating
- Sexual language
- Sexual victimization of others

Cognitive cues

- Drop in school performance
- Suicidal ideation
- More sexual knowledge than is age appropriate
- Fear of males or females

Physical cues

- Complaints of genital or anal itching, pain, or bleeding
- Blood or discharge on undergarments
- Frequent psychosomatic illnesses
- Pregnancy at young age
- STIs at young age
- Older, more sexualized appearance than peers
- Sleep problems or nightmares

Psychological and emotional cues

- Feelings of low self-worth
- Depression
- Anxiety
- Guilt
- Shame
- Hostility
- Flashbacks
- Nightmares

In addition, some researchers have reported children who were victims of CSA but who were without symptoms at the time of their evaluations (e.g., Kendall-Tackett et al., 1993). Reasons for these asymptomatic presentations may include narrowness of symptomology being studied, symptoms that have not yet manifested, or children's perceptions that the CSA was not intolerable, was not threatening, or did not exceed their normal functioning.

INTERVENTION STRATEGIES FOR VICTIMS OF CSA

When working with victims of CSA, it is important that clinicians know and understand the dynamics of not only their own personal work with the client but also how the counseling process might affect the legal and social services processes and professionals that might also be working with the child and family. Crisis counselors must understand how the therapeutic relationship will act in concert with other support services for the child from the initial interview through the reporting and counseling process. Without a thorough understanding, crisis counselors may impede the progress of legal proceedings. In the next sections, intervention strategies are discussed, but it is strongly recommended that crisis counselors become familiar with the local legal and social services entities and professionals with whom they will be interacting so as to understand local procedures and laws regarding CSA.

Initial Disclosure and Interviewing for CSA

When working with a child or adolescent who has recently disclosed CSA, it is important that clinicians not ask leading questions regarding the existence or nature of the abuse. There are specific protocols that CPS workers and law enforcement officers use when working with children and adolescents who have reported abuse, and members of those agencies should be responsible for the investigation of the alleged abuse. Many communities have child advocacy centers in which trained forensic interviewers work in concert with CPS, law enforcement, medical officials, and counselors to interview the child just once and document the interview. Therefore, while it is appropriate to ask probing questions, crisis counselors should not suggest that CSA has occurred or who the perpetrator of the abuse is. Therefore, a question like "It sounds like this was a difficult weekend for you, and you seem really upset. Is there something that I can help you with?" would be more appropriate than "Did someone sexually abuse you this weekend?" or "Sometimes daddies touch little girls and make them feel uncomfortable. Did that happen to you?" In addition, children and adolescents may be afraid of making the disclosure and the potential ramifications the disclosure may have. These fears may be the result of a promise of retaliation by the perpetrator for the disclosure (e.g., a threat to harm the child or a family member), a belief that the perpetrator may go to jail, a fear that the victim will be removed from the home, and feelings of loyalty, attachment, or love for the perpetrator. In addition, the child may feel that the abuse is normal (e.g., a form of sex education, a ritual to initiate one into manhood/womanhood).

It is important when working with a child or adolescent who is disclosing abuse to help the child maintain a sense of control of the information that he or she gives and understand the steps involved in the reporting process. This could include involving the child or adolescent, as appropriate, in making the report to CPS or describing the steps in the process as clearly as possible. It is very important not to make promises that cannot be guaranteed or kept, and crisis counselors may find it helpful to involve appropriate individuals (e.g., CPS social worker, law enforcement officer) in helping lay out when the child can expect to be interviewed, what the potential consequences may be for the perpetrator of the abuse, and what sort of process will be involved if the child is, in fact, removed from the home. Equally important is reiterating, even multiple times, that the child is not at fault, not in trouble, and not to blame in any way. This can help the child maintain some sense of control and stability, even in an unfamiliar circumstance.

Reporting CSA

Every state in the United States has mandated reporting of CSA (Myers, 1998). Mandated reporters may differ by state and typically include mental health professionals, educational personnel, law enforcement officers, and medical personnel (U.S. Department of Health & Human Services, 2008c). Despite the legal responsibility to report child abuse and neglect, there are times when professionals choose not to report child abuse and neglect. This, however, can put the professional in conflict with legal and ethical guidelines (e.g., CAPTA; American Counseling Association, 2005) that require disclosure of suspicion of CSA. It is important for individuals serving children and adolescents to be knowledgeable of their legal and ethical responsibilities regarding CSA. This includes knowing not only the laws governing the reporting of CSA and the statutes of limitations for their particular state(s) but also the policies of the agency, organization, or school in which they practice (see Table 7.3).

TABLE 7.3 Policies to Know Regarding Child Sexual Abuse

- Whom do you notify?
- What specific information do you need to know in order to report?
- What other agency/school personnel should be involved?
- Who makes the report to CPS? How?
- Is there a time frame for making a verbal report followed by a written report?
- Who is responsible for monitoring or receiving feedback from CPS once the report is filed?
- What information should be included in the report? (This is dictated by state law and CPS policy.)
- What does the protocol indicate regarding confidentiality?
- Is the written report kept in a separate location from the client's normal file or cumulative folder?
- What follow-up is expected on reported cases?
- What role will you play in possible community or child protection teams?

ACTIVITY 7.4
Interviewing Activity

Contact a member of Child Protective Services or a member of local law enforcement with experience in working with children and adolescents who have been sexually abused. Interview that individual about the process of making reports, including agency procedures when CSA has been reported, the process involved in interviewing and investigating CSA, and the timeline during which major events occur (e.g., initial interview of child, interview of family and/or alleged perpetrator, filing of legal charges, removal from home).

The mandate for reporting suspicion of CSA can make it difficult to determine when steps should be taken, especially in cases where a child has not disclosed abuse but rather has exhibited some behaviors that seem to demonstrate a potential history of sexual abuse. For clinicians working with children and adolescents, one way to help provide some clarification is to develop professional relationships with contacts within the local CPS agency and local law enforcement, preferably prior to having a client who may be a victim of CSA. This can help the clinician understand the process of local agencies as well as providing an individual or individuals with whom that clinician can discuss hypothetical cases and appropriate action(s) or reporting procedures. This can be especially helpful in cases where the line between CSA (and thus mandated reporting) and statutory rape (for which reporting is not typically mandated) is blurred.

CPS traditionally works with CSA cases involving parents or caregivers, especially those in the home. While CPS may be involved in other CSA cases, CPS's primary focus will typically be on parent/caregiver cases. Law enforcement agencies will typically handle extrafamilial cases or those that involve individuals who are not in a caretaking role. Important information to include in a CSA report is presented in Table 7.4. When making an initial CSA report to CPS, it is important for the mental health professional to document that the report was made, including to whom the report was made (both the agency and the name of the individual taking the report).

TABLE 7.4 Information to Include in an Initial Report of Child Sexual Abuse

- Child's name
- Age
- Sex
- Address
- Parent's name and address
- Nature and extent of the condition observed
- Actions taken by the reporter (e.g., talking with the child)
- Where the act occurred
- Issues of potential risk for the child (e.g., Is the perpetrator in the home? Is there a threat of physical abuse for the child disclosing information? Might the child be kicked out of the home for reporting?)
- Are there other children who might be at risk from the alleged perpetrator?
- Reporter's name, location, and contact information

CPS reports may be filed anonymously. Even if an anonymous report is made, however, counselors are mandated reporters and should document their reports. The documentation should include the report made, the date and time the report was made, and the name of the individual to whom the report was made.

Treatment of Survivors of CSA

There are a number of difficulties in identifying evidence-based practices for effectively treating survivors of CSA, based in part on the range of symptomology presented; the challenges that children have verbalizing their current mental, emotional, and physical states; and the reliance on parent and teacher reports, which may differ substantially both from each other and from the experience of the child (Saywitz, Mannarino, Berliner, & Cohen, 2000). Children and adolescents who have survived sexual abuse, like adult sexual assault survivors, are usually served through a combination of individual and group therapy (Swenson & Chaffin, 2006). As described earlier in this chapter in reference to sexual assault victims, cognitive-behavioral strategies—combining psychoeducation, anxiety management, exposure, and cognitive restructuring techniques—may be beneficial to children and adolescents who are struggling with posttraumatic stress or depression after being sexually abused and are the primary evidence-based practices for treating children and adolescents with posttraumatic symptomology (Chaffin & Friedrich, 2004). Abuse-specific CBT (see Cohen, Mannarino, Berliner, & Deblinger, 2000) focusing on the symptoms presented in the child (e.g., anxiety, depression, traumatic stress) seems to be one of the best available treatments for survivors of CSA (Chaffin & Friedrich, 2004; Saywitz et al., 2000). Play therapy is also a viable and often preferred approach for intervention with young children.

One potential caveat for mental health personnel employing abuse-specific CBT or any type of treatment using exposure therapy is that the process of exposure therapy and systematic desensitization or cognitive restructuring around sexual abuse needs to be done carefully in order to reduce any potential distortion in the child's story, as it could affect court testimony or a CPS investigation (Saywitz et al., 2000). It is best for crisis counselors working with survivors of CSA to avoid the dual relationship inherent in being both investigator and counselor. Crisis counselors should consult with CPS workers and law enforcement officers, avail themselves of training opportunities and continuing education for working with CSA survivors, and research methods of therapy for CSA survivors that limit leading questions or statements that might affect the child's story.

In addition to these strategies, the inclusion of nonoffending parents (i.e., primarily mothers) in the treatment of children who have experienced sexual abuse has been related to a reduction in acting out or other problematic behaviors (Deblinger, Lippman, & Steer, 1996) and an increase in parent support (Berliner & Elliott, 2002), with abuse-specific CBT tailored to parent needs being particularly effective in reducing problem behaviors (Cohen & Mannarino, 1997) and internalizing symptoms (Cohen & Mannarino, 1998). At this point, there is little experimental research on other therapies besides CBT for the inclusion of nonoffending parents (Berliner & Elliott, 2002). It is important, therefore, that crisis counselors continue to follow the professional literature on counseling strategies for CSA survivors and their families. The benefit of including nonoffending fathers is at this time inconclusive, due, in part, to a lack of research on this population (Swenson & Chaffin, 2006).

When working with adults who are disclosing CSA, there are multiple factors that need to be taken into consideration. Crisis counselors need to consider the adult client in her or his own context regarding desired treatment outcomes (e.g., Is the client presenting with sexual dysfunction, relationship issues, difficulty in regulating mood, or PTSD?) and client abuse history (e.g., Who was the perpetrator? When did the abuse take place? What was the duration of the abuse?) as well as factors that might necessitate involving law enforcement or CPS (e.g., Is the abuser still alive? If so, does the abuser have access to children or adolescents who might also be victimized?). Another factor to consider in treatment planning is whether or not the client has previously disclosed her or his abuse and, if so, what the outcome of that disclosure was. Crisis counselors should empower and respect the autonomy of the adult CSA survivor, while also taking necessary steps to protect any children or adolescents who might be at risk. As with the process of reporting sexual abuse disclosed by a child, crisis counselors may need to contact CPS or local law enforcement for clarification of statutes of limitation, local policies and procedures, and the procedure to follow if a perpetrator of sexual abuse is residing in another state. Mandated reporters of a past child sexual abuse incident must comply with the laws in the state where one practices. For example, if the state requires a mandated reporter to report past child sexual abuse, and there is enough identifiable information on a perpetrator, then the mandated reporter must comply with the law.

PERPETRATORS OF SEXUAL ASSAULT AND CHILD SEXUAL ABUSE

When discussing sexual assault and child sexual abuse, it is important to consider not only the survivors but also the perpetrators. In the following section, the prevalence, characteristics, and treatment options regarding perpetrators of sexual assault and child sexual abuse are described.

Prevalence and Characteristics of Sexual Assault Perpetrators

It is common knowledge that the majority of sexual assault perpetrators are male. According to the U.S. Department of Justice's Bureau of Justice Statistics (2008), almost 98% of offenders are male, with only 2% being female. More than 40% of male offenders are over the age of 30 years. The vast majority (85%) of these perpetrators used no weapon during the assaults. In the assaults that used weapons, firearms were typically used. According to the Bureau of Justice Statistics, an examination of four datasets (i.e., arrests in the FBI's Uniform Crime Reports, state felony court convictions, prison admissions, and the National Crime Victimization Survey) reveals that sex offenders are older than other violent offenders (early thirties) and more likely to be White than other violent offenders.

According to Groth (2001), several myths exist regarding rapists: (1) Rapists are sexually compulsive males who see women as provocative and malicious, (2) they are sexually frustrated males reacting to stress that is repressed, and (3) they are "demented sex-fiends" who harbor perverted desires. These myths assume that the perpetrator's primary motivation is based on sexual needs and desires and that rape is the method for gratifying these desires. In reality, the rape of an adult is based on the nonsexual needs of the perpetrator, which include power and control rather than sexual needs. Basic characteristics of perpetrators who commit power, anger, and sadistic rapes are detailed below.

PERPETRATORS OF POWER RAPE   A power rapist may be attempting to validate his masculinity in compensation for feelings of inadequacy. Through rape, he attempts to demonstrate strength, control, and capability. Like the perpetrator of the anger rape, a power rapist finds little sexual gratification with the act; unlike the anger rape perpetrator, however, the power rapist may have fantasized about or planned the event. His fantasy may include a desire that the victim will not protest and will find his sexual prowess difficult to resist. When the victim does resist, the act is disappointing to him because his fantasy did not come to fruition, and he may feel the need to experience another rape in order to continue to pursue his fantasy. The power rape diverges from the anger rape in that the power rape may be premeditated, with the perpetrator often searching for victims or acting on opportunities. Victims of the power rape may be the same age or younger than the perpetrator and are based on availability, accessibility, and vulnerability. The power rapist may deny that the encounter was forced, often believing that the victim actually enjoyed the encounter. He may attempt to show a kind gesture following the encounter as a way to discredit the victim.

PERPETRATORS OF ANGER RAPE   As described earlier in the chapter, the purpose of an anger rape is to hurt, humiliate, or demean the victim. Methods employed by an anger rapist include both physical violence and verbal aggression. This rapist, however, finds that physical and verbal aggression alone do not meet his needs for power and control, and sex becomes a weapon by which he can release his anger. Anger rape may also include other acts thought of by the rapist to be particularly objectionable, such as sodomy or fellatio, or humiliating, such as urinating or ejaculating onto the victim. This rapist may have difficulties with an erection and may find little sexual gratification with the act. Anger rapes are typically short in nature, often unplanned by the rapists, and not a focus of his fantasies prior to the act.

PERPETRATORS OF SADISTIC RAPE   The sadistic rapist finds pleasure with the torment, anguish, suffering, and pain of the victim. The main goal of the sadistic rapist is to achieve sexual gratification through inflicting pain, even finding pleasure in the victim's futile resistance. The sadistic rape is often premeditated, and the perpetrator goes to great precautions to avoid detection, often wearing gloves, wearing disguises, or blindfolding victims. A sadistic rapist is frequently considered a psychopath, although he is often married and employed and can appear personable and friendly. However, even in normal environmental contexts, he may abuse his wife, children, or pets.

Child Sexual Abuse Perpetrators

Perpetrators of CSA are both male and female, and they commit sex crimes against children for a variety of reasons. Some of these may be parallel to the reasons of sexual assault perpetrators, but some are distinctly different. In the following section, male and female perpetrators of CSA are described, with a focus on the motivation that may drive behavior that is sexually abusive toward children or adolescents.

MALE PERPETRATORS OF SEXUAL ABUSE   Like sexual assault perpetrators, individuals who sexually abuse children are predominantly male. Indeed, males are the perpetrators in 75–96% of CSA cases (McCloskey & Raphael, 2005; U. S. Department of Health & Human Services, 2005). Unlike sexual assault perpetrators, individuals who sexually abuse children fall along a continuum of motivation for committing the sexual abuse, ranging from situational to preferential (Lanning, 2001). Situational perpetrators commit sexual abuse because they are driven by basic sexual *and* nonsexual (e.g., power, anger) needs (Lanning, 2001). In the case of situational offenders, the preferred sexual partner is not typically a child; rather, the child is available when the individual perceives that he has a sexual or power-related need that must be met. Thus, the child serves as a sexual substitute and may be part of a larger pattern of abusive behavior. In contrast, preferential perpetrators are compulsive and driven by fantasies about their victims; they may participate in behaviors that groom their potential targets. Preferential perpetrators are more likely than situational perpetrators to sexually abuse children or adolescents. In his behavioral analysis of child molesters, Lanning (2001) describes this continuum as well as subcategories of situational and preferential perpetrators. These motivations and subtypes are meant not for clinical treatment or diagnosis but rather to help law enforcement officials recognize, identify, and gather relevant evidence about individuals who sexually abuse children.

Lanning (2001) identified three patterns of situational perpetrators of sexual abuse: regressed, morally indiscriminate, and inadequate. A situational offender who follows a regressed pattern is driven by a precipitating stressor and may find a readily available child to serve as a sexual substitute for a preferred adult partner. A situational offender who fits a morally indiscriminate pattern abuses individuals in general, so the sexual abuse of a child is less a specific preference for children than the result of a sociopathic level of indiscriminate abuse of people regardless of their age or background. Finally, the inadequate pattern of situational perpetrators is typically followed by an individual perceived as nonmainstream, perhaps with preexisting mental or emotional problems, who may sexually abuse a child out of insecurity or curiosity about sexual behavior.

Those individuals who fall toward the preferential side of the motivation continuum tend to sexually abuse children or adolescents either because children and/or adolescents are their preferred sexual partners or because children and/or adolescents are less threatening individuals with whom they can participate in sexual behaviors that are more bizarre or more shameful to the perpetrator (Lanning, 2001). Not all preferential perpetrators, therefore, are pedophiles; many, however, have a paraphilia, which is defined as a strong sexual preference for nonhuman objects, nonconsenting individuals, or the suffering and/or humiliation of themselves or their partners (American Psychiatric Association, 2000). Not all individuals who have a paraphilia (including pedophilia) commit child sexual abuse; therefore, it is important that clinicians not assume that all, most, or even many individuals who have a paraphilia will sexually abuse children.

In addition to identifying three patterns of situational perpetrators, Lanning (2001) identified the following four patterns of preferential perpetrators: seduction, introverted, diverse, and sadistic. Sexual abuse perpetrators who fit the seduction pattern of preferential motivation form the largest group of acquaintance child molesters and are characterized by an ability to identify with children and groom potential victims. When grooming children, the perpetrator will ply them with gifts and attention, making them feel loved and understood to the point where they may willingly participate in sexual acts. Unlike individuals who fit the seduction pattern, perpetrators who fit the introverted pattern lack the verbal and social skills to seduce children and may resort to the traditionally stereotypical behaviors of lurking around playgrounds or abducting children with whom there is no prior relationship. This pattern parallels the inadequate pattern of situational offenders, but with a specific preference for children. Individuals who fit the diverse pattern of preferential motivation are interested in sexual experimentation, and they choose a child target because of the novelty and/or taboo or because the child is a more vulnerable partner with whom sexual experimentation can take place. Finally, individuals who fit the sadistic pattern of preferential motivation are a small percentage of perpetrators, but they are the most likely to abduct or kill their victims. The sadistic perpetrator is aroused by the infliction of pain, humiliation, and suffering in his victims.

FEMALE PERPETRATORS OF SEXUAL ABUSE   Female sexual abuse perpetrators appear to be fewer in number than their male counterparts, but there are several factors that must be considered. First, females are still socially accepted as the primary caregivers in society, and therefore, they can bathe and touch children without arousing the same type of suspicion as a male who performs comparable activities (Miller-Perrin & Perrin, 2007). Second, there is more of a social acceptance of older females seducing younger males (e.g., the *American Pie* series of movies, the songs "Stacy's Mom" and "That Summer") than there is of similar relationships between older males and adolescent females (e.g., *Lolita*). Law enforcement officers, criminal justice personnel, and mental health providers must be aware of their own biases and stereotypes about the demographic characteristics of sex offenders so as to understand the severity of abuse for the victim and to properly treat the female perpetrator.

Due to the relatively smaller numbers of female perpetrators, the literature on female perpetrators is still sparse compared to that on their male counterparts. Mathews, Matthews, and Speltz (1989) clustered female offenders into three subtypes: male-coerced, predisposed, and teacher/lover. Male-coerced females tend to abuse children in concert with a dominant male partner, and they may grant access to children out of a fear of abandonment by a dominant male partner. Predisposed female abusers typically act alone in victimizing their own children or other easily accessible young children.

They are typically survivors of incestuous relationships with continued psychological problems and deviant or paraphilic sexual fantasies. Teacher/lover female perpetrators have a more regressed pattern of behavior, have strained peer relationships, and perceive themselves as being in romantic relationships or as sexually mentoring their victims, therefore resisting the idea that their actions might be criminal in nature.

Treatment of Sex Offenders

Because there is no evidence-based guidance about the most effective approaches to working with female sexual offenders (Center for Sex Offender Management, 2007), the primary focus of this treatment section will be on male offenders, with "sex offender" referring to males unless specifically stated otherwise. When considering treatment for sex offenders, crisis counselors should consider three aspects: (1) client dynamics, (2) treatment setting, and (3) treatment modality (Groth, 2001). First of all, client dynamics must be assessed through a comprehensive psychological evaluation. This evaluation should include demographics, family background, medical history, education level, military history, interpersonal development (e.g., social, sexual, and marital information), occupational history, and criminal history. In addition, assessments should include behavioral observations, field investigations, medical examination, and psychometric examinations. The clinical assessment must include information about the perpetrator's sexual behavior. This information should include premeditation, victim selection, style of attack, accompanying fantasies, role of aggression, sexual behavior (contact, duration, dysfunction), mood state, contributing factors (stressors), acceptance of responsibility, and recidivism and deterrence.

Second, appropriate treatment settings should be considered (Groth, 2001). Most offenders enter the mental health system through either the criminal justice or the health care system. The perpetrator may have been hospitalized for a mental illness or referred by the courts for treatment. Treatment facilities may typically specialize in the treatment of sex offenders and offer either inpatient or outpatient treatment. Group counseling may be the primary method of delivery of services in order to provide confrontation to a client population that may be prone to denial.

Lastly, there are specific treatment modalities that may be effective when treating sex offenders. However, it is important to recognize that no one treatment modality has been found to be the most effective treatment for sex offenders (Groth, 2001). Crisis counselors should consider court requirements and specific needs of each client to determine a course of treatment and possibly combine treatments in order to find a successful plan of action. Treatment modalities available include (1) chemotherapy, (2) psychotherapy, (3) psychoeducation, (4) behavior modification, (5) incapacitation, and (6) family systems counseling.

CHEMOTHERAPY   Use of chemotherapy in the treatment of sexual offenders includes administering an antiandrogen hormone to reduce interest in sexual activity. The most commonly used forms of chemotherapy include medroxyprogesterone acetate (MPA), available in the United States, and cyproterone acetate (CPA), available in Canada and Europe. This medical intervention is based on the use of synthetic progesterones designed to decrease testosterone levels, which has been shown to lessen deviant sexual fantasies and behaviors as well as reducing libido, erections, and ejaculations (Grossman, Martis, & Fichtner, 1999).

PSYCHOTHERAPY   Various methods of counseling are used to treat sex offenders. Individual counseling, group counseling, and family and marital counseling are all used to help clients develop insight into their inappropriate behavior and poor choices, which are typically thought to be based on internal and emotional conflicts (Groth, 2001). Although counseling may be the most common treatment for sex offenders, counseling has several limitations. First of all, there is no clear evidence that this type of treatment works, particularly in isolation. Second, clients' intellectual functioning can affect their ability to develop insights related to their behavior. In addition, clients' ability to think abstractly, as well as their level of self-awareness, is crucial to the success of counseling. Third, the ability to develop a counseling relationship with clients is important. It is highly possible that this population is distrustful of any professional perceived as punitive. If clients have been required to attend counseling by a third party (e.g., judge), the challenge of developing a relationship increases.

FAMILY SYSTEMS COUNSELING   In the case of incestuous CSA, a family systems approach to treatment may be taken (e.g., Child Sexual Abuse Treatment Program; see Giarretto, 1982 or Hewitt, 1998). This systems-oriented counseling may involve individual counseling for the child, the nonoffending parent(s), and the perpetrator; marital therapy; counseling with the nonoffending parent(s) and child; counseling with the offender and the child; group counseling; and family therapy with the purpose of retaining or reunifying the family (Miller-Perrin & Perrin, 2007).

PSYCHOEDUCATION   Life-skills training involves focusing on several areas where deficiencies may exist, such as (1) sex education, (2) social skills, (3) empathy skills, and (4) emotional regulation (Groth, 2001). Sex education can help the sex offender understand normal sexual functioning, as most experience sexuality in a dysfunctional way. Social skills training allows sex offenders to understand healthy relationships and develop improved interpersonal skills. Empathy skills help the sex offender develop sensitivity to people and recognize the needs of others. Emotional regulation is important for helping sex offenders cope with anger and aggression, which they typically release via a sexual assault. Relaxation techniques may also be used to address their feelings of frustration.

BEHAVIOR MODIFICATION AND COGNITIVE-BEHAVIORAL APPROACHES   Behavior modification for sex offenders primarily involves aversive conditioning in which a sexual response (i.e., erection) is repeatedly paired with a noxious event (e.g., electric shock, an unpleasant smell) (Groth, 2001). One example of behavior modification is to have an offender masturbate to ejaculation while fantasizing about an appropriate, nondeviant sexual encounter and partner and then, postorgasm, continuing to masturbate for an additional hour to a fantasy involving his preferred (and deviant) partner or sexual encounter, thus pairing the pleasurable experience with a socially appropriate partner and the uncomfortable experience with the behavior to be extinguished (Miller-Perrin & Perrin, 2007). Another behavior modification technique for treating sex offenders is covert sensitization in which guided imagery is used to help the client imagine his offense and then imagine a frightening or disgusting event. In both of the treatment modalities, repeating the techniques until the behavior is extinguished is the key to success. Although this is a commonly used approach, there is debate over whether aversion therapy produces permanent results (Laws & Marshall, 2003).

Cognitive-behavioral therapy (CBT) has also been used to treat offender populations, targeting cognitive distortions, deviant sexual practices and preferences, concurrent nonsexual behavioral and social challenges, and relapse prevention (Miller-Perrin & Perrin, 2007). The Sex Offender Treatment and Evaluation Project (SOTEP) is a cognitive-behavioral treatment program for sex offenders in California (see Marques, 1999; Marques, Wiederanders, Day, Nelson, & van Ommeren, 2005) that has tracked participants longitudinally for eight years. Results are mixed, with no statistical difference in rates of recidivism between participants and nonparticipants; however, the treatment is associated with a significant reduction of reoffending in individuals who complete program goals, suggesting that there is potential for cognitive-behavioral approaches to reduce reoffending with at least some segment of sex offenders (Marques et al., 2005).

INCAPACITATION   Incapacitation for the sex offender can take several forms, including neurosurgery, surgical castration, and imprisonment/institutionalization. Neurosurgery involves removing parts of the hypothalamus, which decreases male hormone production

CASE STUDY 7.2

Child Abuse

Imagine that you are a counselor who has a 14-year-old biracial female client, Tina. Tina is the oldest of three children in a home with a single female parent. She has a distant relationship with her father, who has lived in a neighboring town for the past five years. Her presenting concerns for counseling include behavioral issues at school (e.g., threats of fighting another eighth-grade female, back-talking in class, not completing homework assignments). During one of your sessions, Tina is describing her anger at another student, who tried to grab a journal that Tina writes in faithfully. Tina was extremely upset by this.

As you explore the anger and paranoia she expresses, Tina breaks down, telling you that she's having a relationship with an older neighbor. This man, Cameron, is well liked and respected, and Tina has regularly done chores to help him out and earn some money. When you ask about the nature of the relationship that Tina and Cameron have, Tina becomes very guarded but proudly states that Cameron told her that she was "beautiful" and "much more mature" than other girls of her age. After sharing this, Tina closes off and refuses to answer any of your other questions about Cameron.

Trying another approach, you ask Tina if her mother is aware of her relationship with Cameron. Tina states that she is "afraid" of her mother finding out about Cameron because "she'd probably whoop me good."

Discussion Questions

Is this child sexual abuse? Explain.

In this situation, how would you proceed regarding your work with Tina around her relationship with Cameron?

What are the legal and ethical guidelines that will drive your work with Tina?

and diminishes sexual arousal and impulsive behaviors. Surgical castration involves a sex offender losing the functions of his testes. Sex offenders may voluntarily undergo this procedure to help lessen sexual drives. Involuntary castration is extremely controversial, based on legal, moral, and ethical ambiguity. Imprisonment is the most common type of incapacitation (Groth, 2001), in which the confinement of the sex offender prevents commission of future acts.

FEMALE OFFENDERS   Although there is little evidence-based guidance regarding treatment of female sex offenders, female perpetrators have higher rates and more severe experiences of sexual victimization than do male perpetrators (see Center for Sex Offender Management, 2007). Treatment, therefore, may need to address the trauma that these female perpetrators (and male perpetrators who may have sustained similar sexual abuse) have faced. Thus, while addressing victimization issues, it is important for clinicians to be empathetic regarding the abuse that perpetrators have sustained without minimizing or excusing the sexual offenses that they have committed.

Summary

Survivors of sexual violence are a significant minority of society, with some reports estimating that at least 20% of women and up to 10% of men are sexually victimized in their lifetime. Although the definitions of sexual assault, child sexual abuse, and statutory rape may differ by state, it is important for crisis counselors to be aware of legislation, resources, and best practices for working with survivors of sexual violence. Primarily, the need for empathetic understanding, for the use of abuse-specific cognitive-behavioral strategies, and for the connection of survivors to resources in the community that best fit their needs is vital. It is also important to understand that not all victims of sexual violence will react the same way. While some may show immediate physical, cognitive-behavioral, or psychological signs, others may appear without symptoms. It is a crisis counselor's responsibility to provide support to clients in keeping with ethical and legal guidelines, respecting adult clients' right to decide whether or not a sexual assault is reported, and making proper reports to Child Protective Services regarding the sexual abuse of children.

In addition, sexual offenders who perpetrate sexual violence against youth or adults are often perceived as a highly difficult population to treat. By educating themselves about the motivations of these individuals, crisis counselors may be able to better implement treatment strategies or programs to rehabilitate sexual offenders.

8 Addressing Substance Abuse and Dependence Within the Crisis Context

Edward Cannon

PREVIEW

In this chapter, you will read about Substance Use Disorders and the disease of addiction, including causes, manifestations, and treatment. There are numerous models of and theories about the causes of alcoholism and drug addiction, and this chapter will introduce you to the medical model and the moral/legal model as well as important genetic, sociocultural, and psychological theories. As you read this chapter, keep in mind your own belief system about substance abuse and dependence, and reflect on the role that your own culture has played in your understanding of these complex phenomena.

SUBSTANCE ABUSE IN A SOCIETAL CONTEXT

Citizens of the United States have a somewhat ambivalent attitude toward alcohol and other drugs. On the one hand, alcohol use is considered by many to be a "rite of passage" into adulthood, while, on the other hand, excessive use beyond college age is frowned on. In our society, some drugs that we know can kill are legal (e.g., alcohol), while other drugs with some medicinal benefits are illegal (e.g., marijuana). Prescription drugs, which many people consider to be as lethal as so-called street drugs, are seen by others as harmless because they are prescribed by physicians. Often, the use of both legal and illegal drugs can precipitate a crisis in a person's life, causing behavior to spin out of control—and with dire consequences. This is the point at which a crisis counselor typically sees a client who is adversely affected by substance abuse and dependence.

Throughout this text, many definitions have been offered to establish precisely what a crisis is. Later in this chapter, we will discuss a situation that is somewhat unique to the world of Substance Use Disorders: creating a crisis for an addicted person to engage him or her in treatment. For now, we begin with a classic and enduring definition by Caplan (1961): "[P]eople are in crisis when they face an obstacle that is, for a time, insurmountable by the customary methods of problem solving. A period of disorganization ensues, a period of upset, during which many abortive attempts at solutions are made" (p. 18). According to Jacobson, Strickland, and Morley (1968), crisis intervention may be defined as "activities designed to influence the course of crisis so that a more adaptive outcome will result, including the ability to better cope with future crisis" (p. 339). Note the emphasis here on a process that is unfolding over time as well as on the ability to develop strategies for dealing with future crisis. For the friends, family, co-workers, teachers, and others who care for a person struggling with alcoholism or addiction, the "crisis" may, in fact, be months or even years in the making. The point at which the crisis counselor intervenes may be one moment in time but is part of a much larger and more complex process at work. Let's turn our attention now to how this process may look.

ETIOLOGY OF ALCOHOLISM AND DRUG ADDICTION

The etiology of a disease is the cause of that disease, and alcoholism and drug addiction are real diseases. Alcohol and drug use, abuse, dependence, and addiction are all related conditions and can best be considered in terms of a continuum, with abstinence (i.e., no use) on one end and alcoholism/addiction on the other end. In between, there are numerous categories into which an individual may fit, including light use, moderate use, misuse, abuse, and dependence (see Figure 8.1). The American Society of Addiction Medicine (1996) defined alcoholism as follows: "Alcoholism is a primary, chronic disease with genetic, psychosocial, and environmental factors influencing its development and manifestations. The disease is often progressive and fatal. It is characterized by continuous or periodic impaired control over drinking, preoccupation with the drug alcohol, use of alcohol despite adverse consequences, and distortions in thinking, most notably denial" (p. 34).

Culture, social norms, availability, and religion all affect how people use, misuse, and abuse alcohol, and there is no general agreement on the exact nature of the origins of alcoholism in individuals. However, there are three major categories that define how most experts consider the development and manifestation of this disease, and a discussion of these biological, psychological, and social theories follows.

The disease concept or medical model continues to be the most widely accepted biological theory regarding the development and manifestation of alcoholism, and it first gained prominence in the 18th century (Vaillant, 1995). In 1790, Dr. Benjamin Rush described a disease syndrome caused by alcohol and characterized by individual moral and physical decay. According to Rush, the diseased condition of dependence on alcohol could be cured by total abstinence from hard liquor. Proponents of the medical model have considered alcoholism a disease because it fits certain criteria of all diseases: (1) it has a primary nature (e.g., it is caused by consumption of alcohol and is not a secondary symptom of something else, (2) it is progressive (e.g., it gets worse over time with continued alcohol use), and (3) it can be fatal if not arrested.

Today, many treatment professionals and alcoholics in recovery subscribe to the notion that the only way to arrest the disease of alcoholism is through complete

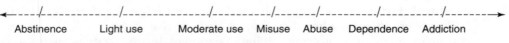

Abstinence   Light use   Moderate use   Misuse   Abuse   Dependence   Addiction

FIGURE 8.1   The Abstinence/Addiction Continuum.

abstinence. Alcoholics Anonymous (AA) is the most well known self-help group for alcoholism and asserts that abstinence should be the major goal of treatment. This program has been used successfully by millions of men and women around the world since its inception in 1935 in Akron, Ohio, by Bill Wilson and Robert Smith, M.D. (Alcoholics Anonymous World Services, 1997). According to this view, because of the progressive nature of alcoholism, an individual seeking treatment must completely stop using alcohol and seek social support from others also in recovery from the disease.

The genetic theory of alcoholism asserts that certain biological or physical factors are present in alcoholics that are not present in nonalcoholics (Stanton, 1999). This theory emphasizes the role of heredity in the development of alcohol problems. For example, alcoholism runs in families, and children of alcoholics have a greater risk of developing alcoholism than do those in the general population. However, most children of alcoholics do not themselves become alcoholics. Among certain ethnic groups, genetic factors are theorized to increase individuals' likelihood of becoming alcohol dependent (e.g., Northern European descent). Individuals in other ethnic groups (e.g., Asian descent) appear to have protective genetic factors that make it less likely that they will ever abuse alcohol (Bonner & Waterhouse, 1996). Other research suggests that in alcoholics, alcohol produces a morphinelike chemical in the brain and that alcoholics have lower-than-normal levels of serotonin (Doweiko, 2003). At the same time, recent studies have shown that the genetic influence is one of degree—and not the sole determinant—with other environmental factors playing a role. One metaphor, or way to look at it, is that while genes may load the gun, it is the environment that pulls the trigger for alcoholism and addiction.

For many years, psychologists and psychiatrists considered alcoholism a symptom of mental illness and not a disease or disorder in itself. Both the American Psychological Association and the American Psychiatric Association consider alcoholism a disease (Vaillant, 1995). The other side of the disease model, which will be presented later in this chapter, is the moral/legal model, which asserts that alcoholism is a sign of mental weakness or a moral failure. While most addiction professionals subscribe to the disease model, the moral/legal model has many proponents, so there is some controversy surrounding this topic. Nevertheless, psychological theories can deepen our understanding of alcoholism and contribute to the development of treatment modalities. Psychological theories of alcoholism include trait or personality theory (i.e., an addictive personality exists that is characterized by low frustration tolerance, low impulse control, and high emotionality); conditioning theory (i.e., alcoholism is a learned behavior); psychodynamic theory (i.e., use of alcohol relieves anxiety by reducing conflicts among the id, ego, and superego); and stress management theory (i.e., individuals self-medicate with alcohol to relieve tension and manage stress) (Bonner & Waterhouse, 1996).

Sociocultural theories assert that it is the environment, family, culture, and economic factors that contribute to the use and abuse of alcohol by individuals. Sociocultural theories view people as primarily social beings, rather than as merely biological or psychological entities. Organization, interaction, interdependency, and integration of parts and elements characterize this view (Goldenberg & Goldenberg, 2004). Imagine that you live in an environment that supports heavy alcohol or drug use and that this is the only way of life you have known since birth. Your parents, siblings, coworkers, and friends drink alcohol, or abuse drugs, heavily and often. For many, this is reality. In many urban centers in the United States, there is a liquor store seemingly on

ACTIVITY 8.1
Making Sense of Models of Alcoholism

Given the fact that alcoholics come from all walks of life, explain how you can use the same theory or model to understand binge drinking by college students and chronic alcohol abuse by homeless people. Which model presented so far makes the most sense to you?

almost every corner, and it is not unusual to find alcohol cheaply priced. In conditions of poverty, hopelessness, and boredom, excessive alcohol consumption is common and even expected (Nash, 1997). Cross-cultural research suggests that the primary function of alcohol in all societies is tension reduction, which is often related to social instability, dysfunction, or change (Milgram, 1996). Given this, it is not surprising that many of the inner cities in the United States have had historically high rates of alcoholism.

Drug use, misuse, abuse, dependence, and addiction (like alcoholism) can best be examined in terms of the continuum from abstinence to addiction described earlier in this chapter, and many of the biological, psychological, and sociocultural theories also apply here. Psychoactive substances (i.e., drugs) are legal or illegal substances that, when ingested, affect the central nervous system and alter mood, perception, cognition, memory, or consciousness (Ksir, Hart, & Ray, 2006). Users experience increased pleasure or diminished pain, both emotional and physical. These substances include central nervous system depressants like alcohol and other sedative, hypnotic, and anxiolytic drugs; central nervous system stimulants, including cocaine, amphetamines, nicotine, and caffeine; opioids in any form, including heroin, morphine, and prescription analgesics; hallucinogens, such as lysergic acid diethylamide (LSD) and phencyclidine hydrochloride (PCP); marijuana, including hashish; and, finally, inhalants, anabolic steroids, and club drugs such as MDMA/ecstasy, gamma-hydroxybutyrate (GHB), and ketamine (Office of National Drug Control Policy, 2008).

Controlled substances are drugs classified by the U.S. Drug Enforcement Agency (DEA) according to their potential for abuse, ability to produce dependence, and medical utility. The classifications range from Schedule I drugs, which have such high potential for abuse that they are unacceptable for legal use, to Schedule V drugs, which have minimal abuse potential. Heroin and LSD are Schedule I controlled substances; buprenorphine (Buprenex), an opioid analgesic, is a Schedule V drug. New substances are added to the schedules every year, and drugs may be moved from one schedule to another. For example, several years ago, propoxyphene (Darvon) was listed as a Schedule V drug, but because of increased abuse, it is now classified as Schedule IV. One of the most controversial classifications is that of marijuana, which is currently Schedule I (no currently acceptable medical use) even though many states allow medical marijuana for cancer and other patients (Ksir et al., 2006).

Similar to alcohol abuse and alcoholism, there is no single precursor of drug addiction that has been universally accepted, but it, too, can be conceptualized in terms of biological, psychological, and sociocultural theories. Historically, there has been a strong societal stigma attached to individuals who use or abuse drugs, and the moral/legal model has widely been used to denigrate and control them. According to extreme proponents of this view, individuals who use and abuse drugs are immoral,

---

ACTIVITY 8.2
Evaluating Addiction Models

Which model, the moral/legal model or the medical model, aligns most closely with your views of alcoholism and drug addiction? Are there any family or cultural influences that affect your response? Make a list of the strengths and weaknesses of each model according to your own views.

---

and addicts are depraved degenerates who should be punished—and not treated (Singer, 1997). Currently, there is a battle going on between proponents of the moral/legal model and those who uphold the medical model. In 1992, the President's Commission on Model State Drug Laws (1993) was formed, with the mission "to develop comprehensive model state laws to significantly reduce, with the goal to eliminate, drug abuse in America through effective use and coordination of prevention, education, treatment, enforcement, and corrections" (p. 2). The commission asserted that tough sanctions are necessary to punish individuals who refuse to abide by the laws. According to the commission, sanctions will deter drug abuse and addiction. The scope of the commission's work reflects the strong influence currently held by the moral/legal model of addiction.

Politics aside, crisis counselors must develop a comprehensive understanding of why and how individuals come to abuse and to become dependent on substances, and that is where theories can provide assistance. Although there is no research evidence that directly links the abuse of drugs to any specific biological cause, specific sites in the brain demonstrate a possible neurochemical basis for the use of substances (Grob, 2000). These sites include the medial forebrain bundle (MFB), the ventral tegmental area (VTA), the nucleus accumbens, and the hypothalamus. It is believed that addiction is fundamentally a chronic and relapsing brain disease, with the regulation of our natural appetites gone haywire. For example, the hypothalamus houses multiple nerve centers that are responsible for keeping us alive, including the pleasure center that converges with the nucleus accumbens and the VTA (Ksir et al., 2006). During repeated drug taking, including alcohol, brain circuits are altered, and even a simple sight or smell can trigger a desire for relapse.

While a biological understanding of the brain is critical, the most comprehensive model of drug addiction today is the biopsychosocial model, which, as the name suggests, encompasses biological, psychological, and sociocultural theories (Gorski, 1995). Rather than viewing addiction from a single perspective, many crisis counselors today employ this model to understand the etiology, expression, treatment, and prevention of addiction from a more comprehensive stance. A biopsychosocial perspective includes and integrates aspects of current biological, psychological, and sociocultural theories and is consistent with a holistic view of the client. By integrating these various elements into their view of each client, crisis counselors are better able to conceptualize prevention and treatment strategies that are individualized and more meaningful to the client. In this way, crisis counselors can increase engagement by clients and can improve outcomes. Specific strategies based on the biopsychosocial model, and related to crisis interventions in various settings, will be presented later in this chapter.

Multicultural Considerations

Culture includes values, beliefs, attitudes, norms, traditions, customs, and practices that a group of people pass from generation to generation (Sue & Sue, 2003). It is critical to keep in mind cultural considerations as you think about working with various populations, especially those whose worldviews may differ from your own. Culture influences an individual's health beliefs and practices, and counselors need to know whether their clients consider the use of alcohol and other drugs to be problematic. For example, Native American cultures have considered the use of psychedelics to be a part of religious or healing rituals. Additionally, counselors must factor in other cultural considerations (including immigrant status) as they think about whether individuals are likely to seek or avoid professional help. According to Sue and Sue, half of African-American clients terminate after one session, compared with 30% of European-American clients. Clearly, crisis counselors must be aware of cultural mistrust and wariness on the part of their minority clients and be ready to respond in a helpful manner. What kinds of assumptions might an African-American client bring to a counseling session? Just like counselors, clients represent a wide range of life experiences and belief systems. It is crucial to keep in mind the difference between salient and nonsalient data—for example, behaviors that may be considered typical of a person from a certain culture versus behaviors unique to an individual.

Another major consideration here is how the interaction of the crisis counselor's culture, the client's culture, and the cultural setting can lead to expectations, meanings, and assumptions resulting in misunderstanding, frustration, and treatment failure. Parham, White, and Amaju (1999) compare seven dimensions of being, presented in Table 8.1, between African Americans and European Americans. Keep in mind that this information does not include all possible differences, nor is it true for all clients; it simply provides a tool for awareness.

Ethnocultural considerations will largely determine alcohol and drug use patterns, as well as treatment engagement, among different groups, and while it is important not to stereotype clients, certain patterns have emerged in the United States. For

TABLE 8.1 Comparison of Dimensions of Being Based on Ethnicity

Dimension	African American	European American
Self	Holistic/integrated	Fragmented/segmented
Feelings	Expressed	Suppressed/controlled
Survival	Collective orientation	Self/competitive
Language	Oral/in relation to other	Written/detached
Time/space orientation	Present-centered/past-referenced	Commodity/future
Universe	Harmony, balance, interrelated	Mastery/control
Death	Transition to next life	Death of body; end
		Desire to preserve life

Source: The Psychology of Blacks: An African Centered Perspective, by T. A. Parham, J. L. White, and A. Amaju, 1999, Upper Saddle River, NJ: Prentice Hall.

example, addiction treatment as we know it today was developed primarily by European-American practitioners, so this group may be the most likely to use addiction treatment (Craig, 2004).

ASSESSMENT OF SUBSTANCE ABUSE AND DEPENDENCE (SUBSTANCE USE DISORDERS)

Use of a substance is considered to be abuse when the substance is used in excess, when the use of the substance may exacerbate existing physical or psychological problems, or when the use of the substance is illegal (Ksir et al., 2006). To diagnose addictive disorders, counselors need information from multiple domains. The most commonly used system for organizing and communicating clinical information about substance abuse and dependence is the *Diagnostic and Statistical Manual of Mental Disorders* (*DSM–IV–TR*; American Psychiatric Association, 2000). The specific categories for substance-related disorders in the *DSM–IV–TR* are divided into two basic groups: the Substance Use Disorders (i.e., Substance Abuse, Substance Dependence) and the Substance-Induced Disorders (e.g., Substance Intoxication and Substance Withdrawal). The main criterion for Substance Abuse includes a "maladaptive pattern of substance use leading to clinically significant impairment or distress, occurring within a 12-month period" (American Psychiatric Association, 2000, p. 182). Areas that the professional counselor should pay particular attention to include changes in work or school performance, use of a substance while driving, and legal problems related to use of a substance as well as interpersonal problems related to use. The diagnosis of Substance Dependence requires more significant impairment due to drug or alcohol use and usually requires evidence of (1) tolerance (e.g., a person needs more of a substance to feel the effects); (2) withdrawal (each class of drugs has its own withdrawal syndrome); (3) loss of control over use; (4) evidence that large amounts of time are spent obtaining, using, or recovering from use; and (5) continued use despite knowledge that it makes a physical or psychological condition worse. To meet criteria for dependence, at least three of these criteria must be met during a 12-month period (American Psychiatric Association, 2000).

Diagnosis should be a collaborative process between the crisis counselor and the client. Using assessment data, collateral information from family and friends (with the permission of the client, of course), and client self-report, the problem is named, and a treatment plan can be written. A reliable diagnosis reflects addiction severity, which means the seriousness of symptoms and the degree of impairment, from moderate to severe. This guides the intensity of treatment. Before we examine the assessment and treatment process, let's look at a few common terms used in the field of addictions counseling.

While the language used to describe addiction has changed over the years, people continue to use words and terms that have inexact meanings. Contributing to this are the negative images people associate with addiction as well as the way people often dilute the concept by saying things like "I am addicted to ice cream" or "I am addicted to shoes." While it is true that there are such things as food addictions and compulsive spending, mental health professionals must be careful to use precise language when discussing clinical issues. A shared vocabulary enhances communication among counselors and between counselors and the general public. Two primary sources inform the terminology and definitions used by addictions counselors: (1) The *DSM–IV–TR* (American Psychiatric Association, 2000) and (2) the American Society of Addiction Medicine's (1996) *Patient Placement Criteria for the Treatment of Substance-Related Disorders*.

Common Terms

Denial is the most common way in which individuals keep the reality of their alcohol or drug use away from immediate consciousness. It stops help-seeking behavior, contributes to treatment failure, and sets up relapse (Kearney, 1996). It is a complex phenomenon that includes minimizing the severity of the problem and that allows individuals to avoid facing the consequences of their use, for both themselves and others. *Craving* is an intense desire beyond rational thought for a drink, a drug, or an addictive activity (e.g., "I don't want to use, but I just can't help it"). Currently, researchers are working to understand the craving phenomenon in order to develop treatments that will curb this process (Craig, 2004). It is hoped that by diminishing the powerful urge to use alcohol or drugs, crisis counselors will be better able to assist clients in the early stages of recovery from alcohol or drugs. *Recovery* means different things to different people but includes optimal client health, well-being, and functioning (Gorski, 1995). It is a term commonly used in the self-help community and refers to an active process of abstinence from substances and addictive behaviors as well as personal growth. Relapse is the recurrence of substance use or addictive behaviors following a period of abstinence and should be considered part of the recovery process. Gorski calls relapse prevention a critical treatment goal that should be framed for clients as a way to learn from mistakes in order to promote self-efficacy and develop emotional maturity.

SCREENING AND ASSESSMENT PROCESS FOR SUBSTANCE ABUSE AND DEPENDENCE

As previously discussed, assessment is a collaborative process between client and counselor in which data are collected about the client, the client's substance use, and the client's environment (Doweiko, 2003). Subjective data provided by clients who use substances include extremes in thoughts, feelings, and behaviors. Individuals may report feeling stimulated or depressed, or they may experience giddiness, euphoria, and grandiosity as well as feelings ranging from anxiety to panic and from fear to paranoia. In a crisis situation where there is not always time to conduct a complete assessment, standardized screening tools can be used to collect as much information as quickly as possible. Screens flag an actual or potential problem and suggest the need for comprehensive assessment. They also help counselors decide whether or not a client is at imminent risk to harm self or others. Three of the most commonly used screening tools are the AUDIT, CAGE Questionnaire, and SMAST.

The AUDIT (Alcohol Use Disorder Identification Test) is a 10-item, multinational test for adults; the cutoff score is 8 points or more, with a range of 0 to 40 points. This test allows counselors to gather information on use and problem history in the past year; it does not detect past alcohol use problems. It is a brief, structured interview, developed by the World Health Organization (WHO), and it contains questions about recent alcohol consumption, dependence symptoms, and alcohol-related problems. Depending on the risk level determined by the results, clients may be provided alcohol education, simple advice about the risks of heavy drinking, brief counseling with continued monitoring, or referral to a specialist for diagnostic evaluation and treatment (WHO, 1993).

The CAGE Questionnaire (Ewing, 1984) is a four-item questionnaire (usually administered verbally) that includes questions related to a history of attempting to *cut down* on alcohol or drug use (C), *annoyance* over criticism of alcohol or drug use (A), *guilt* about behavior under the influence of alcohol or drugs (G), and drinking or drug use in the morning to relieve withdrawal symptoms, sometimes referred to as an *eye-opener* (E). According to Ewing, use of the CAGE questions effectively distinguishes alcoholics from nonalcoholics at or above the 90% range, with one yes response indicating a possibility of alcoholism or drug addiction, two or three yes responses indicating a high suspicion index, and four indicating that an alcoholism or drug-dependence diagnosis is highly likely.

The Short Michigan Alcohol Screening Test (SMAST; Mendelson & Mello, 1985) is a 13-item questionnaire (administered verbally) based on the original MAST (Selzer, 1971), which is the most researched diagnostic instrument for alcoholism. The authors assert that the SMAST has been shown to identify over 90% of alcoholics entering general psychiatric hospitals. Typical questions include "Do you feel you are a normal drinker?" and "Are you able to stop drinking when you want?" (Mendelson & Mello, 1985, p. 56).

While screening tools can provide subjective information for crisis counselors, there is also objective information that merits consideration. What are the signs and symptoms of substance use that family, friends, and counselors observe? In general, individuals who abuse substances neglect their health and personal care; they may present as malnourished and with an unkempt appearance, and they may seem older than their stated age. Biological manifestations of substance use include gastrointestinal problems (e.g., diarrhea or constipation, pain, weight loss), skin problems (e.g., sweating, dehydration, needle marks, lesions), cardiovascular problems (e.g., chest pain, palpitations), and trauma from assaults, accidents, or fighting while under the influence. Other immediate signs to look for include intoxication or intoxicated behavior (e.g., slurred speech, unsteady walk, smell of alcohol, glazed eyes).

Regardless of the setting, crisis counselors should always perform a Mental Status Exam (MSE) with clients upon intake to determine whether they are currently intoxicated as well as how well they are oriented to their surroundings. The MSE can also help rule out coexisting psychiatric disorders and is useful in detecting the direct effects of a Substance Use Disorder, such as persistent or transient hallucinations; mood and affective symptoms; suicidal, violent, or paranoid behavior: and impaired cognitive functioning (Kearney, 1996). The term *dual disorders* (sometimes also called dual diagnosis) refers to clients who have a primary addiction diagnosis plus a second mental health diagnosis, such as alcohol dependence and major depressive disorder. There is some controversy over which diagnosis takes precedence. This will be explored in more depth later in this chapter.

Assessing Motivation for Change

One common assumption frequently made by well-meaning professionals who encounter individuals with addictive behaviors is that resistance to change is the result of a personality trait (e.g., denial) and that people are intrinsically unmotivated to change (Gorski, 1995). By contrast, research conducted by Miller and Rollnick (2002)

CASE STUDY 8.1

Elyse

Imagine you are a crisis counselor at a university counseling center assigned to see walk-in clients. An 18-year-old student, Elyse, arrives one morning and tells you that the prior evening she was out with friends drinking at a club. She appears to be wearing the same clothes from last night, and she has the odor of alcohol about her. During your assessment, she mentions that she has been drinking more lately and that, despite her best efforts, she is unable to cut down. Now she tells you that she does not remember the last part of the evening and fears she may have said some inappropriate things to her friends. She also says she kissed her best friend's boyfriend. She is clearly distraught and remorseful and begins sobbing and shaking in your office. Elyse's responses to the CAGE questionnaire reveal that she has been unable to (C) cut down, and she also reports (G) guilt and remorse over kissing her best friend's boyfriend as well as the inappropriate remarks she may have made to friends while under the influence.

Discussion Question

How can you use crisis intervention skills to help her find adaptive coping skills and a more effective problem-solving approach to her predicament?

---

suggests that motivation should not be thought of as a personality issue (e.g., a trait that the client brings into counseling); rather, it should be seen as a state of readiness to change, which can fluctuate from time to time. For example, a client struggling with her alcohol use (such as Elyse from the earlier case study) may be more motivated to change her behavior following a crisis in which she violates her own personal standards of conduct. Once the crisis passes, she may be less willing to address her alcohol problem.

The good news is that a client's state of readiness to change can be influenced, and Prochaska and DiClemente (1982) originally developed a six-stage model, called the stages of change model, to demonstrate how change occurs. Miller and Rollnick (2002) operationalized this model and developed motivational interviewing, a client-centered, counselor-directed approach based on the stages of change model. Motivational interviewing provides a structure that gives responsibility back to the client for change, relieving crisis counselors of that assumed burden. Once clients have made a commitment for change, crisis counselors can more successfully provide support and strategies to assist clients in achieving their goals. Motivational interviewing is an evidence-based treatment effective across various venues with ethnically and culturally diverse client populations. The stages of change model presents a series of stages through which individuals pass while trying to modify their behavior, whether the behavior is smoking, overeating, or drug and alcohol use. Motivational interviewing provides crisis counselors with specific tasks based on the client's current stage. The five central stages are (1) pre-contemplation, where clients are not ready to change; (2) contemplation, where clients acknowledge the problem and weigh the costs/benefits of changing versus not changing; (3) preparation, where clients develop a firm resolve to change, including developing a plan; (4) action, where clients are actively modifying their behavior; and (5) maintenance, where clients sustain change for six months or more.

ACTIVITY 8.3

Applying the Stages of Change

Think of a time in your life when you tried to change a behavior. It could have been trying to study more, or to lose weight, or to spend less time surfing the Internet. Once you have a behavior in mind, see if you can recall the experience fully and jot down some of the memories and feelings you associate with it. Was there a "crisis" that precipitated your decision to change your behavior? See if you can apply Prochaska and DiClemente's stages of change model to your experience. Are there any cultural implications (e.g., race, gender, religion, sexual orientation) that may have affected your experience?

This model accepts relapse (the sixth stage) as a natural part of the change process that can occur at any time, and clients are encouraged to see it as a learning opportunity rather than as evidence of failure. During relapse, the counselor's task is to assist the client in examining mistakes without becoming demoralized. Naturally, clinicians approach clients differently depending on their current stage of change. For example, a client who does not see any need to modify behavior is said to be in the pre-contemplation stage, and the counselor should primarily provide information and resources. In contrast, a client in the determination stage needs the most help in developing a change strategy that is realistic and achievable, based on client needs and goals. The following section describes how professional counselors can use motivational interviewing to assist clients.

A Single-Session Crisis Intervention Strategy

In Chapter 1, a crisis was defined as an event that is perceived to be so intolerable that it exceeds a person's resources and coping mechanisms. Marino (1995) delineated four stages of crisis: "(a) A critical situation occurs in which a determination is made as to whether a person's normal coping mechanisms will suffice; (b) increasing tension and disorganization around the event escalate beyond the person's coping ability; (c) a demand for additional resources (such as counseling) to resolve the event is needed; and (d) referral may be needed to resolve a major personality disorganization" (p. 40). Roberts and Ottens (2005) have defined a crisis as "[a]n acute disruption of psychological homeostasis in which one's usual coping mechanisms fail and there exists evidence of distress and functional impairment. It often has five components: a hazardous or traumatic event, a vulnerable or unbalanced state, a precipitating factor, an active crisis state based on the person's perception, and the resolution of the crisis" (p. 331).

Keep these definitions in mind throughout the next section, as we examine intervention strategies in various settings using Roberts and Ottens' even-stage crisis intervention model. We will be applying this model to several cases in this chapter. According to Roberts and Ottens (2005), there are seven critical stages through which counselors and clients usually pass on the road to crisis stabilization:

1. Plan and conduct a thorough biopsychosocial and lethality/imminent danger assessment;
2. Make psychological contact and rapidly establish the collaborative relationship;
3. Identify the major problems, including crisis precipitants;
4. Encourage an exploration of feelings and emotions;

5. Generate and explore alternatives and new coping strategies;
6. Restore functioning through implementation of an action plan; and
7. Plan follow-up and booster sessions. (p. 333)

CASE STUDY: CRISIS AT A COMMUNITY MENTAL HEALTH CENTER

Rick is a 35-year-old, married, African-American man who was recently laid off from his job at the local automobile plant. He had worked there for 15 years as a machinist and had earned a pretty good wage. Rick's wife, Laurie, has been concerned about him for the past month because he has been spending more time at the local bar instead of looking for a new job. At the bar, Rick usually consumes between 6 and 10 beers per visit, spaced out over several hours, and, as a large man, he is able to function within a normal range of behavior. Lately, however, Rick has noticed that it takes more beers to feel the same buzz that he enjoys. Despite this increase in consumption, Rick continues to drive home intoxicated, telling himself that he "can handle it." One night Rick is arrested for DUI (Driving Under the Influence), and the judge mandates a visit to you, a counselor at the local community mental health center. Rick is distraught, angry, and clearly upset as he enters your office. How would you approach Rick using Roberts' and Ottens' seven-stage crisis intervention model?

Stage 1: Conduct Psychosocial and Lethality Assessment

Conducting a rapid, but thorough, biopsychosocial assessment is your first priority and should include discussion of Rick's environmental supports and stressors, medical needs and medications, current use of drugs and alcohol, and internal and external coping methods and resources (Roberts & Ottens, 2005). Assessing lethality involves determining whether Rick has actually attempted suicide (e.g., overdose), and, if no suicide attempt is in progress, you should ask about Rick's potential for self-harm. This would include asking about suicidal thoughts and feelings (e.g., "When you say you can't take it anymore, does that mean you are thinking of harming yourself?"). You should also consider any history of suicide attempts, as well as certain risk factors, which in Rick's case include being male and recently experiencing a layoff. Be careful not to ask too many questions, as you do not want to cause Rick to become defensive. You should soon begin to have a clear sense of Rick and of his situation.

Stage 2: Rapidly Establish Rapport

Using your interviewing skills, you should be able to piece together Rick's story without making him feel like he is being judged and, at the same time, allowing him to feel heard and understood. You want to ensure that rapport is built quickly by remembering to engage Rick using genuineness, respect, and acceptance. Other facilitative behaviors include establishing good eye contact, leaning forward slightly, and exhibiting a nonjudgmental tone and attitude (see Chapter 3).

Stage 3: Identify Major Problems or Crisis Precipitants

In Rick's case, the cause (i.e., precipitant) of the current crisis is his arrest for DUI. At the same time, you want to begin to prioritize other issues in the client's life that may be the focus of clinical attention, such as the job layoff and marital problems. While beginning to understand how this event escalated into a crisis, counselors may capture a glimpse of the client's typical coping style (e.g., how he or she usually handles day-to-day problems). This may be useful for the client in the future in order to prevent additional crises.

Stage 4: Deal with Feelings and Emotions

According to Roberts and Ottens (2005), there are two aspects to this stage: (1) allowing the client to express feelings (i.e., to vent) and to tell his story about the current situation and (2) cautiously challenging the client to let go of maladaptive beliefs and consider other behavioral options. In Rick's case, this would mean employing active listening skills such as paraphrasing, reflecting feelings, evoking strengths, and requesting specific examples. At the same time, you want to provide information and play devil's advocate by bringing challenging responses into the conversation (e.g., wondering out loud if Rick's alcohol use may be causing more problems than it is solving). Remember, you are continuing to conduct your assessment throughout the interview so that you can determine a diagnosis for Rick (most likely alcohol abuse or dependence).

Stage 5: Generate and Explore Alternatives

Rick is defensive and in the pre-contemplation stage of behavior change. He quips, "I don't have a drinking problem, I have a judge problem." Your greatest challenge is to help him see the big picture, and by working with him to deal with his feelings and emotions in stage 4, you have laid the foundation for exploring solutions. In this case, you would want to examine the various treatment options available to Rick based on the severity of his alcohol abuse or dependence. These could range from attendance at an alcohol education class to mandated intensive outpatient treatment for six months. Recall from the section on "Assessing Motivation for Change," that it is best to generate alternatives collaboratively so that Rick's intrinsic motivation is tapped, thus increasing the probability of successful treatment.

Stage 6: Implement an Action Plan

It is critical to implement a concrete action plan in order to restore Rick's sense of control and psychological equilibrium. For example, you might consider discussing with Rick his attitude toward Alcoholics Anonymous and whether he would be willing to attend a few meetings. Roberts and Ottens (2005) also emphasize the cognitive dimension, or meaning making, which must be part of the plan. For Rick, this means working through the meaning of his job layoff, his arrest for DUI, and the implications of his use of alcohol to relieve stress. This is critical in order for Rick to gain mastery of the situation and to cope with future setbacks.

Stage 7: Conduct Follow-Up

Evaluating Rick's postcrisis status is critical in order to ensure that he has followed through on your recommendations and is no longer experiencing a crisis. Typically, a booster session may be scheduled about a month after your crisis intervention. In practical terms, this would mean that Rick has stopped using alcohol to cope with stress, is attending Alcoholics Anonymous regularly for support, and is compliant with any other treatment recommendations.

ACTIVITY 8.4
Time for Reflection

What was your initial reaction to working with Rick? Does the fact that he has just been laid off from his job have any impact on how you view his crisis? What are some of the important questions you should ask Rick to assess for suicidal ideation? Are there any cultural factors that might affect your ability to quickly establish rapport? How important do you consider Rick's gender, race, and socioeconomic status to be as factors that might impede or assist your work with him? What emotions are stirred up for you as you recall Rick's initial resistance to taking responsibility for his behavior?

CASE STUDY: CRISIS AT A HIGH SCHOOL

This case will assist you in conceptualizing and applying the Roberts and Ottens (2005) model in a school setting, using the seven critical steps defined earlier. Keep in mind that the school counselor is part of a continuum of care and will be involved as the immediate crisis unfolds and will collaborate with other professionals once it is resolved, monitoring progress of the student when she is back at school.

Ronna is a 17-year-old, second-generation Korean-American senior at the high school where you work as a professional school counselor. She is a member of the varsity soccer team, and her grades are generally excellent. Ronna has an active social life, and she counts numerous individuals among her circle of friends. She reports having alcohol for the first time when she was 15 years old. When asked about this experience, she indicated that it was largely uneventful but that she did enjoy the "buzz" she got from drinking several glasses of rum and coke while at a sleepover at a friend's house. During her junior year, Ronna was arrested for underage drinking and had to serve 20 hours of community service and complete a 16-hour alcohol education program. She reported that the community service was actually enjoyable but that the alcohol education program was "a joke." She continued to use alcohol throughout the time she completed the community service

ACTIVITY 8.5
Questions for Reflection

Given what you know about Asian-American culture and family structure, what might be some factors to keep in mind as you work with Ronna? For example, you may want to assess her family's level of acculturation or listen for the potential role that shame might play in Ronna's family.

How would you approach Ronna using Roberts' and Ottens'(2005) seven-stage crisis intervention model? You may want to jot down some notes now regarding the most pressing concerns, especially regarding a lethality assessment, since Ronna is actively using drugs and alcohol. In this case, stages 1 through 4 will need to occur in rapid succession, usually within about 15 minutes. As a professional school counselor, your primary role when working with Ronna will be as a referral source, but you will first need to assess for any imminent danger. Because she is using alcohol, LSD, and Ritalin, Ronna meets the criteria for danger to self, so her parents should be immediately notified. Once you meet with Ronna and her parents, you can decide together on the most realistic course of action. Most likely, you will act as a link to local mental health resources, which may include hospitalization.

and attended the alcohol education classes, although she did admit to being more discrete as to when, where, and with whom she would drink.

For the past three months, Ronna has been snorting Ritalin in order to keep up with her hectic school, work, and soccer schedule. Last weekend she tried LSD for the first time and said, "I felt like I was losing my mind." She is feeling panicked when she comes to your office today because her parents found her stash of pills and she doesn't know what to do.

COMORBIDITY OF SUBSTANCE ABUSE AND MENTAL ILLNESS

In the United States, between 1998 and 2003, the number of clients diagnosed with both a mental illness and a Substance Use Disorder increased from 210,000 to 800,000, and community mental health centers are playing an increasingly central role in providing services for this population (Druss et al., 2006). Many psychological disorders occur at a higher rate among individuals who abuse or are dependent on alcohol or other drugs. Data from a variety of studies indicate that approximately 50% of individuals with severe mental illness meet lifetime criteria for Substance Use Disorders (Barry et al., 1995). These include anxiety disorders, mood disorders, conduct disorder, depression, and psychosis, among others. Because of this, many clinicians are at odds about which diagnosis should be the primary focus of clinical attention. On the one hand, some argue that if an individual displays symptoms of a serious psychological disorder, the client should immediately be administered a battery of tests. On the other hand, because emotional and psychological problems tend to be made worse by the use and abuse of alcohol and other drugs, others recommend that evaluations to determine independent mental disorders wait until the client has been clean and sober at least 30 days. For example, heavy alcohol use may present as depression, whereas once the individual is sober for a period of time, these symptoms become less severe, and the person will return to his or her emotional baseline.

As previously discussed, depression is very common during bouts of substance abuse and dependence, as well as during periods of abstinence, but it is most frequent, severe, and frightening during the first year of sobriety (Brown, 1985). In a large study of recovering alcoholics and addicts, Brown found that one-third of participants reported feeling suicidal since becoming abstinent. At the same time, respondents reported that their depressions occurred in cycles and grew shorter and less intense as time passed. One of the implications for professional counselors is the need to be aware of this dynamic, whether working with an individual who is actively using substances or one who is sober. Keep in mind that for some, depression (including manic

---

ACTIVITY 8.6
Where Do You Stand?

Which symptoms do you think should take precedence when working with clients who are abusing substances? Is it even possible to determine the extent of an individual's psychological distress while they are currently abusing alcohol or drugs? What are some of the implications of diagnosing someone before he or she has had the time to live drug free?

Spotlight on CHANGES

CHANGES (Levin, Madover, & Wilson, 2006) is an evidence-based program in Oakland, California, that is specifically designed to engage and treat dually diagnosed individuals in the community. Based on the principles of motivational interviewing, CHANGES consists of three types of outreach teams whose involvement depends on the individual client's current stage of change. There is an outreach team for those in the precontemplation or early contemplation stage; a service team for clients in the contemplation, preparation, or action stage; and a self-help component for those in the maintenance stage. The three main goals of this program are to decrease clients' frequent and inappropriate use of psychiatric emergency and acute care services, decrease overall system costs, and empower clients to regain control of their lives. Program effectiveness is measured by successful clinical outcomes and cost savings, and patient-centered care is the hallmark of this innovative program.

episodes), anxiety, and feelings of hopelessness may be a lifelong problem, while for others, these feelings may be part of the recovery process. Facing one's inadequacies, self-doubts, guilt, and shame is all part of the process of developing emotional maturity, but for those who have numbed their feelings with chemicals, the process can be even more daunting. The existence of a co-occurring mental illness only adds to the shame and stigma, creating even more barriers to wellness for many people.

Unfortunately, individuals with a mental illness and a Substance Use Disorder often do not receive adequate services. Studies show that Substance Use Disorders often are not detected in acute care psychiatric settings; for example, only 2% of Substance Use Disorders among severely mentally ill patients were detected in a university emergency room and only 15% in a state hospital (Barry et al., 1995; Drake, Mueser, Clark, & Wallach, 1996). One of the major problems is that assessment instruments such as those described earlier in this chapter were developed and validated on populations without mental illness. Sadly, individuals with dual diagnoses experience frequent crises, rely heavily on psychiatric emergency services, and often end up in jail. As a crisis counselor, part of your task is to advocate for your clients to help reduce the shame and stigma associated with addiction and mental illness. See Spotlight on CHANGES for an example of a community-based program for addressing the needs of clients with a dual diagnosis.

SUBSTANCE ABUSE TREATMENT: ADMISSIONS PROCESS AND TREATMENT OPTIONS

Admitting to oneself and to others that the use of substances has gotten out of control is one of the bravest and most difficult actions an individual can take. It is a process of self-discovery and honesty that often begins with a crisis. Whether it is a soccer mom who crashes her car after too many drinks at lunch, a college student who is admitted to the hospital emergency room after overdosing on methamphetamines, or a nurse caught forging a prescription for opiates, the faces of addiction cross all races, genders, social classes, religions, sexual orientations, and ability statuses. In other words, no one is immune. But what usually happens when a person experiences a crisis and asks for help or is mandated to get help?

Family relationships are often the first casualties of addiction, but it is often within families that interventions occur. Many people who abuse substances have burned all of their bridges, but it is often family members who persevere no matter what. In the 1960s, Johnson pioneered an approach that is so common today there is even a television show based on it: intervention. According to this approach, family and friends do not have to wait until their loved one "hits bottom" and then pick up the pieces (Johnson, 1998). In fact, taking action to prevent a loved one from destroying his or her life (or the lives of others) is the hallmark of an intervention. Family and friends are encouraged to first learn about substance abuse and dependence, through either reading or attending AA or Narcotics Anonymous (NA) meetings. With the help of a trained crisis counselor, family members and concerned others document instances in which the individual's behavior under the influence of substances negatively affected them.

Next, family and friends "present reality to a person out of touch with it in a receivable way" (Johnson, 1998, p. 61). What this means is that family members are careful to be rational, yet loving and nonjudgmental, as they confront their loved one with the impact of his or her behavior. Crisis counselors support and assist family members as they confront their loved one in this moment of truth, citing specific and concrete examples of destructive behavior. At the same time, family members are taught to preface each of their examples with a positive statement in order to reinforce the nonjudgmental atmosphere. Another critical piece of the intervention is to present the loved one with specific options for treatment, including consequences if the person refuses the help that is being offered. Clearly, this is a very emotional experience for all involved, but with the assistance of a trained crisis counselor, many people in crisis because of their substance abuse or dependence can and do receive help.

Another intervention model, the CRAFT intervention program (Smith & Meyers, 2008), uses a different approach: It is "an empirically–based, non-confrontational therapy program designed for the concerned significant other (CSO) who wants to motivate a partner or family member to seek help" (p. 4). This approach is more progressive in its basic premises, practical, and generally applicable to counselors working in a variety of settings. The major difference in this approach is the way the process of enabling is brought to life using a functional analysis of a problem behavior, with the main goal being to alter the identified patient's (IP's) substance use by changing how the CSO interacts with the IP. The model includes rewarding sober behavior and stresses the importance of problem solving and self-care for both the family and the IP. For crisis counselors who may not be confident in their knowledge of drinking/using behavior, the model provides vivid examples and a step-by-step process for getting started, guiding the CSO, identifying short- and long-term consequences for both the IP and the CSO, and, ultimately, helping to get the client who abuses substances into treatment. So what happens when the substance abuser actually enters treatment?

One of the most critical aspects of a crisis counselor's job is the ability to gauge the seriousness of a client's addiction, including the degree of impairment. The American Society of Addiction Medicine (1996) has developed adult and adolescent placement criteria. Another tool that counselors use is the Addiction Severity Index (ASI), a structured clinical interview that assesses client needs and aids in treatment planning (McLellan, 1980). Depending on the results of either the ASAM or the ASI assessment, the counselor (in consultation with other providers) will decide on the appropriate treatment intensity. It is usually best to seek the least restrictive alternative for clients so that they can continue as normal a life as possible while seeking help. Typically, levels of care range from outpatient services (such as those provided to Rick, earlier in this chapter) to medically managed, intensive inpatient services. In between these extremes are intensive outpatient, partial hospitalization, and residential or inpatient services. The best alternative for any given client depends on complex issues such as the client's motivation to enter treatment, whether there is a need for detoxification, how well the client has responded to earlier attempts at treatment, the client's ability to function within a group setting, family resources, and insurance, among others. These are just a few of the issues facing an individual once he or she makes the courageous decision to seek help. One of the greatest rewards of being a counselor is witnessing the rapid changes for the better that can occur once a person enters treatment.

Conflict and Controversy: Harm Reduction Versus Abstinence-Based Models

In the addiction field, there is an ongoing debate between those who believe that abstinence should be the only goal for clients with Substance Use Disorders and those who subscribe to the harm reduction model. Many adherents to 12-step models, such as AA and NA, believe that abstinence is the best and only way for those with a Substance Use Disorder to recover and get well. More recently, proponents of the harm reduction model have argued that this is not a realistic goal for many people, especially younger individuals with a shorter history of abuse. According to Marlatt (1996), there are four basic assumptions central to harm reduction:

> (a) harm reduction is a public health alternative to the moral/criminal and disease models of drug use and addiction; (b) it recognizes abstinence as an ideal outcome but accepts alternatives that reduce harm; (c) it has emerged primarily as a "bottom-up" approach based on addict advocacy, rather than a "top-down" policy established by addiction professionals; and (d) it promotes low threshold access to services as an alternative to traditional high threshold approaches. (p. 780)

Summary

This chapter introduced the various Substance Use Disorders that may precipitate a crisis in a person's life, causing behavior and emotions to spin out of control. This crisis point should be viewed as both a challenge and an opportunity, for it is often during this time that a person is most receptive to making meaningful behavioral and emotional changes. Motivational interviewing was introduced, which helps crisis counselors work with clients to increase intrinsic motivation for behavior change, thus increasing the odds for success. The disease of addiction, including its causes, manifestations, and treatment, was reviewed. There are numerous models of and theories about the causes of alcoholism and drug addiction, and this chapter introduced the medical model and the moral/legal model as well as important genetic, sociocultural, and psychological theories. Roberts' and Ottens'seven-stage crisis intervention model was applied to

various settings with diverse populations. Also presented were two models of intervention: the Johnson model and the CRAFT model. Finally, various substance abuse treatment options and levels of care, as defined by the American Society for Addiction Medicine, were reviewed. These included outpatient services, intensive outpatient services, partial hospitalization services, residential (inpatient) services, and medically managed, intensive inpatient services. Clearly, there is no "one size fits all" when it come to crises involving Substance Use Disorders, and that is why it is important to be able to apply theories and models to understand the best ways to respond when crises do occur. Keep in mind personal belief systems and biases about substance abuse and dependence, and reflect on the role that culture plays in understanding and treating these complex phenomena.

CHAPTER

9

Emergency Preparedness and Response

Jason McGlothlin, Lisa R. Jackson-Cherry, and Michele Garofalo

PREVIEW

Emergency preparedness and effective responses by crisis counselors are reviewed in this chapter. However, the content of this chapter infuses information found in previous chapters to allow readers to synthesize what they have previously read. In the first section of this chapter, crisis intervention models and clinical implications of disasters and hostage situations are explored, including the role of the crisis counselor. In the second part of this chapter, crisis management in the school is explored, including components of a crisis plan and roles of the school counselors and other school officials. Finally, the chapter concludes with an outline of the components that should be implemented when preparing for and providing death notifications.

CHARACTERISTICS OF AND RESPONSES TO DISASTERS, TERRORISM, AND HOSTAGE SITUATIONS

An elevated level of stress is a natural response to a crisis, whether it is a natural disaster, an act of terrorism, or mass destruction. Reactions to a natural disaster, terrorism, and, to some degree, hostage situations create two distinct forms of trauma. Individual trauma affects a person's mental and emotional state and requires the person to react to the event in some compensatory manner. On the other hand, collective trauma occurs on a communitywide level whereby communities either join together and prevail or fragment and possibly create isolation and further conflict. Whether the trauma results from a disaster or act of terrorism, James (2008) provided a timeline of reactions and interventions needed to handle the traumatic event (see Table 9.1). For the purposes of this section, the term *disaster* will stand for a natural disaster or an act of terrorism.

Initially, when a disaster strikes, people experience feelings of shock, fear, panic, confusion, and, possibly, disorientation. Statements such as "I can't believe this is happening" and "This can't be happening" are typical. Almost immediately after the disaster occurs, people transition into preservation mode. Thoughts quickly enter the mind regarding the safety of self

TABLE 9.1   Timeline for Intervening in a Disaster

Time	Possible Response	Intervention Needed
Initial disaster strikes	• Shock • Fear/panic • Self-preservation • Family preservation • Helplessness/hopelessness • Denial/disbelief • Confusion/disorientation	• Evidence of resources available • Evidence of chaos reduction
Hours after disaster	• Same as above • Anger • Grief • Energetic/emotional • Action w/o efficiency • Rumination of disaster	• Evidence of resources available • Evidence of chaos reduction • Organization/control • Ventilation • Problem solving • Connection with loved ones
Days after disaster	• Fear • Denial/disbelief • Anger • Emotional • Rumination of disaster • Cohesion of community • Optimism • Thoughts of pre-disaster life • That which does not kill me makes me stronger!	• Gathering information about loved ones, neighborhoods, etc. • Crisis intervention therapies • Financial/government support
First month after disaster	• Stop talking about disaster • Rumination of disaster • Resiliency • Setbacks can occur	• Prevention of Acute Stress Disorder and possibly Posttraumatic Stress Disorder • Promotion of wellness model • Life is different but can go on
Months after disaster	• Disappointment • Physical and emotional fatigue • Possible onset of Panic Disorder, Anxiety Disorder, suicide, depression, etc. • Moving on!	• Psychotherapy • Resources • Continual support from loved ones
One year after disaster	• Significance of anniversary • Family disputes if family members are not on the same level of recovery from disaster • Move on!	• "Life will go on" focus of counseling • Family therapy

Time	Possible Response	Intervention Needed
Reflection of disaster	• Move on! • Literally move and rebuild? • Grow and build life	• Support • Validation of safety

Source: Crisis Intervention Strategies, 6th ed., by R. K. James, 2008, Belmont, CA: Brooks/Cole.

and family. During this initial time of the disaster, people need to know or be assured that basic survival resources (e.g., safety, food, water) are available. People also need to know that the chaos created by the disaster (e.g., physical or material destruction, communitywide or groupwide panic) will subside. At this point in the disaster, first responders must be visible to increase a sense of hope and reduce feelings of helplessness.

Hours after a disaster strikes, the same emotions and reactions that occurred at the onset of the disaster may continue, although it is anticipated that these reactions would be decreased, even if the decrease is minimal. Feelings of anger and grief may continue, and people may experience an inability to stop thinking about the disaster. Powerful emotions typically prevent victims from organizing an effective response. Likewise, if the crisis turns to chaos, people may not be able to either provide or receive help.

Hours after the disaster people need to vent, express their feelings, and experience a catharsis. During this time period, first responders should help people regain a sense of safety in their lives. First responders can be of substantial help by providing basic problem-solving strategies. Individuals may not be able to solve large or complex problems until personal safety needs have been met. Providing resources, such as connecting people with family members and providing them with resources to meet their basic needs (e.g., shelter, safety), is crucial.

After a few days pass, people may still experience thoughts of fear, denial, disbelief, anger, heightened emotions, and continual rumination over the disaster. However, some people may begin to see optimism in getting past the disaster and moving on with life. At this point, it is beneficial for people to adopt the philosophy of "That which does not kill me makes me stronger." Communitywide efforts may start to emerge to address disaster-related issues. Community efforts instill hope in moving past the disaster and even getting back to a pre-disaster life (e.g., going back to work, buying groceries). First responders should continue to help people gather information about loved ones, neighbors, pets, and others that victims are concerned about. At this point, first responders can use specific crisis intervention counseling strategies with a focus on rebuilding life to a pre-disaster state. Also, financial and government support is needed by victims within days after the disaster.

Months after the disaster, people may stop talking about the disaster as life begins to mirror how life was before the disaster occurred. Resiliency is a positive sign of healthy adjustment. However, some people continue to ruminate over the disaster. Rumination can be a precursor to Posttraumatic Stress Disorder (PTSD) or Acute Stress Disorder. Setbacks to resiliency can occur because some factors are still out of the control of many people (e.g., government assistance does not occur in a timely fashion).

Helping people a month after a disaster requires transition from the role of a first responder to that of a crisis counselor or other mental health clinician. Clinicians at this point should assess for and intervene to address Acute Stress Disorder and prevent PTSD. Clinicians should promote a wellness philosophy that helps people reestablish physical, emotional, and spiritual health and reinforces the perspective that life, although different since the disaster, can continue.

Several months after the disaster is a time when people can either thrive or become stagnant. People who thrive are those who learned from the events surrounding the disaster and feel as if they are stronger because they survived. People who become stagnant at this point can experience physical, emotional, and/or spiritual exhaustion. If this exhaustion persists, it can lead to thoughts of suicide or to symptoms of depression or intense anxiety, especially if life has not returned to a pre-disaster state.

Whether people are thriving or stagnating several months after the disaster, it is critical that family and other loved ones show continual support for those who experienced the disaster and that resources be available to help them move on with their lives. Also at this point in time, people may need to begin formal individual or group psychotherapy in order to prevent or manage symptoms of PTSD, suicide, depression, Panic Disorder, Anxiety Disorder, or other feelings that may impair their functioning.

At the one-year anniversary of the disaster, some victims may have moved on with their lives. However, family disputes may occur when a family member continues to focus on the disaster and continually talks about events surrounding the disaster, while other family members have moved on with their lives. Such conflicts can create distance between some family members. Therefore, family counseling may be warranted, or individual counseling that focuses on wellness, symptom reduction, and the finding of meaning in life may be needed.

A year after the disaster, most individuals will have moved on with life. However, some, especially those who were significantly devastated by the disaster, may need to relocate their residence in order to either distance themselves from the daily reminder of the disaster or rebuild their lives. With these individuals, crisis counselors need to focus on support, validation of safety issues, and possibly continued care connections to counselors in the area where the victims may relocate.

Overall, the results of a disaster can have short- and long-term consequences for people that may be perfectly normal. Everly and Mitchell (1999), along with Alexander (2005), summarized that the typical responses to disaster are:

- *Cognitive reactions:* blaming, uncertainty, poor troubleshooting abilities, poor concentration, disorientation, lessened self-esteem, intrusive thoughts or rumination of the disaster, hypersensitivity, confusion, nightmares, blaming others, and difficulty with memory.
- *Physical reactions:* increased heart rate, tremors, dizziness, weakness, chills, fainting, reduced libido, headaches, vomiting, shock, fatigue, sweating, and rapid breathing.
- *Emotional reactions:* apathy, feelings of being overwhelmed, depression, irritability, anxiety, agitation, panic, helplessness, hopelessness, anger, grief, fear, guilt, loss of emotional control, and denial.
- *Behavioral reactions:* difficulty eating and/or sleeping, restlessness, conflicts with others, withdrawal from others, lack of interest in social activities, and increased drug/alcohol use.

Those who work over a period of time with people who have experienced a disaster need to be able to recognize when "normal reactions" to disaster become substantially debilitating. In order to prevent those normal reactions from becoming debilitating, an immediate response to those exposed to a disaster is critical. The goal of such a response is also to reduce panic and chaos.

Everly and Mitchell (1999) proposed that three essential elements need to take place in order to prevent panic and chaos immediately following a disaster. First, a command post needs to be established in order to help people locate and recognize one centralized location of leadership and organization in a time of chaos and disarray. Second, connections need to be made between those exposed to the disaster and needed resources. Lastly, Everly and Mitchell report that it is essential to communicate with those in need and create an atmosphere in which feelings of helplessness are extinguished.

INTERVENTIONS AFTER A DISASTER OR ACT OF TERRORISM

Little literature exists on the types of therapeutic strategies that are most effective when working with victims of a disaster. Regardless of the modality of intervention, the essential crisis intervention microskills (presented in Chapter 3) are critical to building a therapeutic foundation with clients in crisis. Some argue that cognitive-behavioral therapy (CBT) or eye movement desensitization and reprocessing (EMDR) can be highly effective due to the positive outcomes for adult clients with PTSD (Bradley, Greene, Russ, Dutra, & Westen, 2005; Hamblen, Gibson, Mueser, & Norris, 2006). Hebert and Ballard (2007) state that play therapy is the most beneficial approach with children, as it allows them to express the trauma. In contrast, Harper, Harper, and Stills (2003) contend that meeting a child's basic human needs should be the main concern. Perhaps the most appropriate intervention could be developmental, such as responding initially with a Rogerian approach to allow the client to feel accepted and heard, followed by an existential approach to help the client establish or redefine meaning in his or her life. No matter what type of intervention is implemented, most agree that early interventions increase personal recovery from a disaster (Bonanno, Galea, Bucciarelli, & Vlahov, 2007; Shalev, 2004).

Fortunately, the literature does provide insight into some models for intervening in times of disaster. Psychological First Aid (PFA), Critical Incident Stress Management (CISM), and the Crisis Counseling Program (CCP) have appeared in the literature as models that have been successfully implemented in recent disasters (e.g., the terrorist attacks on September 11, 2001; Hurricane Katrina). A discussion of these models follows.

Psychological First Aid

Everly, Phillips, Kane, and Feldman (2006) stated that "Psychological First Aid (PFA) is emerging as the crisis intervention of choice in the wake of critical incidents such as trauma and mass disaster" (p. 130). According to Ruzek et al. (2007), PFA is "a systematic set of helping actions aimed at reducing initial post-trauma distress and supporting short- and long-term adaptive functioning. Designed as an initial component of a comprehensive disaster/trauma response, PFA is constructed around eight core actions: contact and engagement, safety and comfort, stabilization, information gathering, practical assistance, connection with social supports, information on coping support, and linkage with collaborative services" (p. 17).

PFA is typically an individual approach to treatment; however, Everly et al. (2006) have suggested that group approaches can also be beneficial to those experiencing crisis. Overall, the goals of PFA are to provide resources, education, and information to those in need; promote help-seeking behaviors (especially mental health services); provide empathy and support during the crisis; and aid in moving those in immediate crisis to a pre-crisis state of adjustment (Everly & Flynn, 2005).

Everly and Flynn (2005) reported that PFA begins with helping those in need to meet their basic physical needs (e.g., safety, food, water, shelter). After those physical needs are met, or are about to be met, a crisis counselor practicing PFA attempts to help meet the client's psychological needs (e.g., emotional and behavioral support, empathy, and consolation). Next, connecting the client with friends, family, and other loved ones must take place. In addition, measures to decrease a victim's isolation must occur. Lastly, one practicing PFA should provide avenues for follow-up care. The above steps were successfully used by direct responders after the September 11, 2001, terrorist attack in New York City.

Critical Incident Stress Management

The fundamental components of Critical Incident Stress Management (CISM) are set out in the work of Everly and Mitchell (1997, 1999). This model begins with choosing specific crisis interventions (e.g., venting, debriefing) to best meet the needs of each client; this is called potentiating pairings. Once such interventions are chosen, one specifically chooses in which order to use the potentiating pairings; according to CISM, this is called catalytic sequences. Lastly, the polythetic nature of the situation refers to how one implements the potentiating pairings and the catalytic sequences based on the individual needs of each situation or disaster. Essentially, CISM is an eclectic approach to crisis intervention that takes into consideration the client's individual needs, the interventions available, and the nature of the situation.

According to Castellano and Plionis (2006), CISM was successfully implemented to augment established individual counseling through the following six components:

- *Component 1—Acute Crisis Counseling Provided by Peer Counselors:* Crisis counselors and law enforcement officers with crisis intervention skills provided crisis intervention to law enforcement officers who initially responded to the 9/11 terrorist attack in New York. Component 1 lasted three months after the attack and consisted of traditional crisis intervention techniques.
- *Component 2—Executive Leadership Program:* Because so many senior/superior police officers saw their lower-ranked colleagues die or become devastated by the 9/11 terrorist attack, specific crisis intervention services and educational seminars were developed and delivered to this population.
- *Component 3—The Multidisciplinary Team:* A multidisciplinary team delivered trainings around the clock for everyone working at the site of the 9/11 attack. Crisis intervention seminars and counseling sessions were called "trainings" at the time because they would be better received and attended by those who may have stereotypes about mental health services.
- *Component 4—Acute Traumatic Stress Group Training Sessions:* For the large number of those in need of crisis intervention, two-day psychoeducational group sessions helped to decrease isolation, normalize emotions and reactions to the attack, decrease guilt, and increase coping mechanisms.
- *Component 5—Hotline:* Telephone crisis hotlines were highly emphasized and used to help those who responded to the 9/11 attack. Hotlines are seen as a 24/7

resource that can provide support and information in times when others may not be available. In fact, hotlines are considered to be a necessity in many crisis intervention plans (Wunsch-Hitzig, Plapinger, Draper, & del Campo, 2002).

- *Component 6—Reentry Program:* 9/11 responders who directly witnessed death, carnage, and destruction were deemed to be at high risk and identified as individuals who would have difficulty going back to their daily job and family. The reentry program focused on such high-risk responders to help them get back to their "normal" life.

Crisis Counseling Program

According to Castellano and Plionis (2006), the Crisis Counseling Program (CCP) is frequently used for responses to natural disasters. The CCP model consists of the following components:

- *Assess Strengths:* One must identify not only what the problems are (e.g., stranded people, post-disaster crime) but also what human and material resources are available.
- *Restore Pre-disaster Functioning:* The key to restoring life (especially emotional status) to what it was before the disaster is to attempt to reduce the chaos of the disaster.
- *Accept the Face Value:* One must help clients to reorganize life to accommodate for the impact of the disaster (e.g., Your home was completely destroyed by the hurricane; now how can you move on?)
- *Provide Validation:* The provision of unconditional positive regard, acceptance, and validation is critical to the growth of disaster victims.
- *Provide a Psychoeducational Focus:* The provision of psychoeducation (on both a group and an individual level) regarding the normal (and abnormal) reactions to disaster can play a central role in helping disaster victims monitor their own recovery.

NATURAL DISASTERS

The consequences of natural disasters come in many forms, ranging from power outages resulting from high winds to mass casualties and staggering death tolls resulting from a tsunami. Many crisis intervention strategies (e.g., PFA, CISM, and CCP) can be used. However, when responding to a natural disaster, crisis counselors must be aware of the dynamics of the specific disaster to be better prepared for what to expect from their clients and the environment in the aftermath of the disaster.

In Chapter 2, emphasis was placed on the safety concerns and precautions of crisis counselors and their reactions to crises. This is especially critical when responding to a natural disaster. In a natural disaster, crisis counselors who are at the disaster site may see death and dismemberment, experience remarkable emotional reactions to the crisis, and be exposed to harmful situations. Chapter 2 discusses proactive approaches that a crisis counselor could take when working with clients in crisis. When reading the remainder of this section, reflect back on Chapter 2 and relate what you learned to natural disasters.

In the following sections, a brief overview of specific natural disasters is presented, covering issues that crisis counselors must keep in mind. This information is especially important because many crisis counselors may not have experienced many natural disasters.

Winter Storms

There are many components to a winter storm, and its definition varies in different parts of the United States and the world. However, the consistent elements of a winter storm include heavy snow in a short period of time, high winds, ice (i.e., sleet, freezing rain, accumulated ice), winter flooding due to large amounts of snow melting, and extreme cold temperatures. Winter storms can be localized to a few towns or affect several states (Community Emergency Response Team [CERT], 2003).

The consequences of a winter storm include heart attacks and exhaustion (mostly due to overexertion from shoveling snow), frostbite, hypothermia (mostly in elderly individuals), asphyxiation (due to improper use of heating fuels), and house fires (due to improper use of heating devices). Automobile accidents are also a significant result of winter storms and can be considered the leading cause of death resulting from a winter storm. Winter storms can also close transportation routes (e.g., roads and airports), prolong response time by emergency personnel, create damage to residential and commercial structures, and have a significant economic impact on communities (CERT, 2003).

When crisis counselors work is such conditions, they should be mindful of taking care of their own needs to stay warm and hydrated. They should not stay outdoors for long periods of time; when outdoors, they should make sure all body parts are covered, especially the neck and wrist areas; and they should eat and drink on a regular basis to conserve energy and warmth. Lastly, crisis counselors should be aware of the local resources to counter the effects of a winter storm.

Earthquakes

Earthquakes are caused by movement in the earth's crust. The damage that results from such disasters can range from mild tremors that have little effect to strong shocks that destroy buildings. Depending on its intensity and location, an earthquake can cause power outages, damage to roads and bridges, fires and explosions, structural instability or destruction to buildings, landslides, avalanches, and even tsunamis (CERT, 2003). The vast physical effects of earthquakes include adult respiratory distress syndrome, asphyxiation, burns, death, drowning, extremity injuries, myocardial infarctions, skin injuries, and head trauma (Jones, 2006).

After the initial earthquake, aftershocks often occur: The earth will tremor one or more times initially after the earthquake and up to several weeks after the initial earthquake (CERT, 2003). If an earthquake or aftershock occurs, one should drop to the floor and cover his or her head. Also, be aware of the unstable environment. Depending on the location, one should act accordingly:

- If indoors, stay inside and don't run outdoors.
- If outdoors, go to an area away from buildings, bridges, power lines, trees, and the like.
- If in a car, stay in the car, but pull over to the side of the road.
- If in a multiple-story building, don't use the elevators to leave. Also, one may expect alarms or sprinklers to engage (CERT, 2003).

Regardless of their location, crisis counselors need not only to be mindful of the environment during an earthquake situation but also to be aware of their clients and themselves. They need to make sure that steps are taken to protect themselves and their clients from future aftershocks, check for injuries, and inquire with clients about the location of family members who may be trapped or removed due to the earthquake.

Floods

Floods are caused by heavy rains (either long periods of rain or a very intense rain), poor soil absorption of rain, snowmelt, and failures in dams or levees (CERT, 2003). Floods have been known to cause a variety of physical problems among flood victims, including asphyxiation (by some means other than drowning), drowning, hepatitis A, physical trauma, respiratory infections, suicides, and tetanus (Jones, 2006).

When responding to victims of flooding, counselors need to be prepared for additional flash floods. The best response to a flood is to get to higher ground. It is also important not to walk through any flooded waters, not to drive through water (even if the water does not look high), and to avoid potentially flood-prone areas (e.g., low-lying areas, ditches, storm drains) (CERT, 2003).

The most distinguishing aspect of floods is the psychological effect it has on victims. In the wake of fires, earthquakes, tornados, and other disasters, much of the victim's belongings are completely destroyed and disintegrated—gone—and any remains are not intact. Victims of these natural disasters may have a sense of finality or closure with the notion that "my things are gone and I need to get new things." However, the psychological toll is different for flood victims in that they can see their belongings and how they have been damaged by the flood. Their belongings are not disintegrated and gone, though they are destroyed. Crisis counselors need to pay close attention to how flood victims respond emotionally to revisiting their homes and rebuilding their lives.

Heat Waves

A heat wave is an extensive period of time with excessively high temperatures and high humidity. The consequences of a heat wave can include muscular pains and spasms, heat cramps, heat exhaustion, dehydration, and, ultimately, heat or sun stroke, which is a life-threatening condition in which the body cannot regulate its proper temperature. Such heat waves are especially devastating to the very young and the elderly because their bodies are not physically equipped to work harder to regulate body temperature.

When crisis counselors are working in such conditions, they should attempt to work in air-conditioned facilities, wear lightweight and light-colored clothing, not overexert by doing physical activities, and frequently drink fluids. Also, they should inquire about the client's family members and friends (especially those who are very young or elderly) to ensure their safety.

Hurricanes

Hurricanes consist of high winds, intense rain, and storm surges. They can destroy buildings, damage communities' utility systems, erode the ground, cause tornados and/or floods, displace communities, and devastate the economy (CERT, 2003). Hurricanes have been known to cause a variety of physical problems among their victims, including carbon monoxide poisoning, congestive heart failure, diarrheal disease, drowning, pulmonary conditions, extreme heat exposure, myocardial infarction, injuries to skin and soft tissue, suicide, and trauma (Jones, 2006).

One of the most destructive hurricanes in recent times was Hurricane Katrina in August 2006, which devastated the economy, infrastructure, communities and neighborhoods, and way of life for citizens in New Orleans and along the Gulf Coast. The devastation of Hurricane Katrina created posttraumatic mental health issues that will need to be addressed for years to come (Madrid & Grant, 2008). Therefore, for crisis counselors who respond to large-scale hurricane sites (e.g., Hurricane Katrina), it is important for them to be able to follow up with their clients and connect them with long-standing mental health treatment.

Crisis counselors need to know that, because of the intense damage that hurricanes create, dangerous situations can persist after the initial impact of the hurricane. Therefore, in order to stay safe, they should work only in areas that officials have declared as being safe, not approach or be around downed power lines, and not get separated from others (CERT, 2003).

Tornados

Tornados are powerful funnels of intense circular wind that can be accompanied by severe weather, hailstorms, and gusting winds. Depending on the intensity of the tornado, it can destroy buildings and structures, move cars, destroy utilities, break glass, move concrete blocks, uproot trees and shrubs, and destroy communities (CERT, 2003).

Community counselors must be cautious of working near a site at which a tornado touched down because it can be a dangerous environment. Broken glass, rubble, sharp objects, jagged metal, and unstable structures could be present. When working with a client who has suffered loss due to a tornado, uncertainty about the future and physical heath are the issues of most concern. However, those living in tornado-prone areas (typically known as "tornado alleys") could have existential concerns about when a tornado is going to happen again and why this destruction is happening to them.

Wildfires

There are essentially three types of wildfires: (1) Surface fires are slow moving and burn the forest floor and trees, (2) ground fires are typically started by lightning and burn below the forest's floor, and (3) crown fires are quickly spreading fires that start unnoticed and burn trees, homes, and brush. Depending on the type and intensity of the fire, it can cause asphyxiation, heat exhaustion, smoke damage, burns, and damage to communities and homes (CERT, 2003).

Crisis counselors need to keep safe by staying abreast of how the fire is progressing. Some fires move very quickly, and crisis counselors need to make sure they are staying away from the fire's path. Crisis counselors need to be aware of a client's perception of actual and perceived loss. In other words, some clients might know that their home or community was destroyed by the fire (actual loss). Other clients may have been evacuated before the fire came to their community, so they may not know if their home is gone but they anticipate its loss (perceived loss). This actual or perceived loss includes not only material possessions but also loved ones, pets, and the like. For more information on loss, please refer back to Chapter 4.

With any natural disaster, transitions, displacement, relocation, or rebuilding can occur. The psychological toll that such situations take on victims is monumental. Crisis counselors need to be aware of such consequences of natural disasters (Schuh & Laanan, 2006). For example, in the aftermath of Hurricane Katrina, job sites were gone, colleges and schools were gone, grocery stores were gone, and homes were gone. So clients wonder about many things: Where will I live? Where will I go to school? How will I finish my college degree? Where will I work? How will I get food? A critical task for crisis counselors is to get clients to become aware of and use resources and follow-up services. In addition, helping clients to triage the priorities in their lives is a key element in the direct aftermath of a natural disaster (Araki, Nakane, Ohta, & Kawasaki, 1998; Dugan, 2007).

Besides natural disasters, crisis counselors may be called on to respond to disastrous events that are the result of humankind: for example, house fires or structural fires, chemical spills, nuclear disasters or nuclear meltdowns, contagion, and natural gas explosions. As with natural disasters, crisis counselors need to ensure their own safety as well as attending to the needs of their clients who have experienced these human-made disasters.

CASE STUDY 9.1

Dealing With a Flood

Anton, a 50-year-old Brazilian man, lives in rural Missouri. He has lived alone there for the past 30 years, working in his home as a typesetter. Anton does not have any family left and rarely talks to anyone except his clients. Two years ago his hearing began to diminish, and now he has no hearing in his left ear and only 15% of his hearing in his right ear.

For the past six days, torrential rains have plagued his town. The local news and emergency broadcast system warned of flooding and urged residents to evacuate. Rather than evacuating, Anton began to place sandbags around his home to keep the water out. Unfortunately, the water rose too quickly and spilled over the sandbags. Now Anton's home and business are seven feet under water. He was rescued by the local fire and rescue unit yesterday evening.

As a crisis counselor, you are meeting Anton for the first time just 22 hours after he was rescued. You are meeting him in a school gymnasium that has been converted into a shelter for flood victims.

Discussion Questions

As a crisis counselor, what would be your priority with Anton?

What might be Anton's thoughts, feelings, and behaviors?

What resources do you think Anton needs to be connected with?

What might be some multicultural considerations for Anton, located in rural Missouri?

What might be some long-term effects of this flood on Anton's professional and personal life?

What might be some barriers to his recovery?

What would be some key counseling skills to use with this client? See Chapter 3 for information on such skills.

Referring back to Chapter 5, contemplate Anton's suicidality. Could he be suicidal? If so, at what level of lethality would you think he might be? Discuss various ways to assess Anton for suicide, and think of follow-up strategies to keep Anton safe.

CASE STUDY 9.2

Dealing With a Residential Fire

The Zhang family lives on the sixth floor of a nine-story apartment building in a major metropolitan area. The Zhang family consists of Kane, the 32-year-old father; Miya, the 28-year-old mother; Asa, the 7-year-old daughter; and Kenji, the 3-month-old son.

Last week there was an electrical fire in their neighbor's apartment. As a result, their entire floor caught fire, as did parts of the floors above and below them. The majority of the building experienced significant smoke damage. The Zhang family was awakened at 2:30 A.M. by fire alarms and the smell of smoke. They barely escaped the fire, and Kane and Asa both got second-degree burns and Miya got third-degree burns on 10% of her body. All four family members also experienced significant smoke inhalation.

After the fire was extinguished, the tenants were taken to the hospital and treated. The building was declared to be unsafe, and the Zhang family, along with the rest of the tenants, was told that they could not move back into the building.

As a crisis counselor, you are meeting with the entire Zhang family for the first time three weeks after the fire. They are living with family nearly 40 miles away from their previous home and did not recover any of their belongings from the fire.

Shortly after the fire, Kane started to drink heavily (a minimum of eight beers a day and a maximum of a fifth of bourbon a day). You are meeting them in a group room in a local mental health clinic.

Discussion Questions

As a crisis counselor, what would be your priority with the Zhang family?

What might be some of their thoughts, feelings, and behaviors?

Consider the appropriateness of individual, group, or family counseling for this family. How might each be conducted if found to be appropriate?

How might you facilitate growth in this family?

What might be some developmental concerns for each of the family members?

What might be some multicultural considerations for the family?

What physical concerns might you have for each of the family members?

Refer back to Chapter 8, and consider the reaction and consequence of Kane's recent drinking.

In this and in Case Study 9.1, no one died. However, there was a tremendous amount of loss. Reflect back on the content presented in Chapter 4 which dealt with grieving and loss. What might be some emotions related to loss and grief in each of the case studies? Even though there was no loss of life, could the individuals in the case studies progress through different stages of grief and loss? If so, discuss your responses.

HOSTAGE SITUATIONS

Hostage situations are rare in America; however, there are specific ramifications of such situations that mental health practitioners need to consider, given that over 50% of hostage takers have a mental or emotional disorder (Blau, 1994). Literature on hostage negotiation is vast, and a thorough discussion of specific negotiation strategies is beyond the scope of this chapter. However, a brief discussion of hostage situations may allow mental health practitioners to gain some insight into the experiences of hostages and hostage takers.

There are essentially four stages of a hostage situation (Strentz, 1995): alarm, crisis, accommodation, and resolution (see Table 9.2). The alarm stage occurs at the initial onset of the hostage situation and is typically the most volatile and dangerous period of

TABLE 9.2 Stages of Typical Hostage Situations

Stage	Characteristics of Hostage Takers	Characteristics of Hostages
Alarm	• Volatile • Dangerous • Highly emotional • Highly aggressive • Highly irrational • Abusive to others • Signs of panic create overreactions	• Most traumatized • Confused • Victimized • Shock • Helpless/defenseless • Denial • Paralyzed
Crisis	• Initial reason • Volatile • Dangerous • Grandiose/ridiculous demands • Rants • Secure the area and hostages • Fear of authorities/paranoia • Need for attention • 1st verbal abuse—2nd violence	• Relationship with hostage taker is central to outcome • Denial • Increased fear if hostage taker is unpredictable • Fugue episodes • Claustrophobia • Reliance on hostage takers • Hopelessness
Accommodation	• Long lasting • Fatigue • Increased control of hostages	• Time stands still • Boredom • Brief feelings of terror • Fatigue • Passivity • Possible Stockholm Syndrome
Resolution	• Fatigue • Realization of lost expectations • Contemplate outcome • Possibly suicidal	• Fatigue • Seeing closure

time. Hostage takers believe that terror must be instilled in the hostages in order to keep them under control, and any hint of panic by hostages creates extreme overreactions by hostage takers. During this stage, hostage takers are highly emotional, aggressive, irrational, and abusive.

During the alarm stage, hostages are confused by the sudden turn of events and feel victimized. They suddenly feel like there is no escape from the situation and become paralyzed not only due to threats of physical harm but also due to the severe shock resulting from aggressive actions by the hostage takers. Similar to the experiences of disaster victims, hostages during this stage make comments such as "I can't believe this is happening" (e.g., expressions of denial). As a result of the events that take place during the alarm stage, survivors of hostage situations share similar characteristics with abused children, abused women, and concentration camp survivors (Herman, 1995).

As the alarm stage ends, the crisis stage begins. During the crisis stage of a hostage situation, hostage takers begin to realize the magnitude of the situation. Hostage takers continue to be highly dangerous and volatile but realize that they must secure their surroundings from authorities and attempts by hostages to escape. The crisis stage also begins the hostage takers' interactions with the authorities, and hostage takers frequently make grandiose or ridiculous demands with the expectation that the authorities will meet such demands. Hostage takers during this stage need attention and use attention as a means to show that they are in power. Typically, this showing of power begins with yelling or verbal abuse of the hostages but can quickly escalate to violence.

During the crisis stage, hostages begin to develop a relationship with the hostage takers. They rely on them for everything (e.g., food, water, the ability to use the restroom, freedom). Hostages soon learn that the more cooperative they are, the less violent the hostages takers are toward them. If a hostage shows panic or contradicts a hostage taker, then violence may occur. Hostages still experience hopelessness, denial, and fear, though fear drastically increases if hostage takers are unpredictable or appear disorganized. Occasionally, hostages will experience a significant loss of time or go into a fugue state as a defense mechanism to cope with the trauma. They may also experience a sense of claustrophobia and may feel the need to get out of their situation even though they know there could be dangerous consequences if they do take such action.

The third stage of a hostage situation is the accommodation stage. This stage is marked by time standing still and fatigue for the hostages and the hostage takers. Overall, this stage is somewhat peaceful because dominance over the hostages is established and acts of violence may not be deemed necessary by the hostage takers. Hostages become passive and bored. They may even experience Stockholm Syndrome, a situation in which hostages develop positive feelings for the hostage takers and negative feelings for the authorities, while hostage takers gain concern and positive feelings for the hostages. Everyone is emotionally and physically exhausted. Typically, this is the longest of the four stages of a hostage situation.

The resolution stage is the last stage in a hostage situation. Hostage takers and hostages alike are weary and see that a resolution (whether good or bad) is nearing. Both realize that this situation will not last forever. Hostage takers begin to realize that their demands, or their initial expectations, are not going to be met. The hostage takers contemplate suicide, killing the hostages and themselves, or ending the situation peacefully. No matter what the outcome is, the hostage takers and the hostages typically know that the situation is ending.

Once the hostage situation is over, significant deescalation, ventilation, and self-preservation issues need to be addressed through crisis intervention strategies provided to the hostages and possibly to the hostage takers. Long-term individual and group therapy may need to be implemented to provide preventative measures for PTSD to the hostages.

CASE STUDY 9.3

A Commercial Hostage Situation

In a small convenience store located in an Appalachian town, two men, wearing masks, attempt to rob the store. Both men have guns. Besides the two gunmen, the people in the store are the owner, who is behind the checkout counter, and six customers, located in different aisles in the store. The gunmen ask for money from the cash register, but the owner denies their request. While the gunmen and the owner are arguing, one of the customers calls the police from his cell phone, and within four minutes, a police car pulls up in front of the store. One of the gunmen locks the store's front door, and the robbery has quickly turned into a hostage situation. The hostage situation lasts for seven hours.

Given the information presented earlier, imagine what goes on during those seven hours.

Discussion Questions

Discuss how the hostage takers and the hostages think, feel, and act during the different stages of the situation.

What would be some follow-up resources for the hostages?

What might be some multicultural considerations for the hostages?

What would be some key counseling skills to use with the hostages? See Chapter 3 for information on such skills.

CASE STUDY 9.4

A Family Hostage Situation

Martin is a 38-year-old construction worker who has been married four times and has four children. He has one child (Pat, age 20) from his first wife and three boys (Ben, age 10; Todd, age 6; and Sig, age 4) from his current wife, Michelle. Within the past three weeks, Martin broke his wrist while working, he lost his job because of his anger outbursts and his pushing one of his co-workers after an argument, and he was notified that he needs to pay $22,000 in back taxes to the Internal Revenue Service. Earlier today, Michelle told him that she was leaving him and she was taking the children with her. During this conversation, the police were called because neighbors were concerned about the yelling.

When the police arrived, Martin did not answer the door and told the police that he had a gun and "no one is coming out unless they are in a body bag."

Martin kept Michelle and her three children at gunpoint for three and a half hours. During this time, he yelled, talked as if he was in a rant, cried uncontrollably, put his gun to Michelle's head and threatened to pull the trigger, and slapped Michelle and Ben in the face. After talking to a police negotiator on and off for over two hours, Martin shot himself in the head in front of Michelle and his children.

When the police and the hostage negotiator entered the house, they found Michelle holding her husband's hand, while he lay dead on the floor. Two of her children were sitting on the couch, still afraid to move, while Ben ran out the door into the hands of the police. Michelle and her children spent the next four hours debriefing with the hostage negotiator and other support staff. Later Michelle saw a counselor twice a week for eight months, then once a week for four months, and then once a month thereafter.

Discussion Questions

Overall, what do you think Michelle experienced during this situation? What about her children?

How do you think Michelle and the children experienced each stage of the hostage situation as described above?

What would be some of the emotions, behaviors, and thoughts felt by this family immediately after the hostage situation ended?

How should Martin's child from his first marriage (Pat) be informed of this situation? What should be said?

What would be the crisis counselor's initial treatment goals with Michelle and her children?

How might treatment differ among Michelle, Ben, and the other two children taken hostage?

What do you think was the reason Michelle was able to decrease treatment over time?

CHARACTERISTICS OF AND RESPONSES TO SCHOOL CRISES

Recently, school personnel have faced many crises, both on a national and a local level. As these crises occur, it becomes the responsibility of the school community to respond in a timely manner so that accurate information is provided, while helping the students, parents, teachers, and the community cope with the crisis. According to Johnson (2000), a school crisis "brings chaos" that "undermines the safety and stability of the entire school" (p. 18). Johnson further asserts that a school crisis exposes students and staff to "threat, loss, and traumatic stimulus" and undermines their "security and sense of power" (p. 3). School is a place where students, families, and school staff expect stability and safety. It is expected that when a crisis occurs, school personnel will react in a professional manner to make certain that students are provided with information, nurturance, counseling, and a sense of normalcy. Intervention must occur so that everyone in the school community feels informed, supported, and safe. The school plays a vital role in managing crises and assisting everyone in the school community in coping with these crises. The approach must be organized and sensitive to the needs of students, parents, teachers, and administrators.

The U.S. Department of Education's Office of Safe and Drug-Free Schools (2003) identified four phases that occur regarding a school crisis:

1. *Mitigation/prevention* addresses what schools can do to reduce or eliminate risk to life and property.
2. *Preparedness* refers to the process of planning for a crisis.
3. *Response* refers to the actions taken during the crisis.
4. *Recovery* refers to restoring the school environment after a crisis. (pp. 1–6 & 1–7)

Crises occurring at the national level (e.g., September 11, 2001; Virginia Tech shootings; Hurricane Katrina) or the local level (e.g., the death of a student as a result of an automobile accident, illness, or suicide) may affect the school community as well. When these crises occur, everyone in the school community experiences some level of trauma/loss. The school's response must be organized and coordinated effectively in order to support everyone in the school community. A secondary goal is to prevent additional crises stemming from the initial crisis. For example, if there is a suicide in the school, school officials will not only address the immediate impact of the suicide but also attempt to reduce any other suicide attempts.

Crisis Plan

Every school must have a crisis plan in place that is shared with all faculty and staff prior to any crisis event, implemented quickly in a crisis, reviewed annually and after a crisis event, and updated as needed. School counselors should establish teams within the school and at the district level to develop a comprehensive crisis plan, and stress the importance of the coordination of internal and external crisis workers following the school crisis. The crisis plan should be developed in accordance with the policies and procedures established by the school system. Fitzgerald (1998) identified steps that should be taken in developing and implementing a school crisis plan: (1) determine the composition of the crisis team, (2) gather the crisis team for a planning meeting, (3) decide how to announce the event and discuss or review classroom activities, and (4) hold a team debriefing.

Determine the Composition of the Crisis Team

The crisis team should be composed of individuals who have specialized training in crisis intervention and grief/loss counseling. Professional counselors, social workers, psychologists, and psychiatrists from the community should be a part of this team. These professionals should have been contacted prior to any crisis and asked to agree to be on call during a crisis situation. School counselors, administrators, and school staff should be involved in the plan. Finally, the plan must be shared with parents, guardians, and the community. Frequently, professional school counselors play an important role on the crisis team. Riley and McDaniel (2000) assert that during times of crisis, school counselors are expected to provide counseling for students, coordinate all counseling activities, communicate with teachers and parents, seek support from the crisis team, and contact neighboring schools.

The position statement on immediate response prepared by the American School Counselor Association (ASCA, 2000) states that "the professional school counselor's primary role is to provide direct counseling services during and after the incident." School counselors are expected to serve students and school personnel during times of crisis by providing individual and group counseling; consulting with administrators, teachers, parents, and professionals; and coordinating services within the school and the community (ASCA, 1999; Riley & McDaniel, 2000; Smaby, Peterson, Bergman, Bacig, & Swearinger, 1990). The team should meet at least two times per year to receive training and review the crisis plan. The plan should also be practiced at least three times per year to ensure that it will be effective when it is implemented.

Contact information should be updated at these training sessions so that team members can be reached quickly and easily in the event of a crisis. These training sessions provide an opportunity for team members to become acquainted and share strategies to be implemented when a crisis occurs. Those sessions are also a time to assign specific responsibilities to each team member and to reassign responsibilities if staff or faculty have left their positions. Administrators are responsible for activating the plan.

Gather the Crisis Team Members for a Planning Meeting

The team members should obtain and verify the facts of the incident and designate the person who will continue to gather factual information. At this time, the team should decide on the format for conveying the information to the school community (e.g., large-group meetings, classroom meetings).

Next, the leader(s) of the crisis team should determine the assignments for crisis team members, taking into account team member strengths and comfort levels. Possible roles for team members include direct contact with groups of students, individual counseling sessions, and administrative tasks such as taking phone calls, arranging for transportation, and preparing letters to be sent home to parents/guardians. The letter to parents/guardians should include a description/notification of the event, what the children have been told regarding the event, funeral arrangements (if appropriate), emotional responses parents/guardians may observe in their children as reactions to the event, and resources for parents/guardians to assist their children in coping with the event. Crisis intervention should never be done alone. Team members should always work in pairs. Two crisis team members should observe the class and look for high-risk students. Having two team members working together allows one team member to escort a distressed child out of the room for private counseling, while the other team member continues working with the group. Team members who are experiencing the same intervention are able to debrief each other and can monitor each other's stress levels and react accordingly.

Decide How to Announce the Event and Discuss or Review Classroom Activities

Teams can announce the crisis event via individual classroom sessions, meetings of smaller groups of students, general assemblies, or announcements to larger groups. However, meeting with smaller groups and holding general assemblies are the preferred methods for passing along the information. The public address system should be used only if absolutely necessary.

No matter how the team members decide to inform the student body, important components included below must be integrated into the announcement of the event.

The crisis team members should be introduced to the students. Even if students know the staff, teachers, school counselors, and administrators from other interactions in the school community, students must be made aware that these people are also crisis team members and be apprised of the team members' roles during the crisis event.

Students should be asked if anyone has heard about the event. Allow students to tell what they know or have heard about the event. This will not only allow the sharing of information and the start of the opening-up process but also allow any rumors or half-truths to be spoken in the group so the team can either verify or deny them publicly.

Facts of the event must be delivered in developmentally appropriate terms, and any rumors or incorrect information must be clarified. The team members should provide enough time for students to ask questions. This will assist in decreasing rumors about the event. If students leave the session with questions, they will tend to construct their own answers, which may not include the facts.

When appropriate, children should be allowed to tell their stories about this experience or similar experiences. Team members should list all the feelings voiced on the blackboard and spend some time talking about the normalcy of these feelings.

In crises that may involve another student, students should be allowed to talk about memories they each have of the absent student. Finally, if the event involves a student who may be able to return to school, it is important to discuss what they may encounter when the student returns and how they can help the student.

If the event involves the death of a student, the team members have additional issues to address. The team members must decide what to do with the empty desk. Often, the desk will be left vacant for a period of time; however, a time limit should be established and shared with the other students so they understand the desk eventually will be removed. It is crucial to involve the students in this process.

Information regarding the funeral, including the type of funeral and cultural rituals, may also be shared, if developmentally appropriate. If the school team members decide it would be beneficial to have a memorial service at school and this is approved by the principal, volunteers should be solicited to assist with arrangements. It is essential to provide information regarding the resources that are available at school and in the community and to provide additional handout materials that can be helpful to the students in working through the crisis.

CASE STUDY 9.5

A Student With a Terminal Illness

Laurie was a fifth grader diagnosed with leukemia within the past year. During this time, Laurie was absent from school while receiving chemotherapy treatment for her cancer and had lost her hair. The students were aware of her condition. Her parents just called the school and reported that Laurie died. The principal asks you to call a meeting of the crisis team, teachers, and appropriate staff to discuss how to best approach the other students about Laurie's death. As the leader of this team, decide what must be addressed, what information will be shared, and how this information will be delivered to students and the school community.

Hold a Team Debriefing

Debriefing is a time for the crisis team members to gather and share their unique experiences of the crisis in a private and safe environment. Often, the team members are unintentionally left out of this process, but it is extremely important to allow some time for the crisis team members to share their thoughts and feelings. Team members may have been the teachers, counselors, and mentors of the victims, or the event may have triggered some other unresolved crisis in their life.

It is important for the leader to invite team members to share what happened and what the experience was like, what memory stands out in their mind that is hard to erase, and what each can do to take care of themselves during and after the crisis. Fitzgerald (1998) offered the following suggestions for self-care after a crisis:

- Debrief with your partner, team members, or supervisor.
- Attend regular support meetings.
- Find ways to relax such as music, exercise, meditation, hobbies, reading, or sports.
- Maintain a healthy balance in life: Separate work from leisure time.
- Acknowledge personal feelings.
- Spend quality time with family and friends who are not connected with your crisis work.
- Visit a place that is peaceful such as a church, synagogue, park, or art gallery.
- Write in a journal. (pp. 18–20)

How to Help Students During a Crisis

It is important to offer many coping options for students to feel supported and receive counseling services. Individual counseling and small-group counseling give students an opportunity to express their feelings and receive support. Classroom guidance lessons and class meetings may also be extremely helpful and can provide a forum for students to express emotions and to obtain accurate information and ask questions. In addition, a crisis provides an opportunity to give students suggestions for coping. Brock (1998) developed an intervention program for use in classrooms following a school crisis. This approach focuses on providing facts and dispelling rumors, sharing stories, sharing reactions, empowering students, and providing closure. Fitzgerald (1998) also describes specific activities to be employed with students during and after crisis.

How to Help Parents/Guardians During a Crisis

When there is a crisis at school, parents/guardians must receive accurate information and be offered appropriate suggestions regarding how they might assist their children. It is very helpful to send a letter to parents/guardians that includes accurate information, symptoms, common and uncommon reactions they might observe in their children, and suggestions to help children who are experiencing distress as a result of the crisis. These letters should be developed before a crisis so that, when a crisis occurs, they can be quickly adapted to the uniqueness of the existing crisis and then copied and distributed. These letters can be sent home and put on the school's website; however, the website should never be the only means of communication, since there are many families without this technological resource. Textbox 9.1 provides a sample letter to parents.

Sample Letter to Parents/Guardians

Dear Parents/Guardians:

I regret to inform you of the death of one of our students. Laurie Jones, a fifth grader, died on January 15 of leukemia. I know that you join me in my concern and sympathy for the family.

The students were told of Laurie's death today by their classroom teachers. Crisis counselors visited each class and provided an opportunity for students to talk, ask questions, and share their feelings. Those children who were most upset met privately with counselors for additional counseling and support. Counseling services will continue to be made available to students this week and in the future as needed.

Notes and cards may be sent to the family at the following address:

Mr. and Mrs. David Jones, 2020 Elm Street, Arlington, VA 22207

A memorial service will be held at St. John's Church on Monday, January 19, at 9:00 A.M. The church is located at 1500 Main Street, Arlington, VA 22207. In lieu of flowers, the family is requesting that donations be made to the Leukemia and Lymphoma Society.

Your children may experience a wide range of emotions as a result of Laurie's death. The following suggestions may be helpful as you help your children cope with their grief:

1. Encourage your children to talk about their feelings or to draw pictures to express their emotions.
2. Offer support and let your children know that you are available to talk to them and answer questions.
3. Allow your children to be sad and to cry.
4. Reassure your children that they are healthy, and discuss fears they may have about their own death or the death of a family member.
5. Explain the ritual of funerals and memorial services. If your children express a desire to attend the memorial service, it is recommended that you accompany them.
6. Monitor your children's emotional state and behavior. If you notice prolonged sadness, withdrawal from social contact, changes in eating or sleeping habits, or other behavior unusual for your children, please contact Ms. Smith, our professional school counselor, who will be available to offer support and resources to your children and to you. She can be reached at (571) 248-3607 or Marilyn.Smith@dcps.edu.

If you have questions or concerns, please don't hesitate to contact me.

Sincerely,

Mrs. Helen Tracy, Principal

(703) 571-2438, Helen.Tracy@dcps.edu

Many schools have developed a mechanism to notify parents via e-mail or other communication systems. Some schools will also initiate a "telephone tree" to notify parents of the crisis. Again, these telephone trees should be developed before a crisis occurs and practiced so that they can be implemented quickly and efficiently. Depending on the nature of the crisis, it may be necessary to invite parents/guardians to a group meeting at school so that they can receive accurate information, share feelings and questions, and learn ways to support their children during this difficult time. At this meeting, the crisis team can offer support and suggestions, while also passing along information about services that are available in the community (ASCA, 2003).

Recently, schools have been faced with responding to crises as they are unfolding (e.g., intruder in the school building, terrorist attack, natural disaster). Each school should have a plan for responding to such situations, and each classroom should know how to implement that plan. In addition, parents/guardians should be aware of this plan. A letter or brochure should be developed and sent to parents/guardians explaining this plan so they understand what occurs in lockdown, shelter in place, and so on. It is necessary to inform parents/guardians that the school has thought about and planned for crises and to reassure them that their children are safe at school. While the letter or brochure should not describe specific actions or locations in detail (in case a parent/guardian might be the intruder), it should provide a general overview so that parents/guardians are secure in the knowledge that their children are safe at school.

School Responses to National Crises

Many crises occur miles away from our schools or even in other states. However, such crises may have a tremendous impact on our students. For example, hurricanes, terrorist attacks, school shootings, and war may all have an impact on schools throughout the nation. School personnel must always respond in a way that reassures students, teachers, and parents/guardians. It is important that

- Accurate information is presented in developmentally appropriate ways.
- Students are given opportunities to express feelings and ask questions.
- Information for teachers and parents/guardians is provided so that they can help students/children.
- Service activities are organized so that students, parents/guardians, and members of the school community can provide assistance to victims (e.g., collect money/clothing for victims, send books to children who were affected, have pen pals, organize car washes or other fund-raisers).

During a crisis situation, school personnel have an obligation to intervene in a professional, organized, and efficient manner with students, parents, and the community. The main objective is for school personnel to assist and return the school community to the pre-crisis level of functioning so that the school can continue to be the stable and welcoming environment that it was before the crisis.

Chapter 2 discussed the *Family Educational Rights and Privacy Act* and its implications for crisis counselors. When working in a crisis situation, given the fluidity of crises, it is easy for crisis counselors to try to help everyone in need. However, it is important to be mindful of privacy issues during a crisis.

DEATH NOTIFICATIONS

Historically, crisis counselors seldom acted as first responders in the death notification process. More often, crisis counselors were brought into the counseling process after the notification had taken place and when a referral was made for counseling to assist a person in dealing with the grieving process. However, crisis counselors may be asked to assist with or act as the main notifier of a death. Similarly, as roles and job opportunities become more diverse in the communities for crisis counselors (e.g., in police departments, fire departments, military settings, religious settings, chaplaincies, crisis centers, hospitals, or other agencies such as Red Cross, Green Cross, and Hospice), the likelihood of participating in a death notification increases. With the increasing use of counselors as first responders during recent national crises (Hurricane Katrina, Hurricane Isabel, September 11), counselors have been placed in the role of notifying individuals of family or community deaths more frequently. Even if a counselor intends to work in

ACTIVITY 9.1
Death Notifications

Take a few minutes and reflect on a time when you were notified of a death. Who was the person who died? Who provided the death notification? What were the circumstances? How was the death relayed to you? What were some of your initial feelings or thoughts? What kind of impact did the actual process of the death notification have on you? What made the notification process helpful? What could have improved the death notification process?

a private practice, it is not unforeseen to be asked to assist with a death notification or to be consulted about how to tell another family member about a death. No two death notifications are ever the same due to the actual event, unique relationship, and perception of the death by the survivor. However, the level of preparedness of the crisis counselor for the notification process can affect the initial situation of the notification, how the survivor responds during the crisis state, and whether the survivor seeks professional counseling in the future.

With all of this said, crisis counselors are not to notify anyone of a death unless they are given permission to do so. Such permission is to be given by someone who is their supervisor, their team leader, or above them in the chain of command during a crisis.

Although no crisis counselor who provides a death notification can ever be fully prepared for the response of the person receiving the notification, there are several components that should be included in order to provide a foundation for an effective death notification. As outlined in the training protocol for the Maryland State Police (2001), but adapted for the training of crisis counselors for this section, death notifications should be provided in person and in pairs, in an appropriate time frame and accurately, in plain language, and with compassion.

In Person and In Pairs

Death notifications should always be made in person and not by telephone. The human presence during the notification of the death of a loved one is essential. The presence of a crisis counselor can be crucial if the survivor has a reaction that requires assessment of self-risk or the need for immediate medical attention. Crisis counselors can assist clients during the initial shock, which can be devastating or demobilizing or interrupt intact normal thought processes, and as they formulate a plan to inform others close to the victim of the death. It is helpful to work in pairs in case questions need to be answered, when multiple survivors are present with various needs (age and developmental appropriateness), and as a safety precaution for the members of the notification team.

Team members may be a combination of law enforcement officers, professional counselors, pastoral counselors, clergy, school counselors, case managers, or family members or friends of the victim, depending on the agency or type of death. For example, in homicide/suicide cases, the team ordinarily would consist of law enforcement and possibly a clergy member and/or a professional counselor. More and more police departments are working together with crisis agencies, which use professional counselors for these situations. In a hospital setting, the team may consist of the medical doctor and/or nurse, a chaplain, and a pastoral counselor/professional counselor or social worker. In a school setting, the team may consist of the school counselor, an administrator, and a teacher. Depending on the setting and circumstances of the death in each example, outside professional counselors may be solicited to assist with any crisis situations or death notifications.

In our society, family members do not always live in the same community or even in the same state as one another, which often makes "in person" death notification impossible. In these circumstances, contact can be made with a medical examiner, law enforcement department, member of the clergy, or other friend or family member in the survivor's home area to deliver the notification in person to the next of kin. The person who is initially contacted about the death is preferably someone who has contact with but is not as emotionally involved as the person for whom the death notification is intended.

In Time and with Accurate Information

Timeliness of a death notification is essential so that a person is informed in person by the appropriate individual, rather than by hearing it from outside persons. At the same time, it is imperative to first verify the accuracy of the information to be sure that the correct information regarding the correct person is being given to a survivor. This must be done in a short period of time, given the nature of the event. For example, in law enforcement cases, it is important that relatives (next of kin) be notified in a timely manner and with accurate information so that they do not see or hear the news for the first time on the television or radio. When there is a death on campus or in a school, it is also important for those closest to the deceased to be notified initially. In these instances, it is preferable for administrators, crisis counselors, and faculty to receive the information first so as to prioritize who should be notified (e.g., crisis team members, classmates, close friends) and in what manner (e.g., small groups, teams, homerooms, list serves). This also allows those giving the notification to be able to assess if more intervention is needed for some individuals. Agencies and school settings should, prior to any crisis, designate a contact person or alternate person who will be responsible for collecting and dispensing information. Even if a team is formed to gather information, only one person should be designated as the communicator so differing accounts or information is not relayed. Inaccurate or differing information from several sources could cause chaos, panic, and unneeded crisis responses.

Accuracy of the information does not necessarily mean a crisis counselor has to have the full details, as this depends on the situation. For example, suppose a college student informs a faculty member that another student was killed by a drunk driver the night before. It is premature to send out a message on the list serve without receiving confirmation of the student's death from the family or another firsthand source. At the same time, it is not as crucial to have the details of the circumstances as it is to confirm the identity of the student so the university can respond to the student body in a timely and accurate manner. Perhaps the actual cause of death cannot be confirmed in a timely manner; while this is desirable information, it is not essential for the initial communication. For other situations, more detailed information may be needed at the time of the death notification. The most important point is not to make a wrong notification. Mistaken death notifications may cause undo trauma and in some cases have caused medical complications for the person being informed. Before the notification, move quickly to gather information. Be sure the victim's identity is confirmed, and if administrators need to report the death via a list serve, be sure to include the entire name of the deceased (many first names are common) so as not to cause any further chaos in trying to identify who has died. For example, when using a list serve to provide the initial notification as well as information on any follow-up events (e.g., funeral services, memorial services), give first and last names in all correspondences. Even though multiple previous e-mails were sent out on this person, it should not be assumed that they have all been read by the receivers. Messages may seem redundant, but accuracy is important.

In Plain Language

It is important that the death notification be given to the survivor in a calm, direct, and simple manner by the crisis counselor. Too much information or vague information can cause survivors to panic before getting the information. A crisis counselor can demonstrate care by stating the notification in clear and concise language. For example, "I have some very bad news to tell you" or a similar statement allows a brief but crucial moment for the survivor to prepare for the shock. The follow-up statement should also be provided in plain language, such as "Your daughter, Jill, was in a car crash and she was killed." It is important to avoid vague statements such as "Jill was lost," "Jill was hurt," or "Jill passed away." It is important to include a definitive conclusion as to what occurred, such as "... and she was killed" or "... there were no survivors." This prevents false hope of survival. It is important to refer to the victim by name to provide another level of verification and also to personalize the deceased.

One of the most important gifts a crisis counselor can offer to a survivor is the gift of the crisis counselor's control and calmness during the death notification. Overemotional crisis counselors can increase the potential for panic or chaos. Survivors often have many questions, and some questions may be asked multiple times. Like a child's experience with a death notification, often survivors ask the same question for verification of facts. It is crucial to patiently answer questions about the circumstances regarding the death that a crisis counselor may be privy to, such as the location of the deceased's body, how the deceased's body will be released and transported to a funeral home, and whether an autopsy will be performed. However, the sharing of this information should always take into consideration the developmental stage of the survivor and a clinical assessment of how much he or she can handle at the time of the notification. Oftentimes, the crisis counselor may not know the answer to a survivor's question, and it is better to acknowledge this to the survivor, rather than giving false information. It is important to state that you will attempt to find the answers to any questions you cannot answer. If there are questions you have offered to explore, it is imperative to follow up directly with the survivor even if another agency or office will be contacting the survivor to provide the information.

With Compassion

Presence and compassion may be the only resources a crisis counselor can provide during the initial death notification process. It is important for a crisis counselor to accept the survivor's emotions and reactions to the death notification and also to recognize his or her own personal emotions associated with the notification. Although an overemotional crisis counselor can increase confusion and possibly panic survivors, it is better for a crisis counselor to express appropriate emotion than to appear cold and unfeeling. It is important to relay to the survivor that death is a personal event and that he or she may feel various emotions due to the unique situation, including sadness, anger, frustration, relief, and guilt, to name a few. Normalizing the vast array of emotions survivors may experience during the grief process is an important resource. Print resources that reveal the grieving process, discuss reactions to grief, explain death to a child (if appropriate), and provide referrals for mental health services or a funeral home may be helpful and can be left with the victim. Imposing personal religious beliefs is not helpful and could be harmful. Statements such as "This was God's will," "She led a full life," and "I understand what you are going through" do not demonstrate compassion for the loss or regard for the person's unique grief experiences.

It is essential to take time to provide information, support, and direction to the survivor. Never simply provide a death notification and leave. It is not recommended that persons providing the death notification bring the victim's personal belongings when first meeting with survivors. Survivors often need time before accepting the victim's belongings, but eventually they will want to take possession of these items. Likewise, crisis counselors should never transport survivors unless law enforcement is a part of the notification team and participates in the transportation. One can never truly predict the emotional reaction to the death of a loved one, and the safety of the crisis counselor is always a priority.

Follow-Up

Crisis counselors should always leave their name and telephone number with survivors, and follow-up contact with the survivors should be scheduled for the following day, since most funeral arrangements must be made soon after the death. Some individuals, depending on their social support system, may request assistance from team members with funeral arrangements. If a crisis counselor is asked by the survivor to help with these plans, it is imperative to assist the survivor based on the customs, traditions, religious beliefs, and personal preferences of the family. Most survivors are confused at the initial notification, and others may feel abandoned after the notification. Many survivors will want clarifications or may need more direction on necessary arrangements.

Following up is an important last step in completing the death notification process and may be a crucial factor in enabling a survivor to reach out for continued mental health services. Often, counseling services are necessary for clients to work through the extended or complicated grieving process. A death notification event may be the first exposure a survivor has to a mental health professional, so the interaction could encourage or discourage further connections with crisis counselors. The notification team members should be clear with one another on any follow-up assignments.

Debriefing with Team Members

Debriefing with team members should occur immediately after the death notification process. This debriefing time should be used to plan for any follow-up with the survivors and to review how the death notification process was implemented and received. Processing what went well and what could be improved on will be helpful for

ACTIVITY 9.2
Applying Death Notification Skills

Case A: Community Setting	Case B: School Setting
You are part of a crisis team that has been called to give a death notification to the next of kin of a person who was killed during a random shooting. You are not sure how the person was involved or became a victim of the shooting. Work with your team to plan what needs to be addressed and then role-play a death notification to the family. (This can be done in small groups or as a class role play.)	The principal of your high school contacts you in the morning and states that there was a phone message left last evening that a ninth-grade student (John) was killed in an automobile accident. As a school counselor and a member of the crisis response team for the school, work with your team and decide what needs to be addressed in this process and to whom notifications will be made, if appropriate. (This can be done in small groups or as a class role play.)

future death notifications. Additionally, death notifications can be stressful and emotionally draining for those involved in giving death notifications. The team members should share concerns with one another. It is important to discuss feelings or thoughts associated with the death notifications that may have triggered personal unresolved grief issues. Taking care of oneself is essential when taking care of another person's initial grief. The stages of grief and loss (presented in Chapter 4) can certainly take place among crisis counselors. When debriefing, it is important to take into consideration that crisis counselors experience grief and should be encouraged to process such grief—and consequently the stages of grief. As a culminating activity, choose either case A or case B in Activity 9.2, and prepare a death notification strategy.

Summary

This final chapter began by describing typical responses to disaster and how people's reactions to disaster evolve over time. It could be said that exposure to disaster or trauma plays an important role in one's mental, emotional, cognitive, behavioral, social, and physical functioning. The difficult part of treating individuals is identifying when "normal" responses become significantly detrimental to their functioning.

Various models of crisis intervention were discussed in this book, and all have merit. However, the common thread among these models is that the key to treatment of those who experienced disaster (in all forms) is early intervention. The sooner we respond, reduce panic or chaos, create a sense of hope and support, and establish connections between those in need and appropriate resources, the better.

As with disasters, there are many systematic factors and evolutionary components of a hostage situation. Though hostage situations are relatively rare, those providing mental health services should be aware of the unique characteristics of those who have experienced a hostage situation because it could influence the approach to treatment.

The second portion of this chapter provided a detailed overview of crises in schools and how to respond to such crises. An emphasis was placed on how to create a network of support because school systems have so many stakeholders to address (e.g., students, parents, school staff, principals). The components of a comprehensive school crisis plan include determining the composition of the crisis team, gathering the crisis team members for a planning meeting, deciding how to announce the event and discuss or review classroom activities, and holding a team debriefing.

The death notification process requires a lot of skill and attention to emotional parameters. It is good practice to deliver death notifications in person and in pairs, in time and with accurate information, in plain language, and with compassion. It is also important to follow up with the survivors and incorporate debriefing procedures for the notifiers.

All crises evolve through different stages—and then end. Those who experience crisis, disaster, or trauma also evolve in that they, hopefully, resolve or at least experience a lessened impact of the situation. Crises affect lives in systemic ways; every aspect of one's life can be affected by a crisis.

REFERENCES

Ackard, D. M., & Neumark-Sztainer, D. (2002). Date violence and date rape among adolescents: Associations with disordered eating behaviors and psychological health. *Child Abuse & Neglect, 26,* 455–473.

Ainsworth, M. (1969). Object relations, dependency and attachment: A theoretical review of the infant-mother relationship. *Child Development, 40,* 969–1025.

Alcoholics Anonymous World Services. (1997). *Alcoholics Anonymous 1996 membership survey.* New York: Author.

Alexander, D. A. (2005). Early mental health intervention after disasters. *Advances in Psychiatric Treatment, 11,* 12–18.

Amar, A. F., & Gennaro, S. (2005). Dating violence in college women: Associated physical injury, health-care usage, and mental health symptoms. *Nursing Research, 54,* 235–242.

American Association of Suicidology. (2006a). *Assessing and managing suicide risk.* Washington, DC: Author.

American Association of Suicidology. (2006b). *Suicide in the United States.* Retrieved February 11, 2008, from www.suicidology.org

American Association of Suicidology. (2008). *Elderly suicide fact sheet.* Washington, DC: Author.

American Counseling Association. (2005). *ACA code of ethics.* Alexandria, VA: Author.

American Foundation for Suicide Prevention. (2008). *Surviving a suicide loss: A resource and healing guide* [Brochure]. New York: Author.

American Pet Products Association. (2008). *2007–2008 APPA national pet owners survey.* Retrieved January 7, 2009, from www.americanpetproducts.org/press_industrytrends.asp

American Psychiatric Association. (2000). *Diagnostic and statistical manual of mental disorders* (4th ed., text revision). Washington, DC: Author.

American Psychiatric Association. (2003). *Practice guideline for the assessment and treatment of patients with suicidal behaviors.* Retrieved September 8, 2007, from www.psych.org/psych_pract/treatg/pg/pg_suicidalbehaviors.pdf

American Psychiatric Association. (2004). *Committee on Psychiatric Dimensions of Disaster: Disaster psychiatry handbook.* Retrieved June 28, 2008, from www.psych.org/Resources/DisasterPsychiatry/APADisasterPsychiatryResources/DisasterPsychiatryHandbook.aspx

American Psychiatric Association. (2008). *Psychiatric practice.* Retrieved March 1, 2008, from www.psych.org/MainMenu/PsychiatricPractice.aspx

American School Counselor Association. (1999). *The role of the professional school counselor.* Alexandria, VA: Author.

American School Counselor Association. (2000). *Position statement: Critical incident response.* Alexandria, VA: Author.

American School Counselor Association. (2003). *Counselor immediate response guide.* Retrieved July 15, 2008, from www.cc.ain.com/asca.crisis.htm

American School Counselor Association. (2005). *The ASCA National Model: A framework for school counseling programs* (2nd ed.). Alexandria, VA: Author.

American School Counselor Association. (2008). *The role of the professional school counselor.* Retrieved June 26, 2008, from www.schoolcounselor.org/content.asp?pl=325&sl=133&contentid=240

American Society of Addiction Medicine. (1996). *Patient placement criteria for the treatment of substance-related disorders* (2nd ed.). Chevy Chase, MD: Author.

Amick-McMullen, A., Kilpatrick, D. G., & Resnick, H. S. (1989). Homicide as a risk factor for PTSD among surviving family members. *Behavioral Modification, 15,* 545–559.

Anderson, R. (1974). Notes of a survivor. In S. B. Troop & W. A. Green (Eds.), *The patient, death, and the family* (pp. 73–82). New York: Scribner.

Araki, K., Nakane, Y., Ohta, Y., & Kawasaki, N. (1998). The nature of psychiatric problems among disaster victims. *Psychiatry & Clinical Neurosciences, 52*(Suppl.), s317–s319.

Arata, C. M. (1998). To tell or not to tell: Current functioning of child sexual abuse survivors who disclosed their victimization. *Child Maltreatment, 3*, 63–71.

Armour, M. (2005). Meaning making in the aftermath of homicide. *Death Studies, 27*, 519–540.

Arthur, G. L., Brende, J. O., & Quiroz, S. E. (2003). Violence: Incidents and frequency of physical and psychological assaults affecting mental health providers in Georgia. *Journal of General Psychology, 130*, 22–45.

Asaro, M. R. (2001). Working with adult homicide survivors: Part II: Helping family members cope with murder. *Psychiatric Care, 37*(4), 115–126.

Asian and Pacific Islander Institute on Domestic Violence. (2008). *Fact sheet: Domestic violence in Asian communities*. Retrieved January 15, 2008, from www.apiahf.org/apidvinstitute

Assey, J. L. (1985). The suicide prevention contract. *Perspectives in Psychiatric Care, 23*(3), 99–103.

Australian Academy of Medicine. (2008). *Bereavement, known as sorry business, is a very important part of Aboriginal culture*. Retrieved May 21, 2008, from www.aams.org.au/mark_sheldon/ch7/ch7_sensitive_areas.htm

Barbee, P. W., Ekleberry, F., & Villalobos, S. (2007). Duty to warn and protect: Not in Texas. *Journal of Professional Counseling: Practice, Theory, and Research, 35*(1), 18–25.

Barry, K., Fleming, M., Greenley, J., Widlak, P., Kropp, S., & McKee, D. (1995). Assessment of alcohol and other drug disorders in the seriously mentally ill. *Schizophrenia Bulletin, 21*, 313–321.

Bartlett, M. L. (2006). The efficacy of a no-suicide contract with clients in counseling on an outpatient basis. *Dissertation Abstracts International, 67*, 3438, 06B. (UMI No. 3225247)

Battaglia, T. A., Finley, E., & Liebschutz, J. M. (2003). Survivors of intimate partner violence speak out: Trust in the patient-provider relationship. *Journal of General Internal Medicine, 18*, 617–623.

Bedi, R. P. (2006). Concept mapping the client's perspective on counseling alliance formation. *Journal of Counseling Psychology, 53*, 26–35.

Bennett, L., & Williams, O. (2001). Intervention program for men who batter. In C. Renzetti & J. Edleson (Eds.), *Sourcebook on violence against women* (pp. 261–277). Thousand Oaks, CA: Sage.

Berliner, L., & Elliott, D. M. (2002). Sexual abuse of children. In J. E. B. Myers, L. Berliner, J. Briere, C. T. Hendrix, C. Jenny, & T. A. Reid (Eds.), *The APSAC handbook on child maltreatment* (2nd ed., pp. 55–78). Thousand Oaks, CA: Sage.

Berman, A. L. (1990). Standard of care in assessment of suicidal potential. *Psychotherapy in Private Practice, 8*(2), 35–41.

Berman, A. L. (2006). Risk management with suicidal patients. *Journal of Clinical Psychology, 62*, 171–184.

Berman, A. L., & Cohen-Sandler, R. (1983). Suicide and malpractice: Expert testimony and the standard of care. *Professional Psychology: Research and Practice, 14*(1), 6–19.

Berman, A. L., Jobes, D. A., & Silverman, M. M. (2006). *Adolescent suicide: Assessment and intervention* (2nd ed.). Washington, DC: American Psychological Association.

Berry, D. B. (2000). *The domestic violence sourcebook* (3rd ed.). Los Angeles: Lowell House.

Berzoff, J. N., & Silverman, P. R. (Eds.). (2004). *Living with dying: A handbook for end-of-life healthcare practitioners*. Irvington, NY: Columbia University Press.

Black, H. C. (1979). *Black's law dictionary*. St. Paul, MN: West.

Blake, D. D., Weathers, F. W., Nagy, L. M., Kaloupek, D. G., Gusman, F. D., Charney, D. S., et al. (1995). The development of a clinician administered PTSD scale. *Journal of Traumatic Stress, 8*(1), 75–90.

Blau, T. H. (1994). *Psychological services for law enforcement*. New York: Wiley.

Bober, T., & Regehr, C. (2006). Strategies for reducing secondary or vicarious trauma: Do they work? *Brief Treatment & Crisis Intervention, 6*, 1–9.

Boelen, P. A., de Keijser, J., van den Hout, M. A., & van den Bout, J. (2007). Treatment of complicated grief: A comparison between cognitive-behavioral therapy and supportive counseling. *Journal of Consulting & Clinical Psychology, 75*, 277–284.

Boelen, P. A., van den Bout, J., & de Keijser, J. (2003). Traumatic grief as a disorder distinct from bereavement-related depression and anxiety: A replication study with bereaved mental health care patients. *American Journal of Psychiatry, 160,* 1339–1341.

Bogar, C. B., & Hulse-Killacky, D. (2006). Resiliency determinants and resiliency processes among female adult survivors of childhood sexual abuse. *Journal of Counseling & Development, 84,* 318–327.

Bonanno, G. A., Galea, S., Bucciarelli, A., & Vlahov, D. (2007). What predicts psychological resilience after disaster? The role of demographics, resources, and life stress. *Journal of Counseling & Clinical Psychology, 75,* 671–682.

Bonanno, G. A., & Mancini, A. D. (2008). The human capacity to thrive in the face of potential trauma. *Pediatrics, 121,* 369–375.

Bonanno, G. A., Neria, Y., Mancini, A., Coifman, K. G., Litz, B., & Insel, B. (2007). Is there more to complicated grief than depression and Posttraumatic Stress Disorder? A test of incremental validity. *Journal of Abnormal Psychology, 116,* 342–351.

Bongar, B. (1991). *The suicidal client: Clinical and legal standards of care.* Washington, DC: American Psychological Association.

Bongar, B. (2002). *The suicidal patient: Clinical and legal standards of care* (2nd ed.). Washington, DC: American Psychological Association.

Bongar, B., & Harmatz, M. (1989). Graduate training in clinical psychology and the study of suicide. *Professional Psychology: Research & Practice, 20,* 209–213.

Bongar, B., Maris, R. W., Berman, A. L., & Litman, R. E. (1998). Outpatient standards of care and the suicidal patient. In B. Bongar et al. (Eds.), *Risk management with suicidal patients* (pp. 4–33). New York: Guilford Press.

Bongar, B., Peterson, L. G., Harris, E. A., & Aissis, J. (1989). Clinical and legal considerations in the management of suicidal patients: An integrative overview. *Journal of Integrative & Eclectic Psychotherapy, 8*(1), 53–67.

Bonner, A., & Waterhouse, J. M. (1996). *Addictive behavior: Perspectives on the nature of addiction.* New York: St. Martin's Press.

Boss, P. G. (1987). Family stress: Perception and context. In M. Sussman & S. Steinmetz (Eds.), *Handbook on marriage and family* (pp. 695–723). New York: Plenum Press.

Boss, P. G. (1988). *Family stress management.* Newberry Park, CA: Sage.

Boss, P. G. (2002). *Family stress management: A contextual approach* (2nd ed.). Thousand Oaks, CA: Sage.

Boss, P. G. (2004). Ambiguous loss. In F. Walsh & M. McGoldrick (Eds.), *Living beyond loss: Death in the family* (2nd ed., pp. 237–246). New York: W. W. Norton.

Boss, P. G. (2006). *Loss, trauma, and resilience: Therapeutic work with ambiguous loss.* New York: W. W. Norton.

Bowker, L. H. (1988). Religious victims and their religious leaders: Services delivered to one thousand battered women by the clergy. In A. L. Horton & J. A. Williamson (Eds.), *Abuse and religion: When praying isn't enough* (pp. 229–234). Lexington, MA: Lexington Books.

Bowlby, J. (1960). *Attachment and loss: Vol. 1. Attachment.* New York: Basic Books.

Bowlby, J. (1973). *Attachment and loss: Vol. 2. Separation: Anxiety, and anger.* New York: Basic Books.

Bowlby, J. (1980). *Attachment and loss: Vol. 3. Loss: Sadness and depression.* New York: Basic Books.

Bradley, R., Greene, J., Russ, E., Dutra, L., & Westen, D. (2005). A multi-dimensional meta-analysis of psychotherapy for PTSD. *American Journal of Psychiatry, 162,* 214–227.

Braga, A. A. (2003). Serious youth gun offenders and the epidemic of youth violence in Boston. *Journal of Quantitative Criminology, 19,* 33–54.

Brems, C. (2000). *Dealing with challenges in psychotherapy and counseling.* Belmont, CA: Wadsworth/Thompson Learning.

Brock, S. E. (1998). Helping classrooms cope with traumatic events. *Professional School Counseling, 2,* 110–116.

Brown, S. (1985). *Treating the alcoholic: A developmental model of recovery.* New York: Wiley.

Brownmiller, S. (1975). *Against our will.* New York: Ballantine Books.

Brownridge, D. A., Chan, K. L., Hiebert-Murphy, D., Ristock, J., Tiwan, A., Leung, W., et al. (2008). The elevated risk for non-lethal post-separation violence in Canada: A comparison of separated, divorced, and married women. *Journal of Interpersonal Violence, 23*, 117–135.

Bryant, C. D. (Ed.). (2003). *Handbook of death and dying* (Vol. 1). Thousand Oaks, CA: Sage.

Bryant, J., & Milsom, A. (2005). Child abuse reporting by school counselors. *Professional School Counseling, 9*, 63–71.

Bryant, R. A., Harvey, A. G., Dang, S. T., Sackville, T., & Basten, C. (1998). Treatment of Acute Stress Disorder: A comparison of cognitive-behavioral therapy and supportive counseling. *Journal of Consulting & Clinical Psychology, 66*, 862–866.

Burgess, A. W. (Ed.). (1985). *Rape and sexual assault: A research handbook.* New York: Garland.

Burgess, A. W., & Holmstrom, L. L. (1974). Rape trauma syndrome. *American Journal of Psychiatry, 131*, 981–986.

Burgess, A. W., & Holmstrom, L. L. (1985). Rape trauma syndrome and post traumatic stress response. In A. W. Burgess (Ed.), *Rape and sexual assault: A research handbook* (pp. 46–60). New York: Garland.

Butler, R. N. (1963). The life review: An interpretation of reminiscence in the aged. *Psychiatry, 26*, 65–76.

Buttell, F. P. (2001). Moral development among court-ordered batterers: Evaluating the impact of treatment. *Research on Social Work Practice, 11*(1), 93–107.

Campos-Outcalt, D. (2004). How does HIPAA affect public health reporting? *Journal of Family Practice, 53*, 701–704.

Caplan, G. (1961). *An approach to community mental health.* New York: Grune & Stratton.

Caplan, G. (1964). *Principles of preventive psychiatry.* New York: Basic Books.

Cappuzi, D., & Gross, D. R. (Eds.). (2004). *Youth at risk.* Alexandria, VA: American Counseling Association.

Carey, R. G. (1975). Living until death: A program of service and research for the terminally ill. In E. Kübler-Ross (Ed.), *Death: The final stage of growth* (pp. 73–86). New York: Simon & Schuster.

Carnelley, K. B., Wortman, C. B., Bolger, N., & Burke, C. T. (2006). The time course of grief reactions to spousal loss: Evidence from a national probability sample. *Journal of Personality & Social Psychology, 91*, 476–492.

Carr, J. L. (2005). *American College Health Association campus violence white paper.* Baltimore, MD: American College Health Association.

Carroll, A., Lyall, M., & Forrester, A. (2004). Clinical hopes and public fears in forensic mental health. *Journal of Forensic Psychiatry & Psychology, 15*, 407–425.

Cascardi, M., Avery-Leaf, S., O'Leary, K. D., & Slep, A. M. S. (1999). Factor structure and convergent validity of the Conflict Tactics Scale in high school students. *Psychological Assessment, 11*, 546–555.

Castellano, C., & Plionis, E. (2006). Comparative analysis of three crisis intervention models applied to law enforcement first responders during 9/11 and Hurricane Katrina. *Brief Treatment & Crisis Intervention, 6*, 326–336.

Cavaiola, A. A., & Colford, J. E. (2006). *A practical guide to crisis intervention.* New York: Lahaska Press.

Center for Sex Offender Management. (2007). *Female sex offenders.* Retrieved March 29, 2008, from www.csom.org/pubs/female_sex_offenders_brief.pdf

Centers for Disease Control and Prevention. (2003). *Costs of intimate partner violence against women in the United States.* Retrieved January 10, 2008, from www.cdc.gov/ncipc/pub-res/ipv_cost/ipv.htm

Centers for Disease Control and Prevention. (2005a). Intimate partner violence injuries: Oklahoma, 2002. *Morbidity & Mortality Weekly Report, 54*(41), 1041–1045.

Centers for Disease Control and Prevention. (2005b). *Youth risk behavior surveillance—United States, 2005.* Retrieved January 24, 2008, from www.cdc.gov/mmwr/PDF/SS/SS5505.pdf

Centers for Disease Control and Prevention. (2006). *Intimate partner violence overview.* Retrieved January 10, 2008, from www.cdc.gov/ncipc/factsheets/ipvfacts.htm

Centers for Disease Control and Prevention. (2007). *Suicide facts at a glance.* Retrieved February 15, 2008, from www.cdc.gov/ncipc/dvp/Suicide/ SuicideDataSheet.pdf

Chaffin, M., & Friedrich, B. (2004). Evidence-based treatments in child abuse and neglect. *Children & Youth Services Review, 26,* 1097–1113.

Chang, J. C., Decker, M. R., Moracco, K. E., Martin, S. L., Petersen, R., & Frasier, P. Y. (2005). Asking about intimate partner violence: Advice from female survivors to healthcare providers. *Patient Education & Counseling, 59,* 141–147.

Charles, D. R., & Charles, M. (2006). Sibling loss and attachment style. *Psychoanalytic Psychology, 23,* 72–90.

Chemtob, C. M., Hamada, R. S., Bauer, G. B., Torigoe, R. Y., & Kinney, B. (1988). Patient suicide: Frequency and impact on psychologists. *Professional Psychology: Research & Practice, 19,* 421–425.

Child Abuse Prevention and Treatment Act (CAPTA), Pub. L. No. 93-247. Retrieved June 26, 2008, from www.acf.hhs.gov/programs/cb/ laws_policies/cblaws/capta03/capta_manual.pdf

Child Welfare Information Gateway. (2007). *Recognizing child abuse and neglect: Signs and symptoms.* Retrieved February 29, 2008, from www.childwelfare.gov/pubs/factsheets/ signs.cfm

Chiles, J. A., & Strosahl, K. D. (1995). *The suicidal patient: Principles of assessment, treatment, and case management.* Washington, DC: American Psychiatric Press.

Chung, K., Chung, D., & Joo, Y. (2006). Overview of administrative simplification provisions of HIPAA. *Journal of Medical Systems, 30*(1), 51–55.

Clark, A. H., & Foy, D. W. (2000). Trauma exposure and alcohol use in battered women. *Violence Against Women, 6,* 37–48.

Cohen, E. D., & Cohen, G. S. (1999). *The virtuous therapist: Ethical practice of counseling and psychotherapy.* Belmont, CA: Wadsworth.

Cohen, J. A., & Mannarino, A. P. (1997). A treatment study for sexually abused preschool children: Outcome during a one-year follow-up. *Journal of*

the American Academy of Child & Adolescent Psychiatry, 36, 1228–1235.

Cohen, J. A., & Mannarino, A. P. (1998). Factors that mediate treatment outcome of sexually abused preschool children: Six- and 12-month follow-up. *Journal of the American Academy of Child & Adolescent Psychiatry, 37,* 44–51.

Cohen, J. A., Mannarino, A. P., Berliner, L., & Deblinger, E. (2000). Trauma-focused cognitive-behavioral therapy for children and adolescents: An empirical update. *Journal of Interpersonal Violence, 15,* 1202–1223.

Colangelo, J. J. (2007). Recovered memory debate revisited: Practice implications for mental health counselors. *Journal of Mental Health Counseling, 29*(2), 127–135.

Coley, S. M., & Beckett, J. O. (1988). Black battered women: A review of empirical literature. *Journal of Counseling & Development, 66,* 266–270.

Collins, B. G., & Collins, T. M. (2005). *Crisis and trauma developmental-ecological intervention.* Boston: Houghton Mifflin/Lahaska Press.

Community Emergency Response Team. (2003). *Instructor guide for the Federal Emergency Management Agency (FEMA) Emergency Management Institute, United States Fire Administration.* McLean, VA: Author.

Corey, G., Corey, M., & Callanan, P. (2007). *Issues and ethics in the helping professions* (7th ed.). Belmont, CA: Thomson.

Cornell, D. G. (2007). *Best practices for making college campuses safe* (statement before the U.S. House Committee on Education and Labor, May 15, 2007). Retrieved February 15, 2008, from youthviolence.edschool.virginia.edu/prevention/ congress/testimony%202007.htm

Cowan, P. A., Cowan, C. P., & Schultz, M. S. (1996). Thinking about risk and resilience in families. In E. M. Hetherington & E. A. Blechman (Eds.), *Stress, coping, and resiliency in children and families* (pp. 1–38). Mahwah, NJ: Lawrence Erlbaum.

Craig, R. J. (2004). *Counseling the alcohol and drug dependent client.* New York: Allyn & Bacon.

Creamer, T. L., & Liddle, B. J. (2005). Secondary traumatic stress among disaster mental health workers responding to the September 11 attacks. *Journal of Traumatic Stress, 18*, 89–96.

Crisis Center, Inc. (2008). *Quick-at-a-glance suicide risk assessment*. Birmingham, AL: Author.

Currier, J. M., Holland, J. M., & Neimeyer, R. A. (2006). Sense-making, grief and the experience of violent loss: Toward a meditational model. *Death Studies, 30*, 403–428.

Darby, P. J., Allan, W. D., Kashani, J. H., Hartke, K. L., & Reid, J. C. (1998). Analysis of 112 juveniles who committed homicide: Characteristics and a closer look at family abuse. *Journal of Family Violence, 13*, 365–375.

Dass-Brailsford, P. (2007). *A practical approach to trauma: Empowering interventions*. Thousand Oaks, CA: Sage.

Davidson, M. W., Wagner, W. G., & Range, L. M. (1995). Clinicians' attitudes toward no-suicide agreements. *Suicide & Life-Threatening Behavior, 25*, 410–414.

Davis, R. E. (2002). "The strongest women": Exploration of the inner resources of abused women. *Qualitative Health Research, 12*, 1248–1263.

Deblinger, E., Lippman, J. T., & Steer, R. (1996). Sexually abused children suffering post-traumatic stress symptoms: Initial treatment outcome findings. *Child Maltreatment, 1*, 310–321.

Despenser, S. (2005). The personal safety of the therapist. *Psychodynamic Process, 11*, 429–446.

Deutsch, C. J. (1984). Self-report sources of stress among psychotherapists. *Professional Psychology: Research & Practice, 15*, 833–845.

Dienemann, J., Glass, N., & Hyman, R. (2005). Survivor preferences for response to IPV disclosure. *Clinical Nursing Research, 14*, 215–233.

Doka, K. J. (1996). *Living with grief after sudden loss: Suicide, homicide, accident, heart attack, stroke*. New York: Taylor & Francis.

Doka, K. J. (Ed.). (2000). *Living with grief: Children, adolescents, and loss*. Washington, DC: Hospice Foundation of America.

Doka, K. J. (Ed.). (2002). *Disenfranchised grief: New directions, challenges, and strategies for practice*. San Francisco: Jossey-Bass.

Doka, K. J. (2005, May). New perspectives on grief. *Counseling Today*, 56–57.

Domestic Abuse Project. (1993). *Men's group therapy manual*. Minneapolis, MN: Author.

Doweiko, H. E. (2003). *Concepts of chemical dependency* (5th ed.). Pacific Grove, CA: Brooks/Cole.

Drake, R., Mueser, K., Clark, R., & Wallach, M. (1996). The course, treatment, and outcome of Substance Use Disorder in persons with severe mental illness. *American Journal of Orthopsychiatry, 66*, 42–51.

Drew, B. L. (1999). No-suicide contracts to prevent suicidal behavior in inpatient psychiatric settings. *Journal of the American Psychiatric Nurses Association, 5*(1), 23–28.

Druss, B., Bornemann, T., Fry-Johnson, Y., McCombs, H., Politzer, R., & Rust, G. (2006). Trends in mental health and substance abuse services at the nation's community mental health centers: 1998–2003. *American Journal of Public Health, 96*, 1779–1784.

Dugan, B. (2007). Loss of identity in disaster: How do you say goodbye to home? *Perspectives of Psychiatric Care, 43*(1), 41–46.

Dulit, R. A., & Michels, R. (1992). Psychodynamics and suicide. In D. Jacobs (Ed.), *Suicide and clinical practice* (pp. 147–167). Washington, DC: American Psychiatric Press.

Dunkley, J., & Whelan, T. A. (2006). Vicarious traumatisation: Current status and future directions. *British Journal of Guidance & Counseling, 34*(1), 107–116.

Dutton, D. (1995). *The batterer: A psychological profile*. New York: Basic Books.

Dutton, M., Goodman, L., & Bennett, L. (1999). Court-involved battered women's response to violence: The role of psychological, physical, and sexual abuse. *Violence & Victims, 14*, 89–104.

Egan, G. (2002). *The skilled helper: A problem-management and opportunity-development approach to helping* (7th ed.). Pacific Grove, CA: Brooks/Cole.

Ehrensaft, M. K., Moffitt, T. E., & Caspi, A. (2004). Clinically abusive relationships in an unselected birth cohort: Men's and women's participation and developmental antecedents. *Journal of Abnormal Psychology, 113*, 258–271.

El-Khoury, M. Y., Dutton, M. A., Goodman, L. A., Engel, L., Belamaric, R. J., & Murphy, M. (2004). Ethnic difference in battered women's formal help-seeking strategies: A focus on health, mental health, and spirituality. *Cultural Diversity & Ethnic Minority Psychology, 10*, 383–393.

Elliott, D. M. (1994). Impaired object relations in professional women molested as children. *Psychotherapy, 21*, 79–86.

Ellis, A. (1962). *Reason and emotion in psychotherapy.* New York: Lyle Stuart.

El-Zanaty, F., Hussein, E. M., Shawky, G. A., Way, A. A., & Kishor, S. (1996). *Egypt demographic and health survey—1995.* Cairo: National Population Council.

Erikson, E. H. (1980). *Identity and the life cycle.* New York: W. W. Norton.

Erikson, E. H. (1997). *The life cycle completed.* New York: W. W. Norton.

Eronen, M., Angermeyer, M. C., & Schulze, B. (1998). The psychiatric epidemiology of violent behavior. *Social Psychiatry & Psychiatric Epidemiology, 33*(Suppl.), 13–23.

Essex, N. L. (2004). Confidentiality and student records. *Clearing House, 77*, 111–113.

Evans, D. R., Hearn, M. T., Uhlemann, M. R., & Ivey, A. E. (2008). *Essential interviewing: A programmed approach to effective communication.* Belmont, CA: Brooks/Cole.

Everly, G. S., & Flynn, B. W. (2005). Principles and practices of acute psychological first aid after disasters. In G. S. Everly & C. L. Parker (Eds.), *Mental health aspects of disasters: Public health preparedness and response* (Rev. ed., pp. 79–89). Baltimore, MD: Johns Hopkins Center for Public Health Preparedness.

Everly, G. S., & Mitchell, J. (1997). *Critical incident stress management.* Ellicott City, MD: Chevron.

Everly, G. S., & Mitchell, J. (1999). *Critical incident stress management* (2nd ed.). Ellicott City, MD: Chevron.

Everly, G. S., Phillips, S. B., Kane, D., & Feldman, D. (2006). Introduction to and overview of group psychological first aid. *Brief Treatment & Crisis Intervention, 6*, 130–136.

Ewalt, J. R. (1967). Other psychiatric emergencies. In A. M. Freedman, H. I. Kaplan, & H. S. Kaplan (Eds.), *Comprehensive textbook of psychiatry* (pp. 1179–1187). Baltimore, MD: Williams & Wilkins.

Ewing v. Goldstein, 120 Cal. App. 4th 807 (2004).

Ewing, J. A. (1984). Detecting alcoholism: The CAGE questionnaire. *Journal of the American Medical Association, 252*, 1905–1907.

Fairlie, C. W. (2000). *Civil claims by survivors of sexual abuse.* Retrieved May 31, 2008, from library.findlaw.com/2000/May/1/127159.html

Family Violence Prevention Fund. (1999). *Preventing domestic violence: Clinical guidelines on routine screening.* San Francisco: Author.

Farber, B. A. (1983). Psychotherapist's perceptions of stressful patient behavior. *Professional Psychology: Research & Practice, 14*, 697–705.

Farmer, T. W., Farmer, E. M. Z., Estell, D. B., & Hutchins, B. C. (2007). The developmental dynamics of aggression and the prevention of school violence. *Journal of Emotional & Behavioral Disorders, 15*, 197–208.

Farrow, T. L. (2002). Owning their expertise: Why nurses use no suicide contracts rather than their own assessments. *International Journal of Mental Health Nursing, 11*, 214–219.

Federal Bureau of Investigation. (2005). *Uniform crime reporting program.* Retrieved January 23, 2008, from www.fbi.gov/ucr/05cius/offenses/violent_crime/forcible_rape.html

Federal Bureau of Investigation. (2008). *Uniform crime reports.* Retrieved January 27, 2008, from www.fbi.gov/ucr/ucr.htm

Federal Bureau of Investigation, National Center for the Analysis of Violent Crime. (2001). *Workplace violence: Issues in response.* Retrieved February 10, 2008, from www.fbi.gov/publications/violence.pdf

Federal Emergency Management Agency. (2007). *National preparedness guidelines.* Retrieved February 26, 2008, from www.fema.gov/pdf/government/npg.pdf

Ferrara, F. F. (2002). *Childhood sexual abuse developmental effects across the lifespan.* Pacific Grove, CA: Brooks/Cole.

Few, A. L. (2005). The voices of Black and White rural battered women in domestic violence shelters. *Family Relations, 54,* 488–500.

Fiduccia, B. W., & Wolfe, L. R. (1999). *Violence against disabled women.* Retrieved January 10, 2008, from www.centerwomenpolicy.org

Figley, C. R. (2002). Compassion fatigue: Psychotherapists' chronic lack of self care. *Journal of Clinical Psychology, 58,* 1433–1441.

Fine, M. A., & Sansome, R. A. (1990). Dilemmas in the management of suicidal behavior in individuals with borderline personality. *American Journal of Psychotherapy, 44,* 160–171.

Finkelhor, D. (1981). The sexual abuse of boys. *Victimology, 6,* 76–84.

Finkelhor, D. (1993). Epidemiological factors in the clinical identification of child sexual abuse. *Sexual Abuse & Neglect, 17,* 67–70.

Finkelhor, D. (1994). Current information on the scope and nature of child sexual abuse. *Future of Children, 4*(2), 31–53.

Fisher, B. S., Cullen, F. T., & Turner, M. G. (2000). *The sexual victimization of college women: Research report.* Washington, DC: U.S. Department of Justice.

Fitzgerald, H. (1998). *Grief at school.* Washington, DC: American Hospice Foundation.

Flannery, R. B., & Stone, P. S. (2001). Characteristics of staff victims of patient assault: Ten year analysis of the assaulted staff action program. *Psychiatric Quarterly, 72,* 237–248.

Foa, E. B., Hearst-Ikeda, D., & Perry, K. J. (1995). Evaluation of a brief cognitive-behavioral program for the prevention of chronic PTSD in recent assault victims. *Journal of Consulting & Clinical Psychology, 63,* 948–955.

Foa, E. B., Riggs, D. S., Dancu, C. V., & Rothbaum, B. O. (1993). Reliability and validity of a brief instrument for assessing Post-traumatic Stress Disorder. *Journal of Traumatic Stress, 6,* 459–473.

Foa, E. B., & Rothbaum, B. O. (1998). *Treating the trauma of rape: Cognitive behavioral therapy for PTSD.* New York: Guilford Press.

Foa, E. B., Rothbaum, B. O., Riggs, D. S., & Murdock, T. (1991). Treatment of Posttraumatic Stress Disorder in rape victims: A comparison between cognitive behavioral procedures and counseling. *Journal of Consulting & Clinical Psychology, 59,* 715–723.

Ford, G. G. (2006). *Ethical reasoning for mental health professionals.* Thousand Oaks, CA: Sage.

Foss, L. L., & Warnke, M. A. (2003). Fundamentalist Protestant Christian women: Recognizing cultural and gender influences on domestic violence. *Counseling & Values, 48,* 14–23.

Foster, V., & McAdams, C. (1999). The impact of client suicide in counselor training: Implications for counselor education and supervision. *Counselor Education & Supervision, 39,* 22–33.

Fox, J. A., & Zawitz, M. W. (2004). *Homicide trends in the United States.* Washington, DC: U.S. Department of Justice.

Fox, S. (1988). *Good grief: Helping groups of children deal with loss when a friend dies.* Boston: New England Association for the Education of Young Children.

France, K. (2002). *Crisis intervention* (4th ed.). Springfield, IL: Charles C. Thomas.

Franiuk, R. (2007). Discussing and defining sexual assault: A classroom activity. *College Teaching, 55*(3), 104.

Frankl, V. (1959). *Man's search for meaning.* Boston: Beacon Press.

Freud, S. (1917). *Mourning and melancholia.* London: Hogarth Press.

Fugate, M., Landis, L., Riordan, K., Naureckas, S., & Engel, B. (2005). Barriers to domestic violence help seeking: Implications for intervention. *Violence Against Women, 11,* 290– 310.

Gerbert, B., Capsers, N., Milliken, N., Berlin, M., Bronstone, A., & Moe, J. (2000). Interventions that help victims of domestic violence. *Journal of Family Practice, 49,* 889–895.

Giarretto, H. (1982). A comprehensive child sexual abuse treatment program. *Child Abuse & Neglect, 6,* 263–278.

Gilliland, B. E., & James, R. K. (1997). *Crisis intervention strategies.* Pacific Grove, CA: Brooks/Cole.

Giordano, P. C., Millhollin, T. J., Cernkovich, S. A., Pugh, M. D., & Rudolph, J. L. (1999). Delinquency, identity, and women's involvement in relationship violence. *Criminology, 37,* 17–40.

Gitlin, M. J. (1999). A psychiatrist's reaction to a patient's suicide. *American Journal of Psychiatry, 156,* 1630–1634.

Gladding, S. T. (1997). *Community and agency counseling.* Columbus, OH: Merrill/Prentice Hall.

Gladding, S. T. (2006). *The counseling dictionary: Concise definitions of frequently used terms* (2nd ed.). Upper Saddle River, NJ: Pearson.

Glasser, W. (1965). *Reality therapy: A new approach to psychiatry.* New York: Harper & Row.

Goldenberg, I., & Goldenberg, H. (2004). *Family therapy: An overview* (6th ed.). Pacific Grove, CA: Brooks/Cole.

Gondolf, E. (2002). Service barriers for battered women with male partners in batterer programs. *Journal of Interpersonal Violence, 17,* 217–227.

Gondolf, E., & Fisher, E. (1988). *Battered women as survivors: An alternative to treating learned helplessness.* Lexington, MA: Lexington Books.

Gorski, T. T. (1995). *The phases and warning signs of relapse.* Independence, MO: Herald House/Independence.

Grafanaki, S., Pearson, D., Cini, F., Goldula, D., Mckenzie, B., Nason, S., et al. (2005). Sources of renewal: A qualitative study on the experience and role of leisure in the life of counsellors and psychologists. *Counselling Psychology Quarterly, 18*(1), 31–40.

Granello, D. H., & Granello, P. F. (2007). *Suicide: An essential guide for helping professionals and educators.* Boston: Pearson Education.

Greenberg, L. S., & Pascual-Leone, A. (2006). Emotion in psychotherapy: A practice friendly review. *Journal of Clinical Psychology: In Session, 62,* 611–630.

Greene, G. J., Lee, M., Trask, R., & Rheinscheld, J. (2005). How to work with clients' strengths in crisis intervention: A solution-focused approach. In A. R. Roberts (Ed.), *Crisis intervention handbook: Assessment, treatment, and research* (3rd ed., pp. 64–89). New York: Oxford University Press.

Greenstone, J. L., & Leviton, S. C. (2002). *Elements of crisis intervention: Crises and how to respond to them* (2nd ed.). Pacific Grove, CA: Brooks/Cole.

Griffin, R. M. (2008). *Breaking the silence: Sociologist studies woman-to-woman sexual violence.* Retrieved January 20, 2008, from www.snbw.org/articles/womantowomansexualviolence.htm

Grob, G. S. (2000). Deconstructing ecstasy: The politics of MDMA research. *Addiction Research, 8,* 549–588.

Gross v. Allen, 22 Cal. App. 4th 354, 27 Cal. Rptr. 2d 429 (1994).

Grossman, L. S., Martis, B., & Fichtner, C. G. (1999). *Are sex offenders treatable? A research overview.* Retrieved on January 23, 2008, from www.psychservices.psychiatryonline.org/cgi/reprint/50/3/349.pdf

Groth, A. N. (2001). *Men and rape: The psychology of the offender.* New York: Basic Books.

Gutheil, T. G. (1992). Suicide and suit: Liability after self-destruction. In D. Jacobs (Ed.), *Suicide and clinical practice* (pp. 147–167). Washington, DC: American Psychiatric Press.

Haj-Yahia, M. M. (1998). Beliefs about wife-beating among Palestinian women: The influence of their patriarchal ideology. *Violence Against Women, 12,* 530–545.

Haj-Yahia, M. M. (2002). Beliefs of Jordanian women about wife-beating. *Psychology of Women Quarterly, 26,* 282–291.

Halpern, C. T., Oslak, S. G., Young, M. L., Martin, S. L., & Kupper, L. L. (2001). Partner violence among adolescents in opposite-sex romantic relationships: Findings from the national longitudinal study of adolescent health. *American Journal of Public Health, 91,* 1679–1685.

Hamblen, J. L., Gibson, L. E., Mueser, K. T., & Norris, F. H. (2006). Cognitive behavioral therapy for prolonged postdisaster distress. *Journal of Clinical Psychology: In Session, 62,* 1043–1052.

Hanson, R. F. (2002). Adolescent dating violence: Prevalence and psychological outcomes. *Child Abuse & Neglect, 26,* 447–451.

Harper, F. D., Harper, J. A., & Stills, A. B. (2003). Counseling children in crisis based on Maslow's hierarchy of basic needs. *International Journal for the Advancement of Counselling, 25*(1), 11–25.

Hassouneh-Phillips, D., & Curry, M. A. (2002). Abuse of women with disabilities: State of the science. *Rehabilitation Counseling Bulletin, 45*, 96–104.

Hatton, R. (2003). Homicide bereavement counseling: A survey of providers. *Death Studies, 27*, 427–448.

Haugaard, J. J. (2000). The challenge of defining sexual abuse. *American Psychologist, 55*, 1036–1039.

Hays, D. G., Green, E., Orr, J. J., & Flowers, L. (2007). Advocacy counseling for female survivors of partner abuse: Implications for counselor education. *Counselor Education & Supervision, 46*, 186–198.

Hebert, B. B., & Ballard, M. B. (2007). Children and trauma: A post-Katrina and Rita response. *Professional School Counseling, 11*(2), 140–144.

Hendin, H., Lipschitz, A., Maltsberger, J. T., Haas, A. P., & Wynecoop, S. (2000). Therapists' reactions to patients' suicides. *American Journal of Psychiatry, 157*, 2022–2027.

Herman, J. L. (1995). Complex PTSD: A syndrome in survivors of prolonged and repeated trauma. In G. S. Everly & J. M. Lating (Eds.), *Psychotraumatology: Key papers and core concepts in posttraumatic stress* (pp. 87–100). New York: Plenum.

Hewitt, S. K. (1998). *Small voices: Assessing allegations of sexual abuse in preschool children.* Thousand Oaks, CA: Sage.

Hill, R. (1949). *Families under stress.* Westport, CT: Greenwood Press.

Hill, R. (1958). Social stresses on the family: Generic features of families under stress. *Social Casework, 39*, 139–150.

Hillbrand, M. (2001). Homicide-suicide and other forms of co-occurring aggression against self and others. *Professional Psychology: Research & Practice, 32*, 626–635.

Hines, D. A., & Finkelhor, D. (2007). Statutory sex crime relationships between juveniles and adults: A review of social scientific research. *Aggression & Violent Behavior, 12*, 300–314.

Hines, D. A., & Malley-Morrison, K. (2005). *Family violence in the United States: Defining, understanding and combating abuse.* Thousand Oaks, CA: Sage.

Hipple, J., & Cimbolic, P. (1979). *The counselor and suicidal crisis.* Springfield, IL: Charles C. Thomas.

Holt, M. K., & Espelage, D. L. (2005). Social support as a moderator between dating violence victimization and depression anxiety among African American and Caucasian adolescents. *School Psychology Review, 34*, 309–328.

Holtzworth-Munroe, A., Bates, L., Smultzer, N., & Sandin, E. (1997). A brief review of the research on husband violence. *Aggression & Violent Behavior, 2*, 65–99.

Hooyman, N. R., & Kramer, J. (2006). *Living through loss: Interventions across the lifespan.* New York: Columbia University Press.

Horne, C. (2003). Families of homicide victims: Utilization patterns of extra- and intrafamilial homicide survivors. *Journal of Family Violence, 18*(2), 75–82.

Horne, S. (1999). Domestic violence in Russia. *American Psychologist, 54*, 55–61.

Horner, J., & Wheeler, M. (2005). HIPAA: Impact on clinical practices. *American Speech- Language-Hearing Association Leader, 10*(12), 10–23.

Horowitz, M. J., Wilner, N. J., & Alvarez, W. (1979). Impact of Events Scale: A measure of subjective stress. *Psychosomatic Medicine, 41*, 209–218.

Horvath, A. O., & Bedi, R. P. (2002). The alliance. In J. C. Norcross (Ed.), *Psychotherapy relationships that work: Therapist contributions and responsiveness to patients* (pp. 37–69). New York: Oxford University Press.

Horwitz, A. V., & Wakefield, J. C. (2007). *The loss of sadness: How psychiatry transformed normal sorrow into depressive disorder.* Oxford, England: Oxford University Press.

Howard, D. E., Wang, M. Q., & Yan, F. (2007). Psychosocial factors associated with reports of physical dating violence among U.S. adolescent females. *Adolescence, 42*, 311–324.

Humphreys, C., & Thiara, R. K. (2003). Neither justice nor protection: Women's experiences of post-separation violence. *Journal of Social Welfare & Family Law, 25*, 195–214.

Huprich, S. K., Fuller, K. M., & Schneider, R. B. (2003). Divergent ethical perspectives on the duty-to-warn principle with HIV patients. *Ethics & Behavior, 13*, 263–278.

Imai, H., Nakao, H., Tsuchiya, M., Kuroda, Y., & Katon, T. (2004). Burnout and work environments of public health nurses involved in mental health care. *Occupational & Environmental Medicine, 67*, 764–768.

International Association for Suicide Prevention. (2000). *Guidelines for suicide prevention.* Retrieved September 8, 2007, from www.med.uio.no/iasp/english/guidelines.html

Ivey, A. E., & Ivey, M. B. (2007). *Intentional interviewing and counseling: Facilitating client development in a multicultural society* (6th ed.). Belmont, CA: Brooks/Cole.

Jacobson, G., Strickland, M., & Morley, W. (1968). Generic and individual approaches to crisis intervention. *American Journal of Public Health, 58*, 338–343.

James, R. K. (2008). *Crisis intervention strategies* (6th ed.). Belmont, CA: Brooks/Cole.

Janosik, E. H. (1984). *Crisis counseling: A contemporary approach.* Monterey, CA: Wadsworth.

Jensen, D. G. (2003). HIPAA overview. *Therapist, 15*(3), 26–27.

Jobes, D. A. (2006). *Managing suicidal risk: A collaborative approach.* New York: Guilford Press.

Jobes, D. A. (2007). *How to work effectively with suicidal clients across the age spectrum.* Eau Claire, WI: Health Education Network.

Jobes, D. A., & Berman, A. L. (1993). Suicide and malpractice liability: Assessing and revising policies, procedures, and practice in outpatient settings. *Professional Psychology: Research & Practice, 24*(1), 91–99.

Jobes, D. A., & Drozd, J. F. (2004). The CAMS approach to working with suicidal patients. *Journal of Contemporary Psychotherapy, 34*(1), 73–85.

Johngma, A. E., & Peterson, L. M. (1999). *The complete adult psychotherapy treatment planner* (2nd ed.). New York: Wiley.

Johnson, K. (2000). *School crisis management: A hands-on guide to training crisis response teams* (2nd ed.). Alameda, CA: Hunter House.

Johnson, R. J. (2008). Advances in understanding and treating childhood sexual abuse: Implications for research and policy. *Family & Community Health, 31*(Suppl. 1), S24–S34.

Johnson, V. E. (1998). *Intervention: How to help someone who doesn't want help.* Center City, MN: Hazelden.

Joiner, T. E., Walker, R. L., Rudd, D. M., & Jobes, D. A. (1999). Scientizing and routinizing the assessment of suicidality in outpatient practice. *Professional Psychology: Research & Practice, 30*, 447–453.

Jones, J. (2006). Mother nature's disasters and their health effects: A literature review. *Nursing Forum, 41*(2), 78–87.

Jordan, J. R., & Harpel, J. L. (2007). *Facilitating suicide bereavement support groups: A self-study manual.* New York: American Foundation for Suicide Prevention.

Kaltman, S., & Bonanno, G. A. (2003). Trauma and bereavement: Examining the impact of sudden and violent deaths, *Journal of Anxiety Disorders, 17*, 131–147.

Kanel, K. (2007). *A guide to crisis intervention* (3rd ed.). Belmont, CA: Thomson.

Kaukinen, C. (2004). The help-seeking strategies of female violent-crime victims, the direct and conditional effects of race and the victim-offender relationship. *Journal of Interpersonal Violence, 19*, 967–990.

Kearney, R. J. (1996). *Within the wall of denial: Conquering addictive behaviors.* New York: W. W. Norton.

Keller, E. L. (1996). Invisible victims: Battered women in psychiatric and medical emergency rooms. *Bulletin of the Menninger Clinic, 60*(1), 1–21.

Kelly, K. T., & Knudson, M. P. (2000). Are no suicide contracts effective in preventing suicide in suicidal clients seen by primary care physicians? *Archives of Family Medicine, 9*, 1119–1123.

Kendall-Tackett, K. A., Meyer Williams, L., & Finkelhor, D. (1993). Impact of sexual abuse on children: A review and synthesis of recent empirical studies. *Psychological Bulletin, 113,* 164–180.

Kerr, M. M. (2009). *School crisis, prevention, and intervention.* Columbus, OH: Pearson Merrill Prentice Hall.

Kilpatrick, D. G. (1988). Rape aftermath symptom test. In M. Hersen & A. S. Bellack (Eds.), *Dictionary of behavioral assessment techniques* (pp. 366–367). New York: Pergamon Press.

Kilpatrick, D. G., & Resnick, H. S. (1993). PTSD associated with exposure to criminal victimization in clinical and community populations. In J. R. T. Davidson & E. B. Foa (Eds.), *PTSD in review: Recent research and future directions* (pp. 113–143). Washington, DC: American Psychiatric Press.

Kleespies, P. M. (1998). *Emergencies in mental health practice.* New York: Guilford Press.

Kleespies, P. M., Deleppo, J. D., Gallagher, P. L., & Niles, B. L. (1999). Managing suicidal emergencies: Recommendations for the practitioner. *Professional Psychology: Research & Practice, 30,* 454–463.

Klott, J., & Jongsma, A. E. (2004). *The suicide and homicide risk assessment and prevention treatment planner.* Hoboken, NJ: Wiley.

Knapp, S., & VandeCreek, L. (1982). Tarasoff: Five years later. *Professional Psychology, 13,* 511–516.

Knapp, S., & VandeCreek, L. (1983). Malpractice risks with suicidal patients. *Psychotherapy: Theory, Research & Practice, 20,* 274–280.

Kohlberg, L. (1976). Moral stages and moralization: The cognitive-developmental approach. In T. Lickona (Ed.), *Moral development and behavior: Theory, research, and social issues* (pp. 41–59). New York: Holt, Rinehart, & Winston.

Kohlberg, L. (1984). *The psychology of moral development* (Vol. 2). San Francisco: Harper & Row.

Kohlberg, L., & Candee, D. (1984). The relationship of moral judgment to moral action. In W. M. Kurtines & J. L. Gewirtz (Eds.), *Morality, moral behavior and moral development* (pp. 41–51). New York: Wiley.

Koss, M. P. (1993). Detecting the scope of rape: A review of prevalence research methods. *Journal of Interpersonal Violence, 8,* 198–222.

Koss, M. P., Gidycz, C. A., & Wisniewski, N. (1987). The scope of rape: Incidence and prevalence of sexual aggression and victimization in a national sample of higher education students. *Journal of Consulting & Clinical Psychology, 55,* 162–170.

Kozu, J. (1999). Domestic violence in Japan. *American Psychologist, 54,* 50–54.

Kramer, A., Lorenzon, D., & Mueller, G. (2004). Prevalence of intimate partner violence and health implications for women using emergency departments and primary care clinics. *Women's Health Issues, 14,* 19–29.

Kreitman, N. (1986). The clinical assessment and management of the suicidal patient. In A. Roy (Ed.), *Suicide* (pp. 181–195). Baltimore, MD: Williams & Wilkins.

Krug, E. G., Dahlberg, L. L., Mercy, J. A., Zwi, A. B., & Lozano, R. (Eds.). (2002). *World report on violence and health.* Geneva: World Health Organization.

Ksir, C., Hart, C., & Ray, O. (2006). *Drugs, society, and human behavior* (11th ed.). New York: McGraw Hill.

Kubany, E. S. (1998). Cognitive therapy for trauma-related guilt. In V. M. Follette, J. I. Ruzek, & F. R. Abueg (Eds.), *Cognitive-behavioral therapies for trauma* (pp. 124–161). New York: Guilford Press.

Kübler-Ross, E. (1969). *On death and dying.* New York: Collier Books.

Kübler-Ross, E. (1972). *Questions and answers on death and dying.* New York: Simon & Schuster/ Touchstone.

Kübler-Ross, E. (1975). *Death: The final stage of growth.* Englewood Cliffs, NJ: Prentice-Hall.

Kübler-Ross, E., & Kessler, D. (2005). *On grief and grieving.* New York: Scribner.

Kulwicki, A. (2002). The practice of honor crimes: A glimpse of domestic violence in the Arab world. *Issues in Mental Health Nursing, 23,* 77–87.

Kung, H., Hoyert, D., Xu, J., & Murphy, S. L. (2008). Deaths: Final data for 2005. *National Vital Statistics Reports* (Vol. 56, no. 10). Hyattsville, MD: Centers for Disease Control, National Center for Health Statistics. (Available at www.cdc.gov/nchs/ data/nvsr/nvsr56/nvsr56_10.pdf)

Laajasalo, T., & Hakkanen, H. (2004). Background characteristics of mentally ill homicide offenders: A comparison of five diagnostic groups. *Journal of Forensic Psychiatry and Psychology, 15*, 451–474.

Lambert, M. J., & Ogles, B. M. (1997). The effectiveness of psychotherapy supervision. In J. C. E. Watkins (Ed.), *Handbook of psychotherapy supervision* (pp. 421–446). New York: Wiley.

Lambie, G. W. (2006). Burnout prevention: A humanistic perspective and structured group supervision activity. *Journal of Humanistic Counseling, Education & Development. 45*(1), 32–44.

Langner, T. S. (2002). *Choices for living: Coping with fear of dying.* New York: Kluwer Academic/ Plenum Press.

Lanning, K. (2001). *Child molesters: A behavioral analysis* (4th ed.). Alexandria, VA: National Center for Missing and Exploited Children.

Largen, M. A. (1985). The anti-rape movement—Past and present. In A. W. Burgess (Ed.), *Rape and sexual assault: A research handbook* (pp. 1–13). New York: Garland.

Larson, D. R., & Hoyt, W. T. (2007). What has become of grief counseling? An evaluation of the empirical foundations of the new pessimism. *Professional Psychology: Research & Practice, 38*, 347–355.

Laux, J. M. (2002). A primer on suicidology: Implications for counselors. *Journal of Counseling & Development, 80*, 380–384.

Laws, D. R., & Marshall, W. L. (2003). A brief history of behavioral and cognitive behavioral approaches to sexual offenders: Part 1. Early developments. *Sexual Abuse: A Journal of Research & Treatment, 15*, 75–92.

Lazarus, R. S. (1966). *Psychological stress and the coping process.* New York: McGraw-Hill.

Lazarus, R. S. (1976). *Patterns of adjustment* (3rd ed.). New York: McGraw-Hill.

Leary, M. R., Kowalski, R. M., Smith, L., & Phillips, S. (2003). Teasing, rejection and violence: Case studies of school shootings. *Aggressive Behavior, 29*, 202–214.

Lee, J. B., & Bartlett, M. L. (2005). Suicide prevention: Critical elements for managing suicidal clients and counselor liability without the use of a no-suicide contract. *Death Studies, 29*, 1–19.

Lee, R., Caruso, M., Goins, S., & Southerland, J. (2003). Addressing sexual assault on college campuses: Guidelines for a prevention/awareness week. *Journal of College Counseling, 6*(1), 14.

Lee, R. K., Thompson, V. L. S., & Mechanic, M. B. (2002). Intimate partner violence and women of color: A call for innovations. *American Journal of Public Health, 92*, 530–534.

Lemberg, J. (2002, July 21). Spouse abuse in South Asian marriages may be high. *Women's News.* Retrieved January 11, 2008, from www.women senews.org/article.cfm/dyn/979/context/archive

Leong, F. T. L., & Lau, A. S. L. (2001). Barriers to providing effective mental health services to Asian Americans. *Mental Health Services Research, 3*(4), 201–214.

Leong, F. T. L., & Leach, M. M. (Eds.). (2008). *Suicide among racial and ethnic minority groups: Theory, research, and practice.* New York: Routledge.

Levin, S., Madover, S., & Wilson, S. (2006, July). A recovery approach to bring about "CHANGES." *Behavioral Healthcare.* Retrieved on May 1, 2008, from behavioral.net/Me2/dirmod.asp? sid=9B6FFC446FF7486981EA3C0C3CCE4943& nm=Archives&type=Publishing&mod=Publications %3A%3AArticle&mid=64D490AC6A7D4FE1AEB 453627F1A4A32&tier=4&id=A2580E27DED24A0 7AC0637EAF1DDBA56

Lewis, C. S. (1961). *A grief observed.* London: Faber & Faber.

Liang, B., Goodman, L., Tummala-Narra, P., & Weintraub, S. (2005). A theoretical framework for understanding help-seeking processes among survivors of intimate partner violence. *American Journal of Community Psychology, 36*, 71–84.

Lindemann, E. (1944). Symptomatology and management of acute grief. *American Journal of Psychiatry, 101*, 141–148.

Lipsky, S., Caetano, R., Field, C. A., & Bazargan, S. (2005). The role of alcohol use and depression in intimate partner violence among Black and Hispanic patients in an urban emergency department. *American Journal of Drug & Alcohol Abuse, 31*, 225–242.

Lipsky, S., Caetano, R., Field, C. A., & Larkin, G. L. (2006). The role of intimate partner violence, race, and ethnicity in help seeking behaviors. *Ethnicity & Health, 11*, 81–100.

Loeber, R., Pardini, D., Homish, D. L., Wei, E. H., Crawford, A. M., Farrington, D. P., et al. (2005). The prediction of violence and homicide in young men. *Journal of Consulting & Clinical Psychology, 73*, 1074–1088.

Lord, J. (1997). *Death notification: Breaking the bad news with concern for the professional and compassion for the survivor.* Washington, DC: U.S. Department of Justice, Office for Victims of Crime.

Lutenbacher, M., Cohen, A., & Mitzel, J. (2003). Do we really help? Perspectives of abused women. *Public Health Nursing, 20*(1), 56–64.

MacPhail, D. (1989). The moral education approach in treating adult inmates. *Criminal Justice & Behavior, 16*, 81–97.

Madrid, P. A., & Grant, R. (2008). Meeting mental health needs following a natural disaster: Lessons from Hurricane Katrina. *Professional Psychology: Research & Practice, 39*(1), 86–92.

Madsen, L. H., Blitz, L. V., McCorkle, D., & Panzer, P. G. (2003). Sanctuary in a domestic violence shelter: A team approach to healing. *Psychiatric Quarterly, 74*(2), 155–171.

Mahoney, M. J. (1997). Psychotherapists' personal problems and self-care patterns. *Professional Psychology: Research & Practice, 28*, 14–16.

Mahrer, J., & Bongar, B. (1993). Assessment and management of suicide risk and the use of the no-suicide contract. *Innovations in Clinical Practice: A Source Book, 12*, 277–293.

Maltsberger, J. T. (1986). *Suicide risk: The formulation of clinical judgment.* New York: New York University Press.

Maltsberger, J. T. (1991). The prevention of suicide in adults. In A. A. Leenaars (Ed.), *Lifespan perspectives of suicide: Time-lines in the suicide process* (pp. 295–307). New York: Plenum Press.

Maltsberger, J. T. (1994). Calculated risk-taking in the treatment of suicidal patients: Ethical and legal problems. In A. A. Leenaars, J. T. Maltsberger, & R. A. Neimeyer (Eds.), *Treatment of suicidal people* (pp. 195–205). Washington, DC: Taylor & Francis.

Marino, T. (1995). Crisis counseling: Helping normal people cope with abnormal situations. *Counseling Today, 38*, 40–46.

Marlatt, G. (1996). Harm reduction: Come as you are. *Addictive Behaviors, 21*, 779–788.

Marques, J. K. (1999). How to answer the question, "Does sexual offender treatment work?" *Journal of Interpersonal Violence, 14*, 437–451.

Marques, J. K., Wiederanders, M., Day, D. M., Nelson, C., & van Ommeren, A. (2005). Effects of a relapse prevention program on sexual recidivism: Final results from California's Sex Offender Treatment and Evaluation Project (SOTEP). *Sexual Abuse: A Journal of Research & Treatment, 17*, 79–107.

Marshall, K. (1980). When a patient commits suicide. *Suicide & Life-Threatening Behavior, 10*, 29–40.

Maruish, M. E. (2002). *Essentials of treatment planning.* New York: Wiley.

Maryland State Police. (2001). *Recommended procedures for death notifications: The principles of death notifications.* Annapolis, MD: Author.

Maslach, C. (1982). *Burnout: The cost of caring.* Englewood Cliffs, NJ: Prentice Hall.

Mathews, R., Matthews, J. K., & Speltz, K. (1989). *Female sexual offenders: An exploratory study.* Orwell, VT: Safer Society Press.

Matsakis, A. (1998). *Trust after trauma: A guide to relationships for survivors and those who love them.* Oakland, CA: New Harbinger.

Mattson, S., & Rodriguez, E. (1999). Battering in pregnant Latinas. *Issues in Mental Health Nursing, 20*, 405–422.

Mattson, S., & Ruiz, E. (2005). Intimate partner violence in the Latino community and its effect on children. *Health Care for Women International, 26*, 523–529.

Mayo Clinic. (2008). *Complicated grief.* Retrieved May 31, 2008, from www.mayoclinic.com/health/complicated-grief/DS01023/DSECTION=2

McCann, I. L., & Pearlman, L. A. (1990). Vicarious traumatization: A framework for understanding the psychological effects of working with victims. *Journal of Traumatic Stress, 3*, 131–149.

McClarren, G. M. (1987). The psychiatric duty to warn: Walking a tightrope of uncertainty. *University of Cincinnati Law Review, 56*, 269–293.

McCloskey, K., & Grigsby, N. (2005). The ubiquitous clinical problem of adult intimate partner violence: The need for routine assessment. *Professional Psychology: Research & Practice, 36*, 264–275.

McCloskey, K. A., & Raphael, D. N. (2005). Adult perpetrator gender asymmetries in child sexual assault victim selection: Results from the 2000 National Incident-Based Reporting System. *Journal of Child Sexual Abuse, 14*, 1–24.

McConnell, A., & Drennan, L. (2006). Mission impossible? Planning and preparing for crisis. *Journal of Contingencies & Crisis Management, 14*(2), 59–70.

McCubbin, H. I., & Patterson, J. M. (1982). Family adaptation to crisis. In H. I. McCubbin, A. E. Cauble, & J. M. Patterson (Eds.), *Family stress, coping, and social support* (pp. 26–47). Springfield, IL: Charles C. Thomas.

McFarlane, J., Soeken, K., Reel, S., Parker, B., & Silva, C. (1997). Resource use of abused women following an intervention program: Associated severity of abuse and reports of abuse ending. *Public Health Nursing, 14*, 244–250.

McFarlane, J. M., Groff, J. Y., O'Brien, J. A., & Watson, K. (2005). Prevalence of partner violence against 7,443 African American, White, and Hispanic women receiving care at urban public primary care clinics. *Public Health Nursing, 22*, 98–107.

McKenry, P. C., & Price, S. J. (2005). *Families and change: Coping with stressful events and transitions* (3rd ed.). Thousand Oaks, CA: Sage.

McLeod, A. L., Hays, D. G., & Chang, C. Y. (in press). Experiences of female intimate partner violence survivors: Accessing personal and community resources. *Journal of Counseling & Development.*

McWhirter, P. T. (1999). La violencia privada: Domestic violence in Chile. *American Psychologist, 54*, 37–40.

Meichenbaum, D. H. (1996). Stress inoculation training for coping with stressors. *Clinical Psychologist, 49*, 4–7.

Melby, T. (2004). Duty to warn: A question of loyalty varies by state. *Contemporary Sexuality, 38*(1), 3–6.

Mendelson, J., & Mello, N. (1985). *The diagnosis and treatment of alcoholism.* New York: McGraw Hill.

Meyer, D., & Ponton, R. (2006). The healthy tree: A metaphorical perspective of counselor well-being. *Journal of Mental Health Counseling, 28*, 189–201.

Milgram, G. G. (1996, May/June). Alcohol and other drugs in American society: An overview. *Counselor*, 30–32.

Miller, M. C. (1999). Suicide-prevention contracts: Advantages, disadvantages, and an alternative approach. In D. G. Jacobs (Ed.), *The Harvard Medical School guide to suicide assessment and intervention* (pp. 463–481). San Francisco: Jossey-Bass.

Miller, T., Clayton, R., Miller, J. M., Bilyeu, J., Hunter, J., & Kraus, R. F. (2000). Violence in the schools: Clinical issues and case analysis for high-risk children. *Child Psychiatry & Human Development, 30*, 255–272.

Miller, W. R., & Rollnick, S. (2002). *Motivational interviewing: Preparing people to change addictive behavior* (2nd ed.). New York: Guilford Press.

Miller-Perrin, C. L., & Perrin, R. D. (2007). *Child maltreatment: An introduction* (2nd ed.). Thousand Oaks, CA: Sage.

Mishara, B. L. (2006). Cultural specificity and universality of suicide: Challenges for the International Association for Suicide Prevention. *Crisis, 27* (1), 1–3.

Mitchell, C. W., & Rogers, R. E. (2003). Rape, statutory rape, and child abuse: Legal distinctions and counselor duties. *Professional School Counseling, 6*, 332–338.

Mitchell, R. (2001). *Documentation in counseling records* (2nd ed.). Alexandria, VA: American Counseling Association.

Moline, M. E., Williams, G. T., & Austin, K. M. (1998). *Documenting psychotherapy essentials for mental health practitioners.* Thousand Oaks, CA: Sage.

Mothersole, G. (1996). Existential realities and no-suicide contracts. *Transactional Analysis Journal, 26*(2), 151–159.

Motto, J. A. (1979). Guidelines for the management of the suicidal patient. *Weekly Psychiatric Update Series, 20*(3), 2–8.

Munson Healthcare Organization. (2008). *Partial hospitalization program*. Retrieved February 23, 2008, from www.munsonhealthcare.org/clinical_svcs/behavioral_health/treatments/bh_partial.php

Muran, J. C., & DiGiuseppe, R. A. (1994). Patient pretreatment interpersonal problems and therapeutic alliance in short-term cognitive therapy. *Journal of Consulting & Clinical Psychology, 62*(1), 185–190.

Murphy, C., Meyer, S., & O'Leary, D. (1994). Dependency characteristics of partner assaultive men. *Journal of Abnormal Psychology, 103*, 729–735.

Myer, R. A., Williams, R. C., Ottens, A. J., & Schmidt, A. E. (1992). Crisis assessment: A three-dimensional model for triage. *Journal for Mental Health Counseling, 14*, 137–148.

Myers, J. E. B. (1998). *Legal issues in child abuse and neglect practice* (2nd ed.). Thousand Oaks, CA: Sage.

Nash, J. M. (1997, May 5). Addicted. *Time*, 68–73, 76.

National Center for Victims of Crimes. (2009). *Victim impact statements*. Retrieved January 6, 2009, from www.ncvc.org/ncvc/main.aspx?dbName=DocumentViewer&DocumentID=32515

National Child Advocacy Center. (2008). *Child forensic interview model*. Retrieved May 31, 2008, from www.nationalcac.org/professionals/model/forensic_interview.html

National Coalition of Anti-Violence Programs. (2003). *Lesbian, gay, bisexual and transgender domestic violence in 2002: A report of the National Coalition of Anti-Violence Programs*. Retrieved January 11, 2008, from www.avp.org

Neimeyer, R. A. (1999). Narrative strategies in grief therapy. *Journal of Constructivist Psychology, 12*, 65–85.

Neimeyer, R. A. (2000). Suicide and hastened death: Toward a training agenda for counseling psychology. *Counseling Psychologist, 28*, 551–560.

Neimeyer, R. A. (2001). *Meaning reconstruction and the experience of loss*. Washington, DC: American Psychological Association.

Neimeyer, R. A., & Pfeiffer, A. M. (1994). The ten most common errors of suicide interventionists. In A. A. Leenaars, J. T. Maltsberger, & R. A. Neimeyer (Eds.), *Treatment of suicidal people* (pp. 207–224). Washington, DC: Taylor & Francis.

Norcross, J. C. (2000). Psychotherapist self-care: Practitioner-tested, research-informed strategies. *Professional Psychology: Research & Practice, 31*, 710–713.

Nordstrom, A., Dahlgren, L., & Kullgren, G. (2006). Victims' relations and factors triggering homicides committed by offenders with Schizophrenia. *Journal of Forensic Psychiatry & Psychology, 12*, 192–203.

Norris, F., Friedman, M. J., Watson, P. J., Byrne, C. M., Diaz, E., & Kaniasty, K. (2002). 60,000 disaster victims speak: Part I. An empirical review of the empirical literature, 1998–2001. *Psychiatry: Interpersonal & Biological Processes, 65*, 207–243.

Nugent, F. A., & Jones, K. D. (2005). *Introduction to the counseling profession* (4th ed.). Upper Saddle River, NJ: Pearson.

Nuttall, J. (2002). Modes of therapeutic relationship in brief dynamic psychotherapy. *Journal of Psychodynamic Process, 89*, 505–523.

Office of National Drug Control Policy. (2008). *Drug facts*. Retrieved May 1, 2008, from www.whitehousedrugpolicy.gov/drugfact

Olsen, D. H. (1988). Family types, family stress, and family satisfaction: A family development perspective. In C. J. Falicov (Ed.), *Family transition: Continuity and change over the life cycle* (pp. 55–80). New York: Guilford Press.

O'Toole, M. E. (2000). *The school shooter: A threat assessment perspective*. Retrieved February 4, 2008, from www.fbi.gov/publications/school/school2

Parham, T. A., White, J. L., & Amaju, A. (1999). *The psychology of Blacks: An African centered perspective*. Upper Saddle River, NJ: Prentice Hall.

Parkes, C. M. (1975). Determinants of outcome following bereavement. *Omega, 6*, 303–323.

Parkes, C. M. (2001). *Bereavement: Studies of grief in adult life* (3rd ed.). New York: Routledge.

Parkes, C. M. (2005). *For people affected by natural disasters, terrorist attacks, and other traumatic losses.* Retrieved on May 21, 2008, from www.cruse bereavementcare.org.uk/pdf/cmpadvicecruse%20

Pearlin, L. I., & Schooler, C. (1978). The structure of coping. *Journal of Health & Social Behavior, 19,* 2–21.

Pearlman, D. N., Zierler, S., Gjelsvik, A., & Verhoek-Oftedahl, W. (2003). Neighborhood environment, racial position, and risk of police reported domestic violence: A contextual analysis. *Public Health Reports, 118,* 44–58.

Peled, E., Eisikovits, Z., Enosh, G., & Winstok, Z. (2000). Choice and empowerment for battered women who stay: Toward a constructivist model. *Social Work, 45*(1), 9–25.

Peterman, L. M., & Dixon, C. G. (2003). Domestic violence between same-sex partners: Implications for counseling. *Journal of Counseling & Development, 81,* 40–47.

Piper, W. E., Ogrodniczuk, J. S., Joyce, A. S., McCollum, M., & Rosie, J. S. (2002). Relationships among affect, work and outcome in group therapy for patients with complicated grief. *American Journal of Psychotherapy, 56,* 347–362.

Potoczniak, M. J., Mourot, J. E., Crosbie-Burnett, M., & Potoczniak, D. J. (2003). Legal and psychological perspectives on same-sex domestic violence: A multisystemic approach. *Journal of Family Psychology, 17,* 252–259.

President's Commission on Model State Drug Laws. (1993). *Report of the President's Commission on Model State Drug Laws: Executive summary.* Washington, DC: U.S. Government Printing Office.

Privacy Rule: Standards for Privacy of Individually Identifiable Health Information, 45 C.F.R. §164.502[b][1](2003).

Prochaska, J. O., & DiClemente, C. C. (1982). Transtheoretical therapy: Toward a more integrative model of change. *Psychotherapy: Theory, Research, & Practice, 19,* 276–288.

Psychiatric Solutions, Inc. (2008). *Partial hospitalization program (PHP).* Retrieved February 23, 2008, from www.psysolutions.com/facilities/fremont/php.html

Puleo, S. G., & Wilcoxon, S. A. (1995). Infertility: Issues for counselors with considerations for those in rural communities. *Journal for the Professional Counselor, 10,* 41–50.

Purcell, R., Powell, M. B., & Mullen, P. C. (2005). Clients who stalk psychologists: Prevalence, methods, motives. *Professional Psychology: Research & Practice, 36,* 531–543.

Quinnett, P., & Stover, C. (2007). Suicide prevention training now available online. *Student Affairs Leader, 35*(23), 4–5.

Range, L. M., Campbell, C., Kovac, S. H., Marion-Jones, M., Aldridge, H., Kogas, S., et al. (2002). No suicide contracts: An overview and recommendations. *Death Studies, 26,* 51–74.

Rape, Abuse & Incest National Network. (2008a). *National sexual assault hotline.* Retrieved March 21, 2008, from www.rainn.org/get-help/national-sexual-assault-hotline

Rape, Abuse & Incest National Network. (2008b). *Who are the victims?* Retrieved March 21, 2008, from www.rainn.org/get-information/statistics/sexual-assault-victims

Reid, W. H. (2004). Avoiding the malpractice snare: Documenting suicide risk management. *Journal of Psychiatric Practice, 10*(3), 1–5.

Remley, T. P., & Herlihy, B. (2007). *Ethical, legal, and professional issues in counseling* (2nd ed.). Upper Saddle River, NJ: Pearson.

Rennison, C. M. (2002). *Intimate partner violence, 1993–2001* (Pub. No. NCJ-178247). Washington, DC: U.S. Department of Justice, Bureau of Justice Statistics.

Renzetti, C. M. (1992). *Violent betrayal: Partner abuse in lesbian relationships.* London: Sage.

Resick, P. A., & Schnicke, M. K. (1992). Cognitive processing therapy for sexual assault victims. *Journal of Consulting & Clinical Psychology, 60,* 748–756.

Rest, J., & Navarez, D. (1994). *Moral development in the professions.* Hillsdale, NJ: Lawrence Erlbaum.

Rich, J. M., & DeVitis, J. L. (1985). *Theories of moral development*. Springfield, IL: Charles C. Thomas.

Riger, S., Raja, S., & Camacho, J. (2002). The radiating impact of intimate partner violence. *Journal of Interpersonal Violence, 17*, 184–205.

Riley, P. L., & McDaniel, J. (2000). School violence prevention, intervention, and crisis response. *Professional School Counseling, 4*, 120–125.

Roberts, A. (2006). Classification typology and assessment of five levels of wife battering. *Journal of Family Violence, 21*, 521–527.

Roberts, A. R., & Ottens, A. J. (2005). The seven-stage crisis intervention model: A road map to goal attainment, problem-solving, and crisis resolution. *Brief Treatment & Crisis Intervention, 5*, 329–339.

Robins, E., Murphy, G. E., Wilkinson, R. H., Gassner, S., & Kayes, J. (1996). Some clinical considerations in the prevention of suicide based on a study of 134 successful suicides. In J. T. Maltsberger & M. J. Goldblatt (Eds.), *Essential papers on suicide* (pp. 142–159). New York: New York University Press.

Rock, M., & Rock, J. (2004). *Widowhood: The death of a spouse*. Victoria, BC: Trafford.

Roe, K. J. (2004). *The Violence Against Women Act and its impact on sexual violence public policy: Looking back and looking forward*. Retrieved April 13, 2008, from www.nrcdv.org/docs/Mailings/2004/NRCDVNovVAWA.pdf

Roe-Sepowitz, D. (2007). Adolescent female murderers: Characteristics and treatment implications. *American Journal of Orthopsychiatry, 77*, 489–496.

Rogers, C. R. (1951). *Client-centered therapy*. Boston: Riverside Press.

Rogers, C. R. (1980). *A way of being*. New York: Houghton Mifflin.

Rolland, J. S. (2004). Helping families with anticipatory loss and terminal illness. In F. Walsh & M. McGoldrick (Eds.), *Living beyond loss: Death in the family* (2nd ed., pp. 213–236). New York: W. W. Norton.

Rosenberg, M. S. (2003). Voices from the group: Domestic violence offenders' experience of intervention. *Journal of Aggression, Maltreatment, & Trauma, 7*, 305–317.

Rosenblatt, P. C., Walsh, R. P., & Jackson, D. A. (1976). *Grief and mourning in cross-cultural perspective*. New Haven, CT: Human Relations Area Files Press.

Rosenbluh, E. S. (1981). *Emotional first aid*. Louisville, KY: American Academy of Crisis Interveners.

Rowe, L. P. (2005). What judicial officers need to know about the HIPAA privacy rule. *NASPA Journal, 42*, 498–512.

Rudd, M. D., & Joiner, T. (1998). The assessment, management, and treatment of suicidality: Toward clinically informed and balanced standards of care. *American Psychological Association, 5*(2), 135–150.

Russo, C. J., & Mawdsley, R. D. (2004). Student records. *Education & the Law, 14*, 181–187.

Ruzek, J. L., Brymer, M. J., Jacobs, A. K., Layne, C. M., Vernberg, E. M., & Watson, P. J. (2007). Psychological first aid. *Journal of Mental Health Counseling, 29*(1), 17–27.

Salazar, L. F., Emshoff, J. G., Baker, C. K., & Crowley, T. (2007). Examining the behavior of a system: An outcome evaluation of a community coordinated response to domestic violence. *Journal of Family Violence, 22*, 631–641.

Sarrantakos, S. (2004). Deconstructing self-defense in wife-to-husband violence. *Journal of Men's Studies, 12*, 277–296.

Saywitz, K. J., Mannarino, A. P., Berliner, L., & Cohen, J. A. (2000). Treatment for sexually abused children and adolescents. *American Psychologist, 55*, 1040–1049.

Schmidt, M. C., Kolodinsky, J. M., Carsten, G., Schmidt, F. E., Larson, M., & MacLachlan, C. (2007). Short term change in attitude and motivating factors to change abusive behavior of male batterers after participating in a group intervention program based on the pro-feminist and cognitive-behavioral approach. *Journal of Family Violence, 22*, 91–100.

Schuh, J. H., & Laanan, F. S. (2006). Forced transitions: The impact of natural disasters and other events on college students. *New Directions for Student Services, 114*, 93–102.

Schure, M. B., Christopher, J., & Christopher, S. (2008). Mind-body medicine and the art of self-care: Teaching mindfulness to counseling students through yoga, meditation, and qigong. *Journal of Counseling & Development, 86*, 47–56.

Sedlak, A. J., & Broadhurst, D. D. (1996). *Third National Incidence Study on Child Abuse and Neglect*. Washington, DC: U.S. Department of Health and Human Services.

Seeley, M. F. (1995). The role of hotlines in the prevention of suicide. In M. M. Silverman & R. W. Maris (Eds.), *Suicide prevention toward the year 2000* (pp. 251–270). New York: Guilford Press.

Seligman, L. (1996). *Promoting a fighting spirit: Psychotherapy for cancer patients, survivors, and their families*. San Francisco: Jossey-Bass.

Seligman, L., & Reichenberg, L. (2007). *Selecting effective treatments*. San Francisco: Jossey-Bass.

Seligman, M. E. (1973). Fall into helplessness. *Psychology Today, 7*, 43–48.

Seligman, M. E. (1975). *Helplessness: On depression, development and death*. San Francisco: Freeman.

Selye, H. (1978). *The stress of life*. New York: McGraw-Hill.

Selzer, M. L. (1971). The Michigan Alcohol Screening Test: The quest for a new diagnostic instrument. *American Journal of Psychiatry, 127*, 1653–1658.

Sethi, S., & Uppal, S. (2006). Attitudes of clinicians in emergency room towards suicide. *International Journal of Psychiatry in Clinical Practice, 10*(3), 182–185.

Shalev, A. Y. (2004). Further lessons from 9/11: Does stress equal trauma? *Psychiatry, 67*, 174.

Shea, S. (2002). *The practical art of suicide assessment: A guide for mental health professionals and substance abuse counselors*. Hoboken, NJ: Wiley.

Shein, H. M. (1976). Obstacles in the education of psychiatric residents. *Omega, 7*, 75–82.

Shen, J., Samson, L. F., Washington, E. L., Johnson, P., Edwards, C., & Malone, A. (2006). Barriers of HIPAA regulation to implementation of health services research. *Journal of Medical Systems, 30*(1), 65–69.

Shuchman, M. (2007). Falling through the cracks—Virginia Tech and the restructuring of college mental health services. *New England Journal of Medicine, 357*(2), 105–110.

Simon, R. I. (1988). *Concise guide to clinical psychiatry and the law*. Washington, DC: American Psychiatric Press.

Simon, R. I. (Ed.). (1991). *Review of clinical psychiatry and the law* (Vol. 2). Washington, DC: American Psychiatric Press.

Simon, R. I. (2004). *Suicide risk: Guidelines for clinically based risk management*. Washington, DC: American Psychiatric Publishing.

Singer, J. A. (1997). *Message in a bottle: Stories of men and addiction*. New York: Free Press.

Skovholt, T. M. (2001). *The resilient practitioner: Burnout prevention and self-care strategies for counselors, therapists, teachers and health professionals*. Boston: Allyn & Bacon.

Slaikeu, K. A. (1990). *Crisis intervention: A handbook for practice and research* (2nd ed.). Boston: Allyn & Bacon.

Sleutel, M. R. (1998). Women's experience of abuse: A review of qualitative research. *Issues in Mental Health Nursing, 19*, 525–539.

Smaby, M. H., Peterson, T. L., Bergmann, P. E., Bacig, K. L., & Swearingen, S. (1990). School-based community intervention: The school counselor as lead consultant for suicide prevention and intervention programs. *School Counselor, 37*, 370–377.

Smith, H. I. (2006). *A long shadowed grief: Suicide and its aftermath*. Cambridge, MA: Cowley Publications.

Smith, J. E., & Meyers, R. J. (2008). *The CRAFT intervention program: Motivating substance abusers to enter treatment*. New York: Guilford Press.

Sokoloff, N. J., & Dupont, I. (2005). Domestic violence at the intersections of race, class, and gender: Challenges and contributions to understanding violence against marginalized women in diverse communities. *Violence Against Women, 11*(1), 38–64.

Spencer, P. C., & Munch, S. (2003). Client violence toward social workers: The role of management in community mental health. *Social Work, 48*, 532–544.

Sperry, L. (2007). *The ethical and professional practice of counseling and psychotherapy*. Boston: Pearson.

Sprang, G., Clark, J. J., & Whitt-Woosley, A. (2007). Compassion fatigue, compassion satisfaction, and burnout: Factors impacting a professional's quality of life. *Journal of Loss & Trauma, 12,* 259–280.

Stanford, E. J., Goetz, R. R., & Bloom, J. D. (1994). The no harm contract in the emergency assessment of suicidal risk. *Journal of Clinical Psychiatry, 55,* 410–414.

Stanton, M. D. (1999). Alcohol use disorders. *Clinical Update, 1*(3), 3–5.

Stebnicki, M. A. (2007). Empathy fatigue: Healing the mind, body, and spirit of professional counselors. *American Journal of Psychiatric Rehabilitation, 10,* 317–338.

Strentz, T. (1995). Strategies for victims of hostage situations. In A. R. Roberts (Ed.), *Crisis intervention and time limited cognitive treatment* (pp. 127–147). Newbury Park, CA: Sage.

Sue, D. W., & Sue, D. (1999). *Counseling the culturally different: Theory and practice* (3rd ed.). New York: Wiley.

Sue, D. W., & Sue, D. (2003). *Counseling the culturally diverse: Theory and practice* (4th ed.). New York: Wiley.

Suicide Prevention Action Network USA. (2008). *Quick facts about suicide.* Retrieved February 12, 2008, from www.spanusa.org

Suicide Prevention Resource Center. (2006, March). *Assessing and managing suicide risk.* Newton, MA: Author.

Sullivan, A. M., Bezmen, J., Barron, C. T., Rivera, J., Curley-Casey, L., & Marino, D. C. (2005). Reducing restraints: Alternatives to restraints on an inpatient psychiatric unit utilizing safe and effective methods to evaluate and treat the violent patient. *Psychiatric Quarterly, 76*(1), 51–65.

Swenson, C. C., & Chaffin, M. (2006). Beyond psychotherapy: Treating abused children by changing their social ecology. *Aggression & Violent Behavior, 11,* 120–137.

Tarasoff v. Regents of the University of California, 529 P.2d. 553, 118 Cal. Rptr. 129 (1974), *vacated,* 17 Cal. 3d 425, 551 P.2d 334, 131 Cal. Rptr. 14 (1976).

Tishler, C. L., Gordon, L. B., & Landry-Meyer, L. (2000). Managing the violent patient: A guide for psychologists and other mental health professionals. *Professional Psychology: Research & Practice, 31*(1), 34–41.

Tjaden, P., & Thoennes, N. (2000). *Full report of the prevalence, incidence and consequences of violence against women: Findings from the National Violence Against Women Survey.* Washington, DC: U.S. Department of Justice.

Toray, T. (2004). The human-animal bond and loss: Providing support for grieving clients. *Journal of Mental Health Counseling, 26,* 244–259.

Tower, L. E. (2006). Barriers in screening women for domestic violence: A survey of social workers, family practitioners, and obstetrician-gynecologists. *Journal of Family Violence, 21,* 245–257.

Tower, M. (2007). Intimate partner violence and the health care response: A postmodern critique. *Health Care for Women International, 28,* 438–452.

Towl, G. J., & Crighton, D. A. (1997). Risk assessment with offenders. *International Review of Psychiatry, 9,* 187–193.

Tribbensee, N. E., & McDonald, S. J. (2007). *FERPA allows more than you may realize.* Retrieved February 17, 2008, from insidehighered.com/views/2007/08/07/ferpa

Trickett, P. K. (2006). Defining child sexual abuse. In M. M. Feerick, J. F. Knutson, P. K. Trickett, & S. M. Flanzer (Eds.), *Child abuse and neglect: Definitions, classifications, & a framework for research* (pp. 123–150). Baltimore, MD: Brookes.

Trippany, R. L., White Kress, V. E., & Wilcoxon, A. S. (2004). Preventing vicarious trauma: What counselors should know when working with trauma survivors. *Journal of Counseling & Development, 82*(1), 31–37.

Twemlow, S. W. (2001). Interviewing violent patients. *Bulletin of the Menninger Clinic, 65,* 503–521.

United Nations. (1995). *Report on the world's women 1995: Trends and statistics.* New York: Author.

U.S. Department of Education. (2007). *Safe schools & FERPA.* Retrieved February 17, 2008, from www.ed.gov/policy/gen/guid/fpco/ferpa/safeschools/intex.html

U.S. Department of Education. (2008). *Family Educational Rights and Privacy Act.* Retrieved February 16, 2008, from www.ed.gov/policy/gen/guid/fpco/ferpa/index.html

U.S. Department of Education, Office of Safe and Drug-Free Schools. (2003). *Practical information on crisis planning: A guide for schools and communities.* Retrieved on July 15, 2008, from www.gov/admins/ead/safety/crisisplanning.pdf

U.S. Department of Health and Human Services. (2002). *Standards for privacy of individually identifiable health information: Final rule.* Retrieved February 28, 2008, from www.hhs.gov/ocr/hipaa/privrulepd.pdf

U.S. Department of Health and Human Services. (2003). *Summary of the HIPAA privacy rule.* Retrieved May 24, 2008, from www.hhs.gov/ocr/privacysummary.pdf

U.S. Department of Health and Human Services. (2005). *Child maltreatment 2003.* Washington, DC: U.S. Government Printing Office.

U.S. Department of Health and Human Services. (2006). *National suicide prevention lifeline: After an attempt: A guide for taking care of your family member after treatment in the emergency department* (CMHS-SVP-0159) [Brochure]. Rockville, MD: Center for Mental Health Services, Substance Abuse and Mental Health Services Administration.

U.S. Department of Health and Human Services. (2007). *Child maltreatment 2005.* Retrieved February 26, 2008, from www.acf.hhs.gov/programs/cb/pubs/cm05/table3_6.htm

U.S. Department of Health and Human Services. (2008a). *Hurricane Katrina bulletin: HIPAA privacy and disclosures in emergency situations.* Retrieved February 28, 2008, from www.hhs.gov/ocr/hipaa/KATRINAnHIPAA.pdf

U.S. Department of Health and Human Services. (2008b). *Legal authority for implementation of a federal public health and medical services response.* Retrieved February 28, 2008, from www.hhs.gov/disasters/discussion/planners/legalauthority.html

U.S. Department of Health and Human Services. (2008c). *Mandatory reporters of child abuse and neglect: State statutes series.* Retrieved March 26, 2008, from www.childwelfare.gov/systemwide/laws_policies/statutes/manda.cfm

U.S. Department of Justice, Bureau of Justice Statistics. (2007). *Homicide trends in the United States.* Retrieved February 4, 2008, from www.ojp.usdoj.gov/bjs/homicide/relationhip.htm

U.S. Department of Justice, Bureau of Justice Statistics. (2008). *Definitions.* Retrieved January 21, 2008, from www.ojp.usdoj.gov/bjs/abstract/cvus/definitions.htm#rape_sexual_assault

U.S. Department of Justice, Office for Victims of Crimes. (2006). *OVC fact sheets: The Justice for All Act.* Retrieved June 23, 2008, from www.ojp.usdoj.gov/ovc/publications/factshts/justforall/welcome.html

U.S. Department of Justice, Office for Victims of Crime. (2008). *Help for homicide survivors / co-victims.* Retrieved May 31, 2008, from www.ojp.usdoj.gov/ovc/help/hv.htm

U.S. Department of Justice, Office of Violence Against Women. (2004). *A national protocol for sexual assault medical forensic examinations.* Retrieved January 7, 2009, from www.ncjrs.gov/pdffiles1/ovw/206554.pdf

U.S. Department of Labor, Occupational Safety and Health Administration. (2008). *Safety and health topics: Workplace violence.* Retrieved May 29, 2008, from www.osha.gov/SLTC/workplaceviolence/index.html

Uses and Disclosures of Protected Health Information: General Rules, 45 C.F.R. §164.502 (2002).

Vaillant, G. E. (1995). *The natural history of alcoholism revisited.* Cambridge, MA: Harvard University Press.

Vaillant, L. M. (1997). *Changing character: Short-term anxiety-regulating psychotherapy for restructuring defenses, affects, and attachment.* New York: Basic Books.

VandeCreek, L., Knapp, S., & Herzog, C. (1987). Malpractice risks in the treatment of dangerous patients. *Psychotherapy: Theory, Research, & Practice, 24,* 145–153.

Walker, L. E. (1979). *The battered woman.* New York: Harper & Row.

Walker, L. E. (1994). *Abused women and survivor therapy: A practical guide for the psychotherapist.* Washington, DC: American Psychological Association.

Walker, L. E. (1999). Psychology and domestic violence around the world. *American Psychologist, 54,* 21–29.

Walker, L. E. (2006). Battered woman syndrome: Empirical findings. *Annals of the New York Academy of Sciences, 1087,* 142–157.

Walsh, F. (1998). *Strengthening family resilience.* New York: Guilford Press.

Walsh, F., & McGoldrick, M. (Eds.). (2004). *Living beyond loss: Death in the family.* New York: W. W. Norton.

Wang, C. C. (2007). Person-centered therapy with a bereaved father. *Person-Centered Journal, 14,* 73–97.

Warne, T., & McAndrew, S. (2005). The shackles of abuse: Unprepared to work at the edges of reason. *Journal of Psychiatric & Mental Health Nursing, 12,* 679–686.

Warshaw, R. (1988). *I never called it rape: The* Ms. *report on recognizing, fighting and surviving date and acquaintance rape.* New York: Harper & Row.

Weeks, K. M. (2001). Family-friendly FERPA policies: Affirming parental partnerships. *New Directions for Student Services, 94,* 39–50.

Weiss, A. (2001). The no suicide contract: Possibilities and pitfalls. *American Journal of Psychotherapy, 55,* 414–419.

Werner-Wilson, R. J., Zimmerman, T. S., & Whalen, D. (2000). Resilient response to battering. *Contemporary Family Therapy, 22,* 161–188.

West, C. M., Kanter, G. K., & Jasinski, J. L. (1998). Sociodemographic predictors and cultural barriers to help-seeking behaviors by Latina and Anglo American battered women. *Violence and Victims, 13,* 361–375.

Wettstein, R. M. (1989). Psychiatric malpractice. In A. Tasman, R. E. Hales, & A. J. Frances (Eds.), *Annual review of psychiatry* (Vol. 8, pp. 392–408). Washington, DC: American Psychiatric Press.

Wilson, M., & Daly, M. (1992). *Homicide.* New York: Aldine de Gruyter.

Worden, J. W. (2001). *Children and grief: When a parent dies.* New York: Guilford Press.

Worden, J. W. (2008). *Grief counseling and grief therapy: A handbook for the mental health practitioner* (4th ed.). New York: Springer.

World Health Organization. (1993). *The alcohol use disorders identification test: Guidelines for use in primary care* (2nd ed.). Retrieved May 1, 2008, from whqlibdoc.who.int/hq/2001/ WHO_MSD_MSB_01.6a.pdf

World Health Organization. (2007). *Suicide prevention (SUPRE).* Retrieved February 16, 2008, from www.who.int/mental_health/prevention/ suicide/suicideprevent/en

Wunsch-Hitzig, R., Plapinger, J., Draper, J., & del Campo, E. (2002). Calls for help after September 11: A community mental health hotline. *Journal of Urban Health: Bulletin of the New York Academy of Medicine, 79,* 417–428.

Yalom, I. D. (2008). *Staring at the sun: Overcoming the terror of death.* San Francisco: Jossey-Bass.

Young, M. E. (2005). *Learning the art of helping: Building blocks and techniques* (3rd ed.). Upper Saddle River: NJ: Pearson Education.

INDEX